ATLAS
A-Z

LONDON, NEW YORK, MELBOURNE,
MUNICH, AND DELHI

LONDON, NEW YORK, MELBOURNE,
MUNICH, AND DELHI

FOR THE FIFTH EDITION
Publishing Director Jonathan Metcalf **Art Director** Philip Ormerod
Associate Publishing Director Liz Wheeler **Associate Publisher** Andrew Macintyre
Senior Cartographic Editor Simon Mumford
Designer Nimbus Design
Editors Cambridge International Reference on Current Affairs (CIRCA)
3D Globes Planetary Visions Ltd., London
Production Controller Mandy Inness **Production Editor** John Goldsmid

FOR PREVIOUS EDITIONS
Cartographic Director Andrew Heritage
Cartography Roger Bullen, Rob Stokes, Iorwerth Watkins
Project Editor Sam Atkinson **Art Editor** Karen Gregory

First American Edition, 2001
This revised Edition 2012

Published in the United States by
DK Publishing
375 Hudson Street
New York, New York 10014

12 13 14 15 16 10 9 8 7 6 5 4 3 2 1
181747—March 2012

Published in Great Britain by Dorling Kindersley Limited.

A catalog record for this book is available from the Library of Congress.

ISBN 978-0-7566-8977-3

DK books are available at special discounts when purchased in bulk for sales promotions,
premiums, fund-raising, or educational use. For details, contact: DK Publishing Special Markets,
375 Hudson Street, New York, New York 10014 or SpecialSales@dk.com.

Printed and bound in Singapore by Star Standard

Discover more at
www.dk.com

Key to map symbols

ELEVATION

6000m / 19,686ft

4000m / 13,124ft

2000m / 6562ft

1000m / 3281ft

500m / 1640ft

250m / 820ft

100m / 328ft

0

Below sea level

▲ Mountain

• Depression

BORDERS

———— Full international

----- Disputed de facto

•••••• Territorial claim

×—×—× Cease-fire line

•••••••••• Undefined

———— State/Province

DRAINAGE FEATURES

———— River

----- Seasonal river

———— Canal

⬭ Lake

Seasonal lake

SETTLEMENTS

● Capital city

◉ Major town

○ Minor town

• Major port

COMMUNICATIONS

———— Major road

———— Rail

✈ International airport

◆ Insight; facts, figures, and amazing information from around the world

Atlas contents

North & Central America 16–17

South America 38–39

Africa 50–51

Europe 62–63

Atlas contents

North & West Asia 94–95

South & East Asia 106–107

Australasia & Oceania 124–125

Country Factfiles 138–359

See overleaf for contents

Factfile contents

Factfile contents

The Political World

KEY TO NUMBERS

1. Germany
2. Liechtenstein
3. Czech Republic
4. Austria
5. Slovakia
6. Hungary
7. Slovenia
8. Croatia
9. Bosnia & Herzegovina
10. Serbia
11. Montenegro
12. Kosovo (disputed)
13. San Marino
14. Vatican City

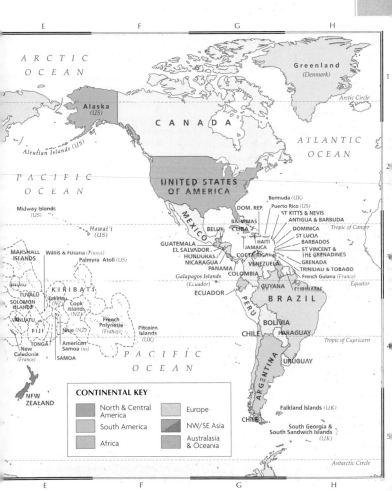

ARCTIC OCEAN

Greenland
(Denmark)

Arctic Circle

Alaska
(US)

CANADA

Aleutian Islands (US)

ATLANTIC OCEAN

PACIFIC OCEAN

UNITED STATES OF AMERICA

Midway Islands
(US)

Hawai'i
(US)

Bermuda *(UK)*

DOM. REP. Puerto Rico *(US)*
ST KITTS & NEVIS
ANTIGUA & BARBUDA

BAHAMAS

MEXICO

BELIZE

CUBA

DOMINICA

ST LUCIA
BARBADOS

HAITI

JAMAICA

ST VINCENT &
THE GRENADINES

Tropic of Cancer

MARSHALL
ISLANDS

Wallis & Futuna (France)

Palmyra Atoll (US)

GUATEMALA
EL SALVADOR
HONDURAS
NICARAGUA

COSTA RICA

GRENADA

PANAMA

VENEZUELA

TRINIDAD & TOBAGO

French Guiana (France)

NAURU

KIRIBATI

Galapagos Islands
(Ecuador)

COLOMBIA

GUYANA

SURINAME

Equator

TUVALU
SOLOMON
ISLANDS

Tokelau
(NZ)

Cook
Islands
(NZ)

ECUADOR

PERU

BRAZIL

VANUATU

French
Polynesia
(France)

Niue (NZ)

Pitcairn
Islands
(UK)

BOLIVIA

FIJI

TONGA

American
Samoa (us)

CHILE

PARAGUAY

Tropic of Capricorn

New
Caledonia
(France)

SAMOA

PACIFIC OCEAN

ARGENTINA

URUGUAY

NEW
ZEALAND

CONTINENTAL KEY

North & Central America	Europe
South America	NW/SE Asia
Africa	Australasia & Oceania

Falkland Islands (UK)

South Georgia &
South Sandwich Islands
(UK)

CHILE

Antarctic Circle

The Physical World

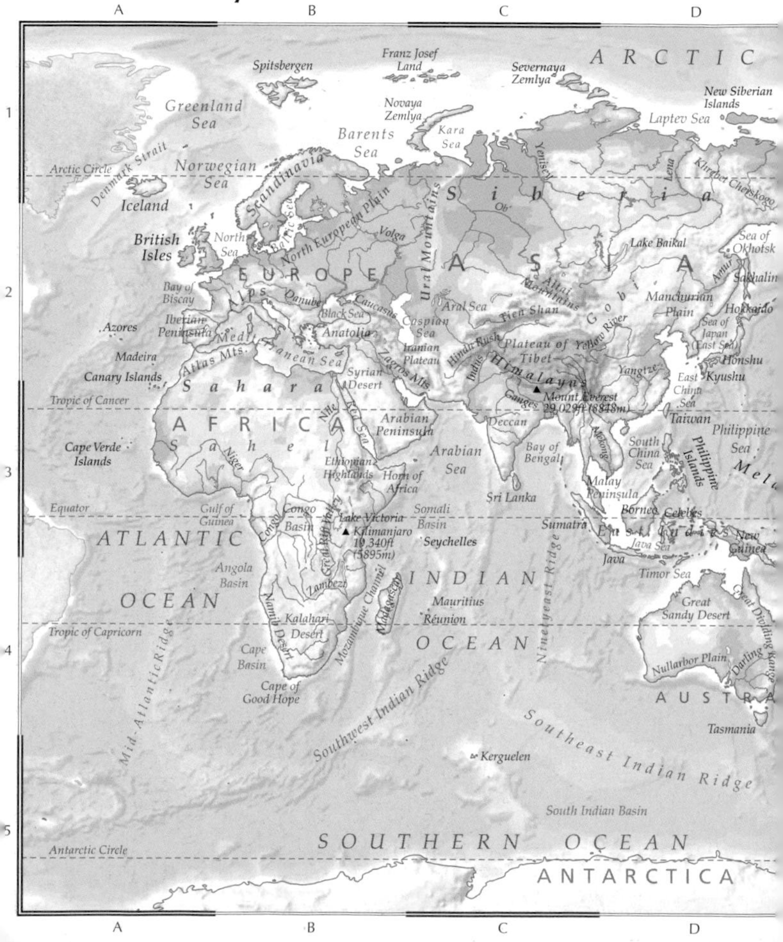
A
B
C
D
1
2
3
4
5
ARCTIC
Franz Josef Land
Spitsbergen
Severnaya Zemlya
New Siberian Islands
Greenland Sea
Novaya Zemlya
Laptev Sea
Barents Sea
Kara Sea
Denmark Strait
Arctic Circle
Norwegian Sea
Scandinavia
Yenisei
Lena
Khrebet Cherskogo
Iceland
North European Plain
Ural Mountains
Siberia
Ob'
British Isles
North Sea
Baltic Sea
Volga
Lake Baikal
Sea of Okhotsk
EUROPE
ASIA
Amur
Sakhalin
Bay of Biscay
Alps
Danube
Caucasus
Altai Mountains
Gobi
Manchurian Plain
Hokkaido
Azores
Iberian Peninsula
Black Sea
Aral Sea
Tien Shan
Caspian Sea
Anatolia
Sea of Japan (East Sea)
Mediterranean Sea
Yellow River
Madeira
Atlas Mts.
Iranian Plateau
Hindu Kush
Plateau of Tibet
Honshu
Zagros Mts
Himalayas
Canary Islands
Sahara
Syrian Desert
Indus
Yangtze
Kyushu
East China Sea
Mount Everest 29,029ft (8848m)
Tropic of Cancer
Ganges
Taiwan
AFRICA
Nile
Red Sea
Arabian Peninsula
Deccan
Philippine Sea
Cape Verde Islands
Sahel
Niger
Arabian Sea
Bay of Bengal
Mekong
South China Sea
Philippine Islands
Ethiopian Highlands
Horn of Africa
Malay Peninsula
Sri Lanka
Equator
Gulf of Guinea
Congo Basin
Great Rift Valley
Lake Victoria
Somali Basin
Sumatra
Borneo
Celebes
East Indies
New Guinea
ATLANTIC
Congo
Kilimanjaro 19,340ft (5895m)
Seychelles
Java Sea
Java
Angola Basin
INDIAN
Ninetyeast Ridge
Timor Sea
Zambezi
Mozambique Channel
Madagascar
OCEAN
Namib Desert
Mauritius
Réunion
Great Sandy Desert
Great Dividing Range
Kalahari Desert
Tropic of Capricorn
OCEAN
Mid-Atlantic Ridge
Cape Basin
Nullarbor Plain
Darling
Southwest Indian Ridge
Cape of Good Hope
AUSTRALIA
Tasmania
Southeast Indian Ridge
Kerguelen
South Indian Basin
SOUTHERN OCEAN
Antarctic Circle
ANTARCTICA

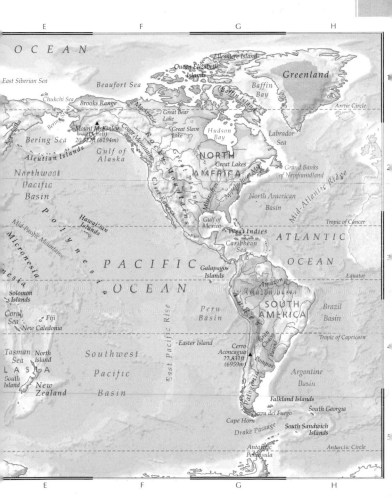

Time Zones

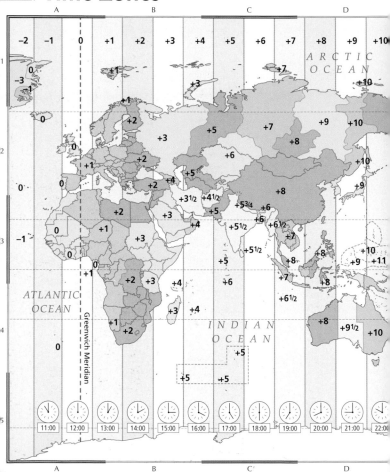

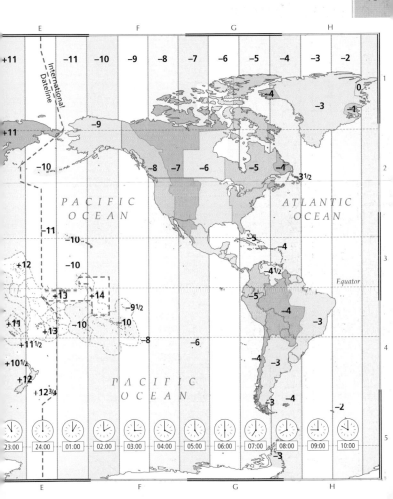

The world's regions

St Pierre & Miquelon *(France)*

ATLANTIC OCEAN

Sargasso Sea

Bermuda *(UK)*

Virgin Islands *(US)*
British Virgin Islands *(UK)*
Anguilla *(UK)*
ANTIGUA & BARBUDA
ST KITTS & NEVIS
Guadeloupe *(France)*
DOMINICA
ST LUCIA
BARBADOS
Montserrat *(UK)*
Martinique *(France)*
ST VINCENT & THE GRENADINES
GRENADA
TRINIDAD & TOBAGO

Turks & Caicos Islands *(UK)*
Puerto Rico *(US)*
DOMINICAN REPUBLIC

48

BAHAMAS

HAITI

Curaçao *(Neth.)*
Aruba *(Neth.)*

SOUTH AMERICA

38

CUBA

Cayman Islands *(UK)*
JAMAICA

Andes

Gulf of Mexico

Great Lakes
Lake Superior
Lake Michigan
Lake Huron
Lake Erie
Lake Ontario

Appalachian Mountains

Ohio

Missouri

Mississippi

UNITED STATES OF AMERICA

Rio Grande

MEXICO

Sierra Madre Oriental

Sierra Madre Occidental

BELIZE
GUATEMALA
HONDURAS
EL SALVADOR
NICARAGUA
COSTA RICA
PANAMA

PACIFIC OCEAN

Galapagos Islands *(Ecuador)*

135

Mount Whitney 14,495ft (4418m)
Death Valley -282ft (-86m)

Colorado

Clipperton Island *(French Polynesia)*

Equator

Tropic of Cancer

0 km   1000
0 miles

134

Western Canada & Alaska

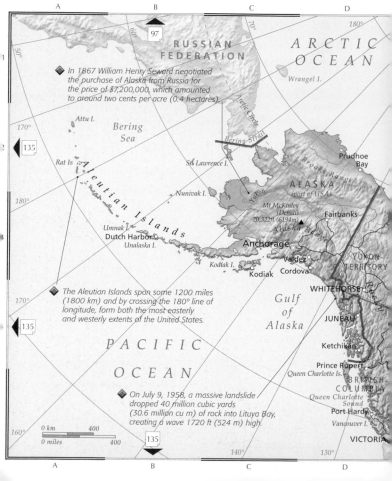

RUSSIAN FEDERATION

ARCTIC OCEAN

In 1867 William Henry Seward negotiated the purchase of Alaska from Russia for the price of $7,200,000, which amounted to around two cents per acre (0.4 hectares).

Wrangel I.

Arctic Circle

Bering Strait

Attu I.

Bering Sea

St Lawrence I.

Prudhoe Bay

Rat Is

Aleutian Islands

Nunivak I.

Brooks Range

ALASKA (part of USA)

Yukon

Umnak I.
Dutch Harbor
Unalaska I.

Mt McKinley (Denali) 20,322ft (6194m) ▲

Fairbanks

Alaska R.

Anchorage

Kodiak I.

Valdez

Cordova

Kodiak

YUKON TERRITORY

WHITEHORSE

The Aleutian Islands span some 1200 miles (1800 km) and by crossing the 180° line of longitude, form both the most easterly and westerly extents of the United States.

Gulf of Alaska

JUNEAU

PACIFIC OCEAN

Ketchikan

Prince Rupert

Queen Charlotte Is.

Queen Charlotte Sound

On July 9, 1958, a massive landslide dropped 40 million cubic yards (30.6 million cu m) of rock into Lituya Bay, creating a wave 1720 ft (524 m) high.

BRITISH COLUMBIA

Port Hardy

Vancouver I.

VICTORIA

0 km 400
0 miles 400

97

135

135

135

◆ Sought by explorers for centuries as a trade route between Europe and Asia, the famous Northwest Passage is now often navigable during the summer months without the need for an icebreaker because of reduced volumes of sea ice.

◆ Despite an area of 808,109 sq miles (2,092,993 sq km), the northerly province of Nunavut has only 530 miles (850 km) of roads and highway.

◆ Only just over 1% of Canada's 3.5 million sq miles (9.1 million sq km) land area is devoted to grain production, yet this yields around 25 million tons (tonnes) of wheat every year.

Greenland (Danish external territory)

Baffin Bay

Davis Strait

Baffin Island

Arctic Circle

IQALUIT (Frobisher Bay)

Hudson Strait

Southampton I.

Rankin Inlet

Hudson Bay

Churchill

QUEBEC

ONTARIO

Ellesmere Island

Axel Heiberg Island

Queen Elizabeth Islands

Bathurst I.

Devon Island

Melville Island

Resolute (Qausuittuq)

Lancaster Sound

Somerset Island

Viscount Melville Sound

Prince of Wales I.

Banks Island

Beaufort Sea

Amundsen Gulf

Victoria Island

King William I.

Inuvik

Kugluktuk (Coppermine)

NUNAVUT

Great Bear Lake

NORTHWEST TERRITORIES

Mackenzie

YELLOWKNIFE

Great Slave Lake

Hay River

Fort Smith

ALBERTA

Fort St John

Fort McMurray

Lake Athabasca

SASKATCHEWAN

MANITOBA

C A N A D A

Grande Prairie

Flin Flon

Thompson

Prince George

EDMONTON

Leduc

Saskatchewan

Red Deer

Prince Albert

Saskatoon

Yorkton

Lake Winnipeg

WINNIPEG

Kamloops

Calgary

REGINA

Brandon

Vancouver

Kelowna

Lethbridge

Estevan

U S A

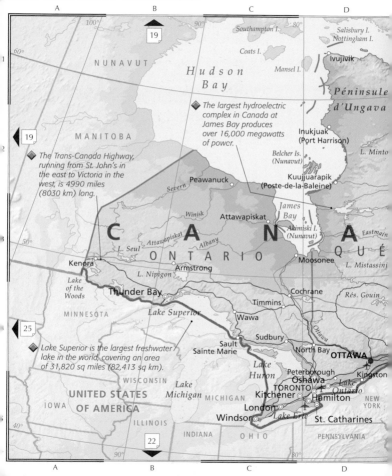

A   B   C   D

19

100°

90°

80°

Southampton I.

Salisbury I.
Nottingham I.

60°

1

NUNAVUT

Coats I.

Ivujivik

H u d s o n
B a y

Mansel I.

Péninsule
d'Ungava

19

MANITOBA

♦ The largest hydroelectric
complex in Canada at
James Bay produces
over 16,000 megawatts
of power.

Inukjuak
(Port Harrison)

2

♦ The Trans-Canada Highway,
running from St. John's in
the east to Victoria in the
west, is 4990 miles
(8030 km) long.

Belcher Is.
(Nunavut)

L. Minto

Peawanuck

Kuujjuarapik
(Poste-de-la-Baleine)

Severn

James
Bay

Attawapiskat

Winisk

Akimiski I.
(Nunavut)

Eastmain

50°

C A N A D A

QUÉ-

Attawapiskat

L. Seul

Albany

ONTARIO

Moosonee

L. Mistassini

3

Kenora

Armstrong

L. Nipigon

Rés. Gouin

Lake
of the
Woods

Thunder Bay

Cochrane

Timmins

MINNESOTA

Lake Superior

Wawa

Ottawa

North Bay

OTTAWA

25

♦ Lake Superior is the largest freshwater
lake in the world, covering an area
of 31,820 sq miles (82,413 sq km).

Sault
Sainte Marie

Sudbury

Peterborough

Kingston

Lake
Huron

Oshawa

Lake

TORONTO

Ontario

WISCONSIN

Lake

MICHIGAN

Kitchener

Hamilton

4

UNITED STATES

Michigan

London

St. Catharines

IOWA

OF AMERICA

Windsor

Lake Erie

NEW
YORK

ILLINOIS

INDIANA

OHIO

PENNSYLVANIA

40°

90°

80°

22

A   B   C   D

Baffin I.

Hudson Strait

Akpatok I.
(Nunavut)

Ungava
Bay

*Labrador
Sea*

64

Canada has the world's longest coastline
(including tens of thousands of islands), with a
total length of 151,019 miles (243,042 km).

Kuujjuaq

Nain

A T L A N T I C

Schefferville

Hopedale
Makkovik

Cartwright

O C E A N

48

Réservoir
Caniapiscau

*Smallwood
Reservoir*

NEWFOUNDLAND
& LABRADOR

Strait of Belle Isle

Newfoundland

Réservoir
Manicouagan

D
E **C**   **A**

Havre-
Saint-Pierre

Île d'Anticosti

Gander

Grand Falls
Corner Brook

ST JOHN'S

Sept-Îles

St. Lawrence

Gulf of St. Lawrence

Channel-Port
aux-Basques

Cape Race

L. Saint-Jean
Jonquière

Gaspé

PRINCE
EDWARD
ISLAND

Cabot Strait

St Pierre
& Miquelon
(French overseas
collectivity)

50°

Chicoutimi

Bathurst
NEW
BRUNSWICK

CHARLOTTETOWN

QUÉBEC

Moncton

NOVA SCOTIA

48

FREDERICTON

Sydney

Trois-Rivières
Sherbrooke

Saint John

Dartmouth
HALIFAX

Montréal

MAINE

Yarmouth

A T L A N T I C

NEW
HAMPSHIRE

O C E A N

40°

VERMONT

The Bay of Fundy has the world's
highest tidal range, with water's rising
20–56 ft (5–17 m) every high tide as
around 115 billion tons (tonnes) of
water flows into the bay.

MASSACHUSETTS

RHODE ISLAND

CONNECTICUT

0 km   300

0 miles   300

48

MINNESOTA

CANADA

ONTARIO

Lake Superior

20

Superior

Ironwood

Marquette

Sault Ste Marie

Iron Mountain

Cheboygan

Lake Huron

Ladysmith

WISCONSIN

MICHIGAN

Eau Claire

Green Bay

Traverse City

La Crosse

Oshkosh

Lake Michigan

Bay City

IOWA

MADISON

Grand Rapids

Saginaw

Flint

Milwaukee

LANSING

Rockford

Waukegan

Ann Arbor

Detroit

The Chicago River originally flowed into Lake Michigan, but was reversed in 1900 by the completion of a canal.

Aurora

Chicago

South Bend

Lake Erie

Erie

Toledo

Cleveland

Joliet

Gary

Youngstown

Rock Island

Fort Wayne

Akron

Galesburg

Peoria

Mansfield

Canton

Wheeling

ILLINOIS

INDIANA

OHIO

SPRINGFIELD

Champaign

Muncie

Decatur

INDIANAPOLIS

Dayton

COLUMBUS

Effingham

Terre Haute

Cincinnati

East St Louis

Bloomington

Huntington

Mt. Vernon

Louisville

CHARLESTON

MISSOURI

Evansville

FRANKFORT

Lexington

WEST VIRGINIA

Carbondale

Owensboro

Richmond

KENTUCKY

Paducah

Hopkinsville

Bowling Green

London

ARKANSAS

30

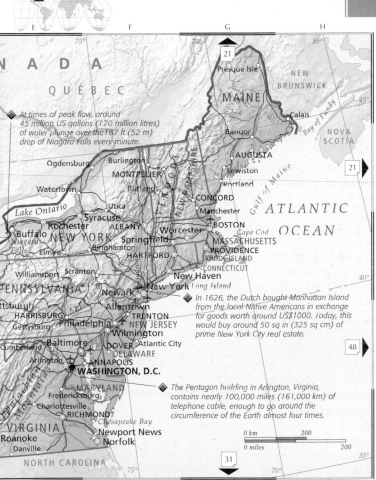

E   F   G   H

CANADA

QUÉBEC

◆ At times of peak flow, around
45 million US gallons (170 million litres)
of water plunge over the 167 ft (52 m)
drop of Niagara Falls every minute.

NEW
BRUNSWICK

Presque Isle

MAINE

Calais

Bay of Fundy

Bangor

NOVA
SCOTIA

AUGUSTA

Ogdensburg   Burlington
Lewiston

MONTPELIER
Portland

Watertown   Rutland

CONCORD

Lake Ontario   Utica   Manchester

Gulf of Maine

Rochester   Syracuse
ALBANY   Worcester   BOSTON   ATLANTIC

Buffalo   NEW YORK   Springfield   Cape Cod   OCEAN

Niagara
Falls   Elmira   Binghamton   HARTFORD   PROVIDENCE

Williamsport   Scranton   RHODE ISLAND

New Haven   CONNECTICUT

PENNSYLVANIA   Newark   New York   Long Island

Pittsburgh   Allentown   ◆ In 1626, the Dutch bought Manhattan Island
from the local Native Americans in exchange
for goods worth around US$1000. Today, this
would buy around 50 sq in (325 sq cm) of
prime New York City real estate.

HARRISBURG   TRENTON
Gettysburg   Philadelphia   NEW JERSEY

Wilmington

Cumberland   Baltimore   DOVER   Atlantic City
DELAWARE

Arlington   ANNAPOLIS
WASHINGTON, D.C.   ◆ The Pentagon building in Arlington, Virginia,
contains nearly 100,000 miles (161,000 km) of
telephone cable, enough to go around the
circumference of the Earth almost four times.

MARYLAND

Fredericksburg

Charlottesville

RICHMOND   Chesapeake Bay

VIRGINIA   Newport News
Norfolk

Roanoke

Danville

NORTH CAROLINA

0 km   200

0 miles   200

E   F   G   H

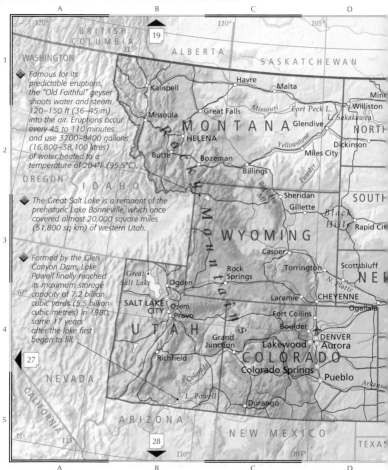

◆ Famous for its predictable eruptions, the "Old Faithful" geyser shoots water and steam 120–150 ft (36–45 m) into the air. Eruptions occur every 45 to 110 minutes and use 3700–8400 gallons (16,800–38,100 litres) of water heated to a temperature of 204°F (95.5°C).

◆ The Great Salt Lake is a remnant of the prehistoric Lake Bonneville, which once covered almost 20,000 square miles (51,800 sq km) of western Utah.

◆ Formed by the Glen Canyon Dam, Lake Powell finally reached its maximum storage capacity of 7.2 billion cubic yards (5.5 billion cubic metres) in 1980, some 17 years after the lake first began to fill.

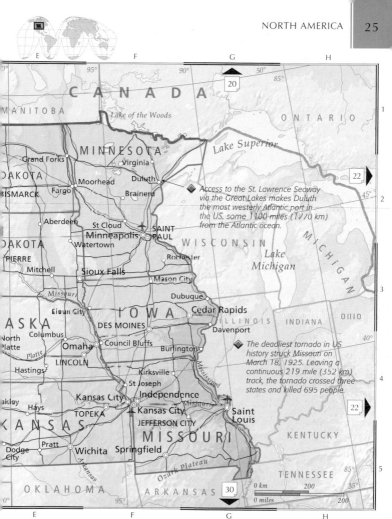

E   95°   F   90°   G   50°   85°   H

20

C A N A D A

MANITOBA   Lake of the Woods   O N T A R I O   1

MINNESOTA   Lake Superior

Grand Forks   Virginia

22

DAKOTA   Moorhead   Duluth   45°
BISMARCK   Fargo   Brainerd   2

♦ Access to the St. Lawrence Seaway via the Great Lakes makes Duluth the most westerly Atlantic port in the US, some 1100 miles (1770 km) from the Atlantic ocean.

Aberdeen   St Cloud   SAINT

DAKOTA   Minneapolis   PAUL   W I S C O N S I N   Lake

Watertown   Rochester   Michigan

PIERRE   M I C H I G A N

Mitchell   Sioux Falls   3

Mason City

Missouri   Dubuque

A S K A   I O W A   Cedar Rapids   OHIO

Sioux City   ILLINOIS   INDIANA

Columbus   DES MOINES   Davenport   40°

North   Council Bluffs

Platte   Omaha   ♦ The deadliest tornado in US history struck Missouri on March 18, 1925. Leaving a continuous 219 mile (352 km) track, the tornado crossed three states and killed 695 people.

Platte   Burlington

LINCOLN

Hastings   Kirksville

St Joseph   4

akloy   Hays   Kansas City   Independence

Kansas City   Saint

TOPEKA   22

JEFFERSON CITY   Louis

KANSAS   M I S S O U R I   KENTUCKY

Dodge   Pratt   Wichita   Springfield   85°
City   5

Arkansas   35°

Ozark Plateau   TENNESSEE

OKLAHOMA   ARKANSAS   30   0 km   200

0 miles   200

90°   E   F   95°   G   H

The Boeing aircraft factory in Everett is the world's largest building by volume at 472 million cu ft (13.3 million cu m), covering 100 acres (40 hectares).

Hells Canyon is the deepest in the US, with cliffs up to 7993 ft (2436 m) high.

At Black Rock Desert on October 15, 1997, ThrustSSC, driven by Andy Green, became the first land vehicle to break the sound barrier by achieving a speed of 763 mph (1228 km/h).

Death Valley is not only the lowest point in North America, at 282 ft (86 m) below sea level, it is also the hottest, with a maximum air temperature of 134°F (57°C) recorded in 1913.

The Golden Gate Bridge, completed in 1937, has 80,000 miles (129,000 km) of wire in its two main cables, weighing a total of 22,200 tons (tonnes).

UTAH

NEVADA

Sierra Nevada

CALIFORNIA

Coast Ranges

PACIFIC OCEAN

ARIZONA

MEXICO

Lake Mead

Colorado

Death Valley

282 ft -86m -418m

Mt Whitney 4,957ft

Mojave Desert

Salton Sea

San Joaquin Valley

Susanville

Elko

Reno
Sparks

Fallon

Hawthorne

CARSON CITY

Pyramid Lake
Walker Lake

Tonopah

Las Vegas

Redding

Chico

Yuba City

Ukiah

Santa Rosa

SACRAMENTO

Stockton

Oakland
Berkeley
San Francisco
San Jose
Santa Cruz
Salinas
Monterey

Modesto

Merced

Fresno

Visalia

Bishop

Bakersfield

Mojave

Lancaster

Santa Barbara

Oxnard

Pasadena

Los Angeles
Long Beach
Huntington Beach

Santa Catalina I.
San Nicolas I.
San Clemente I.

Santa Rosa I.

Pacific Channel Islands

Barstow

San Bernardino
Riverside
Santa Ana
Oceanside

Palm Springs

San Diego
Chula Vista

0 km   200
0 miles   200

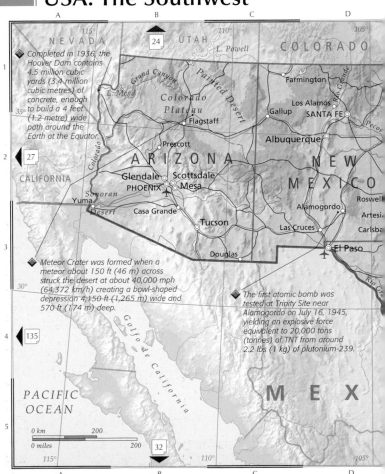

Completed in 1936, the Hoover Dam contains 4.5 million cubic yards (3.4 million cubic metres) of concrete, enough to build a 4 feet (1.2 metre) wide path around the Earth at the Equator.

Meteor Crater was formed when a meteor about 150 ft (46 m) across struck the desert at about 40,000 mph (64,372 km/h) creating a bowl-shaped depression 4,150 ft (1,265 m) wide and 570 ft (174 m) deep.

The first atomic bomb was tested at Trinity Site near Alamogordo on July 16, 1945, yielding an explosive force equivalent to 20,000 tons (tonnes) of TNT from around 2.2 lbs (1 kg) of plutonium-239.

On January 10, 1901, the Lucas Gusher blew oil 150 ft (46 m) into the air, flowing at 100,000 barrels a day until it was eventually capped nine days later.

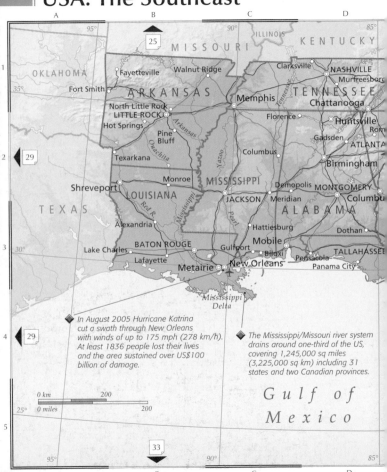

In August 2005 Hurricane Katrina cut a swath through New Orleans with winds of up to 175 mph (278 km/h). At least 1836 people lost their lives and the area sustained over US$100 billion of damage.

The Mississippi/Missouri river system drains around one-third of the US, covering 1,245,000 sq miles (3,225,000 sq km) including 31 states and two Canadian provinces.

Gulf of Mexico

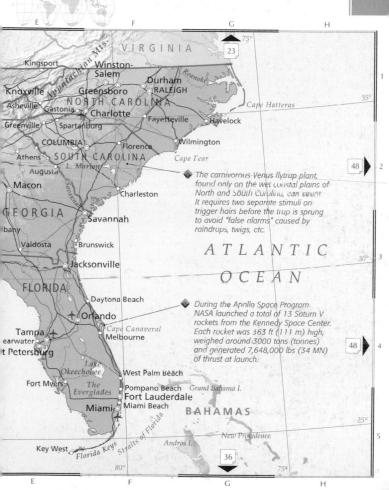

E   F   G   H

75°

23

VIRGINIA

Kingsport

Winston-Salem

Durham

RALEIGH

Roanoke

Knoxville

Greensboro

NORTH CAROLINA

35°

Asheville

Gastonia

Charlotte

Cape Hatteras

Greenville

Spartanburg

Fayetteville

Havelock

COLUMBIA

Florence

Wilmington

Athens

SOUTH CAROLINA

Cape Fear

Augusta

L. Marion

48

Macon

Savannah R.

Charleston

The carnivorous Venus flytrap plant,
found only on the wet coastal plains of
North and South Carolina, can count.
It requires two separate stimuli on
trigger hairs before the trap is sprung
to avoid "false alarms" caused by
raindrops, twigs, etc.

GEORGIA

Savannah

bany

Valdosta

Brunswick

A T L A N T I C

30°

Jacksonville

O C E A N

FLORIDA

Daytona Beach

During the Apollo Space Program
NASA launched a total of 13 Saturn V
rockets from the Kennedy Space Center.
Each rocket was 363 ft (111 m) high,
weighed around 3000 tons (tonnes)
and generated 7,648,000 lbs (34 MN)
of thrust at launch.

Orlando

Tampa

Cape Canaveral

earwater

Melbourne

48

t Petersburg

Lake
Okeechobee

West Palm Beach

Fort Myers

The
Everglades

Pompano Beach

Grand Bahama I.

Fort Lauderdale

Miami

Miami Beach

B A H A M A S

25°

Key West

Florida Keys

Straits of Florida

Andros I.

New Providence

80°

36

75°

E   F   G   H

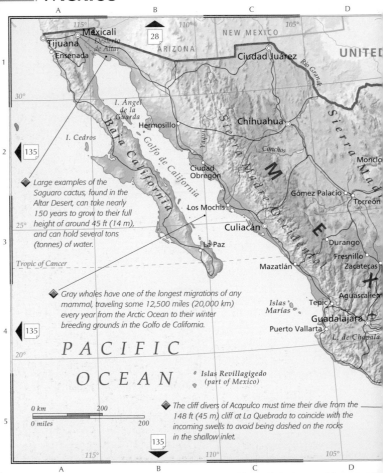

NEW MEXICO

ARIZONA

UNITE

Tijuana
Ensenada
Mexicali
Desierto de Altar

28

Ciudad Juarez

Río Grande

I. Ángel de la Guarda

Hermosillo

Chihuahua

I. Cedros

Baja California

Golfo de California

Conchos

Sierra Madre

Monclo

135

Ciudad Obregón

Gómez Palacio

Torreón

◆ Large examples of the Saguaro cactus, found in the Altar Desert, can take nearly 150 years to grow to their full height of around 45 ft (14 m), and can hold several tons (tonnes) of water.

Los Mochis

M

Culiacán

E

La Paz

Durango

Tropic of Cancer

Fresnillo
Zacatecas

Mazatlán

◆ Gray whales have one of the longest migrations of any mammal, traveling some 12,500 miles (20,000 km) every year from the Arctic Ocean to their winter breeding grounds in the Golfo de California.

Islas Marías

Tepic

Aguascalien

Guadalajara

135

Puerto Vallarta

L. de Chapala

PACIFIC

OCEAN

Islas Revillagigedo
(part of Mexico)

0 km   200

0 miles   200

◆ The cliff divers of Acapulco must time their dive from the 148 ft (45 m) cliff at La Quebrada to coincide with the incoming swells to avoid being dashed on the rocks in the shallow inlet.

135

E   F   G   H

30

95°   90°   85°

LOUISIANA

STATES OF AMERICA

TEXAS

1

Nuevo Laredo

In spring 2001, the Rio Grande stopped flowing
into the Gulf of Mexico for the first time in
recorded history, allowing illegal immigrants
to simply walk into the US.

25°   36

2

Reynosa

Matamoros

G u l f   o f

Monterrey

M e x i c o

Tropic of Cancer

altillo

Ciudad Victoria

It is thought that "The Ballgame," a ritual sport
played by Maya and Aztec civilizations, and a
forerunner of volleyball, often ended
with members of the losing team
being sacrificed

85°

Cancún

3

San Luis
Potosí   Tampico

Ciudad Valles

Río Verde

ón   Dolores Hidalgo   Poza Rica

Querétaro   Tulancingo   Bahía de Campeche

Pachuca

Morelia   Xalapa

MEXICO   Veracruz

CITY   Puebla   Coatzacoalcos

apan   Cuernavaca   Minatitlán

Tehuacán

Balsas   Oaxaca

Sierra Madre del Sur

Acapulco

Campeche

Mérida

20°

Yucatán
Peninsula

Isla
Cozumel

4

Villahermosa

34

BELIZE

Tuxtla

GUATEMALA

Golfo
de
Tehuantepec   Tapachula

15°

HONDURAS

5

100°   15°   95°   90°

34   EL SALVADOR

E   F   G   H

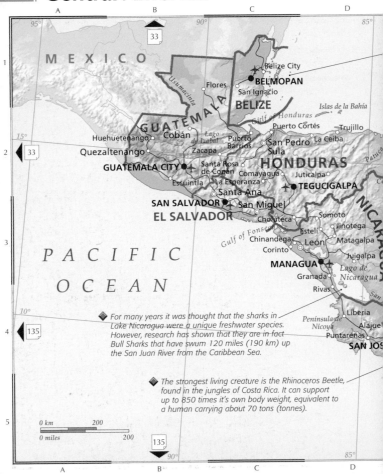

For many years it was thought that the sharks in Lake Nicaragua were a unique freshwater species. However, research has shown that they are in fact Bull Sharks that have swum 120 miles (190 km) up the San Juan River from the Caribbean Sea.

The strongest living creature is the Rhinoceros Beetle, found in the jungles of Costa Rica. It can support up to 850 times it's own body weight, equivalent to a human carrying about 70 tons (tonnes).

◆ The Great Blue Hole in Lighthouse Reef, a submerged cave some 1000 ft (303 m) in diameter and 400 ft (120 m) deep, was originally explored by Jacques Cousteau, co-inventor of the aqualung.

80°   75°

Greater Antilles

HAITI

JAMAICA

Islas Santanilla
(part of Honduras)

Bajo Nuevo
(part of Colombia)

15°

C a r i b b e a n

·Cayos Miskitos

. I. de Providencia
(part of Colombia)

S e a

. I. de San Andrés
(part of Colombia)

· Islas del Maíz

luefields

◆ Each chamber at Gatun Locks on the Panama Canal is 110 ft (33 m) wide and 1000 ft (303 m) long. The locks took four years to build and required 2 million cubic yards (1.5 million cu m) of concrete.

COSTA
RICA

·Limón

tiago

Colón

Gulf
of
Darien

Cordillera
Talamanca

PANAMA

David   Penonomé   PANAMA CITY

Panama
Canal   Isla del
Rey

COLOMBIA

Golfo
de
Chiriquí

Santiago

Chitré

Golfo
de
Panamá

Las Tablas

80°   75°

E   F   G   H

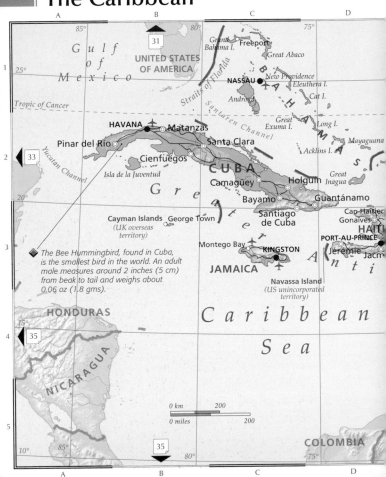

The Bee Hummingbird, found in Cuba, is the smallest bird in the world. An adult male measures around 2 inches (5 cm) from beak to tail and weighs about 0.06 oz (1.8 gms).

Gulf of Mexico

UNITED STATES OF AMERICA

Straits of Florida

Santaren Channel

Grand Bahama I.   Freeport

Great Abaco

New Providence

NASSAU

Eleuthera I.

Cat I.

Andros I.

Great Exuma I.

Long I.

Mayaguana

Acklins I.

Tropic of Cancer

HAVANA   Matanzas

Pinar del Río

Santa Clara

Cienfuegos

Yucatan Channel

Isla de la Juventud

CUBA

Greater

Camagüey

Holguín

Great Inagua

Bayamo

Guantánamo

Cap-Haïtien

Gonaïves

Cayman Islands   George Town
(UK overseas territory)

Santiago de Cuba

Montego Bay

KINGSTON

PORT-AU-PRINCE

Jérémie   Jac

HAITI

Anti

JAMAICA

Navassa Island
(US unincorporated territory)

HONDURAS

Caribbean

Sea

NICARAGUA

0 km   200

0 miles   200

COLOMBIA

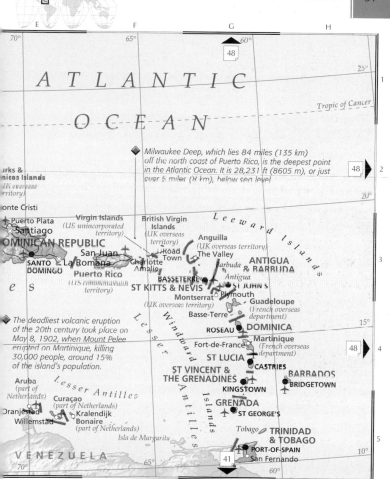

E F G H

70° 65° 60°

48

25°

A T L A N T I C

Tropic of Cancer

O C E A N

Milwaukee Deep, which lies 84 miles (135 km)
off the north coast of Puerto Rico, is the deepest point
in the Atlantic Ocean. It is 28,231 ft (8605 m), or just
over 5 miles (8 km), below sea level

48

20°

Turks &
Caicos Islands
*(UK overseas
territory)*

Monte Cristi

L e e w a r d   I s l a n d s

Puerto Plata
Santiago

DOMINICAN REPUBLIC

Virgin Islands
*(US unincorporated
territory)*

British Virgin
Islands
*(UK overseas
territory)*
Road
Town

Anguilla
(UK overseas territory)
The Valley

SANTO
DOMINGO
La Romana

San Juan

Charlotte
Amalie

Barbuda
Antigua

ANTIGUA
& BARBUDA
ST JOHN'S

Puerto Rico
*(US commonwealth
territory)*

BASSETERRE
ST KITTS & NEVIS

e s

Montserrat
(UK overseas territory)

Plymouth

Guadeloupe
*(French overseas
department)*

L e s s e r

Basse-Terre

The deadliest volcanic eruption
of the 20th century took place on
May 8, 1902, when Mount Pelée
erupted on Martinique, killing
30,000 people, around 15% of
the island's population.

ROSEAU

DOMINICA

15°

W i n d w a r d

Fort-de-France

Martinique
*(French overseas
department)*

48

ST LUCIA

CASTRIES

ST VINCENT &
THE GRENADINES

I s l a n d s

BARBADOS
BRIDGETOWN

4

Aruba
*(part of
Netherlands)*

L e s s e r   A n t i l l e s

KINGSTOWN

GRENADA

Oranjestad

Curaçao
(part of Netherlands)

Kralendijk
Bonaire
(part of Netherlands)

Willemstad

ST GEORGE'S

A n t i l l e s

Isla de Margarita

Tobago

TRINIDAD
& TOBAGO

VENEZUELA

41

PORT-OF-SPAIN
San Fernando

10°

5

E F G H

70° 65° 60°

South America

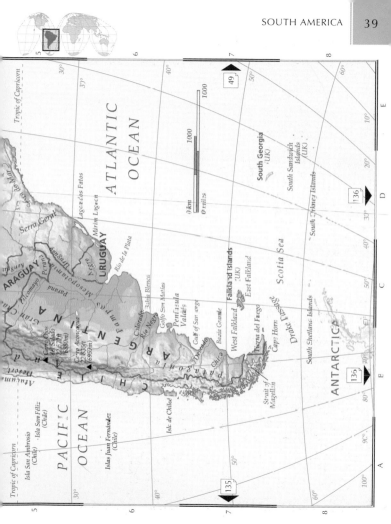

Caribbean Sea

PANAMA

PACIFIC

OCEAN

Santa Marta
Ríohacha
Gulf of Venezuela
Coro
Barranquilla
Maicao
Maracaibo
CARACA
Cartagena
Valledupar
Cabimas
Maracay
Ciudad Ojeda
Lago de Maracaibo
Barquisimeto
Valencia
Sincelejo
Valera
Acarigua
Montería
Mérida
Guanare
San Juan de los Morros
Cúcuta
Barinas
San Cristóbal
San Fernando
Bucaramanga
Arauca
Apure
Bello
Barrancabermeja
Arauca
VEN
Medellín
Quibdó
Itagüí
Tunja
Yopal
Puerto Carreño
Manizales
Meta
Pereira
BOGOTÁ
Armenia
Ibagué
Buenaventura
Villavicencio
COLOMBIA
Cali
Guaviare
Popayán
Neiva
San José del Guaviare
Pasto
Florencia
Mitú
Esmeraldas
Mocoa
Tulcán
Ibarra
Guárico
QUITO
Caquetá
Santo Domingo de los Colorados
Ambato
Manta
Riobamba
Putumayo
Portoviejo
Guayaquil
Milagro
ECUADOR
Cuenca
Golfo de Guayaquil
Machala
PERU
Loja

Cauca
Magdalena

◆ The first coffee seedlings were brought to Colombia in 1804 by Jesui missionaries; today, Colomb produces over 700,000 tons (tonnes) of coffee beans every year.

◆ Nestling between snow capped peaks at 9350 ft (2850 m), Quito is the second highest capital in the world after La Paz in Bolivia which has an elevation of 11,975 ft (3,650 m).

36
35
135
42

ATLANTIC OCEAN

GRENADA

Antilles

65° 60° 55°

Isla de Margarita

Cumaná

Carúpano

Barcelona

TRINIDAD & TOBAGO

Maturín

The Serpent's Mouth

Tucupita

El Tigre

Orinoco

Ciudad Guayana

Ciudad Bolívar

Embalse de Guri

Cuyuní

The Guiana Shield is one of the Earth's oldest surfaces, formed around 2 billion years ago.

(claimed by Venezuela)

Nieuw Amsterdam

St.-Laurent-du-Maroni

GEORGETOWN

New Amsterdam

PARAMARIBO

Sinnamary

Kourou

ZUELA

Caura

Paragua

Salto Ángel

Caroní

G u i a n a

GUYANA

Bartica

Rockstone

Linden

W. J. van Blommesteinmeer

SURINAME

French Guiana

CAYENNE

H i g h l a n d s

Orinoco

Essequibo

Courantyne

Maroni

(French overseas department)

Angel Falls (Salto Ángel) plunge a total of 3212 ft (979 m) to form the world's highest waterfall.

Acarai Mts.

(claimed by Suriname)

(claimed by Suriname)

The European Space Agency launch facility at Kourou takes advantage of the Earth's spin near the equator to gain 10 percent more payload than an equivalent launch at Cape Canaveral in the US.

Equator 0°

A m a z o n

B R A Z I L

B a s i n

2.47 acres (one hectare) of Amazon rain forest can contain more than 750 types of trees and 1500 plant species, amounting to around 900 tons (tonnes) of living plant material.

0 km 200

0 miles 200

37

49

13

43

10°

5°

65° 60° 55°

E F G H

Peru, Bolivia & North Brazil

COLOMBIA

VENEZUELA

Guiana Highlands

Boa Vista

GUYANA

0 km 400
0 miles 400

Equator

ECUADOR

Rio Negro

Represa Balbina

Napo

Putumayo

Amazon

Iquitos

Manaus

Amazon

Juruá

P E R U

Moyobamba

Tarapoto

Marañón

Ucayali

Amazon

Piura

Chiclayo

Saña

Trujillo

Chimbote

Pucallpa

Huaraz

Huánuco

Huacho

La Oroya

Callao

LIMA

Huancayo

Ayacucho

Pisco

Ica

Nazca

Amazon Basin

Madeira

B R A [Z I L]

Purus

Porto Velho

Rio Branco

Madre de Dios

Puerto Maldonado

Riberalta

Beni

Guaporé

Trinidad

BOLIVIA

Puno

Cusco

PACIFIC OCEAN

Arequipa

Lake Titicaca

LA PAZ

Cochabamba

Montero

Santa Cruz

Tacna

Oruro

Lago Poopó

SUCRE

Puerto Suárez

Potosí

Uyuni

Tupiza

Tarija

CHILE

PARAGUAY

ARGENTINA

◆ *Lake Titicaca is the largest lake in South America at 3220 sq miles (8340 sq km). With an altitude of 12,500 ft (3810 m) it is also the world's highest navigable lake.*

BOLIVIA'S TWO CAPITALS

La Paz - legislative and administrative capital

Sucre - legal capital

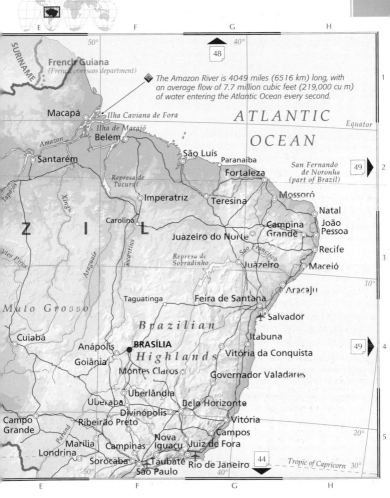

SURINAME

50°   40°

48

French Guiana
(French overseas department)

The Amazon River is 4049 miles (6516 km) long, with
an average flow of 7.7 million cubic feet (219,000 cu m)
of water entering the Atlantic Ocean every second.

Macapá   Ilha Caviana de Fora

ATLANTIC

Amazon   Ilha de Marajó

Belém   Equator

OCEAN

Santarém   São Luís   Paranaiba

Tapajós   Fortaleza   San Fernando   49
de Noronha
(part of Brazil)

Represa de   Mossoró
Tucuruí   Imperatriz   Teresina

Xingu   Carolina   Natal

Z   I   L   Campina   João
Juazeiro do Norte   Grande   Pessoa

Tocantins   São Francisco   Recife

les Pires   Araguaia   Represa de   Juazeiro   Maceió
Sobradinho

Mato Grosso   Taguatinga   Feira de Santana   Aracaju

10°

Salvador

Cuiabá   Brazilian   Itabuna
BRASÍLIA

Anápolis   Highlands   Vitória da Conquista   49

Goiânia   Montes Claros   Governador Valadares

Uberlândia

Uberaba   Belo Horizonte

Campo   Divinópolis   Vitória
Grande   Ribeirão Preto   Campos   20°
Paraná

Marília   Nova   Juiz de Fora

Londrina   Campinas   Iguaçu   44

Sorocaba   Taubaté   Rio de Janeiro   Tropic of Capricorn   30°

50°   São Paulo   40°

E   F   G   H

Paraguay, Uruguay & South Brazil

◆ Formed by river deposits washed down from the Andes and Brazilian Shield, the Gran Chaco is virtually free of stones. It is composed of sand and silt sediments that are up to 10,000 ft (3050 m) thick.

◆ With a maximum height of 269 ft (82 m) and a total width of 1.7 miles (2.7 km) Iguaçu Falls has a peak flow rate of 452,000 cu ft/s (12,799 cu m/s) which would fill five Olympic size swimming pools every second.

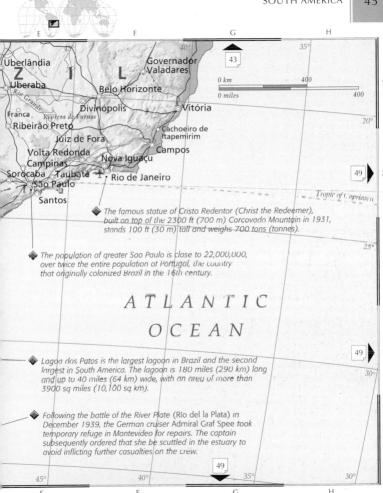

E F G H

Uberlândia

Z I L

Uberaba

Rio Grande

Belo Horizonte

Divinópolis

Franca · Represa de Furnas

Ribeirão Preto · Vitória

Juiz de Fora · Cachoeiro de Itapemirim

Volta Redonda

Campinas · Nova Iguaçu · Campos

Sorocaba · Taubaté

São Paulo · Rio de Janeiro

Santos

Governador Valadares

43

0 km 400

0 miles 400

20°

25°

Tropic of Capricorn

49

49

◆ The famous statue of Cristo Redentor (Christ the Redeemer), built on top of the 2300 ft (700 m) Corcovado Mountain in 1931, stands 100 ft (30 m) tall and weighs 700 tons (tonnes).

◆ The population of greater Sao Paulo is close to 22,000,000, over twice the entire population of Portugal, the country that originally colonized Brazil in the 16th century.

ATLANTIC

OCEAN

49

30°

◆ Lagoa dos Patos is the largest lagoon in Brazil and the second largest in South America. The lagoon is 180 miles (290 km) long and up to 40 miles (64 km) wide, with an area of more than 3900 sq miles (10,100 sq km).

◆ Following the battle of the River Plate (Río de la Plata) in December 1939, the German cruiser Admiral Graf Spee took temporary refuge in Montevideo for repairs. The captain subsequently ordered that she be scuttled in the estuary to avoid inflicting further casualties on the crew.

45° 40° 35° 30°

49

E F G H

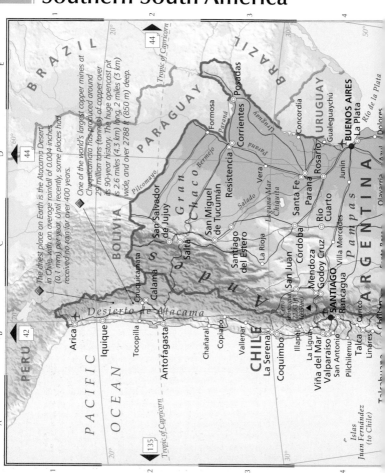

The driest place on Earth is the Atacama Desert in Chile, with an average rainfall of 0.004 inches (0.1 mm) per year. Until recently, some places had received no rain for over 400 years.

One of the world's largest copper mines at Chuquicamata has produced around 29 million tons (tonnes) of copper over its 90-year history. The huge opencast pit is 2.6 miles (4.3 km) long, 2 miles (3 km) wide, and over 2788 ft (850 m) deep.

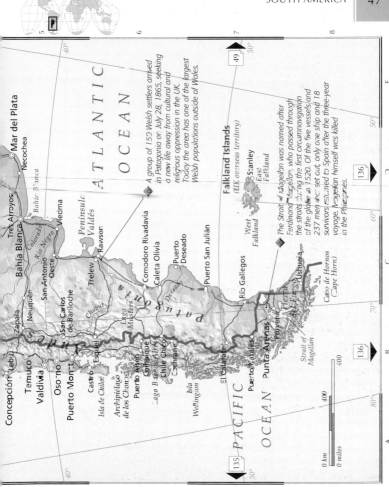

ATLANTIC

OCEAN

A group of 153 Welsh settlers arrived in Patagonia on July 28, 1865, seeking a new life away from cultural and religious oppression in the UK. Today the area has one of the largest Welsh populations outside of Wales.

Mar del Plata

Necochea

Tres Arroyos

Bahía Blanca

Colorado

Río Negro

San Antonio Oeste

Viedma

Península Valdés

Rawson

Trelew

Chubut

Comodoro Rivadavia

Caleta Olivia

Puerto Deseado

Puerto San Julián

Falkland Islands
(UK overseas territory)

Stanley

East Falkland

West Falkland

The Strait of Magellan was named after Ferdinand Magellan, who passed through the straits during the first circumnavigation of the globe in 1520. Of the five vessels, and 237 men who set out, only one ship and 18 survivors returned to Spain after the three-year voyage. Magellan himself was killed in the Philippines.

Concepción (Lebu)

Temuco

Valdivia

Osorno

Puerto Montt

Castro

Isla de Chiloé

Archipiélago de los Chonos

Puerto Aisén

Coihaique

Chile Chico

Cochrane

Lago Buenos Aires

Isla Wellington

El Calafate

Puerto Natales

Punta Arenas

Porvenir

Tierra del Fuego

Ushuaia

Cabo de Hornos (Cape Horn)

Zapala

Neuquén

San Carlos de Bariloche

Esquel

Lago Musters

Patagonia

Río Gallegos

Andes

Strait of Magellan

PACIFIC

OCEAN

Bahía Blanca

0 km   400

0 miles   400

The Atlantic Ocean

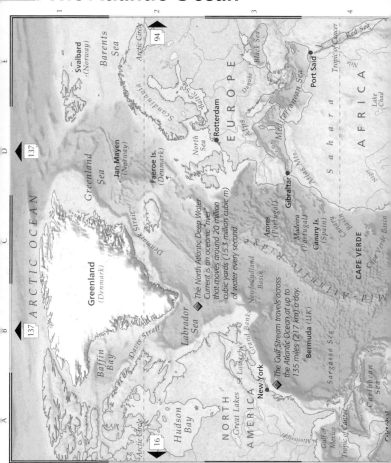

94

ARCTIC OCEAN

Svalbard *(Norway)*

Barents Sea

Arctic Circle

Scandinavia

Baltic Sea

Black Sea

Red Sea

Tropic of Cancer

Port Said

Nile

Danube

Alps

EUROPE

Rotterdam

North Sea

Mediterranean Sea

Sahara

AFRICA

Lake Chad

Niger

137

Greenland Sea

Jan Mayen *(Norway)*

Faeroe Is. *(Denmark)*

Gibraltar

Atlas Mts.

Portugal

Madeira *(Portugal)*

Azores *(Portugal)*

Canary Is. *(Spain)*

Canary Basin

CAPE VERDE

Cape Verde Basin

137

Greenland *(Denmark)*

Denmark Strait

Labrador Sea

◇ The North Atlantic Deep Water Current is an oceanic "river" that moves around 20 million cubic yards (15.3 million cubic m) of water every second.

MID-ATLANTIC RIDGE

Newfoundland Basin

Baffin Bay

Davis Strait

Grand Banks

Bermuda *(UK)*

Sargasso Sea

Caribbean Sea

Hudson Bay

Arctic Circle

NORTH AMERICA

Great Lakes

Labrador

New York

◆ The Gulf Stream travels across the Atlantic Ocean at up to 135 miles (217 km) a day.

Gulf of Mexico

Mississippi

Tropic of Cancer

16

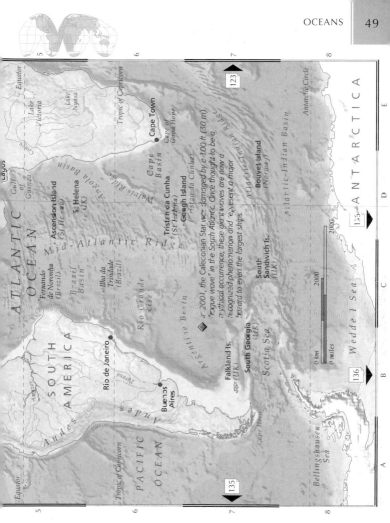

ATLANTIC OCEAN

SOUTH AMERICA

PACIFIC OCEAN

Equator

Tropic of Capricorn

Andes

Pampas

Buenos Aires

Rio de Janeiro

Amazon

Fernando de Noronha (Brazil)

Brazil Basin

Illa da Trindade (Brazil)

Rio Grande Rise

Argentine Basin

Mid-Atlantic Ridge

Ascension Island (St Helena)

St Helena (UK)

Tristan da Cunha (St Helena)

Gough Island (St Helena)

Tristan da Cunha

Walvis Ridge

Cape Basin

Cape Town

Cape of Good Hope

Angola Basin

Gulf of Guinea

Lagos

Lake Victoria

Lake Nyasa

Congo

Equator

Tropic of Capricorn

Falkland Is. (UK)

South Georgia (UK)

Scotia Sea

South Sandwich Is. (UK)

Weddell Sea

Bouvet Island (Norway)

Atlantic-Indian Basin

Atlantic-Indian Ridge

Antarctic Circle

ANTARCTICA

Cape Horn

Bellingshausen Sea

In 2001, the Caledonian Star was damaged by c.100 ft (30 m) "rogue wave" in the South Atlantic. Once thought to be a mythical occurrence, these giant waves are now a recognized phenomenon and represent a major hazard to even the largest ships.

0 km   2000

0 miles   2000

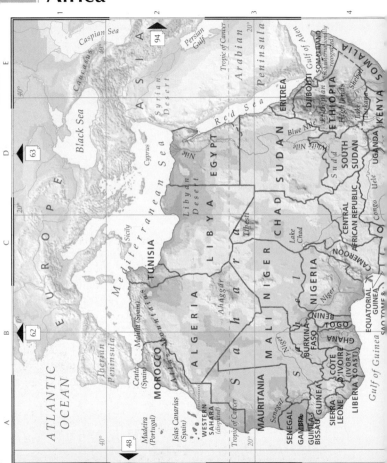

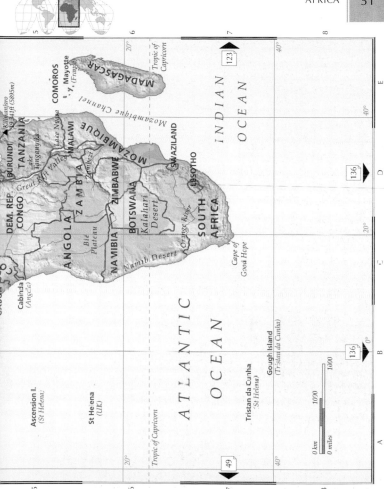

ASCENSION I.
(St Helena)

St Helena
(UK)

Tristan da Cunha
(St Helena)

Gough Island
(Tristan da Cunha)

ATLANTIC

OCEAN

Tropic of Capricorn

CABINDA
(Angola)

GABON

DEM. REP.
CONGO

ANGOLA

Bié
Plateau

NAMIBIA

Namib Desert

BURUNDI

TANZANIA

▲Kilimanjaro
19,341ft (5895m)

Lake
Tanganyika

Great Rift Valley

ZAMBIA

Zambezi

Lake Nyasa

MALAWI

ZIMBABWE

BOTSWANA

Kalahari
Desert

Orange River

SOUTH
AFRICA

Cape of
Good Hope

LESOTHO

SWAZILAND

MOZAMBIQUE

COMOROS

Mayotte
(France)

Mozambique Channel

Tropic of Capricorn

MADAGASCAR

INDIAN

OCEAN

0 km   1000
0 miles   1000

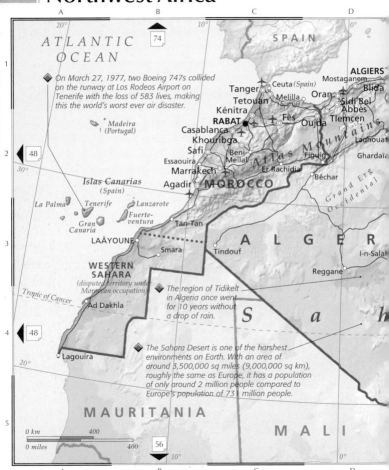

ATLANTIC OCEAN

74

SPAIN

◆ On March 27, 1977, two Boeing 747s collided on the runway at Los Rodeos Airport on Tenerife with the loss of 583 lives, making this the world's worst ever air disaster.

ALGIERS
Mostaganem
Blida
Tanger · Ceuta *(Spain)*
Oran · Sidi Bel
Tetouán · Melilla *(Spain)* · Abbès
Kénitra · Tlemcen
Fès · Oujda
RABAT
Laghoua
Casablanca
Khouribga · Beni-
Safi · Mellal · Figuig
Essaouira · Er Rachidia · Ghardaïa
Marrakech · MOROCCO · Béchar
Agadir

48

Madeira
(Portugal)

Islas Canarias
(Spain)
La Palma · Tenerife · Lanzarote
Gran · Fuerte-
Canaria · ventura
Tan-Tan

LAÂYOUNE
Smara · Tindouf
I-n-Salah

WESTERN
SAHARA
(disputed territory under Moroccan occupation)

Tropic of Cancer

Reggane

◆ The region of Tidikelt in Algeria once went for 10 years without a drop of rain.

Ad Dakhla

S a h

48

◆ The Sahara Desert is one of the harshest environments on Earth. With an area of around 3,500,000 sq miles (9,000,000 sq km), roughly the same as Europe, it has a population of only around 2 million people compared to Europe's population of 731 million people.

Lagouira

MAURITANIA

MALI

0 km   400
0 miles   400

56

ALGER
Grand Erg Occidental
Atlas Mountains

E   F   G   H

87

ITALY
Sicily
GREECE
Crete

Annaba
Bizerte
TUNIS
Constantine
Kairouan
Sousse
MALTA
Mediterranean
Sea

The hottest place ever recorded on earth
was Al 'Aziziyah, Libya, on September 13,
1922 when the air temperature reached
136°F (57.8°C)

Sétif
Batna
Biskra
Gafsa
Sfax
Gabès
Zuwárah
Az Záwiyah
TRIPOLI
Al Khums
Mi~rátah
Gharyán
Yafran
Jurt
Khalij Surt
Banghází
Al Bayçá'
Al Marj
Darnah
Ûubruq
Ajdabiya

54

Shott
Melghir
Tozeur
Médenine
Touggourt
TUNISIA

20°

Touggourt
Ouargla
Grand Erg
Oriental

LIBYA

Great
Sand Sea

EGYPT

Birák
Awbári
Sabhá
Murzuq

L i b y a n

Al Kufrah

Tropic of Cancer

Tassili n Ajjer

S a h a r a

D e s e r t

54

Ahaggar

Tibesti

Tamanrasset

20°

Libya has the largest proven oil reserves
in Africa, estimated at 41.5 billion barrels
in 2008. With a production capacity of
around 1.8 million barrels per day, these
reserves are expected to last for
another 60 years.

NIGER

CHAD

58

E   F   G   H

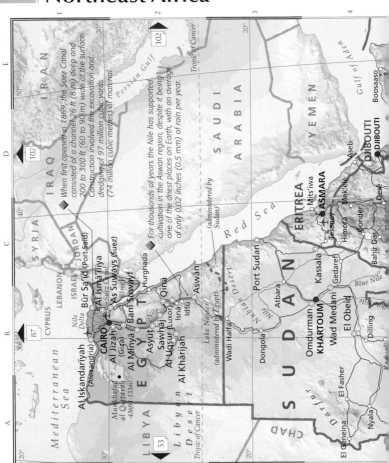

When first opened in 1869, the Suez Canal consisted of a channel 26 ft (8 m) deep and 200 to 300 ft (60 to 90 m) wide at the surface. Construction involved the excavation and dredging of 97 million cubic yards (74 million cubic metres) of material.

For thousands of years the Nile has supported cultivation in the Aswan region, despite it being one of the driest places on Earth, with an average of only 0.02 inches (0.5 mm) of rain per year.

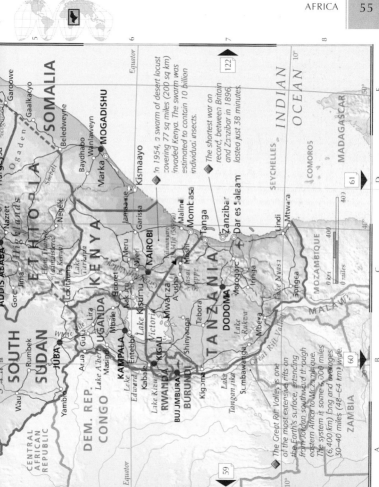

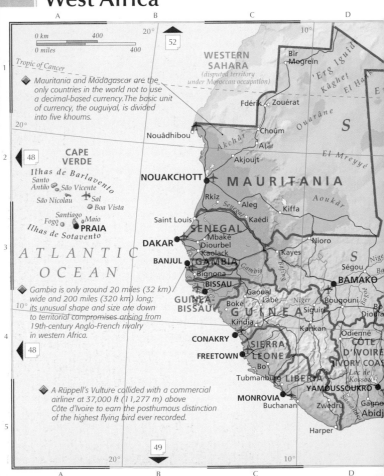

52

WESTERN SAHARA (disputed territory under Moroccan occupation)

Tropic of Cancer

◆ *Mauritania and Madagascar are the only countries in the world not to use a decimal-based currency. The basic unit of currency, the ouguiya, is divided into five khoums.*

20°

Nouâdhibou

Fdérik · Zouérat

Choûm

Atâr

Akjoujt

Bîr Mogrein

'Erg Iguîdî

El Hank

Kâghet

Owarâne

Akchâr

S

El Mreyyé

Aoukâr

48

CAPE VERDE

Ilhas de Barlavento
Santo Antão · São Vicente
São Nicolau · Sal
· Boa Vista
Santiago · Maio
Fogo
PRAIA
Ilhas de Sotavento

NOUAKCHOTT

MAURITANIA

Rkiz
Aleg
Kiffa
Kaédi
Nioro

DAKAR

Saint Louis

Senegal

SENEGAL
Mbaké
Diourbel
Kaolack

Kayes

Ségou

BAMAKO

S

ATLANTIC

OCEAN

BANJUL

GAMBIA

Gambia

Bignona

BISSAU

◆ *Gambia is only around 20 miles (32 km) wide and 200 miles (320 km) long; its unusual shape and size are down to territorial compromises arising from 19th-century Anglo-French rivalry in western Africa.*

10°

GUINEA-BISSAU

Gaoual

Boké

Labé

Niger

Siguiri

Bougouni

Bo

Diou

Kindia

Kankan

Odienné

CÔTE D'IVOIRE
IVORY COAS

CONAKRY

GUINEA

48

FREETOWN

SIERRA LEONE

Bo

Tubmanburg

LIBERIA

Lac de Kossou

YAMOUSSOUKRO

Gagno

Abidj

◆ *A Rüppell's Vulture collided with a commercial airliner at 37,000 ft (11,277 m) above Côte d'Ivoire to earn the posthumous distinction of the highest flying bird ever recorded.*

MONROVIA

Buchanan

Zwedru

Harper

49

20°

10°

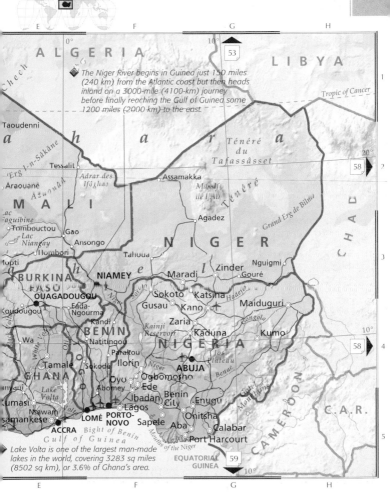

E   F   G   H

0°   10°

A L G E R I A   53   L I B Y A

Chech

◆ The Niger River begins in Guinea just 150 miles
(240 km) from the Atlantic coast but then heads
inland on a 3000-mile (4100-km) journey
before finally reaching the Gulf of Guinea some
1200 miles (2000 km) to the east.

Tropic of Cancer

Taoudenni

a   h   a   r   *Ténéré*
     du
     Tafassâsset   a   20°

Erg I-n-Sâkâne   58

Tessalit

Erg   Araouane   *Azaouad*   *Adrar des*
   Ifôghas   ○Assamakka   *Massif*
     de l'Aïr

M A L I   *Ténéré*   *Grand Erg de Bilma*

Lac
Faguibine   ○Agadez   C H A D
Tombouctou ○Gao
○ *Lac*
Niangay   Ansongo   N I G E R

Mopti   ○Hombori   Tahoua○
   h   *e*   *l*   Zinder○   ○Nguigmi   58

BURKINA   NIAMEY●   Maradi○   ○Gouré   10°
FASO
OUAGADOUGOU●   Sokoto○   Katsina○
  Eda-   Gusau○ ○Kano   ○Maiduguri
Koudougou● ○Ngourma
  Kandi○   Zaria○
Wa○   B E N I N   *Kainji*   ○Kaduna   ○Kumo
     Natitingou○   *Reservoir*   N I G E R I A
  Parakou○   ●ABUJA   *Jos*   C.A.R.
Tamale○   Sokodé○ Ilorin○   *Plateau*
G H A N A   Oyo○ Ogbomosho○   *Benue*
     Abomey○ ○Ede   Benin   ○Enugu
Kumasi○   *Lake*   Ibadan○   City○   ○Onitsha
○Nsawam   *Volta*   Lagos●   ○Aba   ○Calabar
samankese○   LOMÉ● PORTO-   Sapele○   Port Harcourt○
ACCRA●   NOVO●   C A M E R O O N
     Bight of Benin   *Mouths*
     Gulf of Guinea   *of the Niger*

◆ Lake Volta is one of the largest man-made
lakes in the world, covering 3283 sq miles
(8502 sq km), or 3.6% of Ghana's area.

EQUATORIAL
GUINEA   59   10°

E   F   G   H

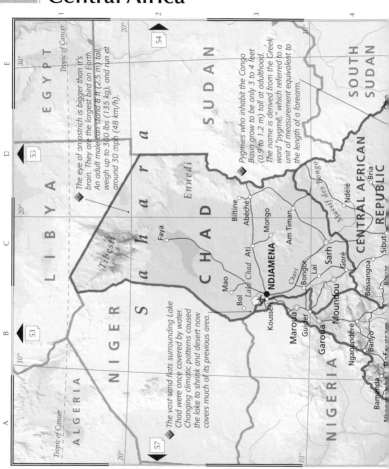

The eye of an ostrich is bigger than it's brain. They are the largest bird on Earth. An adult male can stand 8 ft (2.5 m) tall, weigh up to 300 lbs (135 kg), and run at around 30 mph (48 km/h).

Pygmies who inhabit the Congo Basin grow to be only 3 to 4 feet (0.9 to 1.2 m) tall at adulthood. The name is derived from the Greek word "pygmé," which referred to a unit of measurement equivalent to the length of a forearm.

The vast sand flats surrounding Lake Chad were once covered by water. Changing climatic patterns caused the lake to shrink and desert now covers much of its previous area.

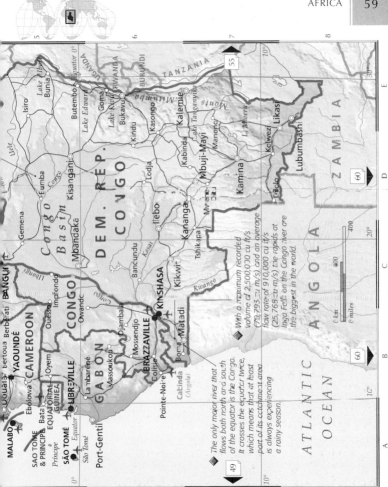

AFRICA

DEM. REP. CONGO

CONGO Basin

CAMEROON
YAOUNDÉ
Ebolowa

EQUATORIAL GUINEA
MALABO
Bata
LIBREVILLE
Oyem
SÃO TOMÉ & PRÍNCIPE
SÃO TOMÉ
Príncipe
São Tomé

GABON
La Mbarené
Port-Gentil

CONGO
Owando
Ouesso
Djambala
Mossendjo
BRAZZAVILLE
Colisie
Pointe-Noire

Cabinda
(Angola)

ANGOLA

ATLANTIC OCEAN

BANGUI
Berbérati
Nola
Yokadouma

Gemena
Eumba
Impfondo
Ubangi
Ubangu

Mbandaka
Kisangani
Butembo
Isiro
Bunia
Lake Albert
Lake Edward
Goma
Lake Kivu
Bukavu
RWANDA
BURUNDI
TANZANIA

UGANDA
Equator 0°

Uele
Congo

Kindu
Kasongo
Kalemie
Mitumba
Monts
Lake Tanganyika
Kalemie
Klemie

Bancundu
Ilebo
Todja
Kabinda
Mbuji-Mayi
Manono
L. Mweru
Kolwezi
Likasi
Lubumbashi

Kikwit
Tshikapa
Kananga
Mwene-Ditu
Kamina

Matadi
Boma
KINSHASA
Kwango
Kwilu
Kesai

ZAMBIA

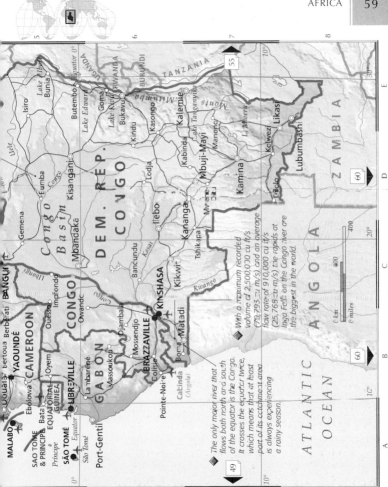

The only major river that flows both north and south of the equator is the Congo. It crosses the equator twice, which means that at least part of its catchment area is always experiencing a rainy season.

With a maximum recorded volume of 2,500,070 cu ft/s (70,793 cu m/s) and an average flow rate of 910,000 cu ft/s (25,768 cu m/s) the rapids at Inga Falls on the Congo river are the biggest in the world.

km 400
0 miles 400

49
55
60
60

Southern Africa

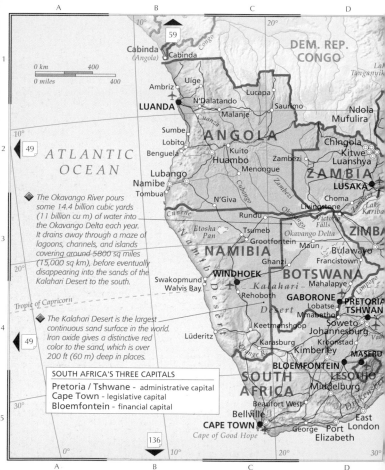

ATLANTIC OCEAN

◆ The Okavango River pours some 14.4 billion cubic yards (11 billion cu m) of water into the Okavango Delta each year. It drains away through a maze of lagoons, channels, and islands covering around 5800 sq miles (15,000 sq km), before eventually disappearing into the sands of the Kalahari Desert to the south.

◆ The Kalahari Desert is the largest continuous sand surface in the world. Iron oxide gives a distinctive red color to the sand, which is over 200 ft (60 m) deep in places.

SOUTH AFRICA'S THREE CAPITALS

Pretoria / Tshwane - administrative capital
Cape Town - legislative capital
Bloemfontein - financial capital

DEM. REP. CONGO

Cabinda (Angola)
Cabinda
Ambriz
Uíge
Lucapa
N'Dalatando
Saurimo
LUANDA
Malanje
Ndola
Mufulira
Sumbe
ANGOLA
Chingola
Lobito
Kuito
Kitwe
Benguela
Huambo
Zambezi
Luanshya
Menongue
ZAMBIA
Lubango
LUSAKA
Namibe
Tombua
N'Giva
Choma
Rundu
Livingstone
Victoria Falls
Cunene
Etosha Pan
Tsumeb
Okavango Delta
ZIMB
Grootfontein
Maun
Bulawayo
NAMIBIA
Ghanzi
Francistown
Swakopmund
WINDHOEK
Kalahari
BOTSWANA
Walvis Bay
Mahalapye
Rehoboth
Desert
GABORONE
PRETORIA
Keetmanshoop
Lobatse
TSHWAN
Mmabatho
Soweto
Lüderitz
Johannesburg
MASERU
Karasburg
Kroonstad
Kimberley
BLOEMFONTEIN
LESOTHO
SOUTH
Middelburg
AFRICA
Beaufort West
Bellville
East London
CAPE TOWN
George
Port Elizabeth
Cape of Good Hope

E F G H

122

◆ Coco de Mer, or the double coconut palm, produces some of the largest seeds in the plant kingdom. Weighing up to 60 lbs (27 kg), they take around 10 years to ripen.

TANZANIA

Mbala
Kasama
MALAWI
Mzuzu
Mpika
LILONGWE
Salima
Blantyre
Tete
Zomba
Nsanje
HARARE
Chitungwiza
Chimoio
Beira
Inhambane
Xai-Xai
MAPUTO
MBABANE
SWAZILAND
Pietermaritzburg
Durban

Rovuma
Mocímboa da Praia
Nacala
Moçambique
Mocuba
Quelimane

MOZAMBIQUE
Mozambique Channel

Lake Nyasa

COMOROS
Grande Comore
● **MORONI**
Mnali *Anjouan*
Mamoudzou
Mayotte
(French overseas department)

Nampula
Mahajanga
Antsohihy

Inner Islands
VICTORIA ✈ *Mahé*
SEYCHELLES

Amirante Islands

Aldabra Group
Farquhar Group

Outer Islands

Antsiranaña

INDIAN

Antalaha

OCEAN

MADAGASCAR

ANTANANARIVO
Morondava
Fianarantsoa
Ihosy
Toliara
Amboasary

Ambositra
Mananjary
Farafangana
Vangaindrano

Fenoarivo Atsinanana
Toamasina

MAURITIUS
PORT LOUIS

Saint-Denis
Réunion
(French overseas department)

Mascarene Islands

Tropic of Capricorn

◆ In 1905, the world's largest rough diamond was discovered at the Cullinan Diamond Mine. Weighing 3106 carats, or about 1.3 pounds (0.6 kg), the diamond was cut into nine smaller stones, including the 530.2 carat "Cullinan I" or "Great Star of Africa," which forms part of the British Crown Jewels and is estimated to be worth over $400 million.

◆ Thought to have been extinct for 70 million years, a living coelacanth was netted in the Indian Ocean in 1938. They are powerful predators, averaging 5 feet (1.5 m) in length and weighing about 100 lbs (45 kg).

123
123
136

40° 50° 60°

E F G H

137
48
48
50

40°
20°
0°
Arctic Circle
Limit of winter pack ice

ICELAND

Lofo

Norwegian Sea

Faeroe Islands
(Denmark)

Outer Hebrides

British Isles

North Sea

DENMARK

Vadero
Vatte

Ireland Isle of Man
(to UK)
IRELAND
Britain

Celtic Sea
UNITED KINGDOM

NETHERLANDS

Nor

GERMANY

Elbe

BELGIUM
LUX.

CZEC
REPUB

English Channel
Channel Is.
(UK)

ATLANTIC OCEAN

40°

Bay of Biscay

Seine

FRANCE

Loire

Massif Central

Rhine

Garonne
Rhône

SWITZ. LIECH

AUSTRI

ALPS

▲ Mont Blanc
15,771ft (4807m)

Po

SLOVEN

CROA

40°

PORTUGAL

Duero

Pyrenees

MONACO

SAN MARINO

BOS
& HE

Tagus

Ebro

ANDORRA

Iberian Peninsula

SPAIN

Corsica

VATICAN CITY

ITALY

20°

*Madeira
(to Portugal)*

Strait of Gibraltar

Gibraltar
(UK)

Balearic Islands

Sardinia

Tyrrhenian Sea

Mediterra

Sicily

*Canary Islands
(to Spain)*

Atlas Mountains

AFRICA

MALTA

0°

E F G H

20° 40° 60° 80° 60°

Barents Sea

North Cape

Ostrov Kolguyev

1

Kola Peninsula

White Sea

80°

FINLAND

Northern Dvina

of Bothnia

Lake Onega

RUSSIAN

2

Åland

Lake Ladoga

ESTONIA

LATVIA

LITHUANIA

FEDERATION

European Plain

Central Russian Upland

Volga Uplands

Ural

3

BELARUS

Volga

Aral Sea

LAND

Pripet Marshes

Bug

Dnieper Lowlands

Don

UKRAINE

Dniester

Dnieper

VAKIA

MOLDOVA

Sea of Azov

Caspian Sea

NGARY

Crimea

Caucasus

4

ROMANIA

El'brus 18,510ft (5042m)

RBIA

Danube

Black Sea

N.

BULGARIA

Balkan Mts.

KOS

TURKEY

MAC

ANIA

A S I A

60°

GREECE

Aegean Sea

Anatolia

5

Peloponnese

e a

Crete

Cyprus

40°

E F G H

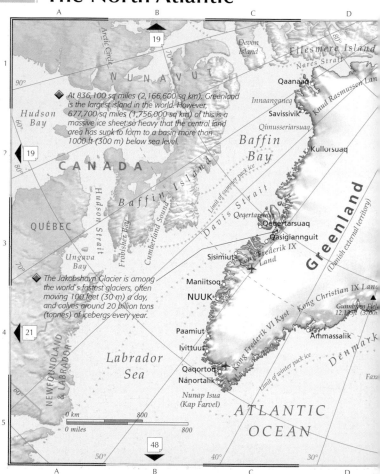

At 836,100 sq miles (2,166,600 sq km), Greenland is the largest island in the world. However, 677,700 sq miles (1,756,000 sq km) of this is a massive ice sheet so heavy that the central land area has sunk to form to a basin more than 1000 ft (300 m) below sea level.

The Jakobshavn Glacier is among the world's fastest glaciers, often moving 100 feet (30 m) a day, and calves around 20 billion tons (tonnes) of icebergs every year.

Greenland *(Danish external territory)*

Arctic Circle

Devon Island

Ellesmere Island

Nares Strait

Qaanaaq

Knud Rasmussen Land

Innaanganeq

Savissivik

Qimusseriarsuaq

Kullorsuaq

Baffin Bay

Hudson Bay

NUNAVUT

CANADA

Baffin Island

Limit of summer pack ice

Davis Strait

Qeqertarsuaq

Qeqertarsuaq

Qasigiannguit

Frederik IX Land

Sisimiut

Maniitsoq

NUUK

Kong Christian IX Land

Gunnbjørn Field
12,139ft (3700m)

Kong Frederik VI Kyst

Paamiut

Ammassalik

Ivittuut

Denmark

Qaqortoq

Nanortalik

Limit of winter pack ice

Nunap Isua
(Kap Farvel)

Faxe

QUÉBEC

Hudson Strait

Frobisher Bay

Cumberland Sound

Ungava Bay

Labrador Sea

NEWFOUNDLAND & LABRADOR

ATLANTIC OCEAN

0 km   800
0 miles   800

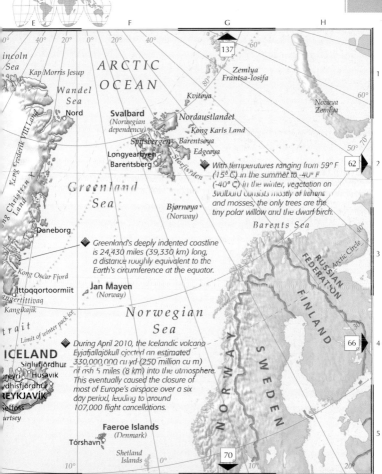

ARCTIC OCEAN

Lincoln Sea

Kap Morris Jesup

Wandel Sea

Nord

Kvitøya

Zemlya Frantsa-Iosifa

Svalbard
(Norwegian dependency)

Nordaustlandet

Novaya Zemlya

Kong Karls Land

Spitsbergen

Barentsøya

Longyearbyen
Barentsberg

Edgeøya

With temperatures ranging from 59° F (15° C) in the summer to -40° F (-40° C) in the winter, vegetation on Svalbard consists mostly of lichens and mosses; the only trees are the tiny polar willow and the dwarf birch.

Greenland Sea

Bjørnøya
(Norway)

Barents Sea

RUSSIAN FEDERATION

Daneborg

Arctic Circle

Greenland's deeply indented coastline is 24,430 miles (39,330 km) long, a distance roughly equivalent to the Earth's circumference at the equator.

Kong Oscar Fjord

Ittoqqortoormiit

Jan Mayen
(Norway)

FINLAND

Kangikajik

Norwegian Sea

Limit of winter pack ice

NORWAY

SWEDEN

ICELAND

During April 2010, the Icelandic volcano Eyjafjallajökull ejected an estimated 330,000,000 cu yd (250 million cu m) of ash 5 miles (8 km) into the atmosphere. This eventually caused the closure of most of Europe's airspace over a six day period, leading to around 107,000 flight cancellations.

Siglufjördhur
Húsavík
REYKJAVÍK
Selfoss

Faeroe Islands
(Denmark)

Tórshavn

Shetland Islands

The North Cape Current warms the northern coasts of Norway, Finland, and Russia's Kola Peninsula with water temperatures of 39–54° F (4–12° C), allowing this area of the Barents Sea to remain free of pack ice throughout the winter.

The sun is continuously visible from late May to late July in Tromsø because of its position well north of the Arctic Circle.

Carved by a massive glacier during the last Ice Age, Sognefjord is 4291 ft (1308 m) deep and 126 miles (203 km) long. Cliffs rise almost vertically from the water to heights of 3,330 ft (1000 m).

ARCTIC OCEAN

Barents Sea

RUSSIAN FEDERATION

Norwegian Sea

Nordkapp (North Cape)

Hammerfest

Tromsø

Narvik

Harstad

Vesterålen

Lofoten

Bodø

Mo i Rana

Steinkjer

Trondheimsfjorden

Vardø

Kirkenes

FINLAND

Sodankylä

Kuusamo

Kajaani

Kemijärvi

Kemi

Rovaniemi

Tornio

Oulu

Oulujärvi

Luleå

Piteå

Skellefteå

Kokkola

Kiruna

Gällivare

Kemijoki

Ounasjoki

Tornio

Muonio

Hyrynsalmi nen

0 km   200
0 miles   200

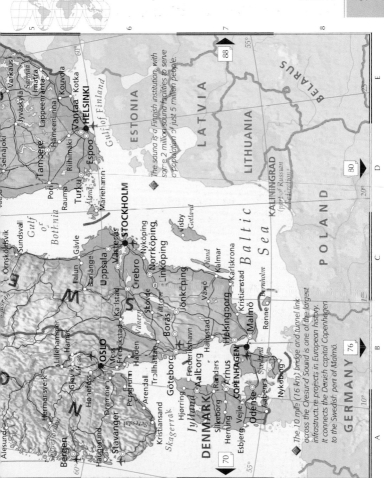

The sauna is a Finnish institution, with some 2 million sauna facilities to serve a population of just 5 million people.

The 10 mile (16 km) bridge and tunnel link across the Oresund Sound is one of the largest infrastructure projects in European history. It connects the Danish capital Copenhagen to the Swedish port of Malmö.

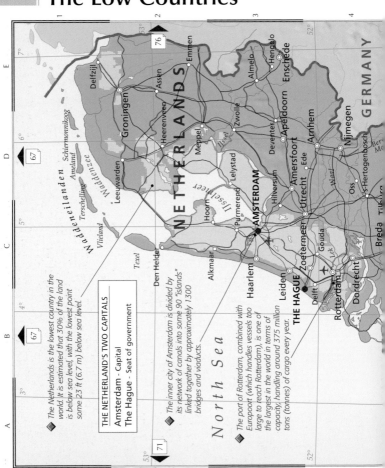

THE NETHERLAND'S TWO CAPITALS

Amsterdam - Capital
The Hague - Seat of government

◆ *The Netherlands is the lowest country in the world. It is estimated that 30% of the land is below sea level, with the lowest point some 23 ft (6.7 m) below sea level.*

◆ *The inner city of Amsterdam is divided by its network of canals into some 90 "islands" linked together by approximately 1300 bridges and viaducts.*

◆ *The port of Rotterdam, combined with Europoort (which handles vessels too large to reach Rotterdam), is one of the largest in the world in terms of capacity, handling around 375 million tons (tonnes) of cargo every year.*

GERMANY

NETHERLANDS

North Sea

Waddeneilanden

Schiermonnikoog
Ameland
Terschelling
Vlieland

Texel

Den Helder

Emmen
Delfzijl
Assen
Groningen
Heerenveen
Hengelo
Almelo
Enschede
Leeuwarden
Meppel
Zwolle
Deventer
Apeldoorn
Arnhem
IJssel
Lelystad
Amersfoort
Ede
Nijmegen
's-Hertogenbosch
Hilversum
Utrecht
Oss
Waal
Hoorn
Purmerend
AMSTERDAM
Breda
Alkmaar
Zoetermeer
Gouda
Haarlem
Leiden
THE HAGUE
Delft
Rotterdam
Dordrecht
Lek

IJsselmeer

Belgium and the Netherlands have an underground boundary that differs from the surface boundary shown on maps. In 1950, the two countries agreed to move the underground boundary so as not to divide coal mines between the two countries

GERMANY

Venlo

Heerlen

Maastricht

Verviers

Geleen

Liège

Seraing

LUXEMBOURG

Diekirch

LUXEMBOURG

Wasserbillig

Our

Sûre

Eisch

Esch-
sur-Alzette

Arlon

Bastogne

0 km 50

0 miles 50

Ardennes

BELGIUM

Antwerpen

Turnhout

Eindhoven

Hasselt

Tienen

Leuven

Mechelen

Namur

Meuse

Sambre

Dinant

Charleroi

La Louvière

Mons

Sint-
Niklaas

Gent

Aalst

Schelde

BRUSSELS

Tournai

Kortrijk

Brugge

Oostende

Zeebrugge

Terneuzen

Westerschelde

Roeselare

Ieper

Mouscron

Flanders

FRANCE

On August 23, 1914, three weeks after Britain entered World War I, the 70,000-strong British Expeditionary Force encountered the advancing German army for the first time at the battle of Mons.

Echternach is the home of the only religious dancing procession remaining in the Western world. Every year since the 15th century, thousands of pilgrims have marched down the streets of the town, performing a ritual dance involving specific movements, music, and prayers.

After the surrender of the German fleet in 1918 and its internment in Scapa Flow, over 50 ships were scuttled by the German crews on June 21, 1919, to prevent them falling into British hands.

With a depth of 788 ft (240 m) and a length of about 23 miles (36 km), Loch Ness contains the largest volume of fresh water in Great Britain.

Midges have the fastest wing-beat of any insect, and are able to flap their wings at around 60,000 beats per minute.

The Giant's Causeway comprises approximately 37,000 interlocking dark basalt polygonal columns; they were formed by volcanic activity some 55 million years ago.

ATLANTIC OCEAN

North Sea

Faeroe Islands

Shetland Islands
Lerwick

Orkney Islands
Kirkwall

Thurso

Ullapool

Isle of Lewis
Stornoway

Outer Hebrides

North Uist
South Uist

Barra

The Little Minch

The Minch

Isle of Skye

Isle of Mull
Oban

Loch Linnhe

Jura

Islay

Greenock

Fort William

Ben Nevis (1343 m)

SCOTLAND

Grampian Mts.

Elgin

Inverness

Loch Ness

Moray Firth

Aberdeen

Dundee

Perth

Stirling

Firth of Forth

EDINBURGH

Isle of Arran
Ayr

Glasgow

Southern Uplands

UNITED KINGDOM

Dumfries

Carlisle

Stranraer

NORTHERN

Londonderry

Newcastle upon Tyne

Every year over 1.8 billion pints (1 billion litres) of Guinness® Irish stout are consumed in over 100 countries around the world.

The River Severn has the second highest tidal range in the world, often giving rise to a tidal bore. In September 1996, one such wave carried a surfer for 5.7 miles (9 km).

Channel Islands (UK crown dependency)

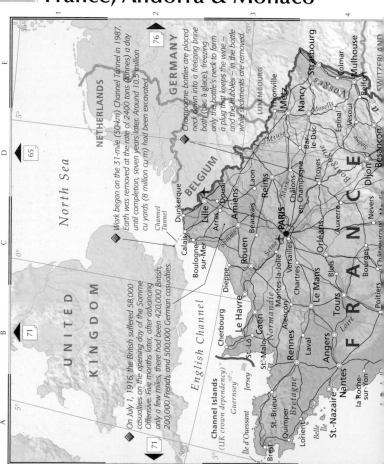

North Sea

NETHERLANDS

GERMANY

BELGIUM

LUXEMBOURG

UNITED KINGDOM

English Channel

F R A N C E

SWITZERLAND

Work began on the 31-mile (50-km) Channel Tunnel in 1987. Earth was removed at the rate of 2400 tons (tonnes) a day until completion, seven years later. Around 10.5 million cu yards (8 million cu m) had been excavated.

Champagne bottles are placed neck down into a freezing brine bath (bac à glace), freezing only the bottle's neck to form a plug that keeps the wine – and the bubbles – in the bottle while sediments are removed.

On July 1, 1916, the British suffered 58,000 casualties on the opening day of the Somme Offensive. Five months later, after advancing only a few miles, there had been 420,000 British, 200,000 French, and 500,000 German casualties.

Channel Islands
(UK crown dependency)
Guernsey
Jersey

Dunkerque
Calais
Boulogne-sur-Mer
Lille
Arras
Douai
Amiens
Beauvais
Rouen
Dieppe
Somme
Channel Tunnel

Cherbourg
Le Havre
Caen
St-Lô
St-Malo
Mantes-la-Jolie
Versailles
PARIS
Chartres
Le Mans
Alençon
Laval
Angers
Tours
Blois
Orléans
Bourges
Poitiers

Rennes
Nantes
la Roche-sur-Yon
St-Nazaire
Loire
Bretagne
St-Brieuc
Quimper
Lorient
Belle
Île
Île d'Ouessant
Brest

Laon
Reims
Châlons-en-Champagne
Marne
Troyes
Auxerre
Nevers

Thionville
Metz
Nancy
Strasbourg
Colmar
Mulhouse
Belfort
Epinal
Vesoul
Bar-le-Duc
Moselle
Meuse
Vosges
Dijon
Besançon
Saône
Bois de

Marne
Seine
Normandie

76
65
71
71

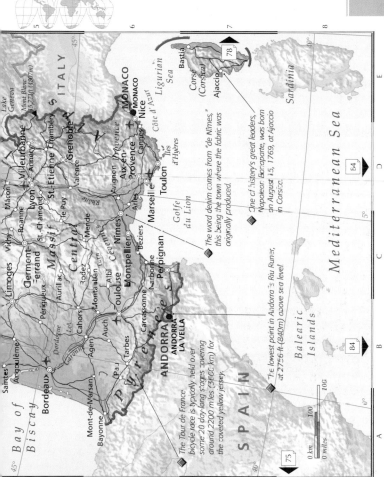

ITALY

Lake Geneva

Mont Blanc (15,771ft [4807m])

Villeurbanne

Chambéry

Annecy

Grenoble

MONACO

MONACO

Nice

Côte d'Azur

Cannes

Aix-en-Provence

Avignon

Provence

Îles d'Hyères

Ligurian Sea

Bastia

Corse (Corsica)

Ajaccio

Sardinia

Mende

Nîmes

Arles

Marseille

Toulon

Golfe du Lion

The word denim comes from "de Nîmes," this being the town where the fabric was originally produced.

One of history's great leaders, Napoleon Bonaparte, was born on August 15, 1769, at Ajaccio in Corsica.

Mâcon

Lyon

St-Étienne

St-Chamond

Le Puy

Roanne

Vichy

Clermont-Ferrand

Limoges

Périgueux

Rodez

Aurillac

Central

Massif

Albi

Montauban

Toulouse

Cahors

Agen

Auch

Tarbes

Béziers

Montpellier

Perpignan

Narbonne

Carcassonne

Cévennes

Mediterranean Sea

Balearic Islands

ANDORRA

ANDORRA LA VELLA

The lowest point in Andorra is Riu Runer, at 2756 ft (840m) above sea level.

SPAIN

Pau

Bayonne

Mont-de-Marsan

Bordeaux

Saintes

Angoulême

Bay of Biscay

Dordogne

Lot

Garonne

Pyrenees

The Tour de France bicycle race is typically held over some 20 day-long stages covering around 2200 miles (3600 km) for the coveted yellow jersey.

0 km   100
0 miles   100

Rhône

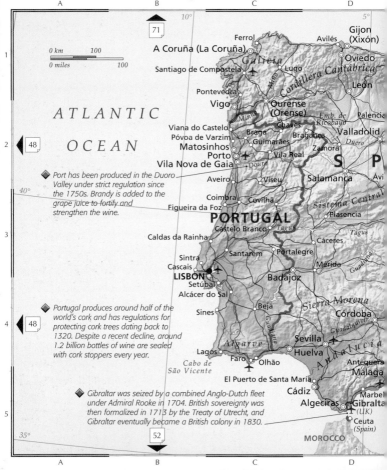

ATLANTIC

OCEAN

Galicia

A Coruña (La Coruña)
Ferrol
Avilés
Gijón (Xixón)
Santiago de Compostela
Lugo
Oviedo
Cordillera Cantábrica
León
Pontevedra
Vigo
Ourense (Orense)
Chaves
Emb. de Ricobayo
Palencia
Viana do Castelo
Braga
Bragança
Valladolid
Póvoa de Varzim
Guimarães
Vila Real
Zamora
Matosinhos
Duero
Porto
Vila Nova de Gaia
Viseu
Salamanca
Aveiro

◆ Port has been produced in the Duoro
Valley under strict regulation since
the 1750s. Brandy is added to the
grape juice to fortify and
strengthen the wine.

Coimbra
Covilhã
Figueira da Foz
PORTUGAL
Sistema Central
Plasencia
Castelo Branco
Tagus
Caldas da Rainha
Cáceres
Santarém
Portalegre
Sintra
Mérida
Cascais
LISBON
Badajoz
Setúbal
Alcácer do Sal

◆ Portugal produces around half of the
world's cork and has regulations for
protecting cork trees dating back to
1320. Despite a recent decline, around
1.2 billion bottles of wine are sealed
with cork stoppers every year.

Sines
Beja
Sierra Morena
Córdoba
Algarve
Sevilla
Lagos
Faro
Olhão
Huelva
Andalucía
Cabo de
São Vicente
El Puerto de Santa María
Antequera
Málaga
Cádiz
Marbe
Algeciras
Gibraltar (UK)

◆ Gibraltar was seized by a combined Anglo-Dutch fleet
under Admiral Rooke in 1704. British sovereignty was
then formalized in 1713 by the Treaty of Utrecht, and
Gibraltar eventually became a British colony in 1830.

Ceuta (Spain)

MOROCCO

0 km   100
0 miles   100

FRANCE

Bay of Biscay

Santander
Bilbao
Donostia-San Sebastián
Vitoria-Gasteiz
Miranda de Ebro
Pamplona (Iruña)
Burgos
Logroño
Huesca
ANDORRA
Soria
Lleida
Zaragoza
Terrassa
Sabadell
Reus
Tarragona
Tortosa
Figueres
Girona (Gerona)
Costa Brava
Mataró
Barcelona
L'Hospitalet de Llobregat

Pyrenees

Cataluña

Sistema Ibérico

Ebro

MADRID
Getafe
Cuenca
Teruel

egovia

Toledo

A I N

Golfe du Lion

Work continues on the Sagrada Família, Gaudí's unfinished cathedral. Begun in 1882, construction passed the mid-point in 2010 and is now due to be completed in around 2025.

Castellón de la Plana
Valencia
Gandia
Albacete
Elda
Cieza
Benidorm
Alicante (Alacant)
Murcia
Elche (Elx)
Lorca
Cartagena
Jaén
Granada
Sierra Nevada
Motril
Almería
Linares
Ciudad Real

País Valenciano

Júcar
Segura

Palma
Menorca
Mallorca
Ibiza
Islas Baleares (Balearic Islands)
Formentera

Seat of many great civilizations throughout history, the name Mediterranean translates as "sea between the lands."

Costa Blanca

Costa del Sol

Mediterranean Sea

A L G E R I A

The Kiel Canal is 61 miles (98 km) long and one of the busiest canals in the world, with around 45,000 ships a year passing between the Baltic and the North Sea.

Early in the morning of Sunday, August 13, 1961, work began on the Berlin Wall, which would eventually run for 66 miles (107 km) between east and west Berlin, cutting through 192 streets.

During what became known as "The Berlin Airlift" a total of 2,326,406 tons (tonnes) of supplies were flown into Berlin over an 18-month period to break a Soviet blockade of the city.

North Sea

Baltic Sea

SWEDEN

DENMARK

Jylland

Sjælland

Bornholm (Denmark)

Fyn

Falster

Fehmarn Belt

Fehmarn

Mecklenburger Bucht

POLAND

Rügen

Stralsund

Greifswald

Rostock

Wismar

Neubrandenburg

Müritz

Schwerin

GERMANY

Flensburg

Kiel

Neumünster

Lübeck

Lüneburg

Hamburg

Elbe

Wolfsburg

Magdeburg

Dessau

Halle

Saale

Potsdam

BERLIN

Spree

Frankfurt an der Oder

Cottbus

Dresden

Leipzig

Jena Gera

Erfurt

Göttingen

Kassel

Braunschweig

Salzgitter

Hildesheim

Hannover

Paderborn

Bielefeld

Hamm

Dortmund

Bochum

Wuppertal

Münster

Osnabrück

Cuxhaven

Bremerhaven

Bremen

Weser

Oldenburg

Emden

Ems

NETHERLANDS

Recklinghausen

Essen

Duisburg

Düsseldorf

Leverkusen

North Frisian Islands

0 km   100

0 miles   100

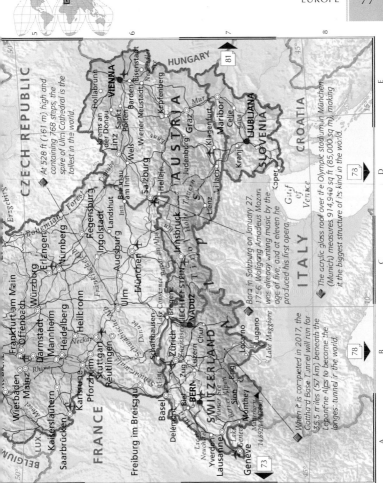

CZECH REPUBLIC

At 528 ft (161 m) high and containing 768 steps, the spire of Ulm Cathedral is the tallest in the world.

HUNGARY

FRANCE

GERMANY area names: Wiesbaden, Mainz, Frankfurt am Main, Offenbach, Darmstadt, Mannheim, Heidelberg, Würzburg, Erlangen, Nürnberg, Regensburg, Ingolstadt, Landshut, Augsburg, München, Ulm, Heilbronn, Stuttgart, Reutlingen, Pforzheim, Karlsruhe, Kaiserslautern, Saarbrücken, Freiburg im Breisgau

Bohemian Forest, Erzgebirge

AUSTRIA area names: Wien (VIENNA), Krems an der Donau, Linz, Wels, Steyr, Salzburg, Bad Ischl, Wiener Neustadt, Eisenstadt, Pollabrunn, Neusiedl, Baden, Kapfenberg, Leoben, Judenburg, Graz, Klagenfurt, Villach, Lienz, Spittal, Zell am See, Innsbruck, Bregenz

Maribor, Celje, Kranj, Koper, LJUBLJANA

SLOVENIA

CROATIA

ITALY

Gulf of Venice

SWITZERLAND area names: Basel, Delémont, Yverdon, Lausanne, Genève, BERN, Biel, Zürich, Zug, Luzern, Chur, Sion, Brig, Lugano, Locarno, Schaffhausen

LIECHTENSTEIN, VADUZ

Lake Constance (Bodensee), Bodensee, Lake Neuchâtel, Lac Léman, Lake Geneva, Thuner See, Brienzer See, Vierwaldstätter See, Lake Maggiore, Lago di Como

Bora in Salzburg on January 27, 1756, Wolfgang Amadeus Mozart was already writing music by the age of five, and at eleven he produced his first opera.

When it is completed in 2017, the Gotthard Base Tunnel will run for 35.5 miles (57 km) beneath the Lepontine Alps to become the longest railway tunnel in the world.

The acrylic glass roof over the Olympic stadium in München (Munich) measures 914,940 sq ft (85,000 sq m), making it the biggest structure of its kind in the world.

Matterhorn 14,692 ft (4,478 m)

Zürichsee, Rhine, Mosel, Neckar, Danube, Inn, Donau, Mur, Drava, Sava, Tirol, ALPS, T I R O L, Ötztaler Alpen

81 · 78 · 73

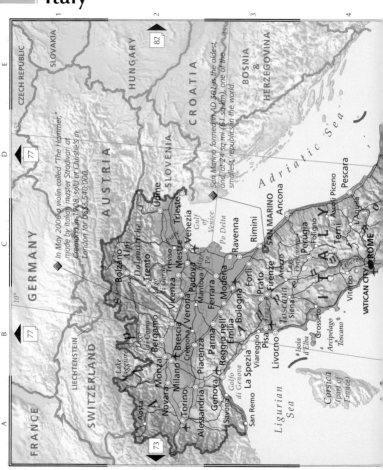

In May 2006 a violin called "The Hammer," made by Italian master Stradivari at Cremona in 1708, sold at Christie's in London for US$3,540,000.

San Marino formed in AD 301, is the oldest, and, at 24 sq mi (61 sq km), one of the smallest, republics in the world.

Mt. Etna began some 300,000 years ago as a submarine volcano and has since grown to a cone with a base 3C miles (48 km) wide and 10,922 ft (3329 m) high.

The medical school at Salerno is the oldest in Europe, established during the 11th and 12th centuries.

The George cross that appears on the Maltese flag was awarded to the islanders by King George VI of Britain for their heroism during World War II.

Strait of Otranto

Bari
Altamura
Brindisi
Lecce
Gallipoli
Taranto
Golfo di Taranto
Crotone
Catanzaro

Ionian Sea

Calabria

Benevento
Salerno
Potenza

Golfo di Salerno

Napoli
Torre del Greco
Isola di Capri

Golfo di Gaeta

Cosenza
Reggio di Calabria
Stretto di Messina

Isola Stromboli
Isola Vulcano
Isole Eolie
Isola Lipari
Cefalù
Messina
Catania
Siracusa

Tyrrhenian Sea

Isola d'Ustica

Palermo

Sicilia (Sicily)

Ragusa

Trapani
Isole Egadi
Marsala
Caltanissetta
Agrigento

Gozo
VALLETTA
MALTA
Malta Channel

Sardegna (Sardinia)

Mediterranean Sea

Isole Pelagie

Isola di Pantelleria

Strait of Sicily

Nuoro
Oristano
Alghero
Iglesias
Cagliari

TUNISIA

0 km   100
0 miles   100

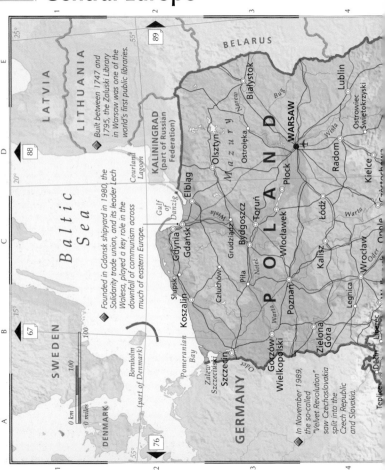

Built between 1747 and 1795, the Zaluski Library in Warsaw was one of the world's first public libraries.

Founded in Gdansk shipyard in 1980, the Solidarity trade union, and its leader Lech Walesa, played a key role in the downfall of communism across much of eastern Europe.

In November 1989, the so-called "Velvet Revolution" saw Czechoslovakia split into the Czech Republic and Slovakia.

LATVIA

LITHUANIA

SWEDEN

DENMARK

Baltic Sea

Bornholm (part of Denmark)

Pomeranian Bay

GERMANY

BELARUS

KALININGRAD (part of Russian Federation)

Courland Lagoon

Gulf of Danzig

POLAND

WARSAW

Białystok

Lublin

Ostrowiec Świętokrzyski

Olsztyn

Ostrołęka

Radom

Kielce

Płock

Elbląg

Gdynia
Gdańsk

Grudziądz

Bydgoszcz

Toruń

Włocławek

Łódź

Słupsk

Koszalin

Człuchów

Piła

Poznań

Kalisz

Wrocław

Opole

Legnica

Zielona Góra

Gorzów Wielkopolski

Zalew Szczeciński

Szczecin

Liberec

Teplice

Warta

Noteć

Odra

Oder

Wisła

Wisła

Narew

Bug

Warta

M a z u r y

Děčín

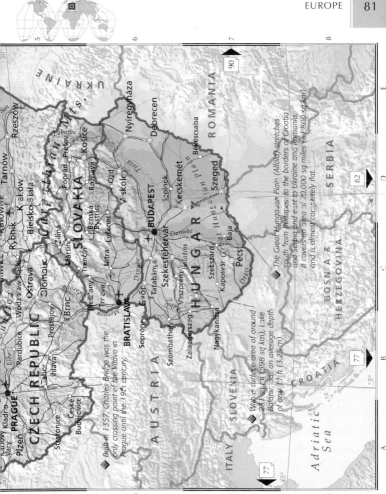

The Great Hungarian Plain (Alföld) stretches south from Budapest to the borders of Croatia and Serbia, and east to Ukraine and Romania. It covers an area of 20,000 sq miles (51,800 sq km) and is almost completely flat.

With a surface area of around 231 sq miles (598 sq km), Lake Balaton has an average depth of only 11 ft (3.25 m).

Built in 1357, Charles Bridge was the only crossing point of the Vltava in Prague until the 19th century.

Southeast Europe

The Danube forms all or part of the border between nine different European nations: Germany, Austria, Slovakia, Hungary, Croatia, Serbia, Romania, Bulgaria, and Ukraine.

At 11:15 am, on June 28, 1914, Archduke Francis Ferdinand and his wife were shot dead by Gavrilo Princip in Sarajevo. This single act precipitated World War I, which eventually lead to the death of almost 10 million troops.

Born in Zagreb in 1892, Marshall Tito was the president of the former Yugoslavia from 1953 until his death in 1980.

BULGARIA

MONTENEGRO • Peje • PRISHTINE
KOSOVO
PODGORICA • Prizren • Feriza • Krmanovo • Strumica
Shkodër • Has Alen-bo • Tetovo • SKOPJE • Stip
Dubrovnik • Veles • Kočani
Lake Scutari • Gostivar • Gevgelija
Lezhë • Kičevo • Kavadarci
MACEDONIA
Drin • Kičevo • Prilep • Strumica
Elbasan • Ohrid • Bitola
TIRANA • Lake Ohrid
Durrës • Korçë • Lake Prespa
ALBANIA
Lushnjë • Berat • Tepelenë
Kuçovë
Fier
Vlorë • Përmet
Gjirokastër • Konispol
Sarandë

GREECE

Palagruza

A d r i a t i c   S e a

Strait of Otranto

I T A L Y

I o n i a n   S e a

◆ Macedonia's capital Skopje, was hit by a
devastating earthquake in 1963. Around
80% of the city's buildings were damaged
or destroyed and over 1000 people killed.

◆ Under an extreme communist regime between
1944 and 1991, Albania was for many years the
only officially atheist state in the world where
all forms of religion were banned by law.

◆ Historically, European eels migrated
thousands of miles from the
Sargasso Sea to live most of their
lives in Lake Ohrid, before returning
to the Atlantic to spawn and die.
Modern hydroelectric projects have
prevented this epic journey, but efforts
are underway to restore access
to the lake.

In February 2008, Kosovo (a UN Protectorate within
Serbia since 1999) declared independence. Although
recognized by several countries, Kosovo's decision has
proved controversial with other states wary of setting a
precedent for separatist groups within their own
borders. It is therefore likely to be some time before
Kosovo becomes universally recognized.

0 km   100
0 miles   100

86
87
79
79

The Mediterranean

A · **B** · **C** · **D**

62

UNITED
KINGDOM
NETHERLANDS
BELGIUM
GERMANY
LUX.
Thames
English Channel
Seine
Rhine
Danube
LIECH.
SWITZ.
FRANCE
A L P S
Loire
Massif
Central
Dordogne
Garonne
Rhône
L. Geneva
Po
SAI
MARINO
Apennines
Genoa
MONACO
Livorno
VATICAN
CITY
Marseille
Golfe
du
Lion
Corsica
Pyrenees
ANDORRA
Ebro
Barcelona
Sardinia
Iberian
SPAIN
Balearic Is.
Medite
Tyrrhenian
Sea
PORTUGAL
Tagus
Peninsula
Valencia
Guadalquivir
ite
Algiers
Tunis
Gibraltar
(UK)
Gibraltar
Oran
TUNISIA
Strait of Gibraltar
Sfax
MOROCCO
Chott el Jerid
Trip
Atlas Mountains
ALGERIA
Madeira
(Portugal)
Grand Erg
Occidental
Grand Erg
Oriental
Canary Is.
(Spain)
A F R I
S a h a a

ATLANTIC
OCEAN
Bay
of
Biscay

48

48

52

0 km 400
0 miles 400

50°
40°
30°
40° 0° 10°
10° 0° 10°

1
2
3
4
5

POLAND

CZECH REP.

EUROPE

UKRAINE

63

SLOVAKIA

USTRIA

HUNGARY

MOLDOVA

Carpathian Mountains

Hungarian Plain

LOVENIA

CROATIA

BOS. & HERZ.

SERBIA

ROMANIA

Dinaric Alps

Adriatic Sea

MON.

KOSOVO (disputed)

Danube

BULGARIA

Balkan Mts.

Danube Delta

Dniester

Crimea

Sea of Azov

RUSSIAN FEDERATION

94

Caucasus

GEORGIA

TALY

Naples

ALBANIA

MACEDONIA

Rhodope Mts.

Black Sea

Bosporus

Pindus Mts.

Aegean Sea

GREECE

Lesbos

Piraeus

Izmir

TURKEY

Anatolia

Lake Van

Ionian Sea

Sicily

Peloponnese

Kos

Taurus Mts.

Euphrates

Tigris

IRAQ

94

MALTA

Rhodes

Cyprus

SYRIA

Crete

LEBANON

Haifa

Anti-Lebanon

Syrian Desert

Gulf of Sirte

ranean Sea

Nile Delta

Port Said

ISRAEL

JORDAN

ASIA

Suez Canal

LIBYA

CA

EGYPT

Libyan Desert

Nile

Red Sea

SAUDI ARABIA

Arabian Peninsula

54

Bulgaria & Greece

Built between 447 and 438 BCE, the Parthenon survived almost unscathed for over 2000 years until in 1687, a gunpowder magazine beneath the building exploded, causing considerable damage.

Sofia's skyline is dominated by the gold domes of the Alexander Nevski Memorial Church, which took craftsmen and artists some thirty years to build between 1882 and 1912.

SERBIA

ROMANIA

Danube

Vidin

Danube

Iskri

Vratsa

Pleven

Lovech

Ruse

Razgrad

Dobrich

Varna

Black
Sea

93

Shumen

Burgas

Yambol

Sliven

Stara Zagora

Kamchiya

Yantra

BULGARIA

Balkan Mountains

Gabrovo

Kazanlŭk

Plovdiv

Haskovo

Pernik

SOFIA

Gorni Iskŭr

Pazardzhik

Velingrad

Rhodope Mountains

Blagoevgrad

Petrich

Drama

Serres

Strymonas

KOSOVO
(disputed)

83

MACEDONIA

Kŭrdzhali

Maritsa

Xanthi

Komotini

Alexandroupoli

Orestiada

Tundzha

Maritsa

TURKEY

Marmara
Denizi

Samothraki

Thracian
Sea

Kavala

Thasos

Akrotirio
Pínes

Akrotirio
Dhepano

Límnos

Vóreies
Sporádes

Lésvos

Mitilíni

40°

90

90

25°

20°

Kilkis

Thessaloniki

Véroia

Kozáni

Flórina

Katerini

Thermaïkós
Kólpos

Akrotirio
Palioúri

Vólos

Lárisa

Trikala

Karditsa

Pineiós

Pindos
Óros

GREECE

ALBANIA

Lake Prespa

Vardar

Ioánnina

Préveza

Kérkyra

Kérkyra

40°

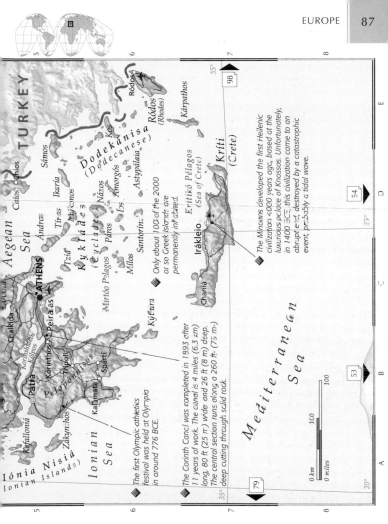

TURKEY

Aegean Sea

Chíos Ochíos

Sámos

Ikaría

Dodekánisa
(Dodecanese)

Kos

Rhodos
(Rhodes)

Kárpathos

ATHENS

Peiraiás

Chalkída

Korinthos

Tripoli

Andros

Tínos

Mýkonos

Kykládes
(Cyclades)

Náxos

Páros

Ios

Amorgós

Astypálaia

Korinthias
Kólpos

Pátra

Pelopónnisos

Kalamáta

Spárti

Mirtóo Pélagos

Mílos

Santoríni

Kýthira

Kritikó Pélagos
(Sea of Crete)

Kríti
(Crete)

Iráklejo

Chaniá

Kefalloniá

Zákynthos

Ιόnia Νissiá
(Ionian Islands)

*Ionian
Sea*

*Mediterranean
Sea*

The Minoans developed the first Hellenic civilization 4000 years ago, based at the luxurious palace of Knossos. Unfortunately, this civilization came to an abrupt end, destroyed by a catastrophic event, probably a tidal wave.

Only about 100 of the 2000 or so Greek Islands are permanently inhabited.

The first Olympic athletics festival was held at Olympia in around 776 BCE.

The Corinth Canal was completed in 1893 after 11 years of work. The canal is 4 miles (6.3 km) long, 80 ft (25 m) wide and 26 ft (8 m) deep. The central section runs along a 260 ft (75 m) deep cutting through solid rock.

0 km   100
0 miles   100

Rich oil shale deposits in northern Estonia are quarried, crushed, and heated to produce almost 7000 barrels of oil a day.

Low salinity and the shallow coastal waters cause pack ice to accumulate at the head of the Gulf of Bothnia and off Finland during most winters; occasionally the ice becomes banked up in pressure ridges that are almost 50 ft (15 m) high.

RUSSIAN

FINLAND

SWEDEN

Gulf of Bothnia

Gulf of Finland

ESTONIA

LATVIA

LITHUANIA

Baltic Sea

Gulf of Riga

Gotland

KALININGRAD
(part of Russian Federation)

92

67

67

67

TALLINN

RIGA

Narva
Kohtla-Järve
Rakvere Bay
Loksa
Tapa
Paide
Viljandi
Tartu
Valga
Võru
Lake Peipus
Lake Pskov
Paldiski
Vormsi
Haapsalu
Virtsu
Pärnu
Valmiera
Cēsis
Ogre
Madona
Jēkabpils
Rēzekne
Daugavpils
Hiiumaa
Saaremaa
Kuressaare
Kolka
Talsi
Saldus
Dobele
Jelgava
Bīržai
Panevėžys
Utena
Ukmergė
Ventspils
Venta
Kuldīga
Mažeikiai
Telšiai
Radviliškis
Šiauliai
Kelmė
Liepāja
Kretinga
Plungė
Šilutė
Tauragė
Jurbarkas
Kaunas
Gusev
Klaipėda
Kaliningrad
Chernyakhovsk
Sovetsk
Courland Lagoon
Neman
Western Dvina
Narva
Narva
Birštono Ežers

20°
25°
30°
60°
55°
60°

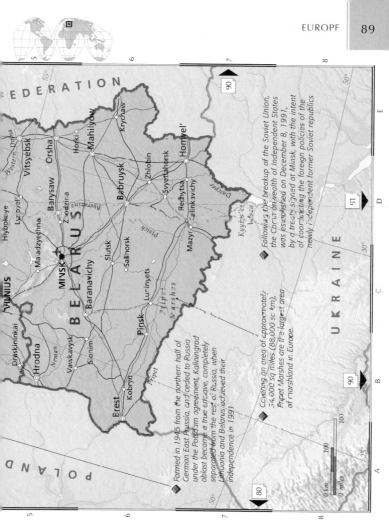

RUSSIAN FEDERATION

BELARUS

LITHUANIA

POLAND

UKRAINE

MINSK

Western Dvina

Daugava

Hlybokaye

Vitsyebsk

Orsha

Horki

Mahilyow

Krychaw

Barysaw

Zhodzina

Babruysk

Zhlobin

Svyetlahorsk

Rechytsa

Kalinkavichy

Homyel'

Mladzyechna

Slutsk

Salihorsk

Byerazina

Ptsich

Dnyapr

Mazyr

Baranavichy

Luninyets

Pinsk

Pripet

Karshas

Kuyezssky Vadas

Drahichyn

Slonim

Vawkavysk

Hrodna

Neman

Kobryn

Brest

Pripet

Druskininkai

VILNIUS

♦ Formed in 1945 from the northern half of
German East Prussia, ceded to Russia
under the Potsdam agreement, Kaliningrad
oblast became a true enclave, completely
separated from the rest of Russia, when
Lithuania and Belarus achieved their
independence in 1991.

♦ Covering an area of approximately
34,000 sq miles (88,000 sq km),
Pripet Marshes are the largest area
of marshland in Europe.

♦ Following the breakup of the Soviet Union,
the Commonwealth of Independent States
was established on December 8, 1991,
by a treaty signed at Minsk, with the intent
of coordinating the foreign policies of the
newly independent former Soviet republics.

0 km   100

0 miles   100

80

90

90

91

Ukraine, Moldova & Romania

On April 25, 1986, engineers accidentally initiated an uncontrolled chain reaction in the number 4 reactor of the Chornobyl' nuclear power plant. The resulting explosion released 8 tons (tonnes) of radioactive material in the world's worst-ever nuclear accident.

Vlad Dracula or Vlad the Impaler was the real-life prince upon whom Bram Stoker based his famous Count Dracula. Dracula was born in Transylvania in 1431 in the town of Sighisoara.

POLAND

BELARUS

Pripet Marshes

Kovel'

Luts'k

Korosten

Rivne

Zhytomyr

L'viv

SLOVAKIA

Ternopil'

U K R

Ivano-Frankivs'k

Khmel'nyts'kyy

Vinnytsya

Uzhhorod

Kam"yanets'-Podil's'ky

Transnist

Chernivtsi

Dnister

Satu Mare

Ribniţa

Baia Mare

Suceava

Botoşani

Bălţi

MOLDOVA

Oradea

Dej

Dubăsari

HUNGARY

Transylvania

Piatra-Neamţ

Iaşi

CHIŞIN

Cluj-Napoca

Tiraspol

Târgu Mureş

Bacău

Tighina

Arad

Alba Iulia

Sighişoara

(Bendery)

Timişoara

Deva

R O M A N I A

Basarabeasca

Sibiu

Focşani

Reşiţa

Carpaţii Meridionali

Braşov

Galaţi

Reni

Râmnicu Vâlcea

Buzău

Tulcea

Târgovişte

Brăila

Drobeta-Turnu Severin

Piteşti

Ploieşti

Craiova

BUCHAREST

Danube

Constan

Corabia

Olt

Eforie Suc

SERBIA

Giurgiu

Mangalia

BULGARIA

93

RUSSIAN FEDERATION

◆ *A monument in central Kiev stands as testament to the 7–12 million Ukrainian peasants who died during the Great Famine, or Holodomor, of 1932–33.*

Shostka

Chernihiv

Chornobyl'

Kyyivs'ke Vdskh.

Sumy

KIEV

Kaniv s'ke Vdskh.

ila Tserkva

Lubny

Kharkiv

A I N E

Cherkasy

Kremenchuts'ke Vdskh.

Poltava

Kremenchuk

Syeverodonets'k

Oleksandriya

Slov''yans'k

Pavlohrad

Horlivka

Luhans'k

Kirovohrad

Kostyantynivka

Dnipropetrovs'k

Yenakiyeve

Makiyivka

Krasnyy Luch

Kryvyy Rih

Nikopol

Donets'k

Zaporizhzhya

Pivdennyy Buh

Kakhovs'ka Vdskh.

Mariupol'

Mykolayiv

Melitopol'

Berdyans'k

Kherson

Kakhovka

Dnieper

Odesa

◆ *In 1872, an iron foundry was established at Donets'k by British industrialist John Hughes (from whom the town's pre-Revolutionary name Yuzovka was derived) to produce rails for the growing Russian transportation network.*

Sea of Azov

Karkinits'ka Zatoka

Kryms'kyy Pivostriv

Kerch

Yevpatoriya

Simferopol'

RUSSIAN FEDERATION

Sevastopol'

Yalta

Black Sea

0 km   100

0 miles   100

Odesa was one of the major flashpoints in the Russian Revolution of 1905, and was the scene of the mutiny on the warship Potemkin, when sailors protesting against the serving of rotten meat eventually killed several of the ship's officers.

98

The port of Murmansk remains ice-free throughout the winter thanks to the Gulf Stream, whereas St. Petersburg, 600 miles (965 km) to the south on the Baltic Sea, is ice-bound between December and May.

ARCTIC OCEAN

Karskoye More

Novaya Zemlya

Barents Sea

Ostrov Vaygach

Ostrov Kolguyev

Murmansk

Vorkuta

Ukhta

Syktyvkar

Usa

Pechora

Mezen'

Arkhangel'sk

Kotlas

(Ural Mountains)

Arctic Circle

RUSSIAN FEDERATION

Kol'skiy Poluostrov

Beloye More

Severnaya Dvina

Pinega

NORWAY

SWEDEN

FINLAND

Ladozhskoye Ozero

Onezhskoye Ozero

Petrozavodsk

Onega

Vologda

Cherepovets

Vytegra

Tver'

Velikiy Novgorod

Nybinskoye Vdkhr.

Yaroslavl'

Arctic Circle

Sankt Peterburg
Sankt Petersburg

Velikiye Luki

Pskov

Smolensk

ESTONIA

LATVIA

LITHUANIA

BELARUS

Gulf of Bothnia

Gulf of Finland

Baltic Sea

Norwegian Sea

0 km   400
0 miles   400

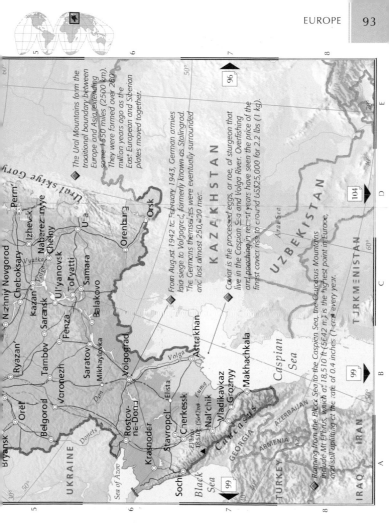

The Ural Mountains form the traditional boundary between Europe and Asia, extending some 1650 miles (2500 km). They were formed over 280 million years ago as the East European and Siberian plates moved together.

Perm'

Izhevsk

Ural'skiye Gory

Naberez'nyye Chelny

Vyatka

Ufa

Orenburg

Orsk

KAZAKHSTAN

From August 1942 to February 1943, German armies laid siege to Volgograd, formerly known as Stalingrad. The Germans themselves were eventually surrounded and lost almost 250,000 men.

Caviar is the processed eggs, or roe, of sturgeon that live in the Caspian Sea and Volga River. Overfishing and poaching in recent years have seen the price of the finest caviar rise to around US$25,000 for 2.2 lbs (1 kg).

UZBEKISTAN

Aral Sea

TURKMENISTAN

Nizhniy Novgorod

Cheboksary

Kazan'

Ul'yanovsk

Tol'yatti

Samara

Balakovo

Saransk

Penza

Ryazan'

Tambov

Saratov

Voronezh

Mikhaylovka

Volgograd

Orël

Belgorod

Don

Donets

Bryansk

UKRAINE

Rostov-na-Donu

Elista

Astrakhan

Volga

Sea of Azov

Krasnodar

Stavropol'

Cherkessk

Nal'chik

Vladikavkaz

Groznyy

Makhachkala

Caspian Sea

Sochi

El'brus 18,510 ft (5642 m)

Kazbek 16,512 ft (5033 m)

Kuma

CAUCASUS

Black Sea

GEORGIA

ARMENIA

AZERBAIJAN

AZ.

TURKEY

IRAN

IRAQ

Running from the Black Sea to the Caspian Sea, the Caucasus Mountains include Mt El'brus, which at 18,510 ft (5642 m) is the highest point in Europe, and still uplifting at the rate of 0.4 inches (1 cm) every year.

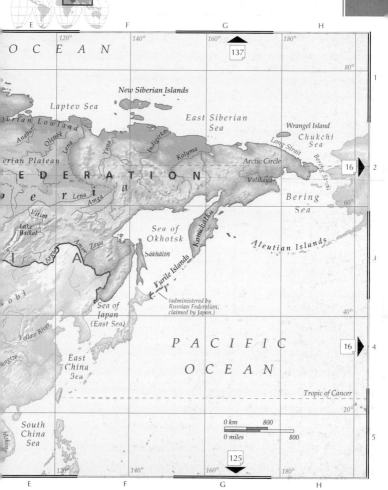

OCEAN

E 120° F 140° G 160° 180° H

137

80° 1

New Siberian Islands

Laptev Sea

East Siberian Sea

...erian Lowland

Anabar Olenëk Lena Yana Indigirka Kolyma

Wrangel Island

Long Strait

Chukchi Sea

...erian Plateau

Arctic Circle

16 2

FEDERATION

Velikaya 60°

...beria Lena Amga

Bering Strait

Bering Sea

Vitim

Sea of Okhotsk

Lake Baikal

Kamchatka

Aldan Argun Zeya

Amur

Sakhalin

Aleutian Islands

A

Kurile Islands

3

...obi

(administered by Russian Federation, claimed by Japan.)

Sea of Japan (East Sea)

East China Sea

PACIFIC

40°

IA

Yellow River

OCEAN

16 4

...ngtze

Tropic of Cancer 20°

South China Sea

0 km 800
0 miles 800

5

Mekong

E 120° F 140° G 160° 180° H

125

0° 100° 120° 140° 160°

OCEAN

◆ Also known as the "Road of Bones," construction of the 1262 mile (2031 km) road between Yakutsk and Magadan took over twenty years and cost the lives of a huge number of prisoners from Stalin's notorious Gulag camps.

Ostrov Vrangelya

18

evernaya Zemlya

Pevek

Anadyr'

Vostochno-Sibirskoye More

Bering Sea

Novosibirskiye Ostrova

Ambarchik

More Laptevykh

oluostrov Taymyr

Ozero Taymyr

Tiksi

134

Ossora

Olenek

Ust'-Kamchatsks

Poluostrov Kamchatka

rednesibirskoye Ploskogor'ye

Magadan

Petropavlovsk -Kamchatskiy

IAN

Okhotsk

Verkhoyanskiy Khrebet

Yakutsk

Sea of Okhotsk

i b i r

Suntar

(Siberia)

Lena

ATION

Sakhalin

Lena

Komsomol'sk-na-Amure

134

ansk

Bratsk

Skovorodno

Ozero Baykal

Yuzhhno-Sakhalinsk

Irkutsk

Chita

Blagoveshchensk

Amur

Khabarovsk

Ulan-Ude

CHINA

JAPAN

Vladivostok

◆ The Trans-Siberian Railroad, completed in 1916, runs 5578 miles (9297 km) between Moscow and Vladivostok. Crossing eight time zones, the journey takes six days.

MONGOLIA

100°   110°   120°   130°

110

0 km   500

0 miles   500

An average of 50,000 commercial ships pass through the Bosporus a year, along with thousands of ferries and smaller passenger boats. The strait is three times busier than the Suez Canal and four times as busy as the Panama Canal.

ROMANIA

Black Sea

BULGARIA

GREECE

Edirne
Kırklareli
Tekirdağ
Sinop
Zonguldak
Küre Dağları
Kastamonu
Samsu
Bosporus
İstanbul
Karabük
Çanakkale Boğazı (Dardanelles)
Marmara Denizi
İzmit
Adapazarı
Çankırı
Çatık Dağlar
Oru
Bursa
Eskişehir
ANKARA
Kızıl Irmak
Çorum
Çanakkale
Balıkesir
Kırıkkale
Tokat
Ayvalık
Kütahya
A
n
a
t
o
l
i
a
T
U
R
K
Sivas
Lésvos
Manisa
Afyon
Chíos
İzmir
Uşak
Tuz Gölü
Nevşehir
Kayseri
Sámos
Aydın
Denizli
İsparta
Konya
Niğde
Kahramanmaraş
Bodrum
Muğla
Ereğli
Osmaniye
Antalya
Toros Dağları
Adana
Gazianteр
Ródos
Dalaman
Mersin
Tarsus
İskenderun
Megísti
Antalya Körfezi
Antaky
Kríti
Kárpathos

TURKISH REPUBLIC OF NORTHERN CYPRUS
(recognized only by Turkey)
Girne (Kyrenia)
NICOSIA
Gazimağusa (Famagusta)
Mediterranean Sea
Paphos
Larnaca
Limassol
CYPRUS
LEBANON

93

RUSSIAN FEDERATION

◆ The Spitak earthquake struck Armenia in 1988, killing at least 25,000 people and devastating the country's infrastructure.

Gagra
Sokhumi
Och'amch'ire
Caspian Sea

Enguri
Kutaisi
CAUCASUS
Poti
GEORGIA
Batumi
TBILISI Rustavi
Hopa
Quba
rabzon Rize
Vanadzor
Gäncä Mingäçevir
Sumqayıt

104

Doğu Karadeniz Dağları
Gyumri
Kars
ARMENIA
YEREVAN
Sevana Lich
AZERBAIJAN
Nagorno-Karabakh
BAKU

Erzurum
Xankändi

Erzincan
Büyükağrı Dağı
(Mount Ararat)
16,853ft (5137m)
Naxçıvan
AZERBAIJAN
Länkäran

◆ Azerbaijan has substantial oil reserves located in and around the Caspian Sea. They were some of the earliest oilfields in the world to be exploited.

Elazığ
Van Gölü
Muş
Van

Güney Doğu Toroslar

102

Malatya
Fırtıs
Siirt
IRAN
Diyarbakır
Batman
Kurdistan
Adıyaman
Mardin
Şanlıurfa

◆ The salty water of Lake Van inhibits all animal life except the Pearl Mullet, a small fish that has adapted to the harsh conditions.

◆ Atatürk Dam, one of the largest dams in the world, was completed in 1990. The reservoir behind the dam covers an area of 315 sq miles (816 sq km) and often requires interruptions in the flow of the Euphrates River to maintain water levels.

SYRIA
IRAQ

0 km   200
0 miles   200

102

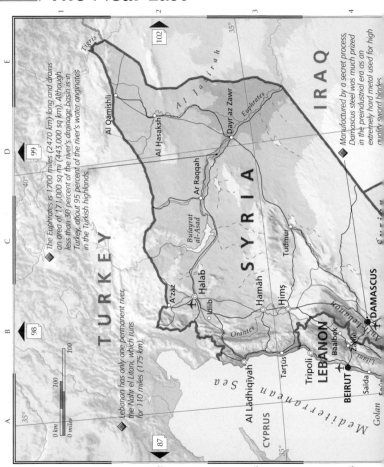

The Euphrates is 1700 miles (2470 km) long and drains an area of 171,000 sq mi (443,000 sq km). Although less than 30 percent of the river's drainage basin is in Turkey, about 95 percent of the river's water originates in the Turkish highlands.

Lebanon has only one permanent river, the Nahr el Litani, which runs for 110 miles (175 km).

Manufactured by a secret process, Damascus steel was much prized in the preindustrial era as an extremely hard metal used for high quality sword blades.

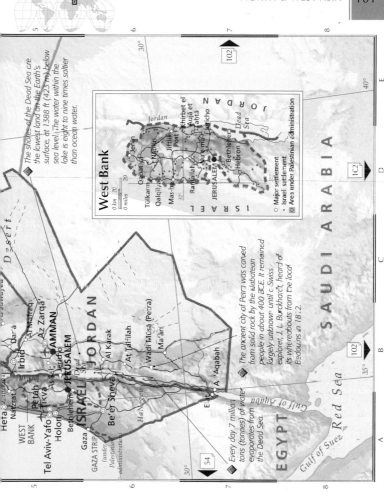

The shores of the Dead Sea are the lowest land on the Earth's surface, at 1388 ft (425 m) below sea level. The water within the lake is eight to nine times saltier than ocean water.

West Bank

0 km   20
0 miles   20

Jordan

Jenin
Qabaṭiya
Ţūlkarm
Nāblus
Jiftlik
Qalqīlyā
Maṣ-ha
Post 14
Khirbet el Auja et Taḥta
Nu'eima
Jericho
Ramallah
JERUSALEM
Bethlehem
Hebron
Dead Sea

ISRAEL
JORDAN

- ⊙ Major settlement
- ● Israeli settlement
- ◎ Area under Palestinian administration

The ancient city of Petra was carved from solid rock by the Nabataean people in about 400 BCE. It remained largely unknown until c. Swiss explorer, J. L. Burckhardt, heard of its whereabouts from the local Bedouins in 1812.

Every day 7 million tons (tonnes) of water evaporates from the Dead Sea.

Desert

Heta'
Natzrat
Irbid
Dar'ā
Al Mafraq
Az Zarqā'
Petaḥ Tiqva
AMMAN
Tel Aviv-Yafo
JERUSALEM
Holon
Jericho
As Salṭ
WEST BANK
Bethlehem
Madaba
ISRAEL
JORDAN
Gaza
GAZA STRIP
(under Palestinian administration)
Be'er Sheva
Al Karak
HaNegev
Aṭ Ṭafīlah
Wādī Mūsā (Petra)
Ma'ān

SAUDI ARABIA

Elat
Al 'Aqabah
Gulf of Aqaba

EGYPT

Gulf of Suez
Red Sea

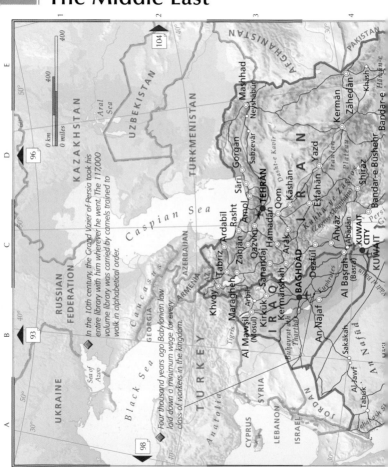

In the 10th century, the Grand Vizier of Persia took his entire library with him wherever he went. The 117,000 volume library was carried by camels trained to walk in alphabetical order.

Four thousand years ago Babylonian law laid down a minimum wage for every class of workers in the kingdom.

RUSSIAN FEDERATION

UKRAINE

KAZAKHSTAN

UZBEKISTAN

TURKMENISTAN

GEORGIA

AZERBAIJAN

ARMENIA

TURKEY

SYRIA

CYPRUS

LEBANON

ISRAEL

JORDAN

IRAQ

I R A N

PAKISTAN

AFGHANISTAN

KUWAIT

Sea of Azov

Black Sea

Caspian Sea

Aral Sea

Anatolia

Caucasus

Mashhad

Neyshābūr

Sabzevār

Gorgān

Sārī

Amol

Ardabīl

Rasht

Qazvīn

Tabrīz

Khvoy

Marāgheh

Zanjān

Hamadān

Sanandaj

Arāk

Arbīl

Kirkūk

Kermānshāh

Al Mawşil
(Mosul)

BAGHDAD

Karbalā'

An Najaf

Dezfūl

Al Başrah
(Basra)

Ahvāz

Abādān

KUWAIT CITY

Qom

TEHRĀN

Kāshān

Eşfahān

Yazd

Shīrāz

Kermān

Zāhedān

Khāsh

Bandar-e Būshehr

Bandar-e
Hājjīān-e

Tigris

Euphrates

Biḩayrat ath Tharthār

An Nafūd

Sakākah

Al Jawf

Tabūk

Dasht-e Kavīr

Dasht-e Lūt

Iranian Plateau

Kūhhā-ye Zāgros
(Zagros Mountains)

Persian Gulf

104

96

93

98

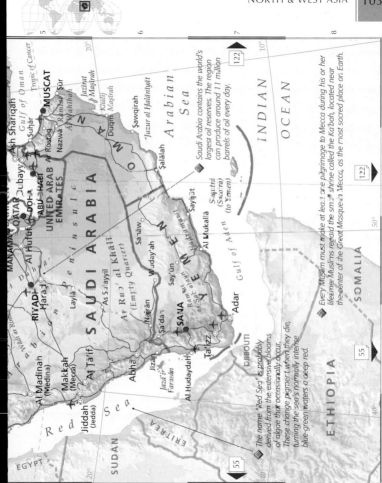

Tropic of Cancer

MUSCAT

Gulf of Oman

Ash Shāriqah

Dubayy

Al Fujayrah

Suhār

Ar Rostāq

Nazwā

Ramlat

Al Wahībah

Jazīrat Maşīrah

Khalīj Maşīrah

Juzur al Halāniyāt

Şawqirah

Duqm Maşīrah

O M A N

Arabian Sea

Şalālah

Saudi Arabia contains the world's largest oil reserves. The region can produce around 11 million barrels of oil every day.

INDIAN OCEAN

QATAR

MANAMA

Al Hufūf

ABU DHABI

DOHA

UNITED ARAB EMIRATES

Saḩḩāḩ

Saywūn

Al Mukallā

Saḩām

Wudayah

Sayḩūt

Şuquţrā (Socotra) (to Yemen)

Peninsula

Dahnā'

SAUDI ARABIA

Haraj

RIYADH

Layla

As Sulayyil

Ar Rub' al Khālī (Empty Quarter)

Ramlat as Sab'atayn

Hadramawt

Gulf of Aden

Adan

Arabian

Najrān

Sa'dah

SANA

Ta'izz

YEMEN

Every Muslim must make at least one pilgrimage to Mecca during his or her lifetime. Muslims regard the small shrine called the Ka'bah, located near the center of the Great Mosque in Mecca, as the most sacred place on Earth.

Wādī ar Rimah

Al Madinah (Medina)

Makkah (Mecca)

Al Ṭā'if

Abhā

Jīzān

Jazā'ir Farasān

Al Ḩudaydah

Jiddah (Jedda)

Red Sea

The name "Red Sea" is probably derived from the extensive blooms of algae that occasionally occur. These change pigment when they die, turning the sea's normally intense blue-green waters a deep red.

ERITREA

DJIBOUTI

ETHIOPIA

SOMALIA

SUDAN

EGYPT

Central Asia

KAZAKHSTAN

Since 1960, the Aral Sea has shrunk by 90 percent, becoming extremely saline and consequently losing all but one of its once-abundant fish species.

Aral Sea

Ustyurt Plateau

Turan Lowland

UZBEKISTAN

Nukus

Köneürgenç

Daşoguz

Urganch

To'rtko'l

Uchquduq

Zaraf\`sǒn

Andarko'l Ko'li

Navoiy

Türkmenbaşy

Hazar

Balkanabat

Bereket

Caspian Sea

Serdar

TURKMENISTAN

Garagum

Buxoro

Seýdi

Samarqar

Qarshi

Baharly

Gökdepe

Abadan

AŞGABAT

Kaka

Tejen

Türkmenabat

Saýat

Mary

Bayramaly

Amu Darya

Atamyrat

Garagumy Kanaly

The desert of Kara Kum (Garagum) occupies over 70 percent of Turkmenistan, severely limiting human settlement across much of the country.

Murgap

Aqchah

Shibirghān

Mazar-e Shar

Maimanah

Bālā Murghāb

Serhetabat

Daryā-ye Murghāb

IRAN

Herāt

Harīrūd

AFGHANISTAN

The Kara Kum (Garagum) Canal, the world's longest irrigation canal, stretches some 850 miles (1375 km) and is known as the "River of Life," since it irrigates large areas of arid land.

Farāh

Gereshk

Qalā

Zaranj

Dasht-e-Mārgow

Kandahar

Daryā-ye Helmand

0 km   200

0 miles   200

96
99
102
102

70°   80°

97

KAZAKHSTAN

Kara-Balta   **BISHKEK**   Tyup
Talas   Tokmak   *Ozero*   Karakol
Issyk-Kul'
KYRGYZSTAN   *Tien Shan*

ASHKENT   Chirchiq
Namangan   Dzhalal-Abad   Naryn   108
Olmaliq   Anatren   Andijon   40°
Qo'qon   Osh
rotepa   **Khujand**   Farg'ona   Khaydarkan
Sulyukta   *Zeravshan*   *Surkhob*

DUSHANBE   **TAJIKISTAN**   *Pamir*

Norak   Danghara   *Bartang*   Murghob   **C H I N A**
Qurghon   Kulob   Khorugh
teppa   Farkhor   *Gunt*
ermez   Faizobod
hulm   Kunduz
    Baghlan   *Hindu Kush*

Pul-e   The "Epic of Manas" is a verbally transmitted
humri   poem of close to 500,000 lines that tells the
hārikār   story of Kyrgyz hero Manas and his
KABUL   Asadābād   descendants and followers.   108
    Jalalābād

Ghazni   Until recent years, people living in remote areas of
Gardēz   Afghanistan were immunized against smallpox by
    having dried powdered scabs from victims of the
    disease blown up their noses. This treatment was
    invented by the Chinese in the 11th century, and is
    thought to be the oldest form of vaccination.

    Despite an area of 251,771 sq miles (652,090 sq km),
    Afghanistan has a limited road network and no
    railroads whatsoever, making access to much
    of the country extremely difficult.

P A K I S T A N   **I N D I A**   30°

70°   116   80°

E   F   G   H

South & East Asia

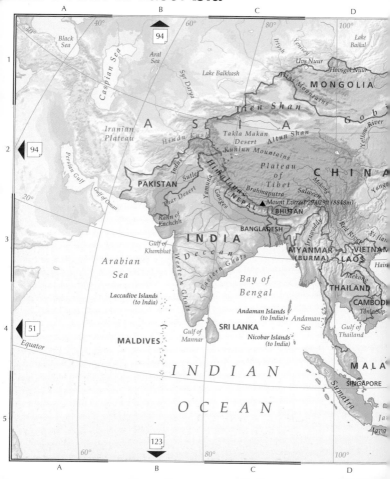

E   F   G   H

120°   140°   160°   180°

95

Amur
Argun
Sakhalin
Zul Khingar Range
Manchuria Plain
Lake Khanka
Hokkaido
Liao He
Yalu
Sea of Japan (East Sea)
JAPAN
NORTH KOREA
SOUTH KOREA
Great Plain of China
Yellow Sea
Korea Strait
Honshu
Shikoku
Kyushu
East China Sea
Ryukyu Islands
TAIWAN
Taiwan Strait

40°

0 km   1000
0 miles   1000

20°

134

P A C I F I C

O C E A N

Luzon Strait
Philippine Sea
Northern Marianas Is. (to US)

Paracel Islands (disputed)
South China Sea
Spratly Islands (disputed)
PHILIPPINES
Luzon
Palawan
Sulu Sea
Mindanao

Guam (to US)

M i c r o n e s i a

Equator

134

BRUNEI
IA
Borneo
Celebes Sea
Halmahera
Moluccas
Seram
Pegunungan Maoke
New Guinea

M e l a n e s i a

Bismarck Archipelago
Solomon Islands

INDONESIA
Celebes
Flores Sea
Lesser Sunda Islands
Banda Sea
Arafura Sea
Timor
EAST TIMOR

Solomon Sea

Coral Sea

124

120°   140°   160°

E   F   G   H

1
2
3
4
5

Western China & Mongolia

96

◆ The Altai Mountains provide one of the last refuges for the endangered snow leopard. There are thought to be only a few thousand animals left in the wild.

KAZAKHSTAN

◆ The Turpan Depression is the lowest and hottest place in China. Temperatures can exceed 117°F (47°C) around the lake of Aydingkol Hu, which lies 505 ft (154 m) below sea level.

96

0 km   400
0 miles   400

RUSSIAN FED

Hövsgöl Nuur

Uvs Nuur
Ulaangom   Hyargas Nuur   Mörön
Olgiy   Har Us Nuur   Tsetserle
Altay   Hovd   MONG
Ulungur   Altay   Bayanhongor
Hu
Karamay   Junggar
Kuytun   Pendi
Yining   Shihezi   ÜRÜMQI
Qitai   Hami   G Gor
Turpan   Dalain Hot
Tien Shan
Korla   Bosten Hu   Xingxingxia
Tarim He   Lop Nur   GANSU
Kashi   Tarim Basin   Qilian Shan
Yengisar   XINJIANG UYGUR
Shache   ZIZHIQU   Ruoqiang
(claimed   Taklimakan   Altun Shan   Qinghai H
by India)   Shamo   Qaidam
Moyu   Pendi   Dulan
Qira   Kunlun Shan   Golmud
Aksai Chin   Qing Zang Gaoyuan   CHI
(administered by China, claimed   (Plateau of Tibet)   Bayan Har Shan   Yushu
by India)   QINGHAI
Rutog   Tongtian He   Mekong   Qamdo
Demchok/Dêmqog   Tanggula Shan   Salween
(administered by China   XIZANG
claimed by India)   ZIZHIQU   Tangra   Amdo
Gar   (Tibet)   Yumco   Siling Co   Naqqu
(Shiquanhe)   Nyima   Nam Co   Damxung
Zanda   Brahmaputra   Arunachal
Lhazê   LHASA   Pradesh
INDIA   Nyainqêntanglha Shan   (claimed by China)
Gyangzê
NEPAL   Mount Everest   BHUTAN   INDIA
29,029ft (8848m)

◆ Although forming around 20 percent of China's landmass, Tibet is sparsely populated, supporting only 1 percent of China's 1.3 billion population.

PAKISTAN
Karakoram Range
AFGH.
TAJIKISTAN
KYRGYZSTAN
Indus

116

117

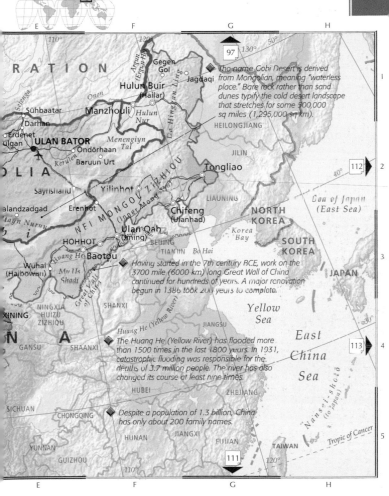

R A T I O N

110°

E

120°

F

130°

G

50°

H

97

Gegen
Gol

Argun (Egun He)

Jagdaqi

Hulun Buir
(Hailar)

Manzhouli

Onon

Sühbaatar

Darhan

Erdenet
Ulgan

ULAN BATOR

Selenga

Hulun
Nur

Da Hinggan Ling

HEILONGJIANG

Ondörhaan

Menengiyn
Tal

Kerulen

Baruun Urt

JILIN

MOLIA

Say'nshand

Yilinhot

N E I M O N G O L Z I Z H I Q U

(Inner Mong.)

Tongliao

LIAONING

112

40°

Sea of Japan
(East Sea)

alandzadgad

tayn Nuruu

Erenhot

Chifeng
(Ulanhad)

NORTH
KOREA

HOHHOT

Ulan Qab
(Jining)

BEIJING

Wuhai
(Haibowan)

Mu Us
Shadi

Baotou

Huang He (Yellow River)

TIANJIN   Bo Hai

Korea
Bay

SOUTH
KOREA

JAPAN

XINING

Great Wall of China

NINGXIA
HUIZU
ZIZHIQU

SHANXI

◆ Having started in the 7th century BCE, work on the
3700 mile (6000 km) long Great Wall of China
continued for hundreds of years. A major renovation
begun in 1386 took 200 years to complete.

Yellow
Sea

N A

GANSU

SHAANXI

Huang He (Yellow River)

JIANGSU

30°

113

East
China
Sea

◆ The Huang He (Yellow River) has flooded more
than 1500 times in the last 1800 years. In 1931,
catastrophic flooding was responsible for the
deaths of 3.7 million people. The river has also
changed its course at least nine times.

HUBEI

ZHEJIANG

SICHUAN

CHONGQING

HUNAN

JIANGXI

FUJIAN

Nansei-shotō
(to Japan)

Tropic of Cancer

TAIWAN

◆ Despite a population of 1.3 billion, China
has only about 200 family names.

YUNNAN

GUIZHOU

111

110°

E

F

120°

G

H

◆ The name Gobi Desert is derived
from Mongolian, meaning "waterless
place." Bare rock rather than sand
dunes typify the cold desert landscape
that stretches for some 500,000
sq miles (1,295,000 sq km).

Eastern China & Korea

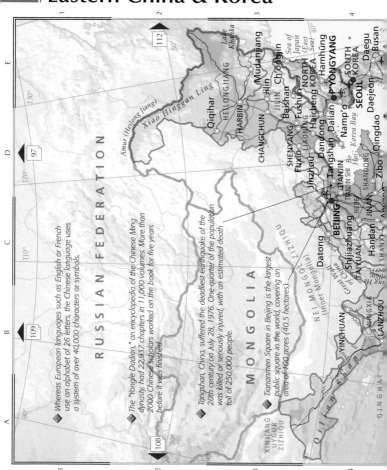

Whereas European languages such as English or French use an alphabet of 26 letters, the Chinese language uses a system of over 40,000 characters or symbols.

The "Yongle Dadian," an encyclopedia of the Chinese Ming dynasty, had 22,937 chapters in 11,000 volumes. More than 2000 Chinese scholars worked on the book for five years before it was finished.

Tangshan, China, suffered the deadliest earthquake of the 20th century on July 28, 1976. One-quarter of the population was killed or seriously injured, with an estimated death toll of 250,000 people.

Tiananmen Square in Beijing is the largest public square in the world, covering an area of 100 acres (40.5 hectares).

RUSSIAN FEDERATION

MONGOLIA

NEI MONGGOL (Inner Mongolia)

NEI MONGGOL ZIZHIQU

XINJIANG UYGUR ZIZHIQU

QINGHAI

Amur (Heilong Jiang)

Xiao Hinggan Ling

Lake Khanka

Qiqihar

HEILONGJIANG

HARBIN

Mudanjiang

CHANGCHUN

JILIN

Jilin

Ch'ŏngjin

Baishan

Fushun

SHENYANG

Fuxin

LIAONING

Haicheng

Dandong

Jinzhou

Dalian

Korea Bay

Sea of Japan (East Sea)

NORTH KOREA

Hamhŭng

PYONGYANG

Namp'o

SOUTH KOREA

SEOUL

Daegu

Busan

Daejeon

Incheon

Qingdao

Zibo

SHANDONG

JINAN

Bo Hai

TIANJIN

TIANJIN SHI

BEIJING

Tangshan

HEBEI

Shijiazhuang

Datong

SHANXI

TAIYUAN

Handan

HENAN

Huang He (Yellow River)

NINGXIA

YINCHUAN

LANZHOU

Qilian Shan

GANSU

109

108

97

112

50°

130°

40°

120°

110°

90°

50°

JAPAN

Jeju-do

Yellow Sea

East China Sea

SHANGHAI

Nanjing Wuxi Yaxing

Ningbo Wenzhou

Okinawa (part of Japan)

Nansei-shoto

Tropic of Cancer

PACIFIC OCEAN

134

PHILIPPINES

(China and Taiwan claim all of each other's territory)

TAIPEI

Taizhong

Taichung

TAIWAN

Tainan

Gaoxiong

Li is the family name for over 87 million people in China.

Parcel Islands (disputed by China, Taiwan and Vietnam.)

Spratly Islands (disputed by China, Malaysia, Philippines, Taiwan and Vietnam.)

South China Sea

Luzon Strait

121

By far the biggest tidal bore in the world occurs on the Qiantang River, in China. At spring tides the wave attains a height of up to 30 ft (9 m) and a speed of 25 mph (40 km/h).

HONG KONG (Xianggang)

Macao (Aomen)

Shantou

Dongguan

GUANGZHOU

HAINAN Hainan Dao

Gulf of Tongking

VIETNAM

NANNING

Red River

118

CAMBODIA

THAILAND

LAOS

The Giant Bamboo is the fastest growing plant in the world, able to grow at the rate of 3 ft (91 cm), a day.

MYANMAR (BURMA)

118

0 km 100
0 miles 100

Japan

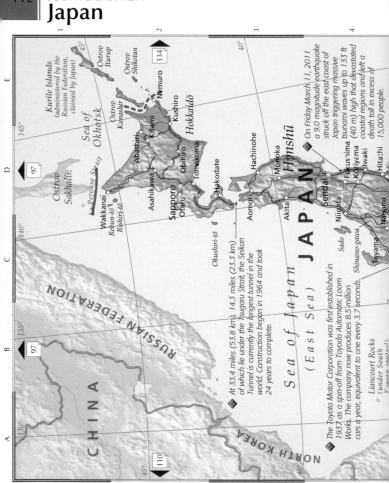

Kurile Islands (administered by the Russian Federation, claimed by Japan)

Ostrov Iturup

Ostrov Shikotan

Ostrov Kunashir

Sea of Okhotsk

Nemuro

Kushiro

Kitami

Abashiri

Hokkaidō

Hachinohe

Ostrov Sakhalin

Perouse Strait

Wakkanai

Rebun-tō

Rishiri-tō

Asahikawa

Obihiro

Tomakomai

Hakodate

Sapporo

Otaru

Okushiri-tō

Aomori

Akita

Monoka

Sendai

Niigata

Fukushima

Kōriyama

Iwaki

Hitachi

Nagano

Toyama

Sado

Shinano-gawa

On Friday March 11, 2011 a 9.0 magnitude earthquake struck off the east coast of Japan triggering massive tsunami waves up to 133 ft (40 m) high that devastated coastal regions and left a death toll in excess of 15,000 people.

At 33.4 miles (53.8 km), 14.3 miles (23.3 km) of which lie under the Tsugaru Strait, the Seikan Tunnel is currently the longest tunnel in the world. Construction began in 1964 and took 24 years to complete.

The Toyota Motor Corporation was first established in 1937 as a spin-off from Toyota Automatic Loom Works. The company now produces 8.5 million cars a year, equivalent to one every 3.7 seconds.

Sea of Japan (East Sea)

JAPAN

Honshū

RUSSIAN FEDERATION

CHINA

NORTH KOREA

Liancourt Rocks (under South

134

97

97

110

The same family has occupied the Imperial Throne of Japan for the last 1300 years. The present-day emperor, Akihito, is the 125th in succession.

On August 12, 1990, Typhoon Winona, combined with the summer vacation rush, created the longest traffic jam in Japan's history, an 84-mile long tailback involving about 15,000 vehicles.

The longest single span suspension bridge in the world is the Akashi Kaikyo Bridge linking Honshu and Shikoku, with a central span of 6352 ft (1991 m); the total length shore to shore is 12,831 ft (3911 m) or 2.4 miles (3.9 km).

SOUTH KOREA

Korea Strait

Tsushima

Shimonoseki
Kitakyūshū   Iki
Fukuoka   Matsuyama
Saseto   Ōita
Nagasaki   Miyazaki
Gotō-rettō
Amakusa-nada
Kagoshima

Ōsumi-shotō

Yaku-shima
Tanega-shima

Kurashiki
Okayama
Hiroshima   Fukuyama
Hamada   Onomichi
Matsue   Tottori
Kurashii
Bingo-nada
Kōbe
Ōsaka
Wakayama
Shingū

Shikoku
Takamatsu
Kōchi
Tokushima
Nakamura

Kyōto
Okazaki
Hamamatsu
Nagoya
Toyota
Yokkaichi

Chiba
Yokohama

Izu-shotō

Hachijō-jima
Aoga-shima

Kumamoto
Kyūshū

East China Sea

Ryukyu-rettō

Tokune-shima
Amami-Ō-shima

Okinawa
Naha

PACIFIC OCEAN

Philippine Sea

PACIFIC OCEAN

0 km   200
0 miles   200

134

134

134

134

111

30°

25°

30°

25°

35°

130°

135°

140°

Southern India & Sri Lanka

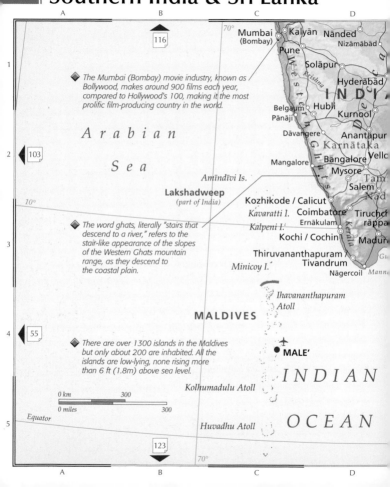

◆ The Mumbai (Bombay) movie industry, known as Bollywood, makes around 900 films each year, compared to Hollywood's 100, making it the most prolific film-producing country in the world.

Arabian

Sea

◆ The word ghats, literally "stairs that descend to a river," refers to the stair-like appearance of the slopes of the Western Ghats mountain range, as they descend to the coastal plain.

MALDIVES

◆ There are over 1300 islands in the Maldives but only about 200 are inhabited. All the islands are low-lying, none rising more than 6 ft (1.8m) above sea level.

0 km   300

0 miles   300

Equator

Mumbai (Bombay)
Kalyān   Nānded
Nizāmābād
Pune
Solāpur
Hyderābād
Belgaum   Hubli   **INDIA**
Pānāji   Kurnool
Dāvangere   Anantāpur
Karnātaka
Mangalore   Bangalore   Vello
Mysore
Amīndīvi Is.   Tam
Nad
Lakshadweep   Salem
(part of India)   Kozhikode / Calicut
Kavaratti I.   Coimbatore   Tiruch
Kalpeni I.   Ernākulam   rāppa
Kochi / Cochin   Madu
Thiruvananthapuram / Tivandrum
Minicoy I.   Nāgercoil   *Manna*

Ihavananthapuram Atoll

✈
● **MALE'**

INDIAN

Kolhumadulu Atoll

OCEAN

Huvadhu Atoll

70°

70°

10°

116

103

55

123

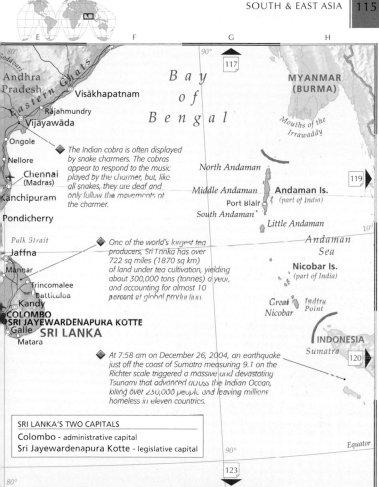

E   F   G   H

Andhra
Pradesh
Godavari

Visākhapatnam

Rājāhmundry

Vijayawāda

Ongole

Nellore

Chennai
(Madras)

Kānchīpuram

Pondicherry

Eastern Ghats

Palk Strait

Jaffna

Mannar

Trincomalee

Batticaloa

Kandy

COLOMBO

SRI JAYEWARDENAPURA KOTTE

Galle

SRI LANKA

Matara

*Bay
of
Bengal*

North Andaman

Middle Andaman

Port Blair

South Andaman

Little Andaman

Andaman Is.
(part of India)

*Andaman
Sea*

Nicobar Is.
(part of India)

Great
Nicobar

Indira
Point

**MYANMAR
(BURMA)**

*Mouths of the
Irrawaddy*

INDONESIA
Sumatra

The Indian cobra is often displayed by snake charmers. The cobras appear to respond to the music played by the charmer, but, like all snakes, they are deaf and only follow the movements of the charmer.

One of the world's largest tea producers, Sri Lanka has over 722 sq miles (1870 sq km) of land under tea cultivation, yielding about 300,000 tons (tonnes) a year, and accounting for almost 10 percent of global production.

At 7:58 am on December 26, 2004, an earthquake just off the coast of Sumatra measuring 9.1 on the Richter scale triggered a massive and devastating Tsunami that advanced across the Indian Ocean, killing over 250,000 people and leaving millions homeless in eleven countries.

SRI LANKA'S TWO CAPITALS

Colombo - administrative capital

Sri Jayewardenapura Kotte - legislative capital

117

119

120

123

Equator

E   F   G   H

North India & Pakistan

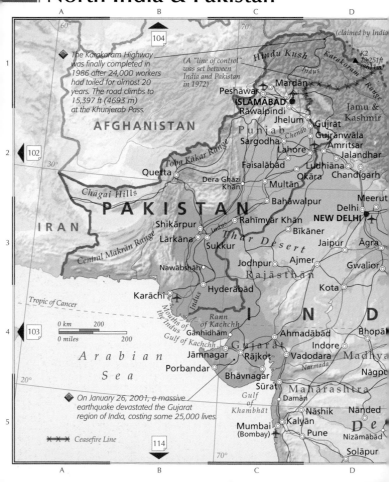

104

◆ The Karakoram Highway was finally completed in 1986 after 24,000 workers had toiled for almost 20 years. The road climbs to 15,397 ft (4693 m) at the Khunjerab Pass.

(A "line of control" was set between India and Pakistan in 1972)

(claimed by India)

K2
28,251 ft
(8611 m)

Hindu Kush

Karakoram Range

Indus

AFGHANISTAN

Jamu & Kashmir

Peshāwar

Mardān

ISLĀMĀBĀD

Rāwalpindi

Jhelum

Gujrāt

Punjab

Gujrānwāla

Toba Kākar Range

Sargodha

Chenāb

Lahore

Amritsar

Jalandhar

102

Quetta

Faisalābād

Ludhiāna

Chandīgarh

Dera Ghāzi Khān

Okāra

Chāgai Hills

Multān

Meerut

PAKISTAN

Bahāwalpur

Delhi

NEW DELHI

IRAN

Shikārpur

Rahīmyār Khān

Bīkāner

Jaipur

Āgra

Central Makrān Range

Lārkāna

Indus

Sukkur

Thar Desert

Jodhpur

Ajmer

Gwalior

Nawābshāh

Rajasthān

Kota

Tropic of Cancer

Karāchi

Hyderābād

I
N
D

0 km   200

0 miles   200

Rann of Kachchh

Ahmadābād

Bhopāl

103

Gāndhidhām

Gujarāt

Indore

Madhya

Gulf of Kachchh

Jāmnagar

Rājkot

Vadodara

Narmada

Nāgpur

Arabian

Porbandar

Bhāvnagar

Sūrat

Mahārāshtra

20°

Gulf of Khambhāt

Dāman

Sea

◆ On January 26, 2001, a massive earthquake devastated the Gujarat region of India, costing some 25,000 lives.

Nāshik

Nānded

Mumbai (Bombay)

Kalyān

De

Pune

Nizāmābād

✕✕✕ Ceasefire Line

Solāpur

114

70°

The northern ranges of the Himalayas contain the highest mountains in the world, with average heights of more than 23,000 ft (7000 m) and many peaks higher than 26,000 ft (8000m).

Cherrapunji, 4872 ft (1484 m) above sea level, has an average annual rainfall of 450 inches (1143 cm), although most of this falls during the monsoon – the winter is a virtual drought. The highest ever seasonal rainfall was 904 inches (2298 cm).

The Kingdom of Bhutan is the only country in the world to measure the happiness of its citizens.

The heaviest hailstones on record, weighing about 2.25 lbs (1 kg), are reported to have killed 92 people in the Gopalganj area of Bangladesh on April 14, 1986.

Mainland Southeast Asia

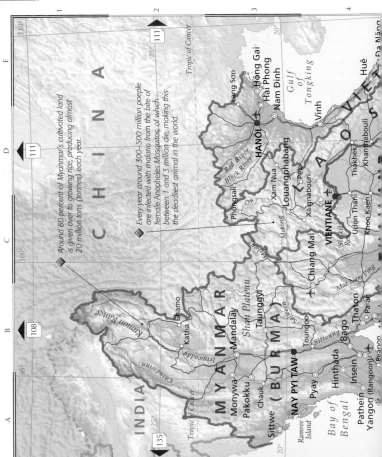

Around 60 percent of Myanmar's cultivated land is given over to growing rice, producing almost 20 million tons (tonnes) each year.

Every year around 300–500 million people are infected with malaria from the bite of the female Anopheles Mosquitos, of which between 1 and 3 million die, making this the deadliest animal in the world.

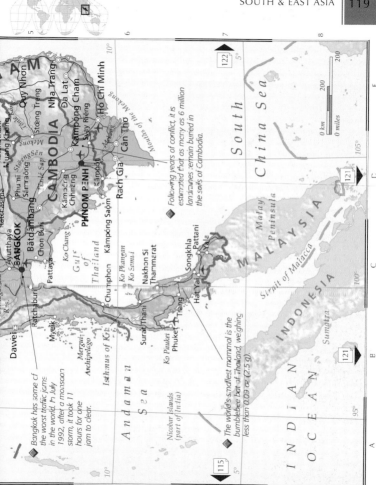

South China Sea

Andaman Sea

INDIAN OCEAN

Gulf of Thailand

MALAYSIA

INDONESIA

Malay Peninsula

Strait of Malacca

Sumatra

Isthmus of Kra

Mergui Archipelago

Nicobar Islands (part of India)

VIETNAM

CAMBODIA

Thailand

BANGKOK

PHNOM PENH

Hô Chi Minh

Quy Nhon

Nha Trang

Đa Lat

Stŏeng Treng

Kâmpóng Cham

Swai Riĕng

Cân Tho

Krâchéh

Kâmpóng Chhnang

Tônlé Sap

Kâmpóng Saôm

Rach Gia

Phumĭ Sâmraông

Bătdâmbâng

Kampôt

Chon Buri

Pattaya

Ko Chang

Chumphon

Ko Phangan

Ko Samui

Nakhon Si Thammarat

Songkhla

Pattani

Hăt Yai

Yala

Sŏng Khla

Ayutthaya

Ratchaburi

Nakhonsawan

Phetchaburi

Dawei

Myeik

Surat Thani

Trang

Phuket

Ko Pauken

Mouths of the Mekong

Mouths of the Mekong

Bangkok has some of the worst traffic jams in the world. In July 1992, after a monsoon storm, it took 11 hours for one jam to clear.

Following years of conflict, it is estimated that as many as 6 million landmines remain buried in the soils of Cambodia.

The world's smallest mammal is the bumblebee bat of Thailand, weighing less than 0.09 oz (2.5 g).

0 km   200

0 miles   200

122

121

121

115

A   B   C   D

90°   100°   110°

MYANMAR (BURMA)

119

Gulf of Tongking

1

0 km   400

0 miles   400

THAILAND

LAOS

VIETNAM

Paracel Islands
(disputed by China, Taiwan, and Vietnam)

South China Sea

MALAYSIA'S TWO CAPITALS

Kuala Lumpur - Capital

Putrajaya - Administrative capital

CAMBODIA

Spratly Islands
(disputed by China, Malaysia, Philippines, Taiwan, and Vietnam)

122

10°

Andaman Sea

Gulf of Thailand

2

Nicobar Islands (to India)

◆ The Rafflesia plant has the largest single flower in the world. The bloom, 3 ft (90 cm) in diameter, attracts insects by imitating the foul smell of rotting flesh.

Bali

Strait of Malacca

George Town

Bandaaceh

Kota Bharu
Kuala Terengganu

Kota Kinabalu
BANDAR SERI BEGAWAN

Taiping   Ipoh   Kuantan

Medan

Klang

KUALA LUMPUR

BRUNEI

Pematangsiantar

Pulau Simeulue

Danau Toba

PUTRAJAYA

MALAYSIA

Sibu

Sarawak

Johor Bahru

Kuching

Sibolga

SINGAPORE

Pulau Nias

Pontianak

Borneo

Equator

Sumatera (Sumatra)

Pekanbaru

Kapuas

Samarir

3

Padang

Pulau Siberut

Batang Hari

Selat Karimata

Kalimantan

Balikpapa

Jambi

Bangka

Pegunungan Barisan

Pematang Menangai

Palembang

Pulau Belitung

Banjarmasin

INDON

4

Bengkulu

I N D

Java Sea

OCEAN

Bandar Lampung

Tegal

Maka

Selat Sunda

JAKARTA

Pekalongan

Semarang

Suraba

10°

◆ In August 1883, a devastating volcanic eruption destroyed most of the island of Krakatau and triggered a tsunami that claimed around 35,000 lives.

Bogor

Sukabumi

Kudus

Matara

Bandung

Jawa (Java)

Cilacap

Magelang

Yogyakarta

Surakarta

Denpasar

Jembe

Malang

Kediri

Madiun

5

Lo

90°   100°   110°

123

A   B   C   D

Luzon Strait

Bahini Channel

120° E

130° F

140° G

H

112

Tuguergarao

Ilagan

Luzon

guio

geles

Dagupan

Cabanatuan

ANILA

tangas

Lucena

Naga

Legazpi City

Mindoro

Sibuyan Sea

Visayan Sea

Roxas City

Calbayog

Tacloban

Iloilo

Cadiz

Bacolod

City

Cebu

Bohol Is.

Butuan

Iligan

Cagayan de Oro

mboanga

Mindanao

Davao

General

Santos

Sulu Archipelago

Kepulauan Talaud

Moro Gulf

Sulu Sea

Princesa

Ileurto

lawan

z Sulu Sea

Wau

Celebes Sea

Philippine Sea

PHILIPPINES

◆ The Philippines take their name from Philip II
of Spain, who was king when the islands were
colonized during the 16th century.

P A C I F I C

O C E A N

Yap

Babeldaob

MICRONESIA

PALAU

◆ Indonesia is the world's largest archipelago,
with over 17,500 islands stretching
3100 miles (5000 km) between the Indian
and Pacific oceans.

Northern
Mariana
Islands
(to US)

Guam *(to US)*

126

126

126

Equator

Gorontalo

Gulf of Tomini

alu

Sulawesi

(Celebes)

Manado

Kepulauan Sangir

Pulau Morotai

Pulau Halmahera

Molucca Sea

Halmahera Sea

Sorong

Jazirah Doberai

Pulau Biak

Sungai Mamberano

Jayapura

Pegunungan Maoke

Maluku (Moluccas)

Ceram Sea

Pulau Seram

Wahai

Ambon

Kendari

Pulau Buru

Kepulauan Banggai

Kepulauan Sula

I N D O N E S I A

Parepare

Pulau Buton

Makassar

Banda Sea

Kepulauan Kai

Pulau Aru

Kepulauan
Aru

Kepulauan Tanimbar

Pulau Yamdena

PAPUA
NEW
GUINEA

New Guinea

Digul

A
Papua
(Irian Jaya)

ores Sea

Nusa

Tenggara

Flores

Wetar Strait

Kepulauan Alor

Kepulauan Leti

Timor

DILI

EAST TIMOR

Sumba

Savu Sea

Kupang

Timor Sea

Arafura Sea

Torres Strait

10°

130

AUSTRALIA

120° E

130° F

140° G

H

The Indian Ocean

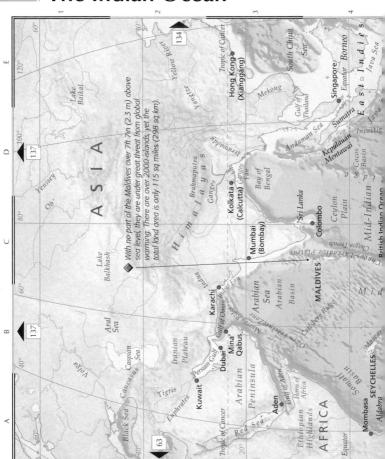

With no part of the Maldives over 7ft 7in (2.3 m) above sea level, they are under great threat from global warming. There are over 2000 islands, yet the total land area is only 115 sq miles (298 sq km).

AUSTRALASIA

Australian Basin

Exmouth Plateau

Tropic of Capricorn

Fremantle

Perth Basin

Naturaliste Plateau

Broken Ridge

Wharton Basin

East Indian Ridge · Ninetyeast Fracture Zone

Southeast Indian Ridge

INDIAN

OCEAN

South Indian Basin

ANTARCTICA

Antarctic Circle

Limit of winter pack ice

Limit of summer pack ice

Osborn Plateau

Islands (to Australia)

Ninetyeast Ridge

Amsterdam Island

Île St-Paul

Every cubic mile (4.3 cu km) of seawater holds over 150 million tons (tonnes) of minerals.

Crozet Basin

French Southern & Antarctic Territories (to France)

Crozet Islands (to France)

Heard & Mcdonald Islands (to Australia)

Kerguelen Plateau

Banzare Seamounts

MAURITIUS

Réunion (to France)

Farafangana

Madagascar Basin

Madagascar Plateau

Southwest Indian Ridge

Enderby Plain

Enderby Plain

The largest animal ever seen alive was a 110 ft (34 m) 170-ton (tonne) female blue whale.

Atlantic-Indian Basin

MADAGASCAR

Netal Basin

Mozambique Chapnet Ridge

Mozambique Plateau

Antarctic Circle

0 km 1500

0 miles

1500

Australasia & Oceania

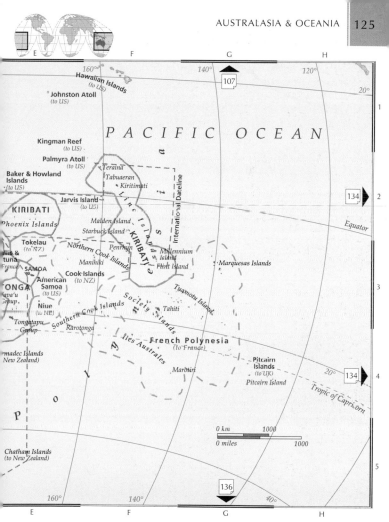

E | F | G | H

160° | 140° | 120° | 20°

107

Hawaiian Islands
(to US)

Johnston Atoll
(to US)

P A C I F I C   O C E A N

Kingman Reef
(to US)

Palmyra Atoll
(to US)

Baker & Howland
Islands
(to US)

Teraina
Tabuaeran
Kiritimati

Jarvis Island
(to US)

134

Equator

KIRIBATI

Phoenix Islands

Malden Island
Starbuck Island

Tokelau
(to NZ)

Penrhyn

Northern Cook Islands

Millennium
Island
Flint Island

Marquesas Islands

Wallis &
Futuna
(to France)

Manihiki

SAMOA

American
Samoa
(to US)

Cook Islands
(to NZ)

Tuamotu Island

TONGA

Vava'u
Group

Niue
(to NZ)

Society Islands

Tahiti

Tongatapu
Group

Southern Cook Islands

Rarotonga

Îles Australes

French Polynesia
(to France)

Pitcairn
Islands
(to UK)

Marotiri

Pitcairn Island

134

20°

Tropic of Capricorn

P O L Y N E S I A

0 km   1000

0 miles   1000

Chatham Islands
(to New Zealand)

160° | 140° | 40°

E | F | G | H

136

The Southwest Pacific

Guam
(US unincorporated territory)
HAGÅTÑA

MARSHALL ISLANDS

Yap

Marianas Trench

Micronesia

Caroline Islands

Chuuk Is.

NGERULMUD

MICRONESIA

Pohnpei
PALIKIR

Kosrae

Majuro

Ralik Chain

Radak Chain

PALAU

BAIRIKI
Tarawa

NAURU

Banab

Equator

The Pitohui bird has a poison on its feathers and skin similar to the poison arrow tree frog, making it the only known example of a poisonous bird.

PAPUA NEW GUINEA

Bismarck Archipelago

New Ireland

INDONESIA

Mt Wilhelm
14,793ft (4509m)

New Guinea

Madang

Bougainville I.

New Britain

Lae

New Georgia Islands

Melanesia

PORT MORESBY

Solomon Sea

HONIARA

Santa Cruz Islands

SOLOMON ISLANDS

Arafura Sea

Torres Strait

Gulf of Carpentaria

Coral Sea

Banks Is.

VANUATU

PORT VILA

Found only in the rainforest of New Guinea, Queen Alexandra's Birdwing, with a wingspan of 11 inches (280 mm), is the largest butterfly in the world.

Great Barrier Reef

Coral Sea Islands
(Australian external territory)

New Caledonia
(French special collectivity)

Îles Loyauté

AUSTRALIA

NOUMÉA

Tropic of Capricorn

P A C I F I C   O C E A N

◆ *In 1995, the International Date Line was repositioned around Kiribati territory, bringing Millennium Island 14 hours ahead of UTC, making it the first landfall for sunrise at the dawn of the new millennium.*

International Dateline

Kingman Reef
(US unincorporated territory)

Palmyra Atoll
(US incorporated territory)

Teraina
Tabuaeran
Kiritimati

Baker & Howland Is.
(US unincorporated territory)

Jarvis I.
(US unincorporated territory)

Line Islands

Equator 0°

K I R I B A T I   *Phoenix Islands*   **KIRIBATI**

◆ *Samoa is home to the world's smallest known spider, the Patu marplesi, which spans a mere 0.017 inches (0.4 mm)*

TUVALU

✈ **FONGAFALE**

Tokelau
(NZ dependent territory)

American Samoa
(US unincorporated territory)

Northern Cook Is.

Vostok I.

Millennium I.

Flint I.

International Dateline

Wallis & Futuna
(French overseas collectivity)

SAMOA

✈ **ÁPIA**

P o l y n e s i a

✈ **PAGO PAGO**

French Polynesia
(French overseas collectivity)

Îles de la Société

FIJI

Vanua Levu

Vava'u Group

Cook Islands
(in free assoc. with NZ)

● **SUVA**

Ha'apai Group

Niue
(in free assoc. with NZ)

✈ **ALOFI**

Southern Cook Is.

PAPEETE ◻ ✈

Tahiti

✈ **TONGA**

● **NUKU'ALOFA**

AVARUA ✈

Rarotonga

0 km   500
0 miles   500

Tropic of Capricorn

On Christmas Day, 1974, Cyclone Tracy devastated Darwin with winds of up to 175 mph (280km/h), resulting in 71 deaths, thousands of injuries, and 95 percent of the city destroyed.

One of the largest states in the world, with an area of more than 1,000,000 sq miles (2.6 million sq km), Western Australia covers a third of the Australian continent and yet supports a population of only 2.3 million people.

The Nullarbor Plain is so flat that the Trans-Australian Railway runs through it in a dead straight line for 297 miles (478 km), the longest section of straight track in the world.

Residents of Coober Pedy have built their homes below ground to escape temperatures that can reach 113°F (45°C) during the summer months.

Around 18 percent of Australia is covered in desert, the biggest being The Great Victoria Desert, which (at 163,905 sq miles (424,400 sq km) is over 10 times the size of Belgium.

Eastern Australia

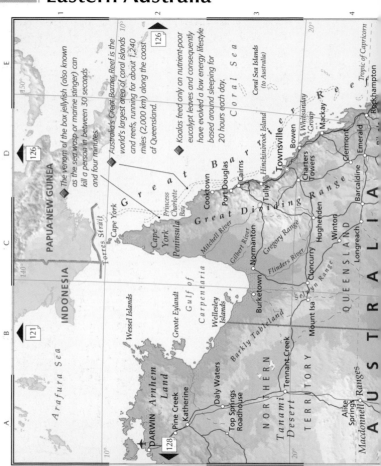

The venom of the box jellyfish (also known as the sea wasp or marine stinger) can kill a person in between 30 seconds and four minutes.

Australia's Great Barrier Reef is the world's largest area of coral islands and reefs, running for about 1,240 miles (2,000 km) along the coast of Queensland.

Koalas feed only on nutrient-poor eucalypt leaves and consequently have evolved a low energy lifestyle based around sleeping for 20 hours each day.

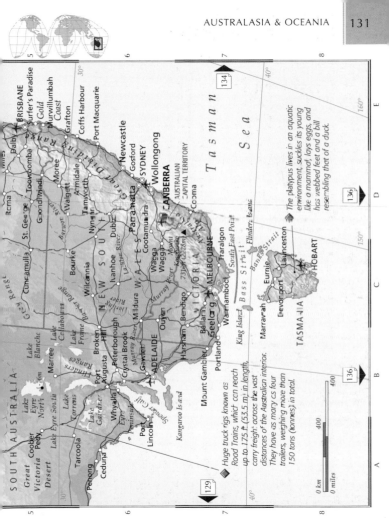

The platypus lives in an aquatic environment, suckles its young like a mammal, lays eggs, and has webbed feet and a bill resembling that of a duck.

Huge truck rigs known as Road Trains, which can reach up to 175 ft (53.5 m) in length, carry freight across the vast distances of the Australian interior. They have as many as four trailers, weighing more than 150 tons (tonnes) in total.

SOUTH AUSTRALIA

Great Victoria Desert

Coober Pedy

Tarcoola

Ceduna

Penong

Lake Eyre North

Lake Eyre South

Marree

Lake Blanche

Lake Frome

Lake Torrens

Lake Gairdner

Whyalla

Port Augusta

Gawler

ADELAIDE

Peterborough

Crystal Brook

Port Lincoln

Eyre Peninsula

Kangaroo Island

Mount Gambier

Portland

Warrnambool

Hamilton

Horsham

Bendigo

Ballarat

Geelong

Ouyen

Mildura

Broken Hill

Wilcannia

Lake Cawndilla

Menindee

Ivanhoe

Balranald

VICTORIA

MELBOURNE

Traralgon

South East Point

Wilsons Promontory

Flinders Island

Bass Strait

King Island

Marrawah

Devonport

Burnie

Launceston

TASMANIA

HOBART

Banks Strait

Tasman Sea

Grey Range

NEW SOUTH WALES

Cunnamulla

St. George

Bollon

Bourke

Cobar

Nyngan

Dubbo

Wagga Wagga

Cootamundra

Mount Kosciuszko 7310ft/2228m

Cooma

CANBERRA

AUSTRALIAN CAPITAL TERRITORY

Parramatta

Wollongong

SYDNEY

Gosford

Newcastle

Port Macquarie

Coffs Harbour

Grafton

Murwillumbah

Gold Coast

Surfers Paradise

BRISBANE

Dalby

Toowoomba

Goondiwindi

Moree

Walgett

Tamworth

Armidale

Roma

Great Dividing Range

Murray River

Darling River

Lachlan River

129

134

136

136

0 km   400

0 miles   400

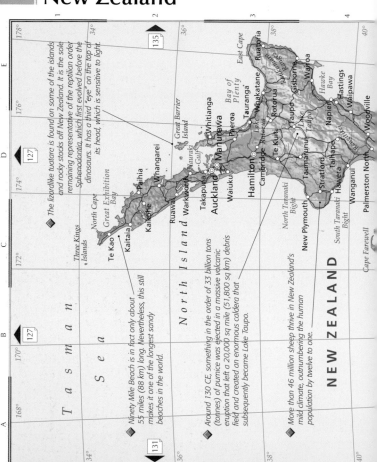

The lizardlike tuatara is found on some of the islands and rocky stacks off New Zealand. It is the sole remaining representative of the reptilian order Sphenodonta, which first evolved before the dinosaurs. It has a third "eye" on the top of its head, which is sensitive to light.

Ninety Mile Beach is in fact only about 55 miles (88 km) long. Nevertheless, this still makes it one of the longest sandy beaches in the world.

Around 130 CE, something in the order of 33 billion tons (tonnes) of pumice was ejected in a massive volcanic eruption that left a 20,000 sq mile (51,800 sq km) debris field and created an enormous caldera that subsequently became Lake Taupo.

More than 46 million sheep thrive in New Zealand's mild climate, outnumbering the human population by twelve to one.

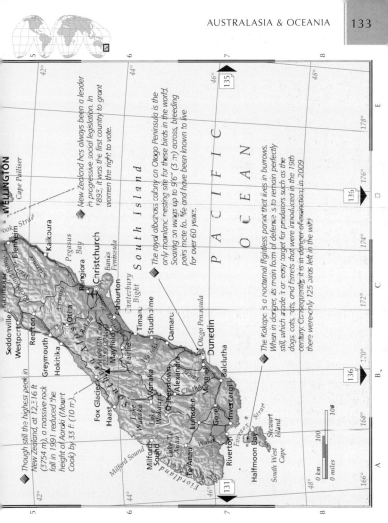

WELLINGTON

Cook Strait

Cape Palliser

New Zealand has always been a leader in progressive social legislation. In 1893, it was the first country to grant women the right to vote.

Though still the highest peak in New Zealand, at 12,316 ft (3754 m), a massive rock fall in 1991 reduced the height of Aoraki (Mount Cook) by 33 ft (10 m).

The royal albatross colony on Otago Peninsula is the only mainland nesting site for these birds in the world. Soaring on wings up to 9.6" (3 m) across, breeding pairs mate for life and have been known to live for over 60 years.

The kakapo is a nocturnal flightless parrot that lives in burrows. When in danger, its main form of defense is to remain perfectly still, which made it an easy target for predators such as the dogs, cats, rats, and ferrets that were introduced in the 19th century. Consequently it is in danger of extinction; in 2009 there were only 125 birds left in the wild.

PACIFIC OCEAN

South Island

Seddonville
Westport
Reefton
Greymouth
Hokitika
Fox Glacier
Haast

Richmond

Blenheim
Kaikoura

Pegasus Bay

Rangiora
Christchurch
Banks Peninsula

Canterbury Bight

Ashburton
Timaru
Studholme
Oamaru

Fairlie
Mayfield
Geraldine

Aoraki (Mt. Cook)
12,283 (3744m)

Lake Wanaka
Lake Hawea
Wanaka
Queenstown
Alexandra
Roxburgh

Lake Wakatipu

Milford Sound
Lake Te Anau
Te Anau
Lumsden

Mossgiel
Balclutha

Otago Peninsula
Dunedin

Gore
Mataura
Invercargill
Riverton

Foveaux Strait

Stewart Island

Halfmoon Bay

South West Cape

Fiordland

0 km   100
0 miles   100

The Pacific Ocean

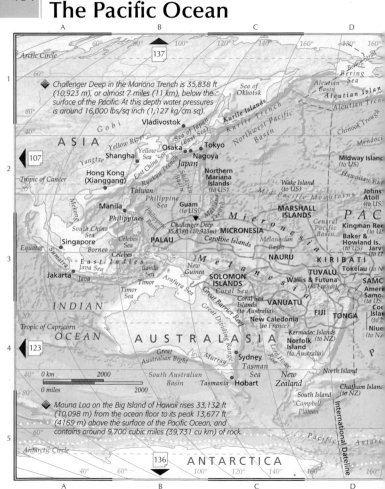

◆ Challenger Deep in the Mariana Trench is 35,838 ft (10,923 m), or almost 7 miles (11 km), below the surface of the Pacific. At this depth water pressures is around 16,000 lbs/sq inch (1,127 kg/cm sq).

◆ Mauna Loa on the Big Island of Hawaii rises 33,132 ft (10,098 m) from the ocean floor to its peak 13,677 ft (4169 m) above the surface of the Pacific Ocean, and contains around 9,700 cubic miles (39,731 cu km) of rock.

Arctic Circle
Bering Strait
Bering Sea
Sea of Okhotsk
Aleutian Basin
Aleutian Islands
Aleutian Trench
Gobi
Vladivostok
Kurile Islands
Kurile Trench
Northwest Pacific Basin
Chinook Trough
ASIA
Sea of Japan (East Sea)
Tokyo
Osaka
Nagoya
Japan
Mendoci
Yellow River
Shanghai
Yellow Sea
East China Sea
Yangtze
Hong Kong (Xianggang)
Taiwan
Northern Mariana Islands (to US)
Wake Island (to US)
Midway Island (to US)
Hawaiian Rid
Johns
Atoll
(to US)
Tropic of Cancer
Ryukyu Trench
Shikoku Basin
Mid
Pacific Mountains
Mekong
Philippine Sea
Guam (to US)
Manila
Philippines
Philippine Basin
Challenger Deep 35,838ft (10,923m)
MICRONESIA
Micronesia
MARSHALL ISLANDS
Central Pacific Basin
PAC
Kingman Ree
(to US)
Baker & Howland Is. (to US)
South China Sea
Singapore
Borneo
Celebes
Celebes Sea
PALAU
Caroline Islands
Melanesian Basin
NAURU
KIRIBATI
Equator
Sumatra
East Indies
Java Sea
Banda Sea
New Guinea
Melanesia
TUVALU
Tokelau (to NZ)
SAMC
Jakarta
Java
Timor
Timor Sea
Arafura Sea
SOLOMON ISLANDS
Coral Sea
Wallis & Futuna (to France)
Amer
Samo
(to US
INDIAN
Great Barrier Reef
Coral Sea Islands (to Australia)
VANUATU
FIJI
TONGA
Coo
Islan
(to N
OCEAN
Tropic of Capricorn
AUSTRALASIA
Great Dividing Range
New Caledonia (to France)
Kermadec Islands (to NZ)
Niue
(to N
AUSTRALIA
Lord Howe Rise
Great Australian Bight
Murray
Sydney
Norfolk Island (to Australia)
P
0 km   2000
0 miles   2000
South Australian Basin
Tasman Sea
North Island
Hobart
Tasmania
New Zealand
Chatham Island (to NZ)
South Island
Campbell Plateau
Pacific
Antar
International Dateline
Antarctic Circle
ANTARCTICA

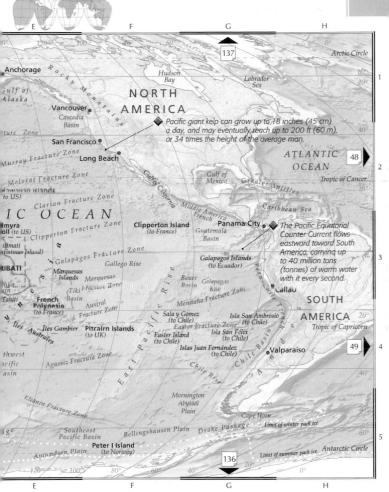

137

Arctic Circle

E   F   G   H

Anchorage

Rocky Mountains

Hudson Bay

Labrador Sea

60°

120°   100°   80°   60°   40°   0°

20°   1

Gulf of Alaska

Cascadia Basin

NORTH AMERICA

Vancouver

...ture Zone

Pacific giant kelp can grow up to 18 inches (45 cm) a day, and may eventually reach up to 200 ft (60 m), or 34 times the height of the average man.

San Francisco

40°

Long Beach

Murray Fracture Zone

ATLANTIC OCEAN

48

Molokai Fracture Zone

Gulf of Mexico

Greater Antilles

Tropic of Cancer   26°   2

...waiian Islands (to US)

Clarion Fracture Zone

Caribbean Sea

...mati ...stmas Island)

IC OCEAN

Middle America French

Clipperton Island (to France)

Panama City

The Pacific Equatorial Counter Current flows eastward toward South America, carrying up to 40 million tons (tonnes) of warm water with it every second.

...myra ...oll (to US)

Clipperton Fracture Zone

Guatemala Basin

RIBATI

Galapagos Fracture Zone

Gallego Rise

Galapagos Islands (to Ecuador)

Bauer Basin

Marquesas Islands   Marquesas

Galapagos Rise

...sin

Tiki Fracture Zone

Callao

Tahiti

Mendaña Fracture Zone

SOUTH

French Polynesia (to France)

Austral Fracture Zone

Sala y Gomez (to Chile)

Isla San Ambrosio (to Chile)

AMERICA   20°

Tropic of Capricorn

49

Îles Gambier

Iles Australes

Pitcairn Islands (to UK)

Easter Fracture Zone   Easter Island (to Chile)

Isla San Félix (to Chile)

Islas Juan Fernández (to Chile)

Valparaiso

...thwest ...arific ...asin

Agassiz Fracture Zone

Chile Rise

40°   4

Mornington Abyssal Plain

Cape Horn

Limit of winter pack ice

Eltanin Fracture Zone

60°

...ge

Southeast Pacific Basin

Bellingshausen Plain

Drake Passage

Peter I Island (to Norway)

Limit of summer pack ice   Antarctic Circle

Amundsen Plain

136

120°   100°   80°   60°   40°   20°   0°

E   F   G   H

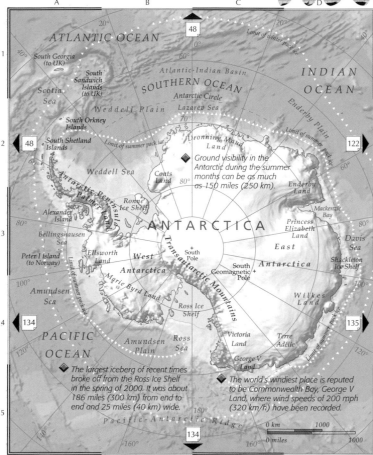

ATLANTIC OCEAN

48

Limit of winter pack ice

INDIAN
OCEAN

South Georgia
(to UK)

South
Sandwich
Islands
(to UK)

Scotia
Sea

Atlantic-Indian Basin

SOUTHERN OCEAN

Antarctic Circle

Weddell Plain

Lazarev Sea

Enderby Plain

South Orkney
Islands

48

South Shetland
Islands

Limit of summer pack ice

Dronning Maud
Land

Limit of summer pack ice

122

Ground visibility in the
Antarctic during the summer
months can be as much
as 150 miles (250 km).

Weddell Sea

Coats
Land

Enderby
Land

Ronne
Ice Shelf

Mackenzie
Bay

Alexander
Island

Bellingshausen
Sea

ANTARCTICA

Princess
Elizabeth
Land

Davis
Sea

Peter I Island
(to Norway)

Ellsworth
Land

West
Antarctica

+ South
Pole

East
Antarctica

Shackleton
Ice Shelf

Amundsen
Sea

Marie Byrd Land

South
Geomagnetic +
Pole

Wilkes
Land

Ross Ice
Shelf

Amundsen
Plain

Ross
Sea

Victoria
Land

Terre
Adélie

PACIFIC
OCEAN

134

George V
Land

135

The largest iceberg of recent times
broke off from the Ross Ice Shelf
in the spring of 2000. It was about
186 miles (300 km) from end to
end and 25 miles (40 km) wide.

The world's windiest place is reputed
to be Commonwealth Bay, George V
Land, where wind speeds of 200 mph
(320 km/h) have been recorded.

Pacific-Antarctic Ridge

134

0 km   1000

0 miles   1000

The Arctic Ocean is the world's smallest ocean, with a total area of 5,440,000 sq miles (15,1000,000 sq km), and is almost permanently covered by pack ice.

The Arctic Lion's Mane is the world's largest jellyfish, 7 ft (2.1 m) in diameter. Its main body trails tentacles up to 180 ft (55 m) in length.

Providentya

ALASKA (part of USA)
NORTH AMERICA
Bering Strait
Chukchi Sea
Arctic Circle
ASIA
RUSSIAN FEDERATION
Ostrov Vrangelya
East Siberian Sea
Tuktoyaktuk
Beaufort Sea
Limit of summer pack ice
Limit of permanent pack ice
Chukchi Plain
Chukchi Plateau
Mendeleyev Ridge
Novosibirskiye Ostrova
Amundsen Gulf
Canada Basin
Victoria Island
CANADA
Queen Elizabeth Islands
Baffin Island
Ellesmere Island
Makarov Basin
ARCTIC
North Pole
OCEAN
Severnaya Zemlya
Kara Sea
Svyataya Anna Trough
Dikson
Ostrov Belyy
Lincoln Sea
Knud Rasmussen Land
Franz Josef Land
Nansen Basin
Novaya Zemlya
East Novaya Zemlya Trough
Baffin Bay
Wandel Sea
Kong Frederik Land
Greenland (to Denmark)
Spitsbergen
Limit of permanent pack ice
Limit of summer pack ice
Svalbard (to Norway)
Longyearbyen
Bjørnøya (to Norway)
Barents Sea
Greenland Sea
North Cape
Murmansk
Jan Mayen (to Norway)
Norwegian Sea
FINLAND
EUROPE
Archangel
Denmark Strait

0 km 500
0 miles 500

The world factfiles

North & Central America

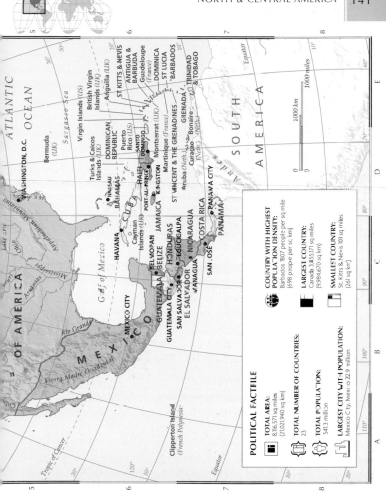

ATLANTIC

OCEAN

Sargasso Sea

Bermuda (UK)

Virgin Islands (US)
British Virgin
Islands (US)
Anguilla (UK)
ST KITTS & NEVIS
ANTIGUA &
BARBUDA
Guadeloupe
(France)
DOMINICA
Turks & Caicos
Islands (UK)
DOMINICAN
REPUBLIC
Puerto
Rico (US)
ST LUCIA
BARBADOS
NASSAU
HAITI   SANTO
DOMINGO
Montserrat (UK)
Martinique (France)
ST VINCENT & THE GRENADINES
GRENADA
TRINIDAD
& TOBAGO
BAHAMAS
PORT-AU-PRINCE KINGSTON
Cayman
Islands (UK)
JAMAICA
Aruba (Neth.) Curaçao
(Neth.)   Bonaire
(Neth.)
HAVANA
CUBA
BELMOPAN
BELIZE
HONDURAS
TEGUCIGALPA
NICARAGUA
MANAGUA
COSTA RICA
SAN JOSÉ
PANAMA CITY
PANAMA
GUATEMALA CITY
GUATEMALA
SAN SALVADOR
EL SALVADOR

SOUTH

AMERICA

Andes

Equator

UNITED STATES
OF AMERICA
WASHINGTON, D.C.
Appalachian Mountains
Ohio
Mississippi
Arkansas
Gulf of Mexico
Rio Grande
MEXICO
MEXICO CITY
Sierra Madre Occidental

Clipperton Island
(French Polynesia)

Tropic of Cancer

Equator

1000 miles

1000 km

POLITICAL FACTFILE

TOTAL AREA:
8,116,571 sq miles
(21,021,940 sq km)

TOTAL NUMBER OF COUNTRIES:
23

TOTAL POPULATION:
541.3 million

LARGEST CITY WITH POPULATION:
Mexico City: Mexico 22.9 million

**COUNTRY WITH HIGHEST
POPULATION DENSITY:**
Barbados 1807 people per sq mile
(698 people per sq km)

LARGEST COUNTRY:
Canada 3,855,171 sq miles
(9,984,670 sq km)

SMALLEST COUNTRY:
St Kitts & Nevis 101 sq miles
(261 sq km)

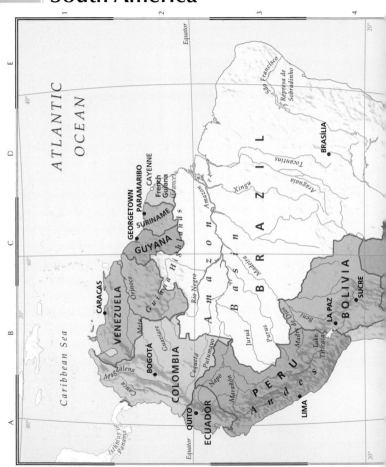

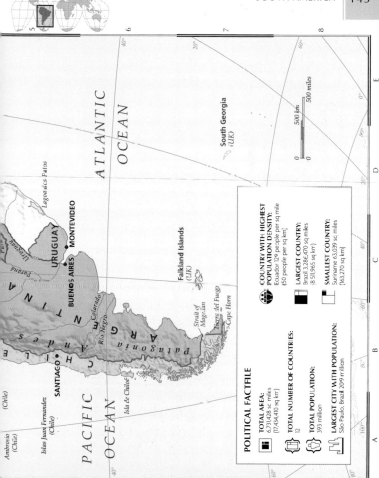

ATLANTIC

OCEAN

South Georgia
(UK)

Lagoa dos Patos

URUGUAY MONTEVIDEO

Paraná

BUENOS AIRES

Falkland Islands
(UK)

A R G E N T I N A

El Colorado

Río Negro

Strait of Magellan

Tierra del Fuego

Cape Horn

Patagonia

C H I L E

SANTIAGO

Andes

Isla de Chiloé

PACIFIC

OCEAN

Islas Juan Fernandez
(Chile)

Ambrosio (Chile)

(Chile)

0   500 km
0   500 miles

POLITICAL FACTFILE

TOTAL AREA:
6,731,428 sc. miles
(17,434,410 sq km)

TOTAL NUMBER OF COUNTRIES:
12

TOTAL POPULATION:
393 million

LARGEST CITY WITH POPULATION:
São Paulo, Brazil 2O9 million

COUNTRY WITH HIGHEST POPULATION DENSITY:
Ecuador 129 people per sq mile
(50 people per sq km)

LARGEST COUNTRY:
Brazil 3,286,470 sq miles
(8,511,965 sq km)

SMALLEST COUNTRY:
Suriname 63,039 sc. miles
(163,270 sq km)

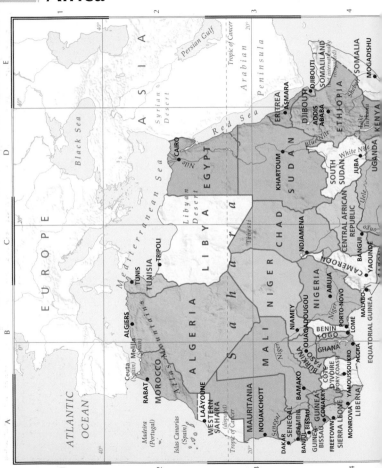

SÃO TOMÉ &
PRINCIPE

Ascension I.
(St Helena)

St Helena
(UK)

ATLANTIC

OCEAN

Tropic of Capricorn

20°

0°

20°

LUANDA•

•Cabinda
(part of Angola)

•BRAZZAVILLE
KINSHASA•

DEM. REP.
CONGO

ANGOLA

NAMIBIA

WINDHOEK•

Kalahari
Desert

Orange River

BOTSWANA

GABORONE•

•BUJUMBURA BURUNDI

TANZANIA

•DODOMA

Lake Nyasa

Lake
Tanganyika

ZAMBIA

LUSAKA•

•LLONGWE
MALAWI

Zambezi

ZIMBABWE

•HARARE

•PRETORIA/TSHWANE
•MBABANE •MAPUTO
SWAZILAND
•BLOEMFONTEIN LESOTHO
•MASERU

SOUTH
AFRICA

CAPE TOWN•

Cape of Good Hope

MOZAMBIQUE

COMOROS
•MORONI
Mayotte
(France)

•ANTANANARIVO

MADAGASCAR

INDIAN

OCEAN

Tropic of Capricorn

20°

40°

1000 km

1000 miles

0

0

POLITICAL FACTFILE

TOTAL AREA:
11,437,865 sq miles
(29,624,100 sq km)

TOTAL NUMBER OF COUNTRIES:
54

TOTAL POPULATION:
1030.8 million

LARGEST CITY WITH POPULATION:
Cairo, Egypt 15.4 million

COUNTRY WITH HIGHEST POPULATION DENSITY:
Mauritius 1811 people per sq mile
(699 people per sq km)

LARGEST COUNTRY:
Algeria 919,590 sq miles
(2,381,740 sq km)

SMALLEST COUNTRY:
Seychelles 176 sq miles
(455 sq km)

Europe

POLITICAL FACTFILE

TOTAL AREA:
3,739,678 sq miles
(9,685,756 sq km)

TOTAL NUMBER OF COUNTRIES:
46

TOTAL POPULATION:
718.3 million

LARGEST CITY WITH POPULATION:
Moscow, European Russia 16 million

COUNTRY WITH HIGHEST POPULATION DENSITY:
Monaco 40,719 people per sq mile
(15,661 people per sq km)

LARGEST COUNTRY:
European Russia 1,527,341 sq miles
(3,955,818 sq km)

SMALLEST COUNTRY:
Vatican City, Italy 0.17 sq miles
(0.44 sq km)

Arctic Circle

REYKJAVÍK
ICELAND

Faeroe Islands
(Denmark)

Norwegian
Sea

Shetland Islands

Outer
Hebrides

Orkney Islands

British
Isles

North
Sea

OSLO

DENMARK
COPENHAGEN

IRELAND
DUBLIN

UNITED
KINGDOM

LONDON

AMSTERDAM
NETH.
THE
HAGUE

BERLIN

GERMANY

Channel Is.
(UK)

BELGIUM
BRUSSELS

Elbe

PRAGUE

PARIS

LUXEMBOURG
LUXEMBOURG

CZECH REPUBLIC

Loire

Rhine

BRATISLAVA

FRANCE

LIECH.

VIENNA
AUSTRIA

ATLANTIC
OCEAN

Bay of Biscay

Garonne

SWITZERLAND

SLOVENIA
LJUBLJANA

ZAGREB
CROATIA

PORTUGAL

Ebro

MONACO

SAN MARINO

SARAJEVO
BOSN.
& HER.

Madeira
(Portugal)

LISBON

MADRID

ANDORRA

Tagus

SPAIN

Corsica

VATICAN CITY
ROME

ITALY

Guadalquivir

Gibraltar
(UK)

Balearic Islands

Sardinia

Canary Islands
(Spain)

Ceuta
(Spain)

Melilla
(Spain)

Mediterranean Sea

Sicily

AFRICA

VALLETTA
MALTA

Asia

Sea of Okhotsk

Kurile Islands

NORTH KOREA

PYONGYANG

SEOUL

JING

SOUTH KOREA

JAPAN

TOKYO

Ryukyu Islands

Tropic of Cancer

TAIPEI

TAIWAN

PACIFIC OCEAN

MANILA

PHILIPPINES

Equator

UNEI

BANDAR SERI BEGAWAN

A

N E S I A

DILI EAST TIMOR

AUSTRALASIA & OCEANIA

POLITICAL FACTFILE

TOTAL AREA:
17,006,354 sq miles
(44,046,472 sq km)

TOTAL NUMBER OF COUNTRIES:
49

TOTAL POPULATION:
4193.9 million

LARGEST CITY WITH POPULATION:
Tokyo, Japan 34.3 million

COUNTRY WITH HIGHEST POPULATION DENSITY:
Singapore 20,339 people per sq mile
(7000 people per sq km)

LARGEST COUNTRY:
Asiatic Russia 5,065,394 sq miles
(13,119,382 sq km)

SMALLEST COUNTRY:
Maldives 116 sq miles
(300 sq km)

0   1000 km
0   1000 miles

Australasia & Oceania

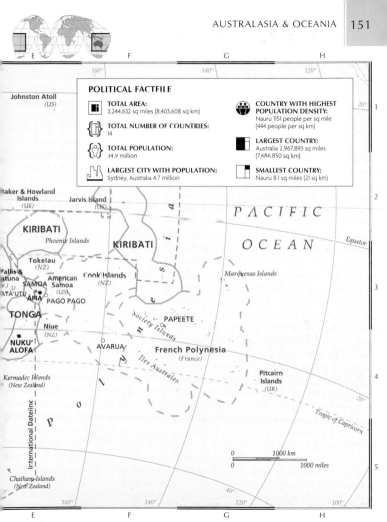

E   **F**   **G**   **H**

160°   140°   120°

POLITICAL FACTFILE

TOTAL AREA:
3,244,632 sq miles (8,403,608 sq km)

TOTAL NUMBER OF COUNTRIES:
14

TOTAL POPULATION:
34.9 million

LARGEST CITY WITH POPULATION:
Sydney, Australia 4.7 million

COUNTRY WITH HIGHEST POPULATION DENSITY:
Nauru 1151 people per sq mile
(444 people per sq km)

LARGEST COUNTRY:
Australia 2,967,893 sq miles
(7,686,850 sq km)

SMALLEST COUNTRY:
Nauru 8.1 sq miles (21 sq km)

Johnston Atoll
(US)

20°   1

Baker & Howland
Islands
(US)

Jarvis Island
(US)

P A C I F I C

2

Micronesia

O C E A N

Equator

KIRIBATI

Phoenix Islands

KIRIBATI

Marquesas Islands

Tokelau
(NZ)

Wallis &
Futuna
(Fr.)

American
Samoa
(US)

Cook Islands
(NZ)

SAMOA

MATA'UTU

ĀPIA   PAGO PAGO

PAPEETE

Society Islands

3

TONGA

Niue
(NZ)

Polynesia

NUKU'
ALOFA

AVARUA

French Polynesia
(France)

Îles Australes

Pitcairn
Islands
(UK)

4

Kermadec Islands
(New Zealand)

30°

International Dateline

Tropic of Capricorn

0   1000 km
0   1000 miles

Chatham Islands
(New Zealand)

40°

5

160°   140°   120°   100°

E   **F**   **G**   **H**

Key to factfile maps

FOREWORD

This factfile is intended as a guide to a world that is continually changing as political fashions and personalities come and go. Nevertheless, all the material in these factfiles has been researched from the most up-to-date and authoritative sources to give an incisive portrait of the geographical, social, and economic characteristics that make each country unique.

KEY TO MAP SYMBOLS

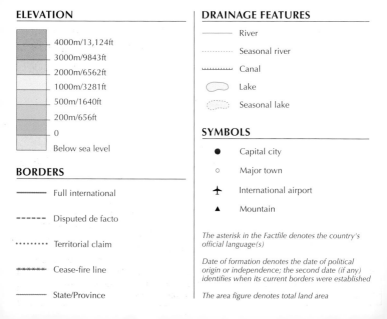

ELEVATION

- 4000m/13,124ft
- 3000m/9843ft
- 2000m/6562ft
- 1000m/3281ft
- 500m/1640ft
- 200m/656ft
- 0
- Below sea level

BORDERS

——— Full international

----- Disputed de facto

·········· Territorial claim

✶✶✶✶✶ Cease-fire line

········· State/Province

DRAINAGE FEATURES

——— River

·········· Seasonal river

ᴗᴗᴗᴗᴗ Canal

⬭ Lake

⬭ Seasonal lake

SYMBOLS

● Capital city

○ Major town

✈ International airport

▲ Mountain

The asterisk in the Factfile denotes the country's official language(s)

Date of formation denotes the date of political origin or independence; the second date (if any) identifies when its current borders were established

The area figure denotes total land area

Afghanistan

About 75% of this landlocked Asian country is
inaccessible. The Islamist *Taliban,* ousted in 2001, continue
to fight a guerrilla war against Afghan and NATO-led forces.

GEOGRAPHY
Predominantly mountainous.
Highest range is the Hindu Kush.
Mountains are bordered by fertile plains.
Desert plateau in the south.

CLIMATE
Harsh continental. Hot, dry
summers. Cold winters with heavy
snow, especially in the Hindu Kush.

PEOPLE & SOCIETY
Mujahideen factions fought first
against Soviet invaders (from 1979), and
then against each other (after 1989).
Taliban insurgents won control in 1996
and imposed a strict Islamist regime:
women were denied all rights and ethnic
tensions were exacerbated. In 2001, a
US-led intervention justified as a "war
on terrorism" helped install an elected
anti-*Taliban* regime. NATO troops led
the anti-insurgency campaign, but aimed
ultimately to hand over and withdraw.

THE ECONOMY
Mainly agricultural, severely
disrupted by war. Illicit opium trade is big
cash earner. Natural gas pipeline planned
from the Caspian Sea to Pakistan.

◆ **INSIGHT:** *The UN estimates that it
could take 100 years to remove the
10 million landmines laid since 1979*

FACTFILE

OFFICIAL NAME: Islamic Republic
of Afghanistan
DATE OF FORMATION: 1919
CAPITAL: Kabul
POPULATION: 29.1 million
TOTAL AREA: 250,000 sq. miles
(647,500 sq. km)

DENSITY: 116 people per sq. mile
LANGUAGES: Pashtu*, Tajik, Dari*, other
RELIGIONS: Sunni Muslim 80%,
Shi'a Muslim 19%, other 1%
ETHNIC MIX: Pashtun 38%, Tajik 25%, Hazara
19%, Uzbek and Turkmen 15%, other 3%
GOVERNMENT: Presidential system
CURRENCY: Afghani = 100 puls

Albania

Lying at the southeastern end of the Adriatic Sea, Albania was the last east European country to liberalize its economy. The regional strife of the 1990s has left a difficult legacy.

GEOGRAPHY
Narrow coastal plain. Interior is mostly hills and mountains. Forest and scrub cover over 40% of the land.

CLIMATE
Mediterranean coastal climate, with warm summers and cool winters. Mountains receive heavy rains or snows in winter.

PEOPLE & SOCIETY
The pace of economic reform remains a major issue. EU membership, applied for in 2009, is a distant prospect. Mosques and churches have reopened in what was once the world's only officially atheist state. The Greek minority in the south suffers much discrimination.

◆ INSIGHT: *The Albanians' name for their country, Shqipërisë, means "Land of the Eagles"*

THE ECONOMY
Oil and natural gas reserves have potential to offset rudimentary infrastructure and lack of foreign investment. Organized crime problem.

FACTFILE

OFFICIAL NAME: Republic of Albania
DATE OF FORMATION: 1912
CAPITAL: Tirana
POPULATION: 3.2 million
TOTAL AREA: 11,100 sq. miles
(28,748 sq. km)
DENSITY: 302 people per sq. mile

LANGUAGES: Albanian*, Greek
RELIGIONS: Sunni Muslim 70%, Albanian Orthodox 20%, Roman Catholic 10%
ETHNIC MIX: Albanian 98%, Greek 1%, other 1%
GOVERNMENT: Parliamentary system
CURRENCY: Lek = 100 qindarka (qintars)

Algeria

On the Mediterranean coast, and independent from France since 1962, Algeria is now Africa's largest country. Its regime used the army to keep Islamists from power in 1992.

GEOGRAPHY

85% of the country lies within the Sahara Desert. Fertile coastal region with plains and hills rises to meet the Atlas Mountains.

CLIMATE

Coastal areas are warm and temperate, with most rainfall during the mild winters. The south is very hot, with negligible rainfall.

PEOPLE & SOCIETY

Algerians are predominantly Arab, under 35 years of age, and urban. Berbers consider the mountainous Kabylia region in the northeast to be their homeland. They have been granted greater ethnic rights in recent years. The Sahara sustains just 500,000 people, mainly oil workers or Tuareg nomads herding goats and camels. A national reconciliation process has followed the suppression of the Islamist challenge to the regime.

THE ECONOMY

Oil and natural gas exports. Political turmoil has led to exodus of skilled foreign labor. Limited agriculture.

◆ **INSIGHT:** *The world's highest dunes are located in the deserts of east central Algeria*

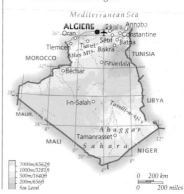

FACTFILE

OFFICIAL NAME: People's Democratic Republic of Algeria

DATE OF FORMATION: 1962

CAPITAL: Algiers

POPULATION: 35.4 million

TOTAL AREA: 919,590 sq. miles (2,381,740 sq. km)

DENSITY: 38 people per sq. mile

LANGUAGES: Arabic*, Tamazight, French

RELIGIONS: Sunni Muslim 99%, Christian and Jewish 1%

ETHNIC MIX: Arab 75%, Berber 24%, European and Jewish 1%

GOVERNMENT: Presidential system

CURRENCY: Algerian dinar = 100 centimes

Andorra

A tiny landlocked principality, Andorra lies high in the eastern Pyrenees between France and Spain. It held its first full elections in 1993. Tourism is the main source of income.

GEOGRAPHY

High mountains, with six deep, glaciated valleys that drain into the Valira River as it flows into Spain.

CLIMATE

Cool, wet springs followed by dry, warm summers. Mountain snows linger until March.

PEOPLE & SOCIETY

Immigration is strictly monitored and restricted by quota to French and Spanish nationals seeking employment in Andorra. Low taxes attract wealthy expatriates. A referendum in 1993 ended 715 years of semifeudal status, but Andorran society remains conservative.

◆ **INSIGHT:** *Andorra's coprincipality status dates from the 13th century. The "princes" are the president of France and the bishop of Urgel in Spain.*

THE ECONOMY

Tourism and duty-free sales dominate the economy. Banking secrecy laws and low consumer taxes promote investment and commerce. France and Spain effectively decide economic policy. The country is dependent on imported food and raw materials.

2000m/6562ft
1000m/3281ft
500m/1640ft

FRANCE

Pyrenees

42°35' Arinsal   Soldeu

Ordino Canillo
        Encamp   Port
                        d'Envalira
        Escaldes

42°30' **ANDORRA LA VELLA**

Valira Sant Julià de Lòria   1°40'

1°35'
1°25'   1°30'   S P A I N

0   5 km
0   5 miles

FACTFILE

OFFICIAL NAME: Principality of Andorra

DATE OF FORMATION: 1278

CAPITAL: Andorra la Vella

POPULATION: 84,825

TOTAL AREA: 181 sq. miles (468 sq. km)

DENSITY: 471 people per sq. mile

LANGUAGES: Spanish, Catalan*, French, Portuguese

RELIGIONS: Roman Catholic 94%, other 6%

ETHNIC MIX: Spanish 46%, Andorran 28%, other 18%, French 8%

GOVERNMENT: Parliamentary system

CURRENCY: Euro = 100 cents

Angola

Located in southwest Africa, Angola suffered a civil war following independence from Portugal in 1975, until a 2002 peace deal. Hundreds of thousands of people died.

GEOGRAPHY
Most of the land is hilly and grass-covered. Desert in the south. Mountains in the center and north.

CLIMATE
Varies from temperate to tropical. Rainfall decreases north to south. Coast is cooler and dry.

PEOPLE & SOCIETY
Civil war pitched the ruling Kimbundu-dominated MPLA against UNITA, representing the Ovimbundu. Multiparty elections in 1991–1992, after the MPLA had abandoned Marxism, failed to stall the war for long. Power-sharing from 2002 ended when the MPLA won the 2008 election. In 2006, separatists in the Cabinda exclave agreed a peace deal.

◆ **INSIGHT:** Angola has the greatest number of amputees (caused by landmines) in the world

THE ECONOMY
Potentially one of Africa's richest countries, but long civil war hampered economic development. Oil and diamonds are exported.

FACTFILE
OFFICIAL NAME: Republic of Angola
DATE OF FORMATION: 1975
CAPITAL: Luanda
POPULATION: 19 million
TOTAL AREA: 481,351 sq. miles (1,246,700 sq. km)
DENSITY: 39 people per sq. mile

LANGUAGES: Portuguese*, Umbundu, Kimbundu, Kikongo
RELIGIONS: Roman Catholic 68%, Protestant 20%, indigenous beliefs 12%
ETHNIC MIX: Ovimbundu 37%, other 25%, Kimbundu 25%, Bakongo 13%
GOVERNMENT: Presidential system
CURRENCY: Readjusted kwanza = 100 lwei

Antarctica

The circumpolar continent of Antarctica is almost entirely covered by ice, some up to 1.2 miles (2 km) thick. It also contains 90% of the Earth's freshwater reserves.

 GEOGRAPHY
The bulk of Antarctica's ice is contained in the Greater Antarctic Ice Sheet – a huge dome that rises steeply from the coast and flattens to a plateau in the interior.

 CLIMATE
Powerful winds create a storm belt around the continent, which brings cloud, fog, and blizzards. Winter temperatures can fall to −112°F (−80°C).

 PEOPLE & SOCIETY
No indigenous population. Scientists and logistical staff work at the 40 permanent, and as many as 100 temporary, research stations. A few Chilean settler families live on King George Island. Tourism is mostly by cruise ship to the Antarctic Peninsula. Annual tourist numbers have reached nearly 40,000.

0   1000 km
0   1000 miles

Territorial Claims:

Chilean claim
Argentinian claim
Brazilian zone of interest
British claim
Norwegian undefined limit

Australian claim

French claim
New Zealand claim

The Antarctic Treaty of 1959 holds all territorial claims in abeyance in the interest of international cooperation

South Orkney Is.
South Shetland Is.
King George I.
Antarctic Peninsula
Weddell Sea
Queen Maud Land
Enderby Land
Ronne Ice Shelf
South Pole
East Antarctica
85° 80° 75° 70° 65° 90°E
90°W
Ellsworth Land
West Antarctica
Transantarctic Mts.
Amundsen Sea
Ross Ice Shelf
Victoria Land
Wilkes Land
Ross Sea
Balleny Is.
South Magnetic Pole
SOUTHERN OCEAN
Antarctic Circle
SOUTHERN OCEAN
SOUTHERN OCEAN
180°

☐ Ice Cap
Permanent Ice

FACTFILE

DATE OF FORMATION: 1961
TOTAL AREA: 5,405,000 sq. miles (14,000,000 sq. km)

◆ **INSIGHT:** *If the ice sheets of Antarctica were to melt, the world's oceans would rise by as much as 200–210 ft (60–65 m)*

Antigua & Barbuda

A former colony of Spain, France, and the UK, Antigua and Barbuda lies at the outer edge of the Leeward Islands group in the Caribbean, and includes the uninhabited islet of Redonda.

GEOGRAPHY
Mainly low-lying limestone and coral islands with some higher volcanic areas. Antigua's coast is indented with bays and harbors.

CLIMATE
Tropical, moderated by trade winds and sea breezes. Humidity and rainfall are low for the region.

PEOPLE & SOCIETY
Population almost entirely of African origin, with small communities of Europeans and South Asians. Women's status has risen as a result of greater access to education. Wealth disparities are small. The Bird family dominated politics from 1960, but lost power to the United Progressive Party (UPP) from 2004.

◆ **INSIGHT:** *In 1865, Redonda was "claimed" by an eccentric Englishman as a kingdom for his son*

THE ECONOMY
Tourism is the main source of revenue and the biggest provider of jobs. Financial services and Internet gambling are expanding. High debt.

FACTFILE

OFFICIAL NAME: Antigua and Barbuda
DATE OF FORMATION: 1981
CAPITAL: St. John's
POPULATION: 87,884
TOTAL AREA: 170 sq. miles
(442 sq. km)
DENSITY: 517 people per sq. mile

LANGUAGES: English*, English patois
RELIGIONS: Anglican 45%,
other Protestant 42%, Roman Catholic 10%,
other 2%, Rastafarian 1%
ETHNIC MIX: Black African 95%,
other 5%
GOVERNMENT: Parliamentary system
CURRENCY: E. Caribbean $ = 100 cents

Argentina

Argentina occupies most of southern South America. After 30 years of intermittent military rule, democracy returned in 1983. Economic crash in 2001 led to largest-ever debt default.

GEOGRAPHY

The Andes form a natural border with Chile in the west. East are the heavily wooded plains (Gran Chaco) and treeless but fertile Pampas plains. Bleak and arid Patagonia lies in the south.

CLIMATE

The Andes are semiarid in the north and snowy in the south. Pampas have a mild climate with summer rains.

PEOPLE & SOCIETY

People are largely of European descent; over one-third are of Italian origin. Indigenous peoples are now a tiny minority, living mainly in Andean regions or in the Gran Chaco. The middle classes were worst hit by the economic meltdown of 2001–2002.

◆ **INSIGHT:** *The Tango originated in the poorer quarters of Buenos Aires at the end of the 19th century*

THE ECONOMY

Agricultural exports restored growth from 2003. Quickly bounced back from drought and global downturn in 2008.

	4000m/13124ft
	3000m/9843ft
	2000m/6562ft
	1000m/3281ft
	200m/656ft
	Sea Level

0   400 km
0   400 miles

FACTFILE

OFFICIAL NAME: Republic of Argentina
DATE OF FORMATION: 1816
CAPITAL: Buenos Aires
POPULATION: 40.7 million
TOTAL AREA: 1,068,296 sq. miles (2,766,890 sq. km)
DENSITY: 39 people per sq. mile

LANGUAGES: Spanish*, Italian, Amerindian languages
RELIGIONS: Roman Catholic 70%, other 18%, Protestant 9%, Muslim 2%, Jewish 1%
ETHNIC MIX: Indo-European 97%, *Mestizo* (European–Amerindian) 2%, Amerindian 1%
GOVERNMENT: Presidential system
CURRENCY: Argentine peso = 100 centavos

Armenia

The smallest of the former USSR's republics, Armenia lies landlocked in the Lesser Caucasus Mountains. After 1988, a confrontation with Azerbaijan dominated national life.

GEOGRAPHY
Rugged and mountainous, with expanses of semidesert and a large lake in the east: Sevana Lich.

CLIMATE
Continental climate, with little rainfall in the lowlands. The winters are often bitterly cold.

PEOPLE & SOCIETY
Christianity is the dominant religion, but minority groups are well integrated. War with Azerbaijan over the enclave of Nagorno Karabakh forced 350,000 Armenians living in Azerbaijan to return home, many to live in poverty. There are close and important ties to the seven-million-strong Armenian diaspora.

◆ INSIGHT: *In the 4th century, Armenia became the first country to adopt Christianity as its state religion*

THE ECONOMY
Overseas remittances and agriculture each account for a sixth of GDP. Main products are wine, tobacco, potatoes, and fruit. Well-developed machine-building and manufacturing – includes textiles and bottling of mineral water.

FACTFILE

OFFICIAL NAME: Republic of Armenia
DATE OF FORMATION: 1991
CAPITAL: Yerevan
POPULATION: 3.1 million
TOTAL AREA: 11,506 sq. miles (29,800 sq. km)
DENSITY: 269 people per sq. mile

LANGUAGES: Armenian*, Azeri, Russian
RELIGIONS: Armenian Apostolic Church (Orthodox) 88%, Armenian Catholic Church 6%, other 6%
ETHNIC MIX: Armenian 98%, Yezidi 1%, other 1%
GOVERNMENT: Parliamentary system
CURRENCY: Dram = 100 luma

Australia

An island continent in its own right, Australia is the world's sixth-largest country. European settlement began over 200 years ago. Most Australians now live in cities along the coast.

GEOGRAPHY

Located between the Indian and Pacific oceans, Australia has a variety of landscapes, including tropical rainforests, the arid plateaus, ridges, and vast deserts of the "red center," the lowlands and river systems draining into Lake Eyre, rolling tracts of pastoral land, and magnificent beaches around much of the coastline. In the far east are the mountains of the Great Dividing Range. Famous natural features include Uluru (Ayers Rock) and the Great Barrier Reef.

CLIMATE

The west and south are semi-arid with hot summers. The arid interior can reach 120°F (50°C) in the central desert areas. The north is hot throughout the year, and humid during the summer monsoon. East, southeast, and southwest coastal areas are temperate.

PEOPLE & SOCIETY

The first settlers arrived in Australia at least 100,000 years ago. Today, the Aborigines make up around 2% of the population. European colonization began in 1788, and was dominated by British and Irish immigrants, some of whom were convicts. White-only immigration drives brought many Europeans to Australia, but since the 1960s multi-culturalism has been encouraged and most new settlers are Asian; Cantonese has overtaken Italian as the second most widely spoken language. Wealth disparities are small, but Aborigines, the exception in an otherwise integrated society, are marginalized: their average life expectancy is around 11 years less than other Australians. The Labor government in power from 2007 overturned right-wing policies on illegal immigration and signed up to limiting greenhouse gas emissions.

FACTFILE

OFFICIAL NAME: Commonwealth of Australia
DATE OF FORMATION: 1901
CAPITAL: Canberra
POPULATION: 21.5 million
TOTAL AREA: 2,967,893 sq. miles (7,686,850 sq. km)

DENSITY: 7 people per sq. mile
LANGUAGES: English*, Cantonese, other
RELIGIONS: Various Protestant 38%, other 36%, Roman Catholic 26%
ETHNIC MIX: European 90%, Asian 7%, Aboriginal 2%, other 1%
GOVERNMENT: Parliamentary system
CURRENCY: Australian dollar = 100 cents

THE ECONOMY

Efficient mining and agriculture: particular success in viticulture. Large resource base: coal, iron ore, bauxite, and most other minerals. Protectionism abandoned to open up Australian markets. Concentration on trade with Asia: China's rapidly expanding demand for minerals means it has now surpassed Japan as Australia's major trading partner.

Upward trend in Asian visitor arrivals has strengthened tourism. The effects of droughts, floods, and cyclones have dented economic growth in recent years.

◆ **INSIGHT:** *Sydney has the world's largest suburban area, a conurbation so vast that the city is twice as large as Beijing and six times the size of Rome*

1000m/3281ft
500m/1640ft
200m/656ft
Sea Level
Below Sea Level

0   400 km

0   400 miles

Austria

Bordering eight countries in the heart of Europe, Austria was created in 1918 after the collapse of the Habsburg Empire. Neutral after World War II, it joined the EU in 1995.

GEOGRAPHY
Mainly mountainous. Alps and foothills cover the west and south. Lowlands in the east are part of the Danube River basin.

CLIMATE
Temperate continental climate. The western Alpine regions have colder winters and more rainfall.

PEOPLE & SOCIETY
Though Austrians speak German, they like to stress their distinctive identity in relation to Germany. Vienna is a major cultural center. Minorities are few; there are some ethnic Croats, Slovenes, and Hungarians, plus refugees from conflict in former Yugoslavia. Though strongly Roman Catholic, Austrian society is less conservative than some southern German *Länder*. Class divisions remain strong.

THE ECONOMY
Large manufacturing base, despite lack of energy resources. The skilled labor force is key to high-tech exports. Eurozone membership since 2002 has boosted investment.

INSIGHT: *Many of the world's great composers were Austrian, including Mozart, Haydn, Schubert, and Strauss*

FACTFILE

OFFICIAL NAME: Republic of Austria
DATE OF FORMATION: 1918
CAPITAL: Vienna
POPULATION: 8.4 million
TOTAL AREA: 32,378 sq. miles (83,858 sq. km)
DENSITY: 263 people per sq. mile

LANGUAGES: German*, Croatian, Slovenian, Hungarian (Magyar)
RELIGIONS: Roman Catholic 78%, nonreligious 9%, other 8%, Protestant 5%
ETHNIC MIX: Austrian 93%, Croat, Slovene, and Hungarian 6%, other 1%
GOVERNMENT: Parliamentary system
CURRENCY: Euro = 100 cents

Azerbaijan

Situated on the western coast of the Caspian Sea, it was the first Soviet republic to declare independence in 1991. Territorial disputes with Armenia have dominated politics since.

GEOGRAPHY
Caucasus Mountains in west, including Naxçivan exclave south of Armenia. Flat, low-lying terrain on the coast of the Caspian Sea.

CLIMATE
Low rainfall. Continental, with bitter winters, inland. Subtropical in coastal regions.

PEOPLE & SOCIETY
Azeris, a Muslim people with ethnic links to Turks, form a large majority. Thousands of Armenians, Russians, and Jews have left since independence. Influx of half a million Azeri refugees fleeing war with Armenia over the disputed enclave of Nagorno Karabakh. Armenians there operate with de facto independence. The status of women deteriorated after the fall of communism but they are slowly regaining their position.

THE ECONOMY
Oil and natural gas exports drive economic growth. Pipeline to Ceyhan, Turkey, has opened up European market. Severe pollution in Baku.

◆ INSIGHT: The fire-worshipping Zoroastrian faith originated in Azerbaijan in the 6th century BCE

FACTFILE
OFFICIAL NAME: Republic of Azerbaijan
DATE OF FORMATION: 1991
CAPITAL: Baku
POPULATION: 8.9 million
TOTAL AREA: 33,436 sq. miles (86,600 sq. km)
DENSITY: 266 people per sq. mile

LANGUAGES: Azeri*, Russian
RELIGIONS: Shi'a Muslim 68%, Sunni Muslim 26%, Russian Orthodox 3%, Armenian Apostolic Church (Orthodox) 2%, other 1%
ETHNIC MIX: Azeri 91%, other 3%, Lazs 2%, Russian 2%, Armenian 2%
GOVERNMENT: Presidential system
CURRENCY: New manat = 100 gopik

Bahamas

Located off the Florida coast in the western
Atlantic, the Bahamas comprises an archipelago of some 700
islands and 2400 cays, only around 30 of which are inhabited.

GEOGRAPHY

Long, mainly flat coral
formations with a few low hills.
Some islands have pine forests,
lagoons, and mangrove swamps.

CLIMATE

Subtropical. Hot summers and
mild winters. Heavy rainfall, especially
in summer. Hurricanes can strike in
July–December.

PEOPLE & SOCIETY
Over 60% of the population live
on New Providence. Tourism employs
over 40% of the labor force. There are
marked wealth disparities, from urban
professionals in the banking sector to
traditional fishermen on outlying islands
and illegal Haitian and Cuban immigrants.
More women are now entering the
professions. Government priorities
are tackling narcotics trafficking and
combating money laundering.

THE ECONOMY
Major tourist destination, especially
for US visitors. Financial services: banking
and insurance.

INSIGHT: *The country's extensive
merchant fleet consists mainly of
"flag-of-convenience" vessels
registered by foreign owners*

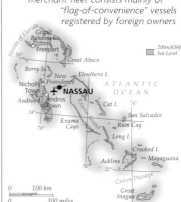

FACTFILE

OFFICIAL NAME: Commonwealth
of the Bahamas
DATE OF FORMATION: 1973
CAPITAL: Nassau
POPULATION: 300,000
TOTAL AREA: 5382 sq. miles
(13,940 sq. km)

DENSITY: 78 people per sq. mile
LANGUAGES: English*, English Creole,
French Creole
RELIGIONS: Baptist 32%, other 29%,
Anglican 20%, Roman Catholic 19%
ETHNIC MIX: Black African 85%, other 15%
GOVERNMENT: Parliamentary system
CURRENCY: Bahamian dollar = 100 cents

Bahrain

Bahrain is an archipelago of 49 islands between the Qatar peninsula and the Saudi Arabian mainland. Only three of the islands are inhabited. It was the first Gulf emirate to export oil.

GEOGRAPHY

All islands are low-lying. The largest, Bahrain Island, is mainly sandy plains and salt marshes.

CLIMATE

Summers are hot and humid. Winters are mild. Low rainfall.

PEOPLE & SOCIETY

The key social division is between the Shi'a majority and Sunni minority. Sunnis hold the best jobs in bureaucracy and business while Shi'as tend to do menial work. Bahrain is socially liberal. The al-Khalifa family has ruled since 1783, but transformed Bahrain into a constitutional monarchy in 2002. Protests calling for greater democracy rocked the country duing the 2011 "Arab Spring"

◆ **INSIGHT:** The 16 Hawar Islands were awarded to Bahrain in 2001 after a lengthy dispute with Qatar

THE ECONOMY

Main exports are refined petroleum and aluminum products. As oil reserves run out, natural gas is of increasing importance. Major Middle East offshore banking center, hit by global banking crisis in 2008–2009.

FACTFILE

OFFICIAL NAME: Kingdom of Bahrain

DATE OF FORMATION: 1971

CAPITAL: Manama

POPULATION: 800,000

TOTAL AREA: 239 sq. miles (620 sq. km)

DENSITY: 2930 people per sq. mile

LANGUAGES: Arabic*

RELIGIONS: Muslim (mainly Shi'a) 99%, other 1%

ETHNIC MIX: Bahraini 63%, Asian 19%, other Arab 10%, Iranian 8%

GOVERNMENT: Mixed monarchical-parliamentary system

CURRENCY: Bahraini dinar = 1000 fils

Bangladesh

Bangladesh lies at the north end of the Bay of Bengal and frequently suffers devastating flood, cyclones, and famine. It seceded from Pakistan in 1971.

GEOGRAPHY
Mostly flat alluvial plains and deltas of the Brahmaputra and Ganges rivers. Southeast coasts are fringed with mangrove forests.

CLIMATE
Hot and humid. During the monsoon, water levels can rise 20 ft (6 m) above sea level.

PEOPLE & SOCIETY
After a period of military rule, Bangladesh returned to democracy in 1991; political instability has continued, however, and corruption is a major problem. Half of the population live in poverty, but living standards are improving. Women are prominent in politics, but their rights are neglected.

◆ INSIGHT: *Torrential monsoon rains flood two-thirds of the country every year*

THE ECONOMY
Agriculture is vulnerable to unpredictable climate. Bangladesh accounts for 90% of world jute fiber exports. Poor infrastructure deters investment. Growing textile industry.

FACTFILE

OFFICIAL NAME: People's Republic of Bangladesh
DATE OF FORMATION: 1971
CAPITAL: Dhaka
POPULATION: 164 million
TOTAL AREA: 55,598 sq. miles (144,000 sq. km)

DENSITY: 3180 people per sq. mile
LANGUAGES: Bengali*, Urdu, Chakma, Marma, Garo, Khasi, Santhali, Tripuri, Mro
RELIGIONS: Muslim (mainly Sunni) 88%, Hindu 11%, other 1%
ETHNIC MIX: Bengali 98%, other 2%
GOVERNMENT: Parliamentary system
CURRENCY: Taka = 100 poisha

Barbados

Barbados is the most easterly of the Caribbean islands. Once solely inhabited by the native Arawak, Barbados was first colonized by British settlers in the 1620s.

 GEOGRAPHY
Encircled by coral reefs. Fertile and predominantly flat, with a few gentle hills to the north.

 CLIMATE
Moderate tropical climate. Sunnier and drier than its more mountainous neighbors.

 PEOPLE & SOCIETY
Independent from the UK since 1966. Some latent tension between the economically dominant white community and the majority black population, but violence is rare. Increasing social mobility has enabled black Barbadians to enter the professions. Despite political stability, and good welfare and education services, pockets of abject poverty remain.

INSIGHT: *Barbados retains a strong British influence and is referred to by its neighbors as "Little England"*

THE ECONOMY
Well-developed tourism sector based on climate and accessibility. Financial services, offshore banking, and information processing are key industries. Sugar production has dwindled. High cost of living.

FACTFILE

OFFICIAL NAME: Barbados
DATE OF FORMATION: 1966
CAPITAL: Bridgetown
POPULATION: 300,000
TOTAL AREA: 166 sq. miles
(430 sq. km)
DENSITY: 1807 people per sq. mile

LANGUAGES: Bajan (Barbadian English), English*
RELIGIONS: Anglican 40%, other 24%, nonreligious 17%, Pentecostal 8%, Methodist 7%, Roman Catholic 4%
ETHNIC MIX: Black African 92%, White 3%, other 3%, mixed race 2%
GOVERNMENT: Parliamentary system
CURRENCY: Barbados dollar = 100 cents

Belarus

Literally "White Russia," Belarus lies landlocked in eastern Europe. It reluctantly became independent when the USSR broke up in 1991. It has few resources other than agriculture.

GEOGRAPHY

Mainly plains and low hills. The Dnieper and Dvina rivers drain the eastern lowlands. Vast Pripet Marshes in the southwest.

CLIMATE

Extreme continental climate. Winters are long, sub-freezing, but mainly dry; summers are hot.

PEOPLE & SOCIETY

Only 2% of people are non-Slav, so ethnic tension is minimal. Russian culture dominates. Belarus was the slowest ex-Soviet state to implement political reform; President Lukashenka has been labeled as Europe's last dictator. Enthusiasm for a merger with Russia has waned. Wealth is held by a small ex-Communist elite. Fallout from the 1986 Chernobyl nuclear disaster in Ukraine still seriously affects health and the environment.

THE ECONOMY

Low unemployment. Industry outmoded and mainly state-owned. Depends on Russia for energy and raw materials: tensions over natural gas prices.

INSIGHT: *The number of cancer and leukemia cases soared after the 1986 Chernobyl disaster*

FACTFILE

OFFICIAL NAME: Republic of Belarus
DATE OF FORMATION: 1991
CAPITAL: Minsk
POPULATION: 9.6 million
TOTAL AREA: 80,154 sq. miles (207,600 sq. km)
DENSITY: 120 people per sq. mile

LANGUAGES: Belarussian*, Russian*
RELIGIONS: Orthodox Christian 80%, Roman Catholic 14%, other 4%, Protestant 2%
ETHNIC MIX: Belarussian 81%, Russian 11%, Polish 4%, Ukrainian 2%, other 2%
GOVERNMENT: Presidential system
CURRENCY: Belarussian rouble = 100 kopeks

Belgium

Belgium lies in northwestern Europe. Its history has been marked by tensions between the majority Dutch-speaking (Flemish) and minority French-speaking (Walloon) communities.

GEOGRAPHY

Low-lying coastal plain covers two-thirds of the country. Land becomes hilly and forested in the southeast (Ardennes).

CLIMATE

Maritime climate with Gulf Stream influences. Mild temperatures, with heavy cloud cover and rain. More rainfall and weather fluctuations at the coast.

PEOPLE & SOCIETY

Since 1970, Flemish regions have become more prosperous than those of the minority Walloons, overturning traditional roles and increasing friction. Belgium moved to a federal system from 1980 in order to contain tensions, but recent fractious politics have raised doubts over the union's survival. Unable to form a government after elections in June 2010, there has been a caretaker government running the country ever since. Brussels hosts key EU institutions.

THE ECONOMY

Variety of industrial exports, including steel, glassware, cut diamonds, and textiles. Very high levels of public debt. Bureaucracy larger than European average

INSIGHT: *Belgium holds the world record for the country with the longest period without a government*

FACTFILE

OFFICIAL NAME: Kingdom of Belgium
DATE OF FORMATION: 1830
CAPITAL: Brussels
POPULATION: 10.7 million
TOTAL AREA: 11,780 sq. miles (30,510 sq. km)
DENSITY: 844 people per sq. mile

LANGUAGES: Dutch*, French*, German*
RELIGIONS: Roman Catholic 88%, other 10%, Muslim 2%
ETHNIC MIX: Fleming 58%, Walloon 33%, other 6%, Italian 2%, Moroccan 1%
GOVERNMENT: Parliamentary system
CURRENCY: Euro = 100 cents

Belize

Belize lies on the eastern shore of the Yucatan Peninsula. Formerly called British Honduras, Belize was the last Central American country to gain its independence, in 1981.

GEOGRAPHY
Almost half the land area is forested. Low mountains in southeast. Flat swampy coastal plains.

CLIMATE
Tropical. Very hot and humid, with May–December rainy season.

PEOPLE & SOCIETY
English-speaking black Creoles are outnumbered by Spanish speakers, including native *mestizos* (European–Amerindian) and immigrants from neighboring states. The Creoles have traditionally dominated society, but high levels of emigration to the US have weakened their influence. The Afro-Carib *garifuna* have their own language. Corruption, and trafficking of people and narcotics, are major problems.

INSIGHT: *Belize's barrier reef is the second-largest in the world*

THE ECONOMY
Tourism, agriculture, and offshore banking. Oil extraction began in 2005. Sugar, textiles, lobsters, and shrimp are exported. Serious hurricane damage is a recurring problem.

FACTFILE

OFFICIAL NAME: Belize
DATE OF FORMATION: 1981
CAPITAL: Belmopan
POPULATION: 300,000
TOTAL AREA: 8867 sq. miles (22,966 sq. km)
DENSITY: 34 people per sq. mile

LANGUAGES: English Creole, Spanish, English*, Mayan, Garifuna (Carib)
RELIGIONS: Roman Catholic 62%, other 20%, Anglican 12%, Methodist 6%
ETHNIC MIX: *Mestizo* 49%, Creole 25%, Maya 11%, other 9%, Garifuna 6%
GOVERNMENT: Parliamentary system
CURRENCY: Belizean dollar = 100 cents

Benin

Benin stretches north from the west African coast. In 1990, Benin became one of the pioneers of African democratization, ending 17 years of one-party Marxist-Leninist rule.

GEOGRAPHY

Sandy coastal region. Numerous lagoons lie just behind the shoreline. Forested plateaus inland. Mountains in the northwest.

CLIMATE

Hot and humid in the south. Two rainy seasons. Hot, dusty *harmattan* winds blow during the December–February dry season.

PEOPLE & SOCIETY

There are 42 different ethnic groups. The southern Fon have tended to dominate politics. Other major groups are the Adja and Yoruba. The northern Fulani follow a nomadic lifestyle. North–south tension is mainly due to the south being more developed. French culture, centered on Cotonou, is highly prized. Substantial differences in wealth reflect a strongly hierarchical society.

THE ECONOMY

Strong agricultural sector: cash crops include cotton, oil palm, and cashew nuts. Large-scale smuggling is a serious problem. France is the main aid donor.

INSIGHT:
Voodoo is thought to have originated in Benin, and was taken to Haiti by slaves

500m/1640ft
200m/656ft
Sea Level

0   100 km
0   100 miles

ATLANTIC OCEAN

FACTFILE

OFFICIAL NAME: Republic of Benin
DATE OF FORMATION: 1960
CAPITAL: Porto-Novo
POPULATION: 9.2 million
TOTAL AREA: 43,483 sq. miles (112,620 sq. km)
DENSITY: 215 people per sq. mile

LANGUAGES: Fon, Bariba, Yoruba, Adja, Houeda, Somba, French*
RELIGIONS: Indigenous beliefs and Voodoo 50%, Christian 30%, Muslim 20%
ETHNIC MIX: Fon 41%, other 21%, Adja 16%, Yoruba 12%, Bariba 10%
GOVERNMENT: Presidential system
CURRENCY: CFA franc = 100 centimes

Bhutan

Perched in the eastern Himalayas between India and China lies the landlocked Kingdom of Bhutan. It is largely closed to the outside world to protect its culture; TV was banned until 1999.

GEOGRAPHY
Low, tropical southern strip rising through fertile central valleys to high Himalayas in the north. Around 70% of the land is forested.

CLIMATE
South is tropical, north is alpine, cold, and harsh. Central valleys warmer in east than west.

PEOPLE & SOCIETY
The king was absolute monarch until 1998, and the first democratic elections were held a decade later. Most people are devoutly Buddhist and originate from Tibet. The Hindu Nepalese settled in the south. Bhutan has 20 languages. In 1988, Dzongkha (a Tibetan dialect native to just 16% of the people) was made the official language. The Nepalese community regard this as "cultural imperialism," causing considerable ethnic tensions.

THE ECONOMY
Reliant on India for trade. Most people farm their own plots of land and herd cattle and yaks. Steep land unsuited for cultivation. Development of cash crops for Asian markets.

INSIGHT: *In 2004 Bhutan became the first country in the world to ban smoking and the sale of tobacco*

4000m/13124ft
3000m/9843ft
2000m/6562ft
500m/3281ft
500m/1640ft
200m/656ft
Sea Level

0   50 km
0   50 miles

FACTFILE

OFFICIAL NAME: Kingdom of Bhutan
DATE OF FORMATION: 1656
CAPITAL: Thimphu
POPULATION: 700,000
TOTAL AREA: 18,147 sq. miles (47,000 sq. km)
DENSITY: 39 people per sq. mile

LANGUAGES: Dzongkha*, Nepali, Assamese
RELIGIONS: Mahayana Buddhist 75%, Hindu 25%
ETHNIC MIX: Drukpa 50%, Nepalese 35%, other 15%
GOVERNMENT: Mixed monarchical–parliamentary system
CURRENCY: Ngultrum = 100 chetrum

Bolivia

Landlocked high in central South America, Bolivia is one of the region's poorest countries. La Paz is the world's highest capital city: 13,385 feet (3631 m) above sea level.

GEOGRAPHY
A high windswept plateau, the *altiplano*, lies between two Andean mountain ranges. Semiarid grasslands to the east; dense tropical forests to the north.

CLIMATE
Altiplano has extreme tropical climate, with night-frost in winter. North and east are hot and humid.

PEOPLE & SOCIETY
Wealthy Spanish-descended families have traditionally controlled the economy. The indigenous majority faces widespread discrimination. Amerindian Evo Morales, president from 2006, is cutting poverty, redistributing land, and pushing for inter-national recognition of legal coca use.

INSIGHT: *Between 1825 and 1982 Bolivia averaged more than one armed coup a year*

THE ECONOMY
Gold, silver, zinc, tin, oil, natural gas: all vulnerable to world price fluctuations. Social issues and nationalization of natural gas sector deter investors. Major coca producer. Lack of manufacturing. Rich eastern provinces want autonomy.

FACTFILE
OFFICIAL NAME: Plurinational State of Bolivia
DATE OF FORMATION: 1825
CAPITALS: La Paz (administrative); Sucre (judicial)
POPULATION: 10 million
TOTAL AREA: 424,162 sq. miles (1,098,580 sq. km)

DENSITY: 24 people per sq. mile
LANGUAGES: Aymara*, Quechua*, Spanish*
RELIGIONS: Roman Catholic 93%, other 7%
ETHNIC MIX: Quechua 37%, Aymara 32%, *Mestizo* (mixed European–Amerindian) 13%, European 10%, other 8%
GOVERNMENT: Presidential system
CURRENCY: Boliviano = 100 centavos

Bosnia & Herzegovina

Perched in the highlands of southeast Europe, Bosnia and Herzegovina was the focus of the bitter ethnic conflict that accompanied the early 1990s dissolution of the Yugoslav state.

GEOGRAPHY

Hills and mountains, with narrow river valleys. Lowlands in the north. Mainly deciduous forest covers about half of the total area.

CLIMATE

Continental. Hot summers and cold, often snowy winters.

PEOPLE & SOCIETY

Despite sharing the same origin and spoken language, Bosnians have been divided by history between Orthodox Serbs, Roman Catholic Croats, and Muslim Bosniaks. Ethnic cleansing was practiced by all sides in the civil war, displacing about 60% of the population. Hopes for EU integration will require further ethnic reconciliation.

 INSIGHT: *The murder of Archduke Ferdinand of Austria in Sarajevo in 1914 triggered the First World War*

THE ECONOMY

Potential to recover status as a thriving market economy with a strong manufacturing base, but still struggles with resettling refugees and the legacy of war. Little foreign investment.

2000m/6562ft
1000m/3281ft
500m/1640ft
200m/656ft
Sea Level

0   50 km
0   50 miles

FACTFILE

OFFICIAL NAME: Bosnia and Herzegovina

DATE OF FORMATION: 1992

CAPITAL: Sarajevo

POPULATION: 3.8 million

TOTAL AREA: 19,741 sq. miles (51,129 sq. km)

DENSITY: 192 people per sq. mile

LANGUAGES: Bosnian*, Serbian*, Croatian*

RELIGIONS: Muslim (mainly Sunni) 40%, Orthodox Christian 31%, Roman Catholic 15%, other 10%, Protestant 4%

ETHNIC MIX: Bosniak 48%, Serb 34%, Croat 16%, other 2%

GOVERNMENT: Parliamentary system

CURRENCY: Marka = 100 pfeninga

Botswana

Landlocked in the heart of southern Africa, Botswana boasts the world's largest inland river delta. Diamonds provide potential wealth, but the country is crippled by HIV/AIDS.

GEOGRAPHY
Lies on vast plateau, high above sea level. Hills in the east. Kalahari Desert in center and southwest. Swamps and salt pans elsewhere and in Okavango Basin.

CLIMATE
Dry and prone to drought. Summer wet season, April–October. Winters are warm, with cold nights.

PEOPLE & SOCIETY
The nomadic San bushmen, the first inhabitants, are marginalized. One in four adults are living with HIV/AIDS: only Swaziland is worse affected. Life expectancy is around 56 years. Diamond revenue has widened wealth inequalities.

◆ INSIGHT: Water, Botswana's most precious resource, is honored in the name of the currency – pula

THE ECONOMY
Overreliance on diamonds: vulnerable to world price fluctuations. Beef is exported to Europe. Tourism aimed at wealthy wildlife enthusiasts. AIDS is devastating the population.

FACTFILE

OFFICIAL NAME: Republic of Botswana
DATE OF FORMATION: 1966
CAPITAL: Gaborone
POPULATION: 2 million
TOTAL AREA: 231,803 sq. miles (600,370 sq. km)
DENSITY: 9 people per sq. mile

LANGUAGES: Setswana, English*, Shona, San, Khoikhoi, isiNdebele
RELIGIONS: Christian 70%, nonreligious 20%, traditional beliefs 6%, other 4%
ETHNIC MIX: Tswana 79%, Kalanga 11%, other 10%
GOVERNMENT: Presidential system
CURRENCY: Pula = 100 thebe

Brazil

Covering almost half of South America, Brazil is the site of the world's largest and ecologically most important rainforest. The country has immense natural and economic resources.

GEOGRAPHY

Rainforest grows around the massive Amazon River and its delta, covering almost half of Brazil's total land area. Apart from the basin of the River Plate to the south, the rest of the country consists of highlands. The mountainous east is part-forested and part-desert. The coastal plain in the southeast has swampy areas. The Atlantic coastline is 1240 miles (2000 km) long.

CLIMATE

Brazil's share of the Amazon Basin has a model tropical equatorial climate, with high temperatures and rainfall all year round. The Brazilian plateau has far greater seasonal variation. The dry northeast suffers frequent droughts, though coastal regions are occasionally flooded by bouts of torrential rain. The south has hot summers and cool winters.

PEOPLE & SOCIETY

Diverse population includes Amerindians, black people of African descent, European immigrants, and those of mixed race. Amerindians suffer prejudice from most other groups. Shanty towns in the cities attract poor migrants from the northeast. Urban crime, violent land disputes, and unchecked development in Amazonia tarnish Brazil's image as a modern nation. Catholicism and the family unit remain strong.

Equator

COLOMB

PERU

THE ECONOMY

Dominant regional economy. Huge potential for growth based on abundant natural resources. A leading exporter of coffee, sugar, soybeans, and orange juice. Social tension threatens stability. Infrastructure needs investment.

FACTFILE

OFFICIAL NAME: Federative Rep. of Brazil
DATE OF FORMATION: 1822
CAPITAL: Brasília
POPULATION: 195 million
TOTAL AREA: 3,286,470 sq. miles (8,511,965 sq. km)
DENSITY: 60 people per sq. mile

LANGUAGES: Portuguese*, German, Japanese, Italian, Spanish, Polish, Amerindian languages
RELIGIONS: Roman Catholic 74%, Protestant 15%, atheist 7%, other 4%
ETHNIC MIX: White 54%, mixed race 38%, Black 6%, other 2%
GOVERNMENT: Presidential system
CURRENCY: Real = 100 centavos

INSIGHT: *Since 1900, a third of Brazil's indigenous Amerindian groups have become extinct due to disease, starvation, or the forceful taking of land by miners, loggers, and settlers*

VENEZUELA

Boa Vista

Guiana Highlands

Rio Negro

SURINAME

French Guiana (France)

GUYANA

ATLANTIC

OCEAN

Macapá

Equator

Ilha de Marajó

Amazon

Manaus

Santarém

A m a z o n

B a s i n

Rio Branco

Madeira

Tapajós

Xingu

Tocantins

Purus

Rondon

São Luís

Parnaíba

Teresina

Fortaleza

Sun Fernando de Noronha

Imperatriz

Porto Velho

Rio Branco

Chapada dos Parecis

Guaporé

Planalto de Mato Grosso

São Manuel

Juazeiro do Norte

Represa de Sobradinho

Natal

João Pessoa

Olinda

Recife

Campina Grande

Maceió

BOLIVIA

Cuiabá

Taguatinga

São Francisco

Aracaju

Feira de Santana

Salvador

Brazilian Highlands

Itabuna

Vitória da Conquista

BRASÍLIA

Goiânia

Montes Claros

Governador Valadares

Uberlândia

Ubetaba

Belo Horizonte

Campo Grande

Bauru

Ribeirão Preto

Vitória

Campos

PARAGUAY

Paraná

Londrina

Campinas

Nova Iguaçu

Duque de Caxias

São Paulo

Santos

Rio de Janeiro

Joinville

Curitiba

Florianópolis

ARGENTINA

Caxias do Sul

Porto Alegre

ATLANTIC

OCEAN

Lagoa dos Patos

Pelotas

Rio Grande

Mirim Lagoon

URUGUAY

2000m/6562ft
1000m/3281ft
500m/1640ft
200m/656ft
Sea Level

0   500 km

0   500 miles

Brunei

Lying on the northern coast of the island of Borneo, Brunei is surrounded and divided in two by the Malaysian state of Sarawak. It has been independent since 1984.

GEOGRAPHY
Mostly dense lowland rainforest and mangrove swamps, with some mountains in the southeast.

CLIMATE
Tropical. Six-month rainy season with very high humidity.

PEOPLE & SOCIETY
Malays benefit from positive discrimination. Many in the Chinese community are stateless. Since a failed rebellion in 1962, Brunei has been ruled by decree of the sultan. In 1990, "Malay Muslim Monarchy" was introduced, promoting Islamic values as state ideology. Women, less restricted than in some Muslim states, usually wear headscarves but not the veil.

◆ **INSIGHT:** *The sultan spent US$350 million building the world's largest palace at Bandar Seri Begawan*

THE ECONOMY
Oil and natural gas production has brought one of the world's highest standards of living. Massive overseas investments. Major consumer of high-tech hi-fi, video equipment, and Western designer clothes.

FACTFILE
OFFICIAL NAME: Sultanate of Brunei
DATE OF FORMATION: 1984
CAPITAL: Bandar Seri Begawan
POPULATION: 400,000
TOTAL AREA: 2228 sq. miles (5770 sq. km)
DENSITY: 197 people per sq. mile

LANGUAGES: Malay*, English, Chinese
RELIGIONS: Muslim (mainly Sunni) 66%, Buddhist 14%, Christian 10%, other 10%
ETHNIC MIX: Malay 67%, Chinese 16%, other 11%, indigenous 6%
GOVERNMENT: Monarchy
CURRENCY: Brunei dollar = 100 cents

Located in southeastern Europe, Bulgaria was under communist rule from 1947 to 1989. Significant political and economic reform since then enabled it to join the EU in 2007.

GEOGRAPHY

Mountains run east—west across center and along southern border. Danube plain in north, Thracian plain in southeast. Black Sea to the east.

CLIMATE

Hot summers, cooler at the coast. Snowy winters, especially in mountains. East winds bring seasonal extremes.

PEOPLE & SOCIETY

The communists tried forcibly to suppress cultural identities; once free movement was allowed in 1989, there was a large exodus of Bulgarian Turks. Privatizations in the 1990s left many Turks landless, prompting further emigration. Roma suffer discrimination at all levels of society. Women have equal rights in theory, but society remains patriarchal. EU accession included caveats demanding further action against organized crime, human trafficking, and corruption.

THE ECONOMY
Good agricultural production, including grapes, for well-developed wine industry, and tobacco. Expertise in software development. Industry and infrastructure are outdated.

INSIGHT: *Archaeologists have found evidence of wine-making in Bulgaria dating back over 5000 years*

FACTFILE
OFFICIAL NAME: Republic of Bulgaria
DATE OF FORMATION: 1908
CAPITAL: Sofia
POPULATION: 7.5 million
TOTAL AREA: 42,822 sq. miles (110,910 sq. km)
DENSITY: 176 people per sq. mile

LANGUAGES: Bulgarian*, Turkish, Romani
RELIGIONS: Bulgarian Orthodox 83%, Muslim 12%, other 4%, Roman Catholic 1%
ETHNIC MIX: Bulgarian 84%, Turkish 9%, Roma 5%, other 2%
GOVERNMENT: Parliamentary system
CURRENCY: Lev = 100 stotinki

Burkina Faso

The west African state of Burkina Faso was known as Upper Volta until 1984. It became a multiparty state in 1991, though former military ruler Blaise Compaoré remains in power.

GEOGRAPHY

The Sahara covers the north of the country. The south is largely savanna. The three main rivers are the Black, White, and Red Voltas.

CLIMATE

Tropical. Dry, cool weather November–February. Erratic rain March–April, mostly in southeast.

PEOPLE & SOCIETY

No single ethnic group is dominant, but the Mossi, from around Ouagadougou, have always played an important part in government. The people from the west are much more ethnically mixed. Extreme poverty has led to a strong sense of egalitarianism. Most women are still denied access to education, though their absence from public life belies their real power and social influence.

THE ECONOMY

Cotton is the major cash crop, but the encroaching Sahara Desert is restricting agriculture. Beneficiary of foreign debt cancellation plans.

INSIGHT: *Droughts and poor soils mean that many Burkinabés seek work southward in Ghana and Côte d'Ivoire*

FACTFILE

OFFICIAL NAME: Burkina Faso

DATE OF FORMATION: 1960

CAPITAL: Ouagadougou

POPULATION: 16.3 million

TOTAL AREA: 105,869 sq. miles (274,200 sq. km)

DENSITY: 154 people per sq. mile

LANGUAGES: Mossi, Fulani, French*, Tuareg, Dyula, Songhai

RELIGIONS: Muslim 55%, Christian 25% traditional beliefs 20%

ETHNIC MIX: Mossi 48%, other 21%, Peul 10%, Lobi 7%, Bobo 7%, Mandé 7%

GOVERNMENT: Presidential system

CURRENCY: CFA franc = 100 centimes

Burundi

Small, densely populated and landlocked, Burundi lies just south of the equator, on the Nile–Congo watershed in central Africa. Its people have the world's lowest per capita income.

GEOGRAPHY
Hilly with high plateaus in center and savanna in the east. Great Rift Valley on western side.

CLIMATE
Temperate, with high humidity. Heavy and frequent rainfall, mostly October–May. Highlands have frost.

PEOPLE & SOCIETY
Burundi has been riven by ethnic conflict between majority Hutu and the Tutsi, who controlled the army – with repeated large-scale massacres: hundreds of thousands of people died between 1993 and 2004. The constitution now guarantees an ethnic balance in the government and army. Twa pygmies were not involved in the conflict.

◆ **INSIGHT:** *Burundi's fertility rate is one of the highest in Africa. On average, women have six children*

THE ECONOMY
Overwhelmingly agricultural economy, mostly subsistence. Small quantities of gold and tungsten. Potential of oil in Lake Tanganyika. Ongoing political fragility.

0   50 km

0   50 miles

2000m/6562ft
1000m/3281ft
500m/1640ft

FACTFILE

OFFICIAL NAME: Republic of Burundi

DATE OF FORMATION: 1962

CAPITAL: Bujumbura

POPULATION: 8.5 million

TOTAL AREA: 10,745 sq. miles (27,830 sq. km)

DENSITY: 858 people per sq. mile

LANGUAGES: Kirundi*, French*, Kiswahili

RELIGIONS: Roman Catholic 62%, traditional beliefs 23%, Muslim 10%, Protestant 5%

ETHNIC MIX: Hutu 85%, Tutsi 14%, Twa 1%

GOVERNMENT: Presidential system

CURRENCY: Burundi franc = 100 centimes

Cambodia

Located on the Indochinese peninsula in southeast Asia, Cambodia has emerged from genocide, civil war, and invasion from Vietnam. Tourism has rebounded, and is a key income earner.

GEOGRAPHY

Mostly low-lying basin. Tônlé Sap (Great Lake) drains into the Mekong River. Forested mountains and plateau east of the Mekong.

CLIMATE

Tropical. High temperatures throughout the year. Heavy rainfall during May–October monsoon.

PEOPLE & SOCIETY

Devastated by US bombing, then by the Khmer Rouge regime, whose extreme Marxist program killed over a million between 1975 and 1979, Cambodia then endured further civil conflict and Vietnamese occupation. The effects are still felt, reflected in the high rates of orphans, widows, and land-mine victims. A fragile stability has lasted since elections in 1993. King Norodom Sihanouk, a key figure in politics, abdicated in 2004.

THE ECONOMY

Economy is heavily aid-reliant, still recovering from civil war. Rubber and timber are exported. Self-sufficient in rice. Garment industry is growing. Land disputes and corruption issues.

INSIGHT: *Cambodia has many impressive temples (including Angkor Wat), which date from when the country was the center of the Khmer Empire*

FACTFILE

OFFICIAL NAME: Kingdom of Cambodia

DATE OF FORMATION: 1953

CAPITAL: Phnom Penh

POPULATION: 15.1 million

TOTAL AREA: 69,900 sq. miles (181,040 sq. km)

DENSITY: 222 people per sq. mile

LANGUAGES: Khmer*, French, Chinese, Vietnamese, Cham

RELIGIONS: Buddhist 93%, Muslim 6%, Christian 1%

ETHNIC MIX: Khmer 90%, Vietnamese 5%, other 4%, Chinese 1%

GOVERNMENT: Parliamentary system

CURRENCY: Riel = 100 sen

Cameroon

Situated in the corner of the Gulf of Guinea, Cameroon was effectively a one-party state for 30 years. Multiparty elections, since 1992, regularly return that same party to power.

GEOGRAPHY

Over half the land is forested: equatorial rainforest in north, evergreen forest and wooded savanna in south. Mountains in the west.

CLIMATE

South is equatorial, with plentiful rainfall, declining inland. Far north is beset by drought.

PEOPLE & SOCIETY

Around 230 ethnic groups; no single group is dominant. The Bamileke is the largest, though it has never held political power. North–south tensions are diminished by the ethnic diversity. There is more rivalry between majority French- and minority English-speakers.

◆ **INSIGHT:** *Cameroon's name derives from the Portuguese word* camarões, *after the shrimp fished by the early European explorers*

THE ECONOMY

Oil reserves. Very diversified agricultural economy – timber, cocoa, bananas, coffee. Fuel smuggling from Nigeria undermines refinery profits. Corruption. Port for Chad and CAR.

FACTFILE

OFFICIAL NAME: Republic of Cameroon

DATE OF FORMATION: 1960

CAPITAL: Yaoundé

POPULATION: 20 million

TOTAL AREA: 183,567 sq. miles (475,400 sq. km)

DENSITY: 111 people per sq. mile

LANGUAGES: Bamileke, Fang, Fulani, French[A], English[M]

RELIGIONS: Roman Catholic 35%, traditional beliefs 25%, Muslim 22%, Protestant 18%

ETHNIC MIX: Cameroon highlanders 31%, other 29%, equatorial Bantu 19%, Kirdi 11%, Fulani 10%

GOVERNMENT: Presidential system

CURRENCY: CFA franc = 100 centimes

Canada

Canada extends from the Arctic to its US border along the 49th parallel. Unified under British rule from 1763, its development and expansion attracted large-scale immigration.

GEOGRAPHY

The world's second-largest country, stretching north to Cape Colombia on Ellesmere Island, south to Lake Erie, and across five time zones from the Pacific seaboard to Newfoundland. Arctic tundra and islands in the far north give way southward to forests, interspersed with lakes and rivers, and then the vast Canadian Shield, which covers over half the area of Canada. Rocky Mountains in west, beyond which are the Coast Mountains, islands, and fjords. Fertile lowlands in the east.

CLIMATE

Ranges from polar and subpolar in the north, to continental in the south. Winters in the interior are colder and longer than on the coast, with temperatures well below freezing and deep snow; summers are hotter. Pacific coast has the mildest winters.

PEOPLE & SOCIETY

Two-thirds of the population live in the Great Lakes–St. Lawrence lowlands, fostering some shared cultural values with the neighboring US. Important differences, however, include wider welfare provision and Commonwealth membership. The French-speaking Québécois wish to preserve their culture and language from further Anglicization, and demand to be recognized as a "distinct society." The government welcomes ethnic diversity among immigrants, promoting a policy that encourages each group to maintain its own culture. Other sizable immigrant groups include Chinese, Italians, Germans, Ukrainians, and Portuguese. Land claims made by the indigenous peoples are being redressed. Nunavut, an Inuit-governed territory that covers nearly a quarter of Canada's land area, was created from a portion of the Northwest Territories in 1999. Women are well represented at most levels of business and government.

FACTFILE

OFFICIAL NAME: Canada
DATE OF FORMATION: 1867
CAPITAL: Ottawa
POPULATION: 33.9 million
TOTAL AREA: 3,855,171 sq. miles
(9,984,670 sq. km)
DENSITY: 10 people per sq. mile

LANGUAGES: English*, French*, Chinese, other
RELIGIONS: Roman Catholic 44%, Protestant 29%, other and nonreligious 27%
ETHNIC ORIGIN: British, French, and other European 87%, Asian 9%, Amerindian, Métis, and Inuit 4%
GOVERNMENT: Parliamentary system
CURRENCY: Canadian dollar = 100 cents

$ THE ECONOMY

Wide-ranging resources, providing exports, cheap energy, and raw materials for manufacturing, underpin a high standard of living, with smaller wealth disparities than in the US. Prices for primary exports fluctuate, but the high oil price has encouraged development of Alberta's vast oil fields. Manufactured exports have flourished under growing global competition, especially since the creation in 1994 of the NAFTA free trade area, but reliance on the US market makes the Canadian economy vulnerable to US slowdowns. Unemployment rose during the 2009 recession, but the economy rebounded quickly.

◆ **INSIGHT:** The Magnetic North Pole, where the dipping needle of a compass stands still, migrates across northern Canada

	3000m/9843ft
	2000m/6562ft
	1000m/3281ft
	500m/1640ft
	200m/656ft
	Sea Level

0   400 km

0   400 miles

Cape Verde

Off the west coast of Africa, in the Atlantic Ocean, lies the group of islands that make up Cape Verde, a Portuguese colony until it gained independence in 1975.

GEOGRAPHY
Ten main islands and eight smaller islets, all of volcanic origin. Mostly mountainous, with steep cliffs and rocky headlands.

CLIMATE
Warm, and very dry. Subject to droughts that can sometimes last for years at a time.

PEOPLE & SOCIETY
Most people are of mixed Portuguese–African origin (*Mestiço*); the rest are descendants of African slaves or more recent immigrants. Creolization of the culture negates ethnic tensions. Almost half of the population live on Santiago. Around 700,000 Cape Verdeans live abroad, mostly in the US.

◆ **INSIGHT:** *Poor soils and lack of surface water mean that Cape Verde is dependent on food aid*

THE ECONOMY
Most people are subsistence farmers. Clothing is the main export. No natural resources. Mid-Atlantic location ensures work maintaining ships and planes.

FACTFILE
OFFICIAL NAME: Republic of Cape Verde
DATE OF FORMATION: 1975
CAPITAL: Praia
POPULATION: 500,000
TOTAL AREA: 1557 sq. miles (4033 sq. km)
DENSITY: 321 people per sq. mile

LANGUAGES: Portuguese Creole, Portuguese*
RELIGIONS: Roman Catholic 97%, other 2%, Protestant (Church of the Nazarene) 1%
ETHNIC MIX: *Mestiço* 71%, African 28%, European 1%
GOVERNMENT: Mixed presidential-parliamentary system
CURRENCY: Escudo = 100 centavos

Central African Republic

The Central African Republic (CAR) is a landlocked country lying between the basins of the Chad and Congo Rivers. Politics has suffered frequent interruption by military coups.

GEOGRAPHY

Comprises a low plateau, covered by scrub or savanna. North is arid. Equatorial rainforests in the south. The Ubangi River forms the border with the Democratic Republic of the Congo.

CLIMATE

The south is equatorial; the north is hot and dry. Rain occurs all year round, with heaviest falls between July and October.

PEOPLE & SOCIETY

The Baya and Banda are the largest ethnic groups, but the lingua franca is Sango, a trading creole spoken by the minorities in the south who have traditionally provided most political leaders. Less than 2% of the population live in the north. Recent rebellions by northern groups have displaced thousands of people.

THE ECONOMY

Dominated by subsistence farming. Exports include diamonds, cotton, timber, and coffee. Aid needed to support refugees. Instability and poor infrastructure hinder progress.

INSIGHT: *"Emperor" Bokassa's eccentric rule from 1965 to 1979 was followed by military dictatorship until democracy was restored in 1993*

1000m/3281ft
500m/1640ft
200m/656ft
Sea Level

FACTFILE

OFFICIAL NAME: Central African Republic
DATE OF FORMATION: 1960
CAPITAL: Bangui
POPULATION: 4.5 million
TOTAL AREA: 240,534 sq. miles (622,984 sq. km)
DENSITY: 19 people per sq. mile

LANGUAGES: Sango, Banda, Gbaya, French[A]
RELIGIONS: Traditional beliefs 35%, Roman Catholic 25%, Protestant 25%, Muslim 15%
ETHNIC MIX: Baya 33%, Banda 27%, other 17%, Mandjia 13%, Sara 10%
GOVERNMENT: Presidential system
CURRENCY: CFA franc = 100 centimes

Chad

Landlocked in north-central Africa, Chad has had a turbulent history since independence from France in 1960. Intermittent periods of civil war followed a military coup in 1975.

GEOGRAPHY
Mostly plateaus sloping west-ward to Lake Chad. Northern third is Sahara. Tibesti Mountains in north rise to 10,826 ft (3300 m).

CLIMATE
Three distinct zones: desert in north, semiarid region in center, and tropics in south.

PEOPLE & SOCIETY
Half the population live in the southern fifth of Chad. The northern third has only 100,000 people, mainly Muslim Toubou nomads. Democracy was restored in 1996 by ex-coup leader Idriss Déby. Instability has continued, first with tension between Muslims and southern Christians and, more recently, with rebellions in the east.

◆ **INSIGHT:** *Lake Chad is slowly drying up – it is now estimated to be just 3% of the size it was in 1970*

THE ECONOMY
The discovery of oil, and the opening of a pipeline to the coast via Cameroon, are transforming Chad's economy, though the new wealth is unlikely to reach most people.

3000m/9843ft
2000m/6562ft
1000m/3281ft
500m/1640ft
200m/656ft
Sea Level

LIBYA
Tibesti
NIGER
Sahara
Bol
Lake Chad
NIGERIA
Abéché
SUDAN
Mongo
NDJAMENA
Bongor
Fianga
Benoy
Sarh
CENTRAL AFRICAN REPUBLIC
CAMEROON
Doba
Moundou

0   200 km
0   200 miles

FACTFILE
OFFICIAL NAME: Republic of Chad
DATE OF FORMATION: 1960
CAPITAL: Ndjamena
POPULATION: 11.5 million
TOTAL AREA: 495,752 sq. miles (1,284,000 sq. km)
DENSITY: 24 people per sq. mile

LANGUAGES: French*, Sara, Arabic*, Maba
RELIGIONS: Muslim 51%, Christian 35%, traditional beliefs 7%, animist 7%
ETHNIC MIX: Other 30%, Sara 28%, Mayo-Kebbi 12%, Arab 12%, Ouaddai 9%, Kanem-Bornou 9%
GOVERNMENT: Presidential system
CURRENCY: CFA franc = 100 centimes

Chile

Chile extends in a ribbon down the west coast of South America. It returned to elected civilian rule in 1989 after a referendum forced out military dictator General Pinochet.

GEOGRAPHY
Fertile valleys in the center between the coast and the Andes. Atacama Desert in north. Deep-sea channels, lakes, and fjords in south.

CLIMATE
Arid in the north. Hot, dry summers and mild winters in the center. Higher Andean peaks have glaciers and year-round snow. Very wet and stormy in the south.

PEOPLE & SOCIETY
Most people are *mestizo* (mixed Spanish–Amerindian descent), and are highly urbanized. Almost a third of the population lives in Santiago, many in large slums. There are three main indigenous groups, including the Rapa Nui of Easter Island. General Pinochet's dictatorship was brutally repressive, but the business and middle classes prospered.

THE ECONOMY
World's biggest copper producer. Growth in foreign investment due to political stability. Exports include wine, fishmeal, fruits, and salmon. Serious earthquake damage in 2010.

INSIGHT:
Chile's Atacama Desert is the driest place on Earth, making it the perfect location for hi-tech space observatories

PERU · BOLIVIA
Arica
Iquique
Antofagasta
PACIFIC OCEAN
Viña del Mar
Valparaíso · SANTIAGO
Rancagua
Talcahuano · Talca
Concepción · Chillán
Temuco
Valdivia
Puerto Montt
Isla de Chiloé
ARGENTINA
Punta Arenas
Strait of Magellan
Cape Horn

70°
20°
30°
40°
50°

4000m/13124ft
3000m/9813ft
2000m/6562ft
1000m/3281ft
Sea Level

0   300 km
0   300 miles

FACTFILE

OFFICIAL NAME: Republic of Chile
DATE OF FORMATION: 1818
CAPITAL: Santiago
POPULATION: 17.1 million
TOTAL AREA: 292,258 sq. miles (756,950 sq. km)
DENSITY: 59 people per sq. mile

LANGUAGES: Spanish*, Amerindian languages
RELIGIONS: Roman Catholic 89%, other and nonreligious 11%
ETHNIC MIX: *Mestizo* and European 90%, other Amerindian 9%, Mapuche 1%
GOVERNMENT: Presidential system
CURRENCY: Chilean peso = 100 centavos

China

Covering a vast area of eastern Asia, China is bordered by 14 countries. A one-party Communist state since 1949, it has recently become a dominant force in global manufacturing.

GEOGRAPHY

A land of huge physical diversity, China has a long Pacific coastline to the east. Two-thirds of the country is uplands. The southwestern mountains include Tibet, the world's highest plateau; in the northwest, the Tien Shan Mountains separate the arid Tarim and Dzungarian basins. The rolling hills and plains of the low-lying east are home to two-thirds of the population.

CLIMATE

China is divided into two main climatic regions. The north and west are semiarid or arid, with extreme temperature variations. The south and east are warmer and more humid, with year-round rainfall. Winter temperatures vary with latitude, but are warmest on the subtropical southeast coast. Summer temperatures are more uniform, rising above 70°F (21°C).

PEOPLE & SOCIETY

Most people are Han Chinese. The rest of the population belong to one of 55 minority nationalities, or recognized ethnic groups. Many of these groups have a disproportionate political significance as they live in strategic border areas. A policy of resettling Han Chinese in remote regions is deeply resented and has led to uprisings in Xinjiang and Tibet. The government has relaxed the one-child family policy, particularly for minorities, after some small groups were brought close to extinction. Chinese society is patriarchal in practice, and generations tend to live together. However, economic change is breaking down the social controls of the Mao Zedong era. Divorce and unemployment are rising. A resurgence of religious belief has occurred in recent years. Materialism has replaced the puritanism of the past; there are now more cell phones in China than in the US.

FACTFILE

OFFICIAL NAME: People's Republic of China
DATE OF FORMATION: 960
CAPITAL: Beijing
POPULATION: 1.35 billion
TOTAL AREA: 3,705,386 sq. miles
(9,596,960 sq. km)
DENSITY: 376 people per sq. mile

LANGUAGES: Mandarin*, other
RELIGIONS: Nonreligious 59%, traditional beliefs 20%, other 13%, Buddhist 6%, Muslim 2%
ETHNIC MIX: Han 92%, other 4%, Hui 1%, Miao 1%, Manchu 1%, Zhuang 1%
GOVERNMENT: One-party state
CURRENCY: Yuan = 10 jiao = 100 fen

$ THE ECONOMY

China has shifted from a centrally planned to a market-oriented economy; liberalization has gone furthest in the south where the emerging business class is based. Exports led annual GDP growth of over 10% in 2003–2007. Faced with a global downturn from 2008, Chinese stimulus packages boosted domestic spending. The buying power of China's huge market for raw materials and consumer goods could drive global recovery. China is now the world's largest exporter and second-largest economy. The Twelfth Five-Year Plan (2011–2015) seeks to limit population growth and improve social infrastructure.

◆ **INSIGHT:** *China has the world's oldest continuous civilization. Its recorded history began 4000 years ago, with the Shang dynasty*

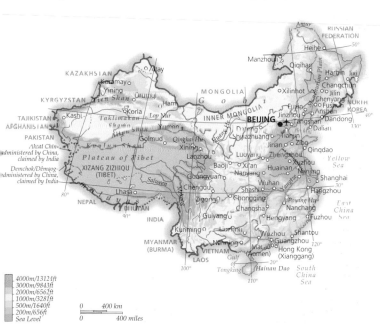

4000m/13124ft
3000m/9843ft
2000m/6562ft
1000m/3281ft
500m/1640ft
200m/656ft
Sea Level

0   400 km
0   400 miles

Colombia

Lying in northwest South America, Colombia has coastlines on both the Caribbean and the Pacific. It is primarily noted for its coffee, emeralds, gold, and cocaine trafficking.

GEOGRAPHY

The densely forested and almost uninhabited east is separated from the western coastal plains by the Andes, which divide into three ranges (cordilleras) with intervening valleys.

CLIMATE

Coastal plains are hot and wet. The highlands are much cooler. The equatorial east has two wet seasons.

PEOPLE & SOCIETY

Most Colombians are of mixed blood. Blacks and Amerindians have the least political representation. Civil conflict over four and a half decades has displaced millions of people, and left over 200,000 dead. The fighting is deeply entwined with the narcotics trade. Violent crime is common.

 INSIGHT: *Over 50% of the world's cocaine is produced in Colombia*

THE ECONOMY

Healthy and diversified export sector – includes coffee and coal. Considerable growth potential, but narcotics-related violence and corruption deter foreign investors.

```
3000m/9843ft
2000m/6562ft
1000m/3281ft
500m/1640ft
Sea Level
```

```
0        200 km
0        200 miles
```

FACTFILE

OFFICIAL NAME: Republic of Colombia

DATE OF FORMATION: 1819

CAPITAL: Bogotá

POPULATION: 46.3 million

TOTAL AREA: 439,733 sq. miles (1,138,910 sq. km)

DENSITY: 115 people per sq. mile

LANGUAGES: Spanish*, Wayuu, Páez, other Amerindian languages

RELIGIONS: Roman Catholic 95%, other 5%

ETHNIC MIX: *Mestizo* (European–Amerindian) 58%, White 20%, European–African 14%, African 4%, African–Amerindian 3%, Amerindian 1%

GOVERNMENT: Presidential system

CURRENCY: Colombian peso = 100 centavos

Comoros

Off the east African coast, between Mozambique and Madagascar, lies the archipelago republic of the Comoros, comprising three main islands and a number of smaller islets.

GEOGRAPHY
Main islands are of volcanic origin and are heavily forested. The remainder are coral atolls.

CLIMATE
Hot and humid all year round, especially on the coasts. November to May is hottest and wettest period.

PEOPLE & SOCIETY
The Comoros has absorbed a diversity of people over the years, including Africans, Arabs, Polynesians, and Persians. There have also been Portuguese, Dutch, French, and Indian immigrants. Ethnic discord is rare, but regional tensions between islands are marked. The country is politically unstable and there have been frequent coups. A fragile new federal system was introduced in 2002, though in 2009 the island presidents were reduced to governors. A political and business elite controls most of the wealth.

THE ECONOMY
One of the world's poorest countries. Subsistence-level farming. Vanilla and cloves are main cash crops. Lack of basic infrastructure.

◆ **INSIGHT:** *The Comoros is the world's largest producer of ylang-ylang – an extract from tree blossom used in manufacturing perfumes*

Grande Comore
(Njazidja)

1000m/3281f
500m/1640ft
200m/656ft
Sea Level

12°30'

Koimbani

✝ **MORONI**

Foumbouni

Dembéni

INDIAN OCEAN

13°

43°30'

Mohéli
(Mwali)

Ouani
Moutsamoudou

Mozambique
Channel

Fomboni

Moya
Anjouan
(Nzwani)

0   20 km

0   20 miles

11°30'

44°

44°30'

FACTFILE

OFFICIAL NAME: Union of the Comoros
DATE OF FORMATION: 1975
CAPITAL: Moroni
POPULATION: 700,000
TOTAL AREA: 838 sq. miles
(2170 sq. km)
DENSITY: 813 people per sq. mile

LANGUAGES: Arabic*, Comoran*, French*
RELIGIONS: Muslim (mainly Sunni) 98%, Roman Catholic 1%, other 1%
ETHNIC MIX: Comoran 97%, other 3%
GOVERNMENT: Presidential system
CURRENCY: Comoros franc = 100 centimes

Congo

Astride the equator in west-central Africa, this former French colony emerged from 20 years of Marxist-Leninist rule in 1990. Democracy was soon overshadowed by years of violence.

GEOGRAPHY
Mostly forest- or savanna-covered plateaus, drained by the Ubangi and Congo river systems. Narrow coastal plain is lined with sand dunes and lagoons.

CLIMATE
Hot, tropical. Temperatures rarely fall below 86°F (30°C). Two wet and two dry seasons. Rainfall is heaviest south of the equator.

PEOPLE & SOCIETY
One of the most tribally conscious and heavily urbanized countries in Africa, with most people living in the Brazzaville–Pointe-Noire region. Main tensions are between the Bakongo in the north and the Mbochi in the south. Relative peace was secured in 1999, and "ninja" rebels in the Pool region, around Brazzaville, signed a peace deal in 2003.

THE ECONOMY
Oil provides over 85% of export revenue. Timber is extracted. Foreign debt high. Substantial industrial base around Brazzaville and Pointe-Noire.

INSIGHT: *In 1970, Congo became the first African country to declare itself a communist state*

FACTFILE

OFFICIAL NAME: Republic of the Congo
DATE OF FORMATION: 1960
CAPITAL: Brazzaville
POPULATION: 3.8 million
TOTAL AREA: 132,046 sq. miles (342,000 sq. km)
DENSITY: 29 people per sq. mile

LANGUAGES: Kongo, Teke, Lingala, French*
RELIGIONS: Traditional beliefs 50%, Roman Catholic 35%, Protestant 13%, Muslim 2%
ETHNIC MIX: Bakongo 51%, Teke 17%, other 16%, Mbochi 11%, Mbédé 5%
GOVERNMENT: Presidential system
CURRENCY: CFA franc = 100 centimes

Congo, Dem. Rep. (DRC)

A former Belgian colony in east-central Africa, the
Democratic Republic of the Congo (DRC) is Africa's second-
largest country and the scene of one of its worst regional wars.

 GEOGRAPHY
Rainforested basin of Congo River
occupies 60% of the land area. High
mountain ranges and lakes stretch down
the eastern border.

CLIMATE
Tropical and humid. Distinct wet
and dry seasons south of the equator.
The north is mainly wet.

PEOPLE & SOCIETY
There are 12 main ethnic groups
and around 190 smaller ones. Civil war
from 1996 drew neighboring countries
into a bloody conflict. The indigenous
forest pygmies, victimized in the war, are
now a marginalized group. A tentative
peace deal in 2003 has been undermined
by intercommunal violence in the east.

 INSIGHT: *The DRC's rainforests
comprise 6% of the world's, and 50% of
Africa's, remaining woodlands*

THE ECONOMY
Rich resource base: minerals
(copper, coltan, cobalt, diamonds)
dominate export earnings. War and
decades of corruption have caused
economic collapse. Food aid is needed
to ease humanitarian crisis.

2000m/6562ft
1000m/3281ft
500m/1610ft
200m/656ft
Sea Level

0   200 km
0   200 miles

FACTFILE

OFFICIAL NAME: Democratic Republic
of the Congo
DATE OF FORMATION: 1960
CAPITAL: Kinshasa
POPULATION: 67.8 million
TOTAL AREA: 905,563 sq. miles
(2,345,410 sq. km)

DENSITY: 77 people per sq. mile
LANGUAGES: Kiswahili, Tshiluba, French*
RELIGIONS: Christian 70%, Kimbanguist 10%,
Muslim 10%, traditional beliefs and other 10%
ETHNIC MIX: Other 55%, Mongo, Luba, Kongo,
and Mangbetu-Azande 45%
GOVERNMENT: Presidential system
CURRENCY: Congolese franc = 100 centimes

Costa Rica

Costa Rica, Central America's most stable country, is rich in pristine scenery and exotic wildlife. Its neutrality in foreign affairs is long-standing, but it has strong ties with the US.

GEOGRAPHY

Coastal plains of swamp and savanna rise to a fertile central plateau, which leads to a mountain range with active volcanic peaks.

CLIMATE

Hot and humid in coastal regions. Temperate central uplands. High annual rainfall.

PEOPLE & SOCIETY

Most people are *mestizo*, of partly Spanish–partly Amerindian origin. There is a black, English-speaking minority and around 35,000 indigenous Amerindians. Plantation owners are the wealthiest group, while one in six people live in poverty. Nonetheless, living standards are high for the region, and education and healthcare provision is good.

◆ **INSIGHT:** *Costa Rica's 1949 constitution bans a national army*

THE ECONOMY

Main exports are bananas, coffee, pineapples, and beef, but all vulnerable to fluctuating world prices. Stability has attracted multinationals. History of high inflation. Pioneer of eco-tourism. Plans to be the world's first carbon neutral country (by 2030).

FACTFILE

OFFICIAL NAME: Republic of Costa Rica

DATE OF FORMATION: 1838

CAPITAL: San José

POPULATION: 4.6 million

TOTAL AREA: 19,730 sq. miles (51,100 sq. km)

DENSITY: 233 people per sq. mile

LANGUAGES: Spanish*, English Creole, Bribri, Cabecar

RELIGIONS: Roman Catholic 71%, Evangelical 14%, nonreligious 11%, other 4%

ETHNIC MIX: *Mestizo* and European 94%, Black 3%, Chinese 1%, Amerindian 1%, other 1%

GOVERNMENT: Presidential system

CURRENCY: C.R. colón = 100 céntimos

Côte d'Ivoire (Ivory Coast)

One of the larger nations along the coast of west Africa, Côte d'Ivoire is the world's biggest cocoa producer. Since 2002 its image of stability has been rocked by civil war and electoral chaos.

GEOGRAPHY
Sandy coastal strip and rainforested interior, with savanna plateau in north.

CLIMATE
Hot all year. Two wet seasons in south; north has one, with lower rainfall.

PEOPLE & SOCIETY

Over 60 tribes; largest is the Baoule (an Akan group). Southern Christians harbor resentment against non-Ivorian Muslims in the north. Plantations employ millions of migrant workers (including children), though thousands fled back to Burkina during the 2002–2005 civil war. Rebels joined a transitional government in 2007. President Gbagbo delayed elections until 2010 and then refused to step down; civil conflict led to his ouster.

◆ **INSIGHT:** *The Basilica of Our Lady of Peace in Yamoussoukro is the largest church in the world*

THE ECONOMY
Main crops are cocoa and coffee. Oil is now major export. Good infrastructure. Lack of professional training. Instability deters investment.

1000m/3281ft
500m/1640ft
200m/656ft
Sea Level

0   100 km
0   100 miles

FACTFILE

OFFICIAL NAME: Republic of Côte d'Ivoire
DATE OF FORMATION: 1960
CAPITAL: Yamoussoukro
POPULATION: 21.6 million
TOTAL AREA: 124,502 sq. miles (322,460 sq. km)
DENSITY: 176 people per sq. mile

LANGUAGES: Akan, French*, Krou, Voltaïque
RELIGIONS: Muslim 38%, Roman Catholic 25%, traditional beliefs 25%, Protestant 6%, other 6%
ETHNIC MIX: Akan 42%, Voltaïque 18%, Mandé du Nord 17%, Krou 11%, Mandé du Sud 10%, other 2%
GOVERNMENT: Presidential system
CURRENCY: CFA franc = 100 centimes

Croatia

Though it was controlled by Hungary from medieval times and was a part of the Yugoslav state for much of the 20th century, Croatia has a very strong national identity.

GEOGRAPHY

Rocky, mountainous Adriatic coastline is dotted with islands. Interior is a mixture of wooded mountains and broad valleys.

CLIMATE

The interior has a temperate continental climate. Mediterranean climate along the Adriatic coast.

PEOPLE & SOCIETY

Croats are distinguished from Bosniaks and Serbs by their Roman Catholic faith and use of the Latin alphabet. Many Serbs fled Croatia during the early 1990s conflict that accompanied Yugoslavia's breakup. Croatia's entry into the EU, delayed by border disputes with Slovenia, is set to go ahead in 2013.

◆ **INSIGHT:** *Croatia only regained control of Serb-occupied Eastern Slavonia, around Vukovar, in 1998*

THE ECONOMY

The war cost the economy an estimated $50 billion. Unemployment has been persistently high. Corruption deters foreign investment. Tourism is mainly on the Dalmatian coast.

FACTFILE

OFFICIAL NAME: Republic of Croatia
DATE OF FORMATION: 1991
CAPITAL: Zagreb
POPULATION: 4.4 million
TOTAL AREA: 21,831 sq. miles (56,542 sq. km)
DENSITY: 202 people per sq. mile

LANGUAGES: Croatian*
RELIGIONS: Roman Catholic 88%, other 7%, Orthodox Christian 4%, Muslim 1%
ETHNIC MIX: Croat 90%, Serb 5%, other 5%
GOVERNMENT: Parliamentary system
CURRENCY: Kuna = 100 lipa

Cuba

A former Spanish colony, Cuba is the largest island in the Caribbean. It became the only communist country in the Americas after Fidel Castro seized power in 1959.

GEOGRAPHY

Mostly fertile plains and basins. Three mountainous areas. Forests of pine and mahogany cover one-quarter of the country.

CLIMATE

Subtropical. Hot all year round, and very hot in summer. Heaviest rainfall in the mountains. Hurricanes can strike in the fall.

PEOPLE & SOCIETY

The Castro regime has reduced formerly extreme wealth disparities, given education a high priority, and established an efficient health service. Political dissent, however, is not tolerated. A dramatic fall in living standards since the late 1980s has led thousands of Cubans to flee to the US, to seek asylum. About 70% of Cubans are of Spanish descent. There is little ethnic tension.

THE ECONOMY

Sugar industry now superseded by tourism and nickel. US trade embargo, since 1961. Shortages drive a black market. Parallel use of US dollar (1993–2004), and then convertible peso, has boosted investment but created a "dollarized" elite.

INSIGHT: *Fidel Castro had become the world's longest-serving non-hereditary ruler before handing power to his brother Raúl in 2006*

FACTFILE

OFFICIAL NAME: Republic of Cuba
DATE OF FORMATION: 1902
CAPITAL: Havana
POPULATION: 11.2 million
TOTAL AREA: 42,803 sq. miles (110,860 sq. km)
DENSITY: 262 people per sq. mile

LANGUAGES: Spanish*
RELIGIONS: Nonreligious 49%, Roman Catholic 40%, atheist 6%, other 4%, Protestant 1%
ETHNIC MIX: Mulatto (mixed race) 51%, White 37%, Black 11%, Chinese 1%
GOVERNMENT: One-party state
CURRENCY: Cuban peso = 100 centavos

Cyprus

Cyprus lies south of Turkey in the eastern Mediterranean. Since 1974, it has been partitioned between the Turkish-occupied north and the Greek-Cypriot south.

GEOGRAPHY

Mountains in the center-west give way to a fertile plain in the east, flanked by hills to the northeast.

CLIMATE

Mediterranean. Summers are hot and dry. Winters are mild, with snow in the mountains.

PEOPLE & SOCIETY

The Greek majority practice Orthodox Christianity. Since the 16th century, a minority community of Turkish Muslims has lived in the north of the island. In 1974 Turkish troops occupied the north and proclaimed the Turkish Republic of Northern Cyprus (TRNC), but it is recognized only by Turkey. Over 100,000 mainland Turks have settled there since. UN-led mediation failed to reunite the island ahead of EU accession in 2004, so the north was left out of membership.

THE ECONOMY

Financial services and tourism. Eurozone member with best economic performance and lowest unemployment in 2009 downturn. North suffers from lack of investment and lower wages.

◆ **INSIGHT:** *The Green Line, which separates north from south, was opened for the first time in 2003*

FACTFILE

OFFICIAL NAME: Republic of Cyprus
DATE OF FORMATION: 1960
CAPITAL: Nicosia
POPULATION: 900,000
TOTAL AREA: 3571 sq. miles (9250 sq. km)
DENSITY: 252 people per sq. mile

LANGUAGES: Greek*, Turkish*
RELIGIONS: Orthodox Christian 78%, Muslim 18%, other 4%
ETHNIC MIX: Greek 81%, Turkish 11%, other 8%
GOVERNMENT: Presidential systems
CURRENCY: Euro = 100 cents (new Turkish lira in TRNC = 100 kurus)

Czech Republic

Once part of Czechoslovakia, a central European communist state in 1948–1989, the Czech Republic peacefully dissolved its union with Slovakia in 1993. It joined the EU in 2004.

GEOGRAPHY

Landlocked in central Europe. Bohemia, the western territory, is a plateau surrounded by mountains. Moravia, in the east, is characterized by hills and lowlands.

CLIMATE
Cool, sometimes cold winters and warm summer months, which bring most of the annual rainfall.

PEOPLE & SOCIETY

Secular and urban society, with high divorce rates. Czechs make up the vast majority of the population, while the next largest group are Moravians. The 300,000 Slovaks left after partition are now permitted dual citizenship. Ethnic tensions are few, but there is widespread hostility toward the Roma minority. A new commercial elite is emerging alongside postcommunist entrepreneurs.

THE ECONOMY
Traditional heavy industries (machinery, iron, car-making) have been successfully privatized. Prague attracts tourists. Skilled workforce. Will join euro in 2017 at earliest.

INSIGHT: *Charles University in Prague was founded in the 13th century*

GERMANY
Liberec
Ústí nad Labem
Karlovy Vary
Kladno
PRAGUE
Plzeň
Hradec Králové
Pardubice
POLAND
Ostrava
Havířov
Olomouc
Bohemia
České Budějovice
Moravia
Zlín
Brno
AUSTRIA
SLOVAKIA

1000m/3281ft
500m/1640ft
200m/656ft
Sea Level

0   50 km

0   50 miles

FACTFILE

OFFICIAL NAME: Czech Republic
DATE OF FORMATION: 1993
CAPITAL: Prague
POPULATION: 10.4 million
TOTAL AREA: 30,450 sq. miles (78,866 sq. km)
DENSITY: 342 people per sq. mile

LANGUAGES: Czech*, Slovak, Hungarian (Magyar)
RELIGIONS: Roman Catholic 39%, atheist 38%, other 18%, Protestant 3%, Hussite 2%
ETHNIC MIX: Czech 90%, other 4%, Moravian 4%, Slovak 2%
GOVERNMENT: Parliamentary system
CURRENCY: Czech koruna = 100 haleru

Denmark

Denmark occupies the Jutland peninsula and over 400 islands in southern Scandinavia. Greenland and the Faeroe Islands are self-governing associated territories.

GEOGRAPHY

Fertile farmland covers two-thirds of the terrain, which is among the flattest in the world. About 100 islands are inhabited.

CLIMATE

Damp, temperate climate with mild summers and cold, wet winters. Rainfall is moderate.

PEOPLE & SOCIETY

Income distribution is the most even in the West: society is egalitarian with few tensions, though cultural clashes have arisen with immigrant minorities. Almost all women now work and Denmark is a world leader in childcare provision. Marriage is becoming less common, even for couples with children.

◆ **INSIGHT:** *Denmark is Europe's oldest kingdom – the monarchy dates back to the 10th century*

THE ECONOMY

Natural gas and oil reserves. Skilled workforce key to high-tech industrial success. Pork, bacon, dairy products are exported. Opted not to join the euro, though its currency is pegged.

FACTFILE

OFFICIAL NAME: Kingdom of Denmark

DATE OF FORMATION: 950

CAPITAL: Copenhagen

POPULATION: 5.5 million

TOTAL AREA: 16,639 sq. miles (43,094 sq. km)

DENSITY: 336 people per sq. mile

LANGUAGES: Danish*

RELIGIONS: Evangelical Lutheran 95%, Roman Catholic 3%, Muslim 2%

ETHNIC MIX: Danish 96%, other (including Scandinavian and Turkish) 3%, Faeroese and Inuit 1%

GOVERNMENT: Parliamentary system

CURRENCY: Danish krone = 100 øre

Djibouti

A city-state with a desert hinterland, Djibouti lies in northeast Africa on the Red Sea. Once known as the French Territory of the Afars and Issas, independence came in 1977.

 GEOGRAPHY
Mainly low-lying desert and semidesert, with a volcanic mountain range in the north.

 CLIMATE
Almost no rain, though the monsoon is very humid. The 109°F (45°C) heat of summer is unbearable.

 PEOPLE & SOCIETY
The main ethnic groups are the Issas in the south, and the nomadic Afars in the north. Tensions between them developed into a guerrilla war in 1991–1994. Smaller tribal groups make up the rest of the population, and the rural peoples are mostly nomadic. Wealth is concentrated in Djibouti city. France exerts considerable influence in Djibouti, supporting it financially and maintaining a naval base and a military garrison.

 THE ECONOMY
Djibouti's major assets are its ports in a key Red Sea location.

INSIGHT: *Chewing the leaves of the mildly narcotic qat shrub is an age-old social ritual in Djibouti*

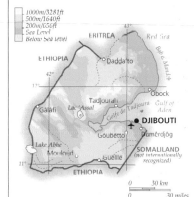

FACTFILE

OFFICIAL NAME: Republic of Djibouti
DATE OF FORMATION: 1977
CAPITAL: Djibouti
POPULATION: 900,000
TOTAL AREA: 8494 sq. miles (22,000 sq. km)
DENSITY: 101 people per sq. mile

LANGUAGES: Somali, Afar, French*, Arabic*
RELIGIONS: Muslim (mainly Sunni) 94%, Christian 6%
ETHNIC MIX: Issa 60%, Afar 35%, other 5%
GOVERNMENT: Presidential system
CURRENCY: Djibouti franc = 100 centimes

Dominica

Dominica is renowned as the Caribbean island that resisted European colonization until the 18th century. It achieved independence from the UK in 1978.

GEOGRAPHY
Mountainous and densely forested. Volcanic activity has given the land very fertile soils, hot springs, geysers, and black sand beaches.

CLIMATE
Tropical, cooled by constant trade winds. Heavy annual rainfall. Tropical depressions and hurricanes are likely June–November.

PEOPLE & SOCIETY
The majority of Dominicans are descendants of African slaves brought over to work on banana plantations. The Carib Territory on the northeast of the island is home to the only surviving indigenous community in the Caribbean. Wealth disparities are not as marked as elsewhere in the region, but the alleviation of poverty has become a major plank of government policy.

THE ECONOMY
Based on bananas, but has lost preferential access to EU market. Some diversification: flowers, coffee, fruit. Agriculture vulnerable to hurricanes. Eco-tourism. Some offshore banking.

◆ **INSIGHT:** Dominica is known as "Nature Island," due to its spectacular flora and fauna

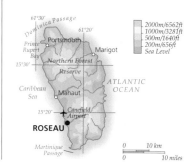

FACTFILE

OFFICIAL NAME: Commonwealth of Dominica
DATE OF FORMATION: 1978
CAPITAL: Roseau
POPULATION: 72,969
TOTAL AREA: 291 sq. miles (754 sq. km)
DENSITY: 252 people per sq. mile

LANGUAGES: French Creole, English*
RELIGIONS: Roman Catholic 77%, Protestant 15%, other 8%
ETHNIC MIX: Black 87%, mixed race 9%, Carib 3%, other 1%
GOVERNMENT: Parliamentary system
CURRENCY: East Caribbean dollar = 100 cents

Dominican Republic

The Dominican Republic occupies the eastern two-thirds of the island of Hispaniola in the Caribbean. Spanish-speaking, it seeks closer ties to the anglophone West Indies.

GEOGRAPHY

Highlands and rainforested mountains – including the highest peak in the Caribbean, Pico Duarte – interspersed with fertile valleys. Extensive coastal plain in the east.

CLIMATE

Hot and humid close to sea level, cooler at altitude. Heavy rainfall, especially in the northeast.

PEOPLE & SOCIETY

White landowners – especially those descended from the original Spanish settlers – form the wealthy elite. The mixed-race majority controls commerce and forms the bulk of the professional middle classes. White and mixed race women are entering the professions. Great disparities of wealth exist; the black and Haitian-immigrant populations occupy the bottom of the social ladder.

THE ECONOMY

Mining (nickel and gold), sugar, and textiles. Tourism, remittances, and exports all rely heavily on US market. Hidden economy based on trans-shipment of narcotics to the US.

INSIGHT: *Santo Domingo is the oldest city in the Americas. It was founded in 1496 by the brother of Christopher Columbus*

2000m/6562ft	
1000m/3281ft	
500m/1640ft	
200m/656ft	
Sea Level	

FACTFILE

OFFICIAL NAME: Dominican Republic

DATE OF FORMATION: 1865

CAPITAL: Santo Domingo

POPULATION: 10.2 million

TOTAL AREA: 18,679 sq. miles (48,380 sq. km)

DENSITY: 546 people per sq. mile

LANGUAGES: Spanish*, French Creole

RELIGIONS: Roman Catholic 95%, other and nonreligious 5%

ETHNIC MIX: Mixed race 73%, European 16%, Black African 11%

GOVERNMENT: Presidential system

CURRENCY: Dominican Republic peso = 100 centavos

East Timor

East Timor occupies the once Portuguese-owned eastern half of the island of Timor. Invaded by Indonesia in 1975, it became independent in 2002 following a long struggle.

GEOGRAPHY

A narrow coastal plain gives way to forested highlands. The mountain backbone rises to 9715 ft (2963 m).

CLIMATE

Tropical. Heavy rain in wet season (December–March), then dry and hot, particularly in the north.

PEOPLE & SOCIETY

The population is almost entirely Roman Catholic. The Timorese are a mix of Malay and Papuan peoples, and many indigenous Papuan tribes survive. There is an urban Chinese minority, and ethnic Indonesian settlers became numerous after annexation in 1975. Preindependence violence in 1999 was politically rather than ethnically motivated. Women do not have access to the professions and levels of domestic violence are notably high. Living standards are low.

THE ECONOMY

Widespread poverty. Violence in 1999 damaged infrastructure. Riots in 2006 undermined stability, further deterring foreign investment. Agreement with Australia on division of oil revenue from the Timor Sea.

INSIGHT: *Once dependent on sandalwood, the economy is being transformed by oil under the Timor Sea*

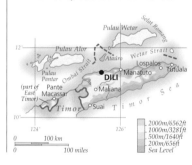

FACTFILE

OFFICIAL NAME: Democratic Republic of Timor-Leste

DATE OF FORMATION: 2002

CAPITAL: Dili

POPULATION: 1.2 million

TOTAL AREA: 5756 sq. miles (14,874 sq. km)

DENSITY: 213 people per sq. mile

LANGUAGES: Tetum* (Portuguese/Austronesian), Bahasa Indonesia, Portuguese*

RELIGIONS: Roman Catholic 95%, other (including Muslim and Protestant) 5%

ETHNIC MIX: Malay/Papuan groups c. 85%, Indonesian c. 13%, Chinese 2%

GOVERNMENT: Parliamentary system

CURRENCY: US dollar = 100 cents

Ecuador

Once part of the Inca heartland, Ecuador lies on the western coast of South America. Its territory includes the fascinating Galápagos Islands, 610 miles (970 km) to the west.

 GEOGRAPHY
Broad coastal plain, inter-Andean central highlands, dense jungle in upper Amazon basin.

 CLIMATE
The climate is hot and moist on the coast, cool in the Andes, and hot equatorial in the Amazon basin.

 PEOPLE & SOCIETY
Most people are of Amerindian–Spanish extraction (*mestizo*). Black communities exist on the coast. The strong and largely unified Amerindian movement leads the pressure for social reform; one in eight people live in extreme poverty. Recent left-wing policies have given greater rights to women, the poor, and Amerindians.

◆ **INSIGHT:** *Darwin's study on the Galápagos Islands in 1856 played a major part in his theory of evolution*

THE ECONOMY
Oil provides over half of export earnings. World's biggest banana exporter. Use of US dollar offers stability, but less control. Defaulted on debt in 2008, prioritizing social spending.

FACTFILE

OFFICIAL NAME: Republic of Ecuador

DATE OF FORMATION: 1830

CAPITAL: Quito

POPULATION: 13.8 million

TOTAL AREA: 109,483 sq. miles (283,560 sq. km)

DENSITY: 129 people per sq. mile

LANGUAGES: Spanish*, Quechua, other Amerindian languages

RELIGIONS: Roman Catholic 95%; Protestant, Jewish, and other 5%

ETHNIC MIX: *Mestizo* 77%, White 11%, Amerindian 7%, Black African 5%

GOVERNMENT: Presidential system

CURRENCY: US dollar = 100 cents

Egypt

Occupying the northeast corner of Africa, Egypt is divided by the highly fertile Nile Valley. Mubarak's military-backed regime was ousted in a popular uprising in the "Arab Spring" of 2011.

GEOGRAPHY
Fertile Nile Valley separates arid Libyan Desert from smaller semiarid eastern desert. Sinai peninsula has mountains in south.

CLIMATE
Summers are very hot, but winters are cooler. Rainfall is negligible, except on the coast.

PEOPLE & SOCIETY
Despite a long tradition of ethnic and religious tolerance, the rise of Islam has sparked clashes between Muslims and Copts (Coptic Christianity is one of the Church's earliest branches). Women play a full part in education and the economy, though this is threatened by Islamism. Rapidly growing population is a problem. Poverty is rife around Cairo.

 INSIGHT: *In 450 BCE Herodotus visited the already-ancient pyramids*

THE ECONOMY
Oil and gas. Cotton. Tolls from the Suez Canal. Successful tourist industry, in spite of terrorist attacks. High birth-rate and rural poverty.

FACTFILE

OFFICIAL NAME: Arab Republic of Egypt

DATE OF FORMATION: 1936

CAPITAL: Cairo

POPULATION: 84.5 million

TOTAL AREA: 386,660 sq. miles (1,001,450 sq. km)

DENSITY: 220 people per sq. mile

LANGUAGES: Arabic*, French, English, Berber

RELIGIONS: Muslim (mainly Sunni) 90%, Coptic Christian and other 10%

ETHNIC MIX: Egyptian 99%, other (Nubian, Armenian, Greek, Berber) 1%

GOVERNMENT: Transitional regime

CURRENCY: Egyptian pound = 100 piastres

El Salvador

El Salvador is Central America's smallest and most densely populated country. Already struggling to recover from a civil war in the 1980s, it was badly struck by earthquakes in 2001.

GEOGRAPHY

El Salvador is a narrow coastal belt backed by two mountain ranges. There is a central plateau. The country is located within a seismic zone, and there are more than 20 volcanic peaks.

CLIMATE

Tropical coastal belt is very hot, with seasonal rains. Cooler, temperate climate in highlands.

PEOPLE & SOCIETY

Population is largely *mestizo*; ethnic tensions are few. The 1981–1991 civil war was fought between the US-backed right-wing government and left-wing FMLN guerrillas over gross economic disparities, which still exist despite some reform. During the war, 75,000 people died, many of whom were unarmed civilians, and human rights abuses were widespread. The FMLN won the presidency in 2009.

THE ECONOMY

Coffee, sugar. Garment industry. Remittances from overseas. Frequent natural disasters damage infrastructure and homes and deepen country's reliance on aid. Five-year anti-poverty program for north from 2007.

INSIGHT: *Independent since 1841, El Salvador is named after Jesus Christ, "the savior" of Christians*

FACTFILE

OFFICIAL NAME: Republic of El Salvador

DATE OF FORMATION: 1841

CAPITAL: San Salvador

POPULATION: 6.2 million

TOTAL AREA: 8124 sq. miles (21,040 sq. km)

DENSITY: 775 people per sq. mile

LANGUAGES: Spanish*

RELIGIONS: Roman Catholic 80%, Evangelical 18%, other 2%

ETHNIC MIX: *Mestizo* (European–Amerindian) 90%, White 9%, Amerindian 1%

GOVERNMENT: Presidential system

CURRENCY: Salvadorean colón = 100 centavos; US dollar = 100 cents

Equatorial Guinea

Comprising the mainland territory of Río Muni and five islands on the west coast of central Africa, Equatorial Guinea, despite its name, lies just north of the equator.

GEOGRAPHY

The islands are mountainous and volcanic. The mainland is lower, with mangrove swamps along the coast.

CLIMATE

The island of Bioko is extremely wet and humid. The mainland is only marginally drier and cooler.

PEOPLE & SOCIETY

Equatorial Guinea is the only Spanish-speaking country in Africa. Río Muni is sparsely populated and most people there are Fang, an ethnic group also found in Cameroon and northern Gabon. Bioko is populated by Bubi and a minority of Creoles known as Fernandinos. Tensions between the two territories have been reignited by the discovery of oil off Bioko. Wealth is concentrated in the ruling clan; oil revenue in the last decade has made little impact on most people.

THE ECONOMY

Oil and gas now account for 94% of exports; the government has promised to reinvest the new funds in development. Timber, cocoa, coffee.

INSIGHT: *In 2003, state radio declared President Obiang Nguema to be "like God in Heaven"*

2000m/6562ft
1000m/3281ft
500m/1640ft
200m/656ft
Sea Level

MALABO

3°30'N · Isla da Bioko

Bight of Biafra 9°

ATLANTIC OCEAN

CAMEROON

Micomeseng

Gulf of Guinea · Bata · Niefang

Mbini

R í o   M u n i

Mongomo
Uolo

Cabo San Juan · Etembue · Cogo

Nsoc

Isla de Corisco

GABON

10°

0   40 km
0   40 miles

FACTFILE

OFFICIAL NAME: Republic of Equatorial Guinea

DATE OF FORMATION: 1968

CAPITAL: Malabo

POPULATION: 700,000

TOTAL AREA: 10,830 sq. miles (28,051 sq. km)

DENSITY: 65 people per sq. mile

LANGUAGES: Spanish*, Fang, Bubi, French*

RELIGIONS: Roman Catholic 90%, other 10%

ETHNIC MIX: Fang 85%, other 11%, Bubi 4%

GOVERNMENT: Presidential system

CURRENCY: CFA franc = 100 centimes

Eritrea

Lying along the southwest shore of the Red Sea, Eritrea won a long war for independence from Ethiopia in 1993. The two neighbors fought a bitter border war in 1998–2000.

GEOGRAPHY
Mostly consists of rugged mountains, bush, and the Danakil Desert, which falls below sea level.

CLIMATE
Warm in the mountains; desert areas are hot. Droughts from July onward are common.

PEOPLE & SOCIETY

Tigrinya-speakers, mainly Orthodox Christians, are the most numerous of nine main ethnic groups. A strong sense of nationhood has been forged by war. Women played a vital role in combat. Over 80% of people are subsistence farmers. Multiparty elections, due under the 1997 constitution, are yet to be held.

◆ **INSIGHT:** *Eritrea was modern Italy's first African colony. It's named for the ancient Greek for Red Sea: Erythra Thalassa*

THE ECONOMY
Legacy of disruption and destruction from wars; resettlement of refugees. Susceptible to drought and famine, dependent on food aid. Most of the population live at subsistence level. Potential for extraction of gold, copper, and oil. Red Sea location: port at Massawa.

0	100 km
0	100 miles

SUDAN
Kerora
Red Sea
40°
Dahlak Archipelago 16°
Ak'ordat Keren Mitsiwa (Massawa)
Barentu
Teseney ✈ ● ASMARA
Adi Ugri
ETHIOPIA Suwa Red Sea
Danakil
Aseb
DJIBOUTI

2000m/6562ft
1000m/3281ft
500m/1640ft
200m/656ft
Sea Level
Below Sea Level

FACTFILE
OFFICIAL NAME: State of Eritrea
DATE OF FORMATION: 1993
CAPITAL: Asmara
POPULATION: 5.2 million
TOTAL AREA: 46,842 sq. miles (121,320 sq. km)
DENSITY: 115 people per sq. mile

LANGUAGES: Tigrinya*, English*, Tigre, Afar, Arabic*, Saho, Bilen, Kunama, Nara, Hadareb
RELIGIONS: Christian 50%, Muslim 48%, other 2%
ETHNIC MIX: Tigray 50%, Tigre 31%, other 9%, Saho 5%, Afar 5%
GOVERNMENT: Transitional regime
CURRENCY: Nakfa = 100 cents

Estonia

The smallest and most Western-oriented of the former Soviet-ruled Baltic states, Estonia is also the most developed, but its standard of living is well below the EU average.

GEOGRAPHY
Estonia's terrain is flat, boggy, and partly forested, with over 1500 islands. Lake Peipus forms much of the eastern border with Russia.

CLIMATE
Maritime, with some continental extremes. Harsh winters, with cool summers and damp springs.

PEOPLE & SOCIETY
Estonians are related ethnically and linguistically to the Finns. Friction between ethnic Estonians and the large Russian minority led to a reassertion of Estonian culture and language. Outright discrimination against the Russian language was only ended in 2000. Estonians are predominantly Lutheran. Families are small and divorce rates are high. Market reforms have increased prosperity; a few people have become very rich.

THE ECONOMY
Timber and oil shale. Good productivity. Strong growth accompanied EU accession in 2004, but first EU country to enter recession in 2008. Drastic spending cuts aided quick revival. Joined eurozone in 2011. Low debt burden.

INSIGHT: *Estonia pioneered online voting in 2007, and voting by cell phone in 2011*

FACTFILE

OFFICIAL NAME: Republic of Estonia
DATE OF FORMATION: 1991
CAPITAL: Tallinn
POPULATION: 1.3 million
TOTAL AREA: 17,462 sq. miles (45,226 sq. km)
DENSITY: 75 people per sq. mile

LANGUAGES: Estonian*, Russian
RELIGIONS: Evangelical Lutheran 56%, Orthodox Christian 25%, other 19%
ETHNIC MIX: Estonian 69%, Russian 25%, other 4%, Ukrainian 2%
GOVERNMENT: Parliamentary system
CURRENCY: Euro = 100 cents

Ethiopia

The former empire of Ethiopia once dominated northeast Africa. A Marxist regime in 1974–1991, now a free-market democracy, it has suffered economic, civil, and natural crises.

GEOGRAPHY

Great Rift Valley divides mountainous northwest region from desert lowlands in northeast and southeast. Ethiopian Plateau is drained mainly by the Blue Nile.

CLIMATE

Moderate, with summer rains. Highlands are warm, with night frost and snowfalls on the mountains.

PEOPLE & SOCIETY

76 Ethiopian nationalities speak 286 languages. Oromo (or Gallas) are the largest group. Ethnic representation is a major political issue. Orthodox Christianity has a very ancient history in Ethiopia. Former emperor Haile Selassie inspired Rastafarianism.

INSIGHT: *King Solomon and the Queen of Sheba are said to have founded the Kingdom of Abyssinia (Ethiopia) c. 1000 BCE*

THE ECONOMY

Overwhelmingly dependent on agriculture; coffee is main export crop. War-damaged infrastructure and periodic serious droughts and famines undermine growth. There is a heavy reliance on food aid. Landlocked since secession of Eritrea.

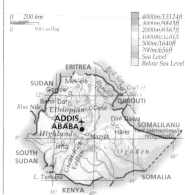

4000m/13124ft	
3000m/9843ft	
2000m/6562ft	
1000m/3281ft	
500m/1640ft	
200m/656ft	
Sea Level	
Below Sea Level	

FACTFILE

OFFICIAL NAME: Federal Democratic Republic of Ethiopia

DATE OF FORMATION: 1896

CAPITAL: Addis Ababa

POPULATION: 85 million

TOTAL AREA: 435,184 sq. miles (1,127,127 sq. km)

DENSITY: 198 people per sq. mile

LANGUAGES: Amharic*, Tigrinya, other

RELIGIONS: Orthodox Christian 40%, Muslim 40%, traditional beliefs 15%, other 5%

ETHNIC MIX: Oromo 40%, Amhara 25%, other 13%, Sidima 9%, Tigray 7%, Somali 6%

GOVERNMENT: Parliamentary system

CURRENCY: Birr = 100 cents

Fiji

A volcanic archipelago in the South Pacific, with two large islands and 880 islets. Tensions between native Fijians and the Indian minority have sparked a succession of coups.

 GEOGRAPHY
Main islands are mountainous, fringed by coral reefs. Remainder are limestone and coral formations.

CLIMATE
Tropical. High temperatures all year round. Cyclones are a hazard.

PEOPLE & SOCIETY
The British introduced workers from India in the late 19th century, and by 1946 their descendants outnumbered the indigenous Fijian population. Ethnic-Fijian nationalism is strong. Many Indo-Fijians left after the 1987 coup, restoring ethnic Fijians to a majority. In 2000, the first Indian-dominated government was ousted. The army led another coup in 2006. Women are lobbying for more rights.

INSIGHT: *Both Fijians and Indians practice fire-walking; Indians walk on hot embers, Fijians on heated stones*

THE ECONOMY
Tourism was main sector, though damaged by instability. Coups have also caused international isolation. All sectors struggling: sugar production, gold mining, textiles, timber, and commercial fishing.

FACTFILE

OFFICIAL NAME: Republic of the Fiji Islands
DATE OF FORMATION: 1970
CAPITAL: Suva
POPULATION: 900,000
TOTAL AREA: 7054 sq. miles (18,270 sq. km)
DENSITY: 128 people per sq. mile

LANGUAGES: Fijian, English*, Hindi, Urdu, Tamil, Telugu
RELIGIONS: Hindu 38%, Methodist 37%, Roman Catholic 9%, Muslim 8%, other 8%
ETHNIC MIX: Melanesian (Fijian) 51%, Indian 44%, other 5%
GOVERNMENT: Transitional regime
CURRENCY: Fiji dollar = 100 cents

Finland

Finland's language and national identity have been influenced by both its Scandinavian and Russian neighbors. Once aligned with the USSR, Finland is now a member of the EU.

GEOGRAPHY
South and center are flat, with low hills and many lakes. Uplands and low mountains in the north. 60% of the land area is forested.

CLIMATE
Long, harsh winters with frequent snowfalls. Short, warmer summers. Rainfall is low, and decreases northward.

PEOPLE & SOCIETY
One in four of the population lives in the Greater Helsinki region. Swedish-speakers live mainly in the Åland Islands in the southwest. The Sámi (Lapps) lead a seminomadic existence inside the Arctic Circle. Women make up 48% of the labor force, continuing a long tradition of equality between the sexes. Families tend to be close-knit, though marriage is becoming less common.

THE ECONOMY
Strong engineering and electronics sectors: home of Nokia. Wood, pulp, and paper production.

 INSIGHT: Finland has Europe's largest inland waterway system

FACTFILE

OFFICIAL NAME: Republic of Finland
DATE OF FORMATION: 1917
CAPITAL: Helsinki
POPULATION: 5.3 million
TOTAL AREA: 130,127 sq. miles (337,030 sq. km)
DENSITY: 45 people per sq. mile

LANGUAGES: Finnish*, Swedish*, Sámi
RELIGIONS: Evangelical Lutheran 83%, other 15%, Orthodox Christian 1%, Roman Catholic 1%
ETHNIC MIX: Finnish 93%, other (including Sámi) 7%
GOVERNMENT: Parliamentary system
CURRENCY: Euro = 100 cents

France

Stretching across western Europe, from the English Channel (la Manche) to the Mediterranean Sea, France was Europe's first modern republic, and is still a leading industrial power.

GEOGRAPHY

Broad plain covers northern half of the country. High mountain ranges in the east and southwest, with a mountainous plateau in the center.

CLIMATE

Three main climates: temperate and damp northwest; continental east; and Mediterranean south.

PEOPLE & SOCIETY

Strong French national identity coexists with pronounced regional differences, including local languages. Immigration laws have been tightened since the 1970s, but ethnic minorities growing up in city suburbs feel increasingly alienated. New rules aim to bring more women into politics.

◆ **INSIGHT:** *France is the most popular tourist destination in the world, with over 70 million visitors a year*

THE ECONOMY

Chemicals, electronics, heavy engineering, cars, and aircraft typify a strong and diversified export sector. World leader in cosmetics, perfumes, and quality wines. Modernized agriculture.

3000m/9843ft	
2000m/6562ft	
1000m/3281ft	
500m/1640ft	
200m/656ft	
Sea Level	

0   100 km
0   100 miles

FACTFILE

OFFICIAL NAME: French Republic
DATE OF FORMATION: 987
CAPITAL: Paris
POPULATION: 62.6 million
TOTAL AREA: 211,208 sq. miles (547,030 sq. km)
DENSITY: 295 people per sq. mile
LANGUAGES: French*, Provençal, German, Breton, Catalan, Basque
RELIGIONS: Roman Catholic 88%, Muslim 8%, Protestant 2%, Jewish 1%, Buddhist 1%
ETHNIC MIX: French 90%, North African 6%, German (Alsace) 2%, Breton 1%, other 1%
GOVERNMENT: Mixed presidential–parliamentary system
CURRENCY: Euro = 100 cents

Gabon

Gabon is a former French colony straddling the equator on Africa's west coast. Independent since 1960, it returned to multiparty politics in 1990, after 22 years of one-party rule.

GEOGRAPHY

Low plateaus and mountains lie beyond the coastal strip. Two-thirds of the land is covered by rainforest.

CLIMATE

Hot and tropical, with little distinction between seasons. Cold Benguela current cools the coast.

PEOPLE & SOCIETY
Some 40 different languages are spoken. The Fang, who live mainly in the north, are the largest ethnic group, but have yet to gain control of the government. Oil wealth has led to the growth of an affluent middle class, but one in three people still live in poverty. Menial jobs are done by immigrant workers. Education follows the French system. With 85% of people living in towns, Gabon is one of Africa's most urbanized countries. The government is encouraging population growth.

THE ECONOMY
Oil accounts for 81% of exports, but reserves are dwindling: not much post-oil planning. High debt problem. Tropical hardwoods and manganese.

◆ **INSIGHT:** *Libreville was founded as a settlement for freed French slaves in 1849*

FACTFILE

OFFICIAL NAME: Gabonese Republic
DATE OF FORMATION: 1960
CAPITAL: Libreville
POPULATION: 1.5 million
TOTAL AREA: 103,346 sq. miles (267,667 sq. km)
DENSITY: 15 people per sq. mile
LANGUAGES: Fang, French*, Punu, Sira, Nzebi, Mpongwe

RELIGIONS: Christian (mainly Roman Catholic) 55%, traditional beliefs 40%, other 4%, Muslim 1%
ETHNIC MIX: Fang 26%, Shira-punu 24%, other 24%, foreign residents 15%, Nzabi-duma 11%
GOVERNMENT: Presidential system
CURRENCY: CFA franc = 100 centimes

Gambia

Gambia is a riverbank state on the west coast of Africa, almost entirely surrounded by Senegal. It was renowned for its stability until its government was overthrown in a coup in 1994.

GEOGRAPHY

Located on the narrow strip of land bordering the Gambia River. Long, sandy beaches are backed by mangrove swamps along the river. Savanna and tropical forests higher up.

CLIMATE

Subtropical, with wet, humid months July–October, and warm, dry season November–May.

PEOPLE & SOCIETY

Little tension between various ethnic groups. The largest group, the Mandinka, has traditionally held power. Islam is a strong social influence, though there is no official state religion. A small expatriate community from the UK lives on the coast. Seasonal migrants come from neighboring states to harvest groundnuts each year. Women are very active as traders.

THE ECONOMY

Around 75% of the labor force is involved in agriculture. Groundnuts are the principal crop. Fish stocks are declining. Eco-tourism is promoted, though most visitors come for the beaches. Banjul is one of west Africa's finest deepwater ports: significant re-export trade. Smuggling problems.

◆ INSIGHT: *Overfishing in the waters off Gambia and Senegal, mainly by foreign vessels, is a growing problem*

FACTFILE

OFFICIAL NAME: Republic of the Gambia

DATE OF FORMATION: 1965

CAPITAL: Banjul

POPULATION: 1.8 million

TOTAL AREA: 4363 sq. miles (11,300 sq. km)

DENSITY: 466 people per sq. mile

LANGUAGES: Mandinka, Fulani, Wolof, Jola, Soninke, English*

RELIGIONS: Sunni Muslim 90%, Christian 8%, traditional beliefs 2%

ETHNIC MIX: Mandinka 42%, Fulani 18%, Wolof 16%, Jola 10%, Serahuli 9%, other 5%

GOVERNMENT: Presidential system

CURRENCY: Dalasi = 100 butut

Georgia

Located on the eastern shore of the Black Sea, Georgia has been torn by civil war and ethnic disputes since achieving independence from the Soviet Union in 1991.

GEOGRAPHY
Kura Valley lies between Caucasus Mountains in the north and Lesser Caucasus range in south. Lowlands along the Black Sea coast.

CLIMATE
Subtropical along the coast, changing to continental extremes at high altitudes. Rainfall is moderate.

PEOPLE & SOCIETY
Paternalistic society, with strong family, cultural, and literary traditions. Georgia was converted to Christianity in 326 CE. Armenians in the south are the poorest group. Civil conflicts in the early 1990s against Abkhaz and Osset separatists displaced 300,000 people. Abkhazia and South Ossetia now effectively operate as separate states, backed up by Russian forces since the 2008 war. Russia opposes Georgian hopes of joining the EU and NATO.

THE ECONOMY
Transit revenues from pipelines taking oil to the West. Long-established and booming wine industry. Political instability. Fast pace of reforms in late 2000s, at cost of high unemployment.

◆ **INSIGHT:** *Western Georgia was the land of the legendary Golden Fleece of Greek mythology*

FACTFILE

OFFICIAL NAME: Georgia
DATE OF FORMATION: 1991
CAPITAL: Tbilisi
POPULATION: 4.2 million
TOTAL AREA: 26,911 sq. miles (69,700 sq. km)
DENSITY: 156 people per sq. mile
LANGUAGES: Georgian*, Russian, Azeri, Armenian, Mingrelian, Ossetian, Abkhazian
RELIGIONS: Georgian Orthodox 74%, Muslim 10%, Russian Orthodox 10%, Armenian Apostolic Church (Orthodox) 4%, other 2%
ETHNIC MIX: Georgian 84%, Armenian 6%, Azeri 6%, Russian 2%, Ossetian 1%, other 1%
GOVERNMENT: Presidential system
CURRENCY: Lari = 100 tetri

Germany

Europe's strongest industrial power and its most populous nation, Germany was divided after military defeat in 1945 into a free-market west and a communist east, but reunified in 1990.

GEOGRAPHY

Central European coastal plains in the north, rising to rolling hills of central region and Alps in far south.

CLIMATE

Damp, temperate in northern and central regions. Continental extremes in mountainous south.

PEOPLE & SOCIETY

Regionalism is strong. The north is mainly Protestant, while the south is staunchly Roman Catholic. Social and economic differences still exist between east and west. Turks are the largest single ethnic minority; many came as guest workers in the 1950s–1970s. Immigration rules now favor skilled workers. Feminism is strong.

◆ **INSIGHT:** *Germany's rivers and canals carry as much freight as its busy highways*

THE ECONOMY

Major exporter of electronics, heavy engineering, chemicals, and cars. Worst recession for 60 years in 2008–2009. Aging population.

```
2000m/6562ft
1000m/3281ft
500m/1640ft
200m/656ft
Sea Level

0        100 km
0        100 miles
```

FACTFILE

OFFICIAL NAME: Federal Republic of Germany

DATE OF FORMATION: 1871

CAPITAL: Berlin

POPULATION: 82.1 million

TOTAL AREA: 137,846 sq. miles (357,021 sq. km)

DENSITY: 608 people per sq. mile

LANGUAGES: German*, Turkish

RELIGIONS: Protestant 34%, Roman Catholic 33%, other 30%, Muslim 3%

ETHNIC MIX: German 92%, other 3%, other European 3%, Turkish 2%

GOVERNMENT: Parliamentary system

CURRENCY: Euro = 100 cents

Ghana

The heartland of the ancient Ashanti kingdom, Ghana in west Africa was once known as the Gold Coast. It has experienced intermittent periods of military rule since independence in 1957.

GEOGRAPHY

Mostly low-lying. The west is covered in rainforest. One of the world's largest artificial lakes – Lake Volta – was created by damming the White Volta River.

CLIMATE

Tropical. There are two wet seasons in the south, but the north is drier, and has just one.

PEOPLE & SOCIETY

Around 75 cultural-linguistic groups. The largest is the Akan, who include the Ashanti and Fanti peoples. Southern peoples are richer and more urban than those of the north. There are few tribal tensions. Family ties are strong. Women play a major role in market trading. The 2000 election saw Ghana's first peaceful handover of power. Poverty levels have been significantly reduced.

THE ECONOMY

World's second-largest cocoa producer. Oil discovered in 2007: on stream from 2010. Hardwood trees such as maple and sapele. Gold mining.

INSIGHT: Ghana was the first colony in west Africa to gain independence

FACTFILE

OFFICIAL NAME: Republic of Ghana
DATE OF FORMATION: 1957
CAPITAL: Accra
POPULATION: 24.3 million
TOTAL AREA: 92,100 sq. miles
(238,540 sq. km)
DENSITY: 274 people per sq. mile

LANGUAGES: Twi, Fanti, Ewe, Ga, Adangbe, Gurma, Dagomba (Dagbani), English*
RELIGIONS: Christian 69%, Muslim 16%, traditional beliefs 9%, other 6%
ETHNIC MIX: Akan 49%, Mole-Dagbani 17%, Ewe 13%, other 13%, Ga and Ga-Adangbe 8%
GOVERNMENT: Presidential system
CURRENCY: Cedi = 100 pesewas

Greece

The Balkan state of Greece is bounded on three sides by the Mediterranean, Aegean, and Ionian seas. It has a strong seafaring tradition, with some of the world's richest shipowners.

GEOGRAPHY
Mountainous peninsula and over 2000 islands. Large plain along the mainland's Aegean coast.

CLIMATE
Mainly Mediterranean, with dry, hot summers. Alpine climate in northern mountain areas.

PEOPLE & SOCIETY
Postwar industrial development altered the dominance of agriculture and seafaring. Rural exodus to cities has been stemmed but a third of the population lives in Athens. Age-old culture and Greek Orthodox Church balance social mobility. Civil marriage and divorce only legalized in 1982. There has been much recent civil unrest against severe austerity measures.

◆ INSIGHT: *The modern Olympics, first held in Athens in 1896, evolved from Olympia's ancient Greek games*

THE ECONOMY
Public debt and budget deficit very high: EU bailouts to avoid bankruptcy. World's largest shipping fleet. One of Europe's top tourist destinations. Fruit, vegetables, olives. Large black economy.

FACTFILE

OFFICIAL NAME: Hellenic Republic
DATE OF FORMATION: 1829
CAPITAL: Athens
POPULATION: 11.2 million
TOTAL AREA: 50,942 sq. miles
(131,940 sq. km)
DENSITY: 222 people per sq. mile

LANGUAGES: Greek*, Turkish, Macedonian, Albanian
RELIGIONS: Orthodox Christian 98%, Muslim 1%, other 1%
ETHNIC MIX: Greek 98%, other 2%
GOVERNMENT: Parliamentary system
CURRENCY: Euro = 100 cents

Grenada

The southernmost of the Windward Islands, Grenada
made world headlines in 1983 when the US and Caribbean
allies mounted an invasion to sever links with Castro's Cuba.

GEOGRAPHY
Volcanic in origin, with densely
forested central mountains. Its territory
also includes the islands of Carriacou and
Petite Martinique.

CLIMATE
Tropical, tempered by trade winds.
Hurricanes are a hazard in the July–
November wet season

PEOPLE & SOCIETY
Grenadians are mainly of African
origin; their traditions remain strong,
especially on Carriacou. Inter-ethnic
marriage has reduced tensions between
the groups. Extended families, often
headed by women, are the norm. Wealth
disparities are not marked, but levels of
poverty are growing.

◆ **INSIGHT:** *Known as "the spice island
of the Caribbean," it is the world's
second-largest nutmeg producer*

THE ECONOMY
Severe damage from Hurricane Ivan
in 2004 to crops and 90% of buildings;
reconstruction taking years. Nutmeg,
cocoa, bananas, and mace. Smuggling
is a serious problem.

FACTFILE

OFFICIAL NAME: Grenada

DATE OF FORMATION: 1974

CAPITAL: St. George's

POPULATION: 108,419

TOTAL AREA: 131 sq. miles
(340 sq. km)

DENSITY: 828 people per sq. mile

LANGUAGES: English*, English Creole

RELIGIONS: Roman Catholic 68%,
Anglican 17%, other 15%

ETHNIC MIX: Black African 82%, Mulatto
(mixed race) 13%, East Indian 3%, other 2%

GOVERNMENT: Parliamentary system

CURRENCY: East Caribbean dollar =
100 cents

Guatemala

The largest and most populous nation on the Central American isthmus, Guatemala returned to civilian rule in 1986 after 32 years of violent and repressive military rule.

GEOGRAPHY

Narrow Pacific coastal plain. Central highlands with volcanoes. Short coast on the Caribbean Sea. Tropical rainforests in the north.

CLIMATE

Tropical: hot and humid in coastal regions and north. More temperate in central highlands.

PEOPLE & SOCIETY

Amerindians, concentrated in the highlands, form a majority. Power, wealth, and land are controlled by *ladinos* (Westernized Amerindians and *mestizos*). Catholicism is predominant, mixed with Amerindian beliefs. Literacy levels are low. Half of the population lives on less than $2 a day. Violent crime is a problem.

◆ **INSIGHT:** *Guatemala, which means "land of trees," was the center of the ancient Mayan civilization*

THE ECONOMY

Coffee, sugar, and bananas are top exports. Tourism. Damage from natural disasters. Marked wealth inequalities inhibit domestic market.

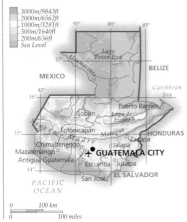

- 3000m/9843ft
- 2000m/6562ft
- 1000m/3281ft
- 500m/1640ft
- 200m/656ft
- Sea Level

FACTFILE

OFFICIAL NAME: Republic of Guatemala

DATE OF FORMATION: 1838

CAPITAL: Guatemala City

POPULATION: 14.4 million

TOTAL AREA: 42,042 sq. miles (108,890 sq. km)

DENSITY: 344 people per sq. mile

LANGUAGES: Quiché, Mam, Cakchiquel, Kekchí, Spanish*

RELIGIONS: Roman Catholic 65%, Protestant 33%, other and nonreligious 2%

ETHNIC MIX: Amerindian 60%, *Mestizo* (European–Amerindian) 30%, other 10%

GOVERNMENT: Presidential system

CURRENCY: Quetzal = 100 centavos

Guinea

Located on the west coast of Africa, Guinea was the first French colony in Africa to gain independence, in 1958. The country was under military rule from 1984 to 1995.

GEOGRAPHY
Coastal plains and mangrove swamps in west rise to forested or savanna highlands in the south. Semidesert in the north.

CLIMATE
Tropical, with a wet season April–October. Conakry is especially rainy. Hot, dry *harmattan* wind blows from Sahara during dry season.

PEOPLE & SOCIETY
Peul and Malinké make up most of the population, but rivalries between them have allowed coastal peoples such as the Soussou to dominate politics. Daily life revolves around the extended family. Women acquired influence under Marxist party rule between 1958 and 1984, but the Muslim revival since then has reversed the trend. Private enterprise has created a business class.

THE ECONOMY
Substantial gold, diamond, and especially bauxite reserves. Cash crops: bananas, coffee, pineapples, palm oil. Poor infrastructure. Instability.

INSIGHT: *The colors of Guinea's flag represent the three words of the country's motto: work (red), justice (yellow), and solidarity (green)*

FACTFILE

OFFICIAL NAME: Republic of Guinea
DATE OF FORMATION: 1958
CAPITAL: Conakry
POPULATION: 10.3 million
TOTAL AREA: 94,925 sq. miles (245,857 sq. km)
DENSITY: 109 people per sq. mile

LANGUAGES: Pulaar, Malinké, Soussou, French*
RELIGIONS: Muslim 85%, Christian 8% traditional beliefs 7%
ETHNIC MIX: Peul 40%, Malinké 30%, Soussou 20%, other 10%
GOVERNMENT: Presidential system
CURRENCY: Guinea franc = 100 centimes

Guinea-Bissau

Known as Portuguese Guinea while a colony, Guinea-Bissau lies on Africa's west coast. Since 1994, its nascent democracy has been plagued by coups and rebellions.

GEOGRAPHY

Low-lying, apart from savanna highlands in northeast. Rainforests and swamps are found along coastal areas.

CLIMATE

Tropical, with wet season May-November and dry season December-April. Hot, dry *harmattan* desert wind blows during dry season.

PEOPLE & SOCIETY

The largest ethnic group is the Balante, who live in the south. Though only around 1% of the population, the mixed race Portuguese--African *mestiços* dominate the top ranks of government and bureaucracy. Most people live and work on small family farms, grouped in self-contained villages. The bulk of the urban population live in Bissau, where they face economic hardship. Narcotics traffickers are taking advantage of the ongoing instability.

THE ECONOMY

Mostly subsistence farming. Lack of sufficiency in rice staple. Main cash crop is cashew nuts. Major cocaine transit route from South America to Europe. Offshore oil as yet untapped. Fisheries and timber potential.

◆ **INSIGHT:** *In 1974, Guinea-Bissau became the first Portuguese colony to gain independence*

FACTFILE

OFFICIAL NAME: Republic of Guinea-Bissau
DATE OF FORMATION: 1974
CAPITAL: Bissau
POPULATION: 1.6 million
TOTAL AREA: 13,946 sq. miles (36,120 sq. km)
DENSITY: 147 people per sq. mile

LANGUAGES: Portuguese Creole, Balante, Fulani, Malinké, Portuguese*
RELIGIONS: Traditional beliefs 50%, Muslim 40%, Christian 10%
ETHNIC MIX: Balante 30%, Fulani 20%, other 16%, Mandyako 14%, Mandinka 13%, Papel 7%
GOVERNMENT: Presidential system
CURRENCY: CFA franc = 100 centimes

Guyana

On the northeast coast of South America, Guyana is the continent's only English-speaking country. Independent since 1966, it has close ties with the anglophone Caribbean.

GEOGRAPHY
Mainly artificial coast, reclaimed by dikes and dams from swamps and tidal marshes. Forests cover 85% of the interior, rising to savanna uplands and mountains.

CLIMATE
Tropical. Coast cooled by sea breezes. Lowlands are hot, wet, and humid. Highlands are a little cooler.

PEOPLE & SOCIETY
Guyana is a complex multiracial society. Tension exists between the Afro-Guyanese, descended from slaves, and the Indo-Guyanese, descendants of laborers brought over after slavery was abolished. Politics is highly polarized around this split and has often spilled over into violence on the streets. Amerindian subsistence farmers are the poorest people in society and have little representation.

THE ECONOMY
Diverse exports: gold, sugar, fish, bauxite, rice, timber, diamonds. Debt relief granted. Narcotics transit zone.

◆ INSIGHT: Guyana means "land of many waters," reflecting its dense network of rivers

FACTFILE

OFFICIAL NAME: Cooperative Republic of Guyana
DATE OF FORMATION: 1966
CAPITAL: Georgetown
POPULATION: 800,000
TOTAL AREA: 83,000 sq. miles (214,970 sq. km)
DENSITY: 11 people per sq. mile

LANGUAGES: English Creole, Hindi, Tamil, Amerindian languages, English*
RELIGIONS: Christian 57%, Hindu 28%, Muslim 10%, other 5%
ETHNIC MIX: East Indian 43%, Black African 30%, mixed race 17%, Amerindian 9%, other 1%
GOVERNMENT: Presidential system
CURRENCY: Guyanese dollar = 100 cents

Haiti

Formerly a French colony, Haiti shares the Caribbean island of Hispaniola with the Dominican Republic. At independence in 1804, it became the world's first black republic.

 GEOGRAPHY
Predominantly mountainous, with forests and fertile plains.

 CLIMATE
Tropical, with rain throughout the year. Humid in coastal areas, much cooler in the mountains.

PEOPLE & SOCIETY
Most Haitians are of African descent. A few have European roots, primarily French. The rigid class structure maintains vast disparities of wealth. The majority of the population live in extreme poverty; Haiti is one of the poorest countries in the Americas. A combination of political oppression and a collapsing economy led thousands to seek asylum in the US or the Dominican Republic. Though most are Christians, many Haitians practice Voodoo, which was recognized as an official religion in 2003.

THE ECONOMY
Fragile economy completely shattered by 2010 earthquake. Ongoing problems of instability, hurricane damage, high unemployment, narcotics trafficking.

◆ **INSIGHT:** *A slave rebellion headed by Toussaint Louverture in 1791 led to Haiti's independence*

FACTFILE

OFFICIAL NAME: Republic of Haiti
DATE OF FORMATION: 1804
CAPITAL: Port-au-Prince
POPULATION: 10.2 million
TOTAL AREA: 10,714 sq. miles (27,750 sq. km)
DENSITY: 959 people per sq. mile

LANGUAGES: French Creole*, French*
RELIGIONS: Roman Catholic 55%, Protestant 28%, other (including Voodoo) 16%, nonreligious 1%
ETHNIC MIX: Black African 95%, *Mulatto* (mixed race) and European 5%
GOVERNMENT: Presidential system
CURRENCY: Gourde = 100 centimes

Honduras

Straddling the Central American isthmus, Honduras returned to democratic rule in 1984, after a period of military government. Hurricane Mitch devastated the country in 1998.

GEOGRAPHY
Narrow plains along both coasts, with a mountainous interior, cut by river valleys. Tropical forests, swamps, and lagoons in the east.

CLIMATE
Tropical coastal lowlands are hot and humid, with May–October rains. Interior is cooler and drier.

PEOPLE & SOCIETY
The majority of the population is *mestizo* (mixed European–Amerindian). An English speaking *garífuna* (black) community and Miskito Amerindians struggle to preserve their rights to land along the remote Caribbean coast. Women's status remains low. Wealth inequalities are large and poverty is at the root of social tension. About 65% of the population live in poverty. The army ousted the president in 2009. Violent crime is a major issue.

THE ECONOMY
Garments, coffee, bananas, and shellfish are exported. Remittances account for a fifth of GDP. Debt relief from 2005. Mineral potential. High underemployment and corruption.

INSIGHT: *The Honduran currency is named after a Lenca Indian chief who was the main leader of resistance to the Spanish conquest in the 16th century*

FACTFILE

OFFICIAL NAME: Republic of Honduras
DATE OF FORMATION: 1838
CAPITAL: Tegucigalpa
POPULATION: 7.6 million
TOTAL AREA: 43,278 sq. miles
(112,090 sq. km)
DENSITY: 176 people per sq. mile

LANGUAGES: Spanish*, Garífuna (Carib), English Creole
RELIGIONS: Roman Catholic 97%, Protestant 3%
ETHNIC MIX: *Mestizo* 90%, Black African 5%, Amerindian 4%, White 1%
GOVERNMENT: Presidential system
CURRENCY: Lempira = 100 centavos

Hungary

Landlocked in central Europe, Hungary was one of the twin centers of the once-great Habsburg Empire. It lost two-thirds of its historical territory for supporting Germany in World War I.

 GEOGRAPHY

Landlocked. Fertile plains in east and northwest; west and north are hilly. The Danube River cuts through the country and the capital.

 CLIMATE

Continental, with wet springs, late but very hot summers, and cold, cloudy winters. The transition between seasons tends to be sudden.

 PEOPLE & SOCIETY

Hungary's population shrank in the 1990s. Mostly ethnic Hungarian (Magyar), there are small minorities of Germans, Jews, and neighboring peoples. Roma face particular discrimination. The government is greatly concerned about the fate of ethnic Hungarians in Romania, Serbia, and Slovakia. Hungary joined the EU in 2004. Working hours are longer than in western Europe.

THE ECONOMY

Strong industrial base. Hard-hit in 2007–2009 by global downturn. Currency plummeted, $25 billion bailout from IMF to avoid meltdown. Tough spending cuts needed to keep on path to join euro.

INSIGHT: *The Hungarian language is Asian in origin and is most closely related to Finnish*

FACTFILE

OFFICIAL NAME: Republic of Hungary
DATE OF FORMATION: 1918
CAPITAL: Budapest
POPULATION: 10 million
TOTAL AREA: 35,919 sq. miles (93,030 sq. km)
DENSITY: 280 people per sq. mile

LANGUAGES: Hungarian (Magyar)*
RELIGIONS: Roman Catholic 52%, Calvinist 16%, other 15%, nonreligious 14%, Lutheran 3%
ETHNIC MIX: Magyar 90%, Roma 4%, German 3%, Serb 2%, other 1%
GOVERNMENT: Parliamentary system
CURRENCY: Forint = 100 fillér

Iceland

Europe's westernmost country, Iceland's strategic ocean location straddles the Mid-Atlantic Ridge. Its spectacular landscape is largely uninhabited, aside from coastal towns.

GEOGRAPHY

Grassy coastal lowlands, with fjords in the north. Central plateau of cold lava desert, geothermal springs, and glaciers. Around 200 volcanoes, with numerous geysers and solfataras.

CLIMATE

Its location in the middle of the Gulf Stream moderates the climate. Mild winters and brief, cool summers.

PEOPLE & SOCIETY

Icelanders share a strong national identity, with few foreign residents. Their language has changed little in 700 years, in part due to the country's isolation. There is high social mobility, free health care, and low-cost heating (geothermal and hydropower). Iceland's recent banking collapse and near financial ruin has swung the long-running debate over EU membership in favor of joining.

THE ECONOMY

Once reliant on fish. Aluminum smelting. Tourism. Banks overexposed in 2007–2009 global downturn. Nation bankrupt, króna depreciated 90%.

INSIGHT: The word geyser is taken from Geysir (the "gusher") in southwest Iceland

| 1000m/3281ft |
| 500m/1640ft |
| 200m/656ft |
| Sea Level |
| Ice Cap |

FACTFILE

OFFICIAL NAME: Republic of Iceland
DATE OF FORMATION: 1944
CAPITAL: Reykjavík
POPULATION: 300,000
TOTAL AREA: 39,768 sq. miles (103,000 sq. km)
DENSITY: 8 people per sq. mile

LANGUAGES: Icelandic*
RELIGIONS: Evangelical Lutheran 84%, nonreligious 3%, Roman Catholic 3%, other (mostly Christian) 10%
ETHNIC MIX: Icelandic 94%, other 5%, Danish 1%
GOVERNMENT: Parliamentary system
CURRENCY: Icelandic króna = 100 aurar

India

India is the world's second most populous country and largest democracy. Despite some success in reducing the birth rate, its population will probably overtake China's by 2030.

GEOGRAPHY

Separated from northern Asia by the Himalaya mountain range, India forms a subcontinent. As well as the Himalayas, there are two other main geographical regions, the Indo-Gangetic plain, which lies between the foothills of the Himalayas and the Vindhya Mountains, and the central-southern Deccan plateau. The Ghats are smaller mountain ranges located on the east and west coasts.

CLIMATE

Varies greatly according to latitude, altitude, and season. Most of India has three seasons: hot, wet, and cool. Summer temperatures in the north can reach 104°F (40°C). Monsoon rains normally break in June, petering out in September to October. In the cool season, the weather is mainly dry. The climate in the warmer south is less variable than in the north.

PEOPLE & SOCIETY

India's planners, overseeing an economic revolution, see its growing population rather than environmental constraints as the main brake on development. Nationwide awareness campaigns promote birth control but cultural and religious pressures encourage large families. Rural deprivation spurs urban migration, to live in sprawling slums. Over 70% of people survive on less than $2 a day. The majority of Indians are Hindu. Various attempts to reform the Hindu caste system, which determines social standing and even marriage, have met with violent opposition. Severe tensions exist between Hindus and the Muslim minority, especially in Kashmir and Gujarat. Smaller ethnic groups exist in the northeast, and many struggle for greater autonomy. Over two million people are living with HIV/AIDS.

FACTFILE

OFFICIAL NAME: Republic of India
DATE OF FORMATION: 1947
CAPITAL: New Delhi
POPULATION: 1.21 billion
TOTAL AREA: 1,269,338 sq. miles (3,287,590 sq. km)
DENSITY: 1058 people per sq. mile

LANGUAGES: Hindi*, English*, Urdu, Bengali, Marathi, Telugu, Tamil, Bihari, Gujarati, Kanarese
RELIGIONS: Hindu 81%, Muslim 13%, Christian 2%, Sikh 2%, Buddhist 1%, other 1%
ETHNIC MIX: Indo-Aryan 72%, Dravidian 25%, Mongoloid and other 3%
GOVERNMENT: Parliamentary system
CURRENCY: Indian rupee = 100 paise

THE ECONOMY

One of Asia's fastest-growing economies. Protectionism has given way to free-market economics. Tea, gems, textiles exported. High-tech industries, outsourcing center. Success of "Bollywood" films. Cheap labor. Huge market, held back by poverty.

INSIGHT: *India's national animal, the tiger, was depicted as early as 4000 years ago by the Mohenjo-Daro civilization*

5000m/16405ft
4000m/13124ft
3000m/9843ft
2000m/6562ft
1000m/3281ft
500m/1640ft
200m/656ft
Sea Level

A 'line of control was agreed between India and Pakistan in 1972

Srinagar
Jammu and Kashmir

Aksai Chin - administered by China, claimed by India

Demchok/Dêmqog - administered by China, claimed by India

Much of Arunāchal Pradesh is claimed by China

Amritsar
Jalandhar
Ludhiāna
Chandīgarh
CHINA
NEPAL
BHUTAN
MYANMAR (BURMA)

PAKISTAN

Meerut
Delhi
Bareilly
Shiligurī
Brahmaputra
Assam

NEW DELHI
Agra
Lucknow
Patna
BANGLADESH
Imphāl

Jodhpur
Jaipur
Kānpur
Ganges

Kota
Gwalior
Vārānasi
Dhanbād
Hāora

Gulf of Kachchh
Ahmadābād
Indore
Bhopāl
Jabalpur
Rānchi
Kolkata Calcutta

Jāmnagar
Rājkot
Vadodara
Nāgpur
Jamshedpur
Mouths of the Ganges

Sūrat
Narmada
Mahānadi

Gulf of Khambhāt
Kalyān
Nānded
Cuttack

Mumbai (Bombay)
Pune
Deccan
Godāvari
Visākhapatnam
Bay of Bengal

Hyderābad
Krishna
Arabian Sea
Solāpur
Panaji

Hubli

Andaman Islands
North Andaman
Middle Andaman

Chennai (Madras)
South Andaman
Port Blair
Little Andaman

Lakshadweep (Laccadive Is.)
Bangalore
Salem
INDIAN OCEAN

Mysore
Coimbatore
Nicobar Islands

Kochi/Cochin
Madurai
Indira Point
Great Nicobar

0   200 km
0   200 miles

Indonesia

Formerly called the Dutch East Indies, Indonesia is the world's largest archipelago, with 18,108 islands scattered across 3000 miles (5000 km). It is the world's fourth most populous nation.

GEOGRAPHY

Indonesia is highly mountainous, with numerous tropical swamps. The land is covered with dense rainforest, especially on New Guinea, where it remains largely unexplored. There are more than 200 volcanoes, many of which are still active. Earthquakes, eruptions, and tsunamis are hazards. The islands of Java, Bali, Lombok, Sumatra, and Borneo were once joined together by dry land, which has since been submerged by rising sea levels. Coastal lowland development distinguishes some of the large islands.

CLIMATE

The climate is predominantly tropical monsoon. Variations relate mainly to differences in latitude and altitude; hilly areas are cooler overall. Rain falls throughout the year, often in thunderstorms, but there is a relatively dry season from June to September.

PEOPLE & SOCIETY

The basic Melanesian–Malay ethnic division disguises a diverse society. Bahasa Indonesia, the national language, coexists with at least 250 other spoken languages or dialects. Attempts by the Javanese

FACTFILE

OFFICIAL NAME: Republic of Indonesia
DATE OF FORMATION: 1949
CAPITAL: Jakarta
POPULATION: 232 million
TOTAL AREA: 741,096 sq. miles
(1,919,440 sq. km)
DENSITY: 335 people per sq. mile

LANGUAGES: Javanese, Sundanese, Madurese, Bahasa Indonesia*, Dutch
RELIGIONS: Sunni Muslim 86%, Christian 9%, Hindu 2%, other 2%, Buddhist 1%
ETHNIC MIX: Javanese 41%, other 32%, Sundanese 15%, coastal Malays 12%
GOVERNMENT: Presidential system
CURRENCY: Rupiah = 100 sen

political elite to suppress local cultures have been vigorously opposed, especially by the Aceh of northern Sumatra, and the Papuans. Religious and interethnic hostility is a problem, with clashes between Christians and Muslims in many areas, and discrimination against ethnic Chinese leading to mob attacks on their businesses. Gender equality is enshrined in law; women are active in public life.

💲 THE ECONOMY

Varied resources, especially natural gas. Cheap and plentiful labor pool. Sizable state-owned sector, and state control of prices of basic goods. Large foreign debt rescheduled. Bureaucracy and corruption damage business confidence. Regional conflicts and terrorist attacks deter tourists and investors. Piracy is rife. The 2004 tsunami, which killed over 130,000 people, devastated northern Sumatra.

4000m/13124ft
3000m/9843ft
2000m/6562ft
1000m/3281ft
500m/1640ft
Sea Level

◆ **INSIGHT:** *Indonesia has a very youthful population: almost 30% of its people are under 15 years of age*

0   500 km
0   500 miles

Iran

Since the 1979 Islamic fundamentalist revolution led by Ayatollah Khomeini, the Middle Eastern country of Iran has been the world's largest theocracy.

GEOGRAPHY

High desert plateau with large salt pans in the east. West and north are mountainous. Coastal land bordering Caspian Sea is rainy and forested.

CLIMATE

Desert climate. Hot summers, and bitterly cold winters. Area around the Caspian Sea is more temperate.

PEOPLE & SOCIETY

Many ethnic groups, including Persians, Azaris (ethnically related to Azeris), and Kurds. Militant Shi'a Islamism has dominated since the 1979 revolution. The mullahs' belief that adherence to religious values is more important than economic welfare has resulted in declining living standards. Female emancipation has been reversed. Student-backed demonstrations favoring greater liberalism have been suppressed.

THE ECONOMY

A leading oil producer: 80% of exports. Government restricts contact with the West, blocking acquisition of vital technology. High unemployment and inflation. Sizable black market.

◆ **INSIGHT:** *More than a hundred offenses carry the death penalty*

3000m/9843ft
2000m/6562ft
1000m/3281ft
500m/1640ft
200m/656ft
Sea Level

0   200 km
0   200 miles

FACTFILE

OFFICIAL NAME: Islamic Republic of Iran
DATE OF FORMATION: 1502
CAPITAL: Tehran
POPULATION: 75.1 million
TOTAL AREA: 636,293 sq. miles (1,648,000 sq. km)
DENSITY: 119 people per sq. mile

LANGUAGES: Farsi*, Azeri, Luri, Gilaki, Arabic, Mazanderani, Kurdish, Turkmen, Baluchi
RELIGIONS: Shi'a Muslim 89%, Sunni Muslim 9%, other 2%
ETHNIC MIX: Persian 51%, Azari 24%, other 10%, Lur and Bakhtiari 8%, Kurd 7%
GOVERNMENT: Islamic theocracy
CURRENCY: Iranian rial = 100 dinars

Iraq

Oil-rich Iraq is situated in the central Middle East. The last 50 years have been dominated by dictatorship, war, and civil strife. A US-led Coalition ousted Saddam Hussein in April 2003.

GEOGRAPHY
Mainly desert. The Tigris and Euphrates rivers water fertile regions and create the southern marshland. Mountains along northeast border.

CLIMATE
Southern deserts have hot, dry summers and mild winters. North has dry summers, but winters can be harsh in the mountains. Rainfall is low.

PEOPLE & SOCIETY
Carved out of remnants of the Ottoman Empire, Iraq is home to Arab Muslims (mainly Shi'a, some Sunni), northern Kurds (who were persecuted under Saddam's regime), and smaller minorities. After Saddam's removal, sectarian violence overshadowed efforts to build democracy. Improved security allowed the final US forces to withdraw by the end of 2011. After years of war and sanctions, poverty is widespread.

THE ECONOMY
Economy and infrastructure have been destroyed. Given stability and aid for reconstruction, hopes of recovery rest on massive oil reserves.

INSIGHT: *As Mesopotamia, Iraq was the site where the Sumerians established the world's first civilization*

FACTFILE

OFFICIAL NAME: Republic of Iraq
DATE OF FORMATION: 1932
CAPITAL: Baghdad
POPULATION: 31.5 million
TOTAL AREA: 168,753 sq. miles (437,072 sq. km)
DENSITY: 187 people per sq. mile

LANGUAGES: Arabic*, Kurdish*, Turkic languages, Armenian, Assyrian
RELIGIONS: Shi'a Muslim 60%, Sunni Muslim 35%, other (including Christian) 5%
ETHNIC MIX: Arab 80%, Kurdish 15%, Turkmen 3%, other 2%
GOVERNMENT: Parliamentary system
CURRENCY: New Iraqi dinar = 1000 fils

Ireland

In the Atlantic Ocean off the west coast of Britain, the Irish Republic governs about 85% of the island of Ireland, with the remainder (Northern Ireland) being part of the UK.

GEOGRAPHY

Low mountain ranges along an irregular coastline surround an inland plain punctuated by lakes, undulating hills, and peat bogs.

CLIMATE

The Gulf Stream accounts for the mild and wet climate. Snow is rare, except in the mountains.

PEOPLE & SOCIETY

Though homogeneous in ethnicity and Roman Catholic by religion, society has undergone a major generational change, liberalizing birth control, divorce, abortion, and general attitudes. Traditionally an emigrant nation, there is now net immigration. The Good Friday peace agreement over Northern Ireland was reached in 1998.

INSIGHT: *About 40% of Irish people can speak Irish Gaelic*

THE ECONOMY

Efficient agriculture, electronics, and food-processing industries. Rapid growth until 2008: housing bubble burst, banks faltered. Large EU bailouts to avoid bankruptcy. Struggling with budget deficit.

1000m/3281ft
500m/1640ft
200m/656ft
Sea Level

FACTFILE

OFFICIAL NAME: Ireland
DATE OF FORMATION: 1922
CAPITAL: Dublin
POPULATION: 4.6 million
TOTAL AREA: 27,135 sq. miles (70,280 sq. km)
DENSITY: 173 people per sq. mile

LANGUAGES: English*, Irish Gaelic*
RELIGIONS: Roman Catholic 87%, other and nonreligious 10%, Anglican 3%
ETHNIC MIX: Irish 99%, other 1%
GOVERNMENT: Parliamentary system
CURRENCY: Euro = 100 cents

Israel

Created as a new state in 1948, Israel lies on the eastern shore of the Mediterranean. Palestinian resistance to Israeli occupation has led to years of fierce violence.

 GEOGRAPHY
Coastal plain. Desert in the south. In the east lie the Great Rift Valley and the Dead Sea – the lowest point on the Earth's land surface.

 CLIMATE
Summers are hot and dry. Wet season, March–November, is mild.

PEOPLE & SOCIETY
Large numbers of Jews settled in Palestine before Israel was founded in 1948. After World War II, there was a massive increase in immigration. Sephardi Jews from the Middle East and Mediterranean are now in the majority, but Ashkenazi Jews from central Europe still dominate business and politics. Palestinians in Gaza and Jericho gained limited autonomy in 1994 but Israeli–Palestinian talks on a two-state solution, backed by most of the world, have repeatedly foundered.

THE ECONOMY
High-tech industries, modern infrastructure, and educated workforce, but hampered by conflict and boycotts.

 INSIGHT: *All Jews worldwide have the right to Israeli citizenship*

FACTFILE

OFFICIAL NAME: State of Israel

DATE OF FORMATION: 1948

CAPITAL: Jerusalem (not internationally recognized)

POPULATION: 7.3 million

TOTAL AREA: 8019 sq. miles (20,770 sq. km)

DENSITY: 930 people per sq. mile

LANGUAGES: Hebrew*, Arabic*, Yiddish, German, Russian, Polish, Romanian, Persian

RELIGIONS: Jewish 76%, Muslim (mainly Sunni) 16%, other 4%, Christian 2%, Druze 2%

ETHNIC MIX: Jewish 76%, Arab 20%, other 4%

GOVERNMENT: Parliamentary system

CURRENCY: Shekel = 100 agorot

Italy

The Italian peninsula was home to the Roman Empire, one of the greatest ancient civilizations. The south has two famous volcanoes, Vesuvius and Etna.

GEOGRAPHY

The Appennines form the backbone of a rugged peninsula, extending from the Alps into the Mediterranean Sea. Alluvial plain in the north.

CLIMATE

Mediterranean in the south. Seasonal extremes in the mountains and on the northern alluvial plain.

PEOPLE & SOCIETY

Ethnically homogeneous, but with a gulf between the prosperous, industrial north and the poorer, agricultural south. Strong regional identities persist, especially on Sicily and Sardinia. Family ties remain strong, though the influence of the Roman Catholic Church has lessened.

◆ **INSIGHT:** *Italy was a collection of dukedoms, monarchies, and city-states before unification in the 1860s*

THE ECONOMY

World leader in industrial and product design, fashion, textiles. Strong tourism and agriculture sectors. Large public sector debt: austerity packages adopted in attempt to balance budget by 2013.

	3000m/9843ft
	2000m/6562ft
	1000m/3281ft
	500m/1640ft
	200m/656ft
	Sea Level

SWITZERLAND
AUSTRIA
SLOVENIA
Bolzano
Trieste
FRANCE
Torino
Milano
Verona
Venezia
Genova
Parma
Bologna
Rimini
Golfo di
Venezia
SAN MARINO
Pisa
Firenze
Ancona
Perugia
Adriatic Sea
ROME
VATICAN CITY
Bari
Sassari
Napoli
Taranto
Lecce
Sardegna
(Sardinia)
Salerno
Cagliari
Tyrrhenian Sea
Cosenza
Ionian Sea
Messina
Mediterranean Sea
Palermo
Sicilia
(Sicily)
Siracusa

0   100 km
0   100 miles

FACTFILE

OFFICIAL NAME: Italian Republic
DATE OF FORMATION: 1861
CAPITAL: Rome
POPULATION: 60.1 million
TOTAL AREA: 116,305 sq. miles (301,230 sq. km)
DENSITY: 529 people per sq. mile

LANGUAGES: Italian*, German, French, Rhaeto-Romanic, Sardinian
RELIGIONS: Roman Catholic 85%, other and nonreligious 13%, Muslim 2%
ETHNIC MIX: Italian 94%, other 4%, Sardinian 2%
GOVERNMENT: Parliamentary system
CURRENCY: Euro = 100 cents

Jamaica

First colonized by the Spanish and then by the English, the Caribbean island of Jamaica achieved independence in 1962. It remains an influential force in Caribbean politics.

GEOGRAPHY

Mainly mountainous, with lush tropical vegetation. Inaccessible limestone area in the northwest. Low, irregular coastal plains are broken by hills and plateaus.

CLIMATE

Tropical. Hot and humid at sea level, with temperate mountain areas. Hurricanes are likely June–November.

PEOPLE & SOCIETY

Social tensions result from vast disparities in wealth, rather than race. Economic and political life is dominated by a few wealthy, long-established families. Many women hold senior positions in public life. Armed crime, much of it narcotics-related, is a problem. Large areas of Kingston, which have their own patois, are ruled by violent gangs. Jamaican music styles are influential worldwide.

THE ECONOMY

Major bauxite producer, though sector vulnerable to changes in world prices. Tourism and light industry. Sugar, bananas, coffee, and rum are exported. Debt burden dominates budget. High underemployment.

INSIGHT: *Jamaica's Rastafarians revere the late emperor of Ethiopia, Haile Selassie, as their spiritual leader, and see Africa as their spiritual home*

FACTFILE

OFFICIAL NAME: Jamaica
DATE OF FORMATION: 1962
CAPITAL: Kingston
POPULATION: 2.7 million
TOTAL AREA: 4243 sq. miles (10,990 sq. km)
DENSITY: 646 people per sq. mile
LANGUAGES: English Creole, English*

RELIGIONS: Other and nonreligious 45%, other Protestant 20%, Church of God 18%, Baptist 10%, Anglican 7%
ETHNIC MIX: Black African 91%, *Mulatto* (mixed race) 7%, European and Chinese 1%, East Indian 1%
GOVERNMENT: Parliamentary system
CURRENCY: Jamaican dollar = 100 cents

Japan

Japan is located off the east Asian coast and comprises four principal islands and over 3000 smaller ones. A powerful economy, it has an emperor as ceremonial head of state.

GEOGRAPHY

The terrain is predominantly mountainous, with fertile coastal plains; over two-thirds is woodland. There is no single continuous mountain range; the mountains divide into many small land blocks separated by lowlands and dissected by numerous river valleys. The islands lie on the Pacific "Ring of Fire," and earthquakes and volcanic eruptions are frequent. The Pacific coast is vunerable to *tsunamis*. There are numerous hot springs.

CLIMATE

Generally temperate–oceanic. Spring is warm and sunny, while summer is hot and humid, with high rainfall. In western Hokkaido and northwest Honshu, winters are very cold, with heavy snowfall. Freak storms and damaging floods in recent years have raised concern over global climate changes.

PEOPLE & SOCIETY

One of the most racially homogeneous societies in the world. A sense of order and social structure was founded on a strongly ingrained respect for elders and social superiors. In business, this underpinned the now much-diluted "lifetime employer" concept, where company allegiance determined social life as well as career. There is little tradition of generational rebellion, but the youth market is powerful and current fashions focus on teenagers. The education system is highly pressurized. Nongraduates have difficulty reaching management-level jobs, so competition for university places is intense. Long-term jobs for women are now the norm. One of the world's best healthcare systems and increased longevity have led to an aging population, with one in five people already over 65. The cost of living is high, especially in Tokyo.

FACTFILE

OFFICIAL NAME: Japan
DATE OF FORMATION: 1590
CAPITAL: Tokyo
POPULATION: 127 million
TOTAL AREA: 145,882 sq. miles (377,835 sq. km)
DENSITY: 874 people per sq. mile

LANGUAGES: Japanese*, Korean, Chinese
RELIGIONS: Shinto and Buddhist 76%, Buddhist 16%, other (including Christian) 8%
ETHNIC MIX: Japanese 99%, other (mainly Korean) 1%
GOVERNMENT: Parliamentary system
CURRENCY: Yen = 100 sen

THE ECONOMY

World's third-largest economy. Market leader in high-tech electronic goods and cars. Global spread of business – especially to EU, US. Once-revolutionary management and production methods. Talent for developing ideas from abroad. Long-term research and development. Trade surplus causes international tension. Protectionism in domestic economy. Reform of financial sector obstructed by traditional economic power brokers. Major aid donor. Largest coal importer. Retreat from nuclear power after massive damage caused by 2011 earthquake and tsunami.

INSIGHT: *The Japanese are among the world's most avid newspaper readers, with daily sales around 67 million copies*

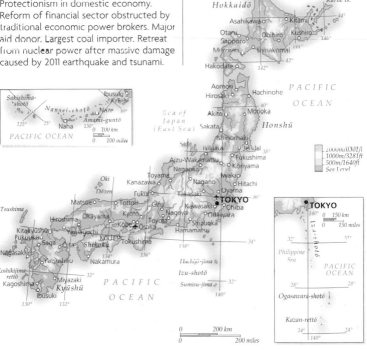

Jordan

The Kingdom of Jordan lies east of Israel, and borders the Palestinian West Bank. Its relations with its Arab neighbors are troubled by its relatively close ties to the US.

GEOGRAPHY

Mostly desert plateaus, with occasional salt pans. Lowest parts lie along the eastern shores of the Dead Sea and the Jordan River.

CLIMATE

Hot, dry summers. Cool, wet winters. Areas below sea level very hot in summer, and warm in winter.

PEOPLE & SOCIETY

Jordan is predominantly Muslim with a strong national identity, but its people have Bedouin roots. There is a Christian minority, while Palestinians who have emigrated from Israeli-occupied territory make up over a third of the population. Jordan ceded its claim to the West Bank to the aspiring Palestinian state in 1988. The monarchy's power base lies among the rural tribes, which also provide the backbone of the military. Political reforms were proposed in 2011.

THE ECONOMY

Lack of water. Exports garments, potash, fertilizers, and phosphates. Tourism hit by regional instability.

INSIGHT: *The Nabataean ruins of the ancient city of Petra attract thousands of tourists every year*

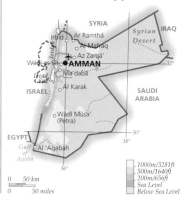

FACTFILE

OFFICIAL NAME: Hashemite Kingdom of Jordan
DATE OF FORMATION: 1946
CAPITAL: Amman
POPULATION: 6.5 million
TOTAL AREA: 35,637 sq. miles (92,300 sq. km)

DENSITY: 189 people per sq. mile
LANGUAGES: Arabic*
RELIGIONS: Sunni Muslim 92%, Christian 6%, other 2%
ETHNIC MIX: Arab 98%, Circassian 1%, Armenian 1%
GOVERNMENT: Monarchy
CURRENCY: Jordanian dinar = 1000 fils

Kazakhstan

Kazakhstan was the last of the former Soviet
republics to declare independence. Foreign investment in
the oil and natural gas sector is strengthening its regional power.

GEOGRAPHY

Mainly steppe. Volga Delta and
Caspian Sea in the west. Central plateau.
Inhospitable Altai Mountains in the east.
Semidesert in the south.

CLIMATE

Dry continental. Temperature
variations between desert south and
northern steppes are large. Winters are
mildest near the Caspian Sea.

PEOPLE & SOCIETY

Kazakhstan's ethnic diversity
arose mainly from forced settlements
there during Soviet times. Since
independence, the proportion of ethnic
Russians has dropped. Many emigrated
while ethnic Kazakhs arrived from
neighboring states. Very few Kazakhs
maintain a traditional nomadic lifestyle,
but Islam and loyalty to clans remain
strong. There are significant disparities
of wealth.

THE ECONOMY

Vast mineral resources: natural gas,
oil, bismuth, uranium, and cadmium. Oil
pipelines to China and Black Sea. Many
Western investors. Wheat exported. Sale
of farmland legal only since 2003.

INSIGHT: *The Soviet-built Baykonyr
space center is still an important launch
site for international missions*

FACTFILE

OFFICIAL NAME: Republic of Kazakhstan
DATE OF FORMATION: 1991
CAPITAL: Astana
POPULATION: 15.8 million
TOTAL AREA: 1,049,150 sq. miles
(2,717,300 sq. km)
DENSITY: 15 people per sq. mile

LANGUAGES: Kazakh*, Russian, Ukrainian,
German, Uzbek, Tatar, Uighur
RELIGIONS: Muslim (mainly Sunni) 47%,
Orthodox Christian 44%, other 9%
ETHNIC MIX: Kazakh 57%, Russian 27%,
other 8%, Ukrainian 3%, Uzbek 3%, German 2%
GOVERNMENT: Presidential system
CURRENCY: Tenge = 100 tiyn

Kenya

Kenya straddles the equator on Africa's east coast. After nearly 40 years in power, the KANU party was soundly defeated in elections in 2002. Corruption is a serious issue.

GEOGRAPHY

A central plateau is divided by the Great Rift Valley. North of the equator is mainly semidesert. To the east lies a fertile coastal belt.

CLIMATE

The coast and the Great Rift Valley are hot and humid. The plateau interior is temperate. The northeastern desert is hot and dry. Rain usually falls April–May and October–November.

PEOPLE & SOCIETY

70 ethnic groups share about 40 languages. Strong clan and family links in rural areas are being weakened by urban migration. Poverty, severe drought, and years of high population growth exacerbate ethnic tensions.

INSIGHT: *Kenya has more than 50 game reserves, national parks, and marine reservations*

THE ECONOMY

Tourism: image damaged by 2008 post-election violence. Flowers, tea, and coffee. Diversified manufacturing sector. Needs food aid, especially to cope with 2011 famine. Sizable informal economy.

FACTFILE

OFFICIAL NAME: Republic of Kenya

DATE OF FORMATION: 1963

CAPITAL: Nairobi

POPULATION: 40.9 million

TOTAL AREA: 224,961 sq. miles (582,650 sq. km)

DENSITY: 187 people per sq. mile

LANGUAGES: Kiswahili*, English*, Kikuyu, Luo, Kalenjin, Kamba

RELIGIONS: Christian 80%, Muslim 10% traditional beliefs 9%, other 1%

ETHNIC MIX: Other 28%, Kikuyu 22%, Luhya 14%, Luo 14%, Kalenjin 11%, Kamba 11%

GOVERNMENT: Mixed presidential–parliamentary system

CURRENCY: Kenya shilling = 100 cents

Kiribati

Situated in the mid-Pacific, the islands adopted the name Kiribati (pronounced "Keer-ee-bus," a corruption of their former name "Gilberts") upon independence from Britain in 1979.

 GEOGRAPHY
Kiribati consists of three groups of tiny, very low-lying coral atolls scattered across 1,930,000 sq. miles (5 million sq. km) of ocean. Most of the 33 atolls have central lagoons.

 CLIMATE
Central islands have a maritime equatorial climate. Those to north and south are tropical, with constant high temperatures. There is little rainfall.

 PEOPLE & SOCIETY
Officially I-Kiribati, many local people still refer to themselves as Gilbertese. Almost all are Micronesian, apart from the inhabitants of the island of Banaba, who employed anthropologists to establish their racial distinction. Most people are poor subsistence farmers and many travel abroad to work. The islands are effectively ruled by traditional chiefs.

THE ECONOMY
Since exhaustion of Banaba's phosphate deposits in 1980, copra (dried coconut) and fish have become the main exports. Foreign aid and remittances are vital to compensate for Kiribati's isolation and lack of resources.

◆ **INSIGHT:** *In 1981, the UK paid A$10 million to Banabans for the destruction of their island by mining*

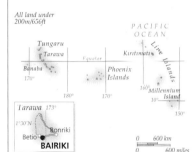

All land under 200m/656ft

PACIFIC OCEAN

Tungaru
Tarawa
Equator Kiritimati
Banaba Line Islands
170° Phoenix Islands
180° 170° 160° Millennium Island
10°
150°

Tarawa 173°
1°30'N
Bonriki
Betio
BAIRIKI

0   600 km
0   600 miles

FACTFILE

OFFICIAL NAME: Republic of Kiribati
DATE OF FORMATION: 1979
CAPITAL: Bairiki (Tarawa Atoll)
POPULATION: 100,743
TOTAL AREA: 277 sq. miles (717 sq. km)
DENSITY: 368 people per sq. mile

LANGUAGES: English^, Kiribati
RELIGIONS: Roman Catholic 55%, Kiribati Protestant Church 36%, other 9%
ETHNIC MIX: Micronesian 99%, other 1%
GOVERNMENT: Elections involving informal groupings
CURRENCY: Australian dollar = 100 cents

North Korea

Separated from the democratic South by the world's most heavily defended border, the Stalinist North Korean state has been isolated from the outside world since 1948.

 GEOGRAPHY
Mostly mountainous, with fertile plains in the southwest.

 CLIMATE
Continental. Warm summers and cold winters, especially in the north, where snow is common.

 PEOPLE & SOCIETY
Life is heavily regulated. Cult of personality is more powerful than the state-controlled religions, which include Korea's own Chondogyo. Women are expected to work and to run the home. Children are looked after in state-run crèches. The Korean Worker's Party is the sole party. Its elite have a privileged lifestyle. Globally condemned for its nuclear weapons development, its grip on power perpetuates its pariah status.

 INSIGHT: *Only the political elite are allowed phones and private cars*

THE ECONOMY
Minerals are only resource. Vital aid streams lost with global collapse of communism after 1989. Decades of economic mismanagement have led to chronic food shortages. Lack of fuel. Disproportionate defense budget.

2000m/6562ft
1000m/3281ft
500m/1640ft
200m/656ft
Sea Level

FACTFILE

OFFICIAL NAME: Democratic People's Republic of Korea
DATE OF FORMATION: 1948
CAPITAL: Pyongyang
POPULATION: 24 million
TOTAL AREA: 46,540 sq. miles (120,540 sq. km)

DENSITY: 516 people per sq. mile
LANGUAGES: Korean*
RELIGIONS: Government-controlled religions include Chondogyo, Buddhism, and Christianity
ETHNIC MIX: Korean 100%
GOVERNMENT: One-party state
CURRENCY: North Korean won = 100 chon

South Korea

South Korea occupies the southern half of the Korean peninsula. Under US sponsorship, it was separated from the communist North in 1948 and is now a capitalist economy.

 GEOGRAPHY

Over 80% is mountainous and two-thirds is forested. The flattest and most populous parts lie along the west coast and in the extreme south.

 CLIMATE

There are four distinct seasons. Winters are dry, and bitterly cold. Summers are hot and humid.

PEOPLE & SOCIETY

Inhabited for the last 2000 years by a single ethnic group. The nuclear family is replacing traditional extended households. Since the 1953 armistice, the Koreas have remained technically at war. Reunification is the ultimate goal but in 2009 the South became less conciliatory and the North retaliated by ending its offer of cooperation.

◆ **INSIGHT:** *Half of all Koreans are named Kim, Lee, Park, or Choi*

THE ECONOMY

World's biggest shipbuilder. High-tech goods and cars: rising demand from China. Strong regional competition. Aging population.

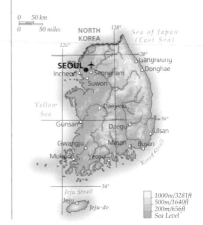

FACTFILE

OFFICIAL NAME: Republic of Korea
DATE OF FORMATION: 1948
CAPITAL: Seoul
POPULATION: 48.5 million
TOTAL AREA: 38,023 sq. miles
(98,480 sq. km)
DENSITY: 1272 people per sq. mile

LANGUAGES: Korean*
RELIGIONS: Mahayana Buddhist 47%, Protestant 38%, Roman Catholic 11%, Confucianist 3%, other 1%
ETHNIC MIX: Korean 100%
GOVERNMENT: Presidential system
CURRENCY: South Korean won = 100 chon

Kosovo

Once part of the former Yugoslav state, Kosovo seceded from Serbia in 2008. International recognition, mainly from Western countries, is strongly opposed by Serbia and Russia.

GEOGRAPHY

Landlocked and mountainous, with two plains in the east and west.

CLIMATE

Continental, with warm, sunny summers and cold, snowy winters.

PEOPLE & SOCIETY

The balance of Albanians to Serbs in Kosovo has changed dramatically over centuries, both groups suffering interethnic violence at various times. Attacks against Albanians in the late 1990s caused a million to flee. After NATO stepped in, many Serbs left: Albanians now form a 92% majority. Most Albanians are Muslim. Serbs dominate three northern provinces, which have threatened to secede.

◆ **INSIGHT:** *The UN administered Kosovo in 1999–2008 after NATO intervention to stop Serb ethnic cleansing*

THE ECONOMY

One of the two poorest countries in Europe. Aid and remittances cover a large trade deficit. Organized crime: smuggling of fuel, cigarettes, and cement. Uncertain status deters foreign investors. High unemployment. Use of euro has kept inflation low. Lignite deposits. Inefficient agriculture.

1000m/3281ft
500m/1640ft
200m/656ft

0   50 km
0   50 miles

FACTFILE

OFFICIAL NAME: Republic of Kosovo
DATE OF FORMATION: 2008
CAPITAL: Prishtinë
POPULATION: 1.83 million
TOTAL AREA: 4212 sq. miles (10,908 sq. km)
DENSITY: 433 people per sq. mile

LANGUAGES: Albanian*, Serbian*, Bosniak, Gorani, Roma, Turkish
RELIGIONS: Muslim 92%, Roman Catholic 4%, Orthodox Christian 4%
ETHNIC MIX: Albanian 92%, Serb 4%, Bosniak and Gorani 2%, Turkish 1%, Roma 1%
GOVERNMENT: Parliamentary system
CURRENCY: Euro = 100 cents

Kuwait

Kuwait lies at the northwest tip of the Gulf, dwarfed by its neighbors Iraq, Iran, and Saudi Arabia. It was a British protectorate until 1961, when full independence was granted.

GEOGRAPHY

Terrain is low-lying desert. The lowest land is in the north. Cultivation is only possible along the coast.

CLIMATE

Summers are very hot and dry. Winters are cooler, with some rain and occasional frost at night.

PEOPLE & SOCIETY

Oil-rich monarchy, ruled by the al-Sabah family. It is a conservative Sunni Muslim society, but women are relatively free. Nonetheless, a 1999 decree giving women the vote was blocked for six years in parliament by Islamic traditionalists. Immigrant workers, from other Arab states, India, and Pakistan, now outnumber native citizens. US-led forces rescued Kuwait after the 1990 Iraqi invasion, and later used it as a launchpad for the 2003 invasion to oust Saddam Hussein.

THE ECONOMY

Oil and natural gas dominate the economy. Skilled workforce, raw materials, and food are imported. High standard of living. Financial services: stock market lost 40% of value in 2008.

◆ **INSIGHT:** *During the 1991 Gulf War, Iraq deliberately set fire to 800 of Kuwait's 950 oil wells*

FACTFILE

OFFICIAL NAME: State of Kuwait
DATE OF FORMATION: 1961
CAPITAL: Kuwait City
POPULATION: 3.1 million
TOTAL AREA: 6880 sq. miles (17,820 sq. km)
DENSITY: 451 people per sq. mile

LANGUAGES: Arabic*, English
RELIGIONS: Sunni Muslim 45%, Shi'a Muslim 40%, Christian, Hindu, and other 15%
ETHNIC MIX: Kuwaiti 45%, other Arab 35%, South Asian 9%, other 7%, Iranian 4%
GOVERNMENT: Monarchy
CURRENCY: Kuwaiti dinar = 1000 fils

Kyrgyzstan

A small and mountainous landlocked state in central Asia, Kyrgyzstan is one of the least urbanized ex-Soviet republics, and was slow to develop its own sense of cultural identity.

GEOGRAPHY

The mountainous spurs of the Tien Shan range contain glaciers, alpine meadows, forests, and narrow valleys. Semidesert in the west.

CLIMATE

Varies from permanent snow and cold deserts at high altitudes, to hot deserts in low regions.

PEOPLE & SOCIETY

Ethnic Kyrgyz have only been in the majority since the late 1980s – due to a high birth rate and the emigration of ethnic Russians. Wary of losing skills vital to the economy, the government has attempted to deter Russians from leaving; concessions include making Russian an official language. There are some tensions between Kyrgyz and Uzbeks, and a trend toward greater Islamization, particularly in the poorer south.

THE ECONOMY

Mainly still under state control; corruption issues. Agriculture employs half of the labor force. Cotton, wool, meat, and tobacco exports. Mercury, gold, and antimony are mined. Great potential for hydroelectric power.

◆ **INSIGHT:** *Kyrgyz folklore is based around the 1000-year-old poem, Manas, which takes a week to recite*

FACTFILE

OFFICIAL NAME: Kyrgyz Republic
DATE OF FORMATION: 1991
CAPITAL: Bishkek
POPULATION: 5.6 million
TOTAL AREA: 76,641 sq. miles (198,500 sq. km)
DENSITY: 73 people per sq. mile

LANGUAGES: Kyrgyz*, Russian*, Uzbek, Tatar, Ukrainian
RELIGIONS: Muslim (mainly Sunni) 70%, Orthodox Christian 30%
ETHNIC MIX: Kyrgyz 69%, Uzbek 14%, Russian 9%, other 6%, Dungan 1%, Uighur 1%
GOVERNMENT: Transitional regime
CURRENCY: Som = 100 tyiyn

Laos

A French colony prior to 1953, Laos lies landlocked in southeast Asia. Heavily bombed during the Vietnam War, it fell in 1975 to communist insurgents, whose regime remains in power.

GEOGRAPHY
Largely forested mountains, broadening in the north to a plateau. Lowlands along the Mekong Valley.

CLIMATE
Monsoon rains September–May. The rest of the year is hot and dry.

PEOPLE & SOCIETY
There are over 60 ethnic groups. Lowland Laotians (Lao Loum) live along the Mekong River and are rice farmers. Upland and highland Laotians (Lao Theung and Lao Soung) traditionally employ environmentally damaging slash-and-burn farming, and grow illegal cash crops (notably opium). Government efforts to reform these practices are resisted.

◆ **INSIGHT:** *Three small Laotian kingdoms were unified under French control in 1899*

THE ECONOMY
One of world's least developed nations. Poor infrastructure. Gold, copper, electricity, timber, garments, and coffee are exported. Levels of foreign investment are rising.

FACTFILE

OFFICIAL NAME: Lao People's Democratic Republic
DATE OF FORMATION: 1953
CAPITAL: Vientiane
POPULATION: 6.4 million
TOTAL AREA: 91,428 sq. miles (236,800 sq. km)
DENSITY: 72 people per sq. mile

LANGUAGES: Lao*, Mon-Khmer, Yao, Vietnamese, Chinese, French
RELIGIONS: Buddhist 65%, other (including animist) 34%, Christian 1%
ETHNIC MIX: Lao Loum 66%, Lao Theung 30%, Lao Soung 2%, other 2%
GOVERNMENT: One-party state
CURRENCY: New kip = 100 at

Latvia

Latvia lies on the east coast of the Baltic Sea. Like its Baltic neighbors, it regained independence from Moscow in 1991, and joined the EU and NATO in 2004.

GEOGRAPHY
A flat coastal plain which is deeply indented by the Gulf of Riga. Poor drainage creates many bogs and swamps in the forested interior.

CLIMATE
Temperate, with warm summers and cold winters. There is steady rainfall throughout the year.

PEOPLE & SOCIETY
Latvians make up just over half of the population and are mostly Lutheran. They have been officially favored by the state since 1991 over the largely Orthodox Christian Russian minority. Latvian was declared the only official language in 2000 and has been used exclusively in schools since 2004. This discrimination has strained relations with neighboring Russia. Women enjoy full equality. The divorce rate is high.

THE ECONOMY
Services now account for 69% of GDP. EU's fastest-growing economy in 2004–2006. Global credit crunch brought Latvia to verge of bankruptcy in 2008: banks were bailed out, stringent austerity measures imposed. Worst recession in EU ensued, but lats remains pegged to euro.

INSIGHT: *Ethnic Latvians are outnumbered by Russians in Riga*

FACTFILE

OFFICIAL NAME: Republic of Latvia
DATE OF FORMATION: 1991
CAPITAL: Riga
POPULATION: 2.2 million
TOTAL AREA: 24,938 sq. miles (64,589 sq. km)
DENSITY: 88 people per sq. mile

LANGUAGES: Latvian*, Russian
RELIGIONS: Other 43%, Lutheran 24%, Roman Catholic 18%, Orthodox Christian 15%
ETHNIC MIX: Latvian 59%, Russian 28%, Belarussian 4%, other 4%, Ukrainian 3%, Polish 2%
GOVERNMENT: Parliamentary system
CURRENCY: Lats = 100 santimi

Lebanon

Once a vibrant cultural hotspot, Lebanon suffered badly from years of civil war and occupation until a 1989 peace deal. Reconstruction was reversed by Israeli bombardment in 2006.

GEOGRAPHY
Behind a narrow Mediterranean coastal plain, two parallel mountain ranges run the length of the country, separated by the fertile Beqaa Valley.

CLIMATE
Winters are mild and summers are hot, with high coastal humidity. Snow falls on high ground in winter.

PEOPLE & SOCIETY
Politics has long been dominated by divisions between Sunni and Shi'a Muslims and the traditional ruling Maronite Christians. Power-sharing ended 14 years of civil war in 1989. Syria acted as power broker until made to withdraw in 2005. Israel attacked in 2006 in a botched bid to crush Iran-backed Hezbollah militants. Recent short-lived governments added to instability. Huge gulf exists between the poor and a small, rich elite. Lebanon hosts over 400,000 Palestinian refugees.

THE ECONOMY
Much infrastructure destroyed. Instability undermines Beirut's role as regional financial center. Wine and fruit production. High public debt.

◆ **INSIGHT:** *The Cedar of Lebanon has been the nation's symbol for more than 2000 years*

FACTFILE

OFFICIAL NAME: Republic of Lebanon
DATE OF FORMATION: 1941
CAPITAL: Beirut
POPULATION: 4.3 million
TOTAL AREA: 4015 sq. miles (10,400 sq. km)
DENSITY: 1089 people per sq. mile

LANGUAGES: Arabic*, French, Armenian, Assyrian
RELIGIONS: Muslim 60%, Christian 39%, other 1%
ETHNIC MIX: Arab 95%, Armenian 4%, other 1%
GOVERNMENT: Parliamentary system
CURRENCY: Lebanese pound = 100 piastres

Lesotho

The landlocked Kingdom of Lesotho is entirely surrounded by – and economically dependent on – South Africa, which even sent in troops to restore calm after rioting in 1998.

GEOGRAPHY
A high mountainous plateau, cut by valleys and ravines. The Maluti Range runs through the center. The Drakensberg Range lies to the east.

CLIMATE
Temperate. Summers are hot with torrential rain storms. Snow is frequent in the mountains in winter.

PEOPLE & SOCIETY
The overwhelming majority of people are Sotho, though there are some South Asians, Europeans, and Chinese. A strong sense of national identity has tended to minimize ethnic tensions. Many men work as migrant laborers in South Africa, leaving women to run households.

◆ INSIGHT: *Lesotho has one of the highest literacy rates in Africa – but one of the highest rates of HIV/AIDS too*

THE ECONOMY
Dependent on South Africa. Water and energy exported from new Highlands Water Scheme. Subsistence farming. Garment exports struggle to compete. HIV/AIDS is depleting workforce.

3000m/9843ft
2000m/6562ft
1000m/3281ft

0   50 km
0   50 miles

FACTFILE

OFFICIAL NAME: Kingdom of Lesotho
DATE OF FORMATION: 1966
CAPITAL: Maseru
POPULATION: 2.1 million
TOTAL AREA: 11,720 sq. miles (30,355 sq. km)
DENSITY: 179 people per sq. mile

LANGUAGES: English*, Sesotho*, isiZulu
RELIGIONS: Christian 90%, traditional beliefs 10%
ETHNIC MIX: Sotho 99%, European and Asian 1%
GOVERNMENT: Parliamentary system
CURRENCY: Loti = 100 lisente

Liberia

Liberia, on Africa's Atlantic coast, was founded as a republic of freed slaves. A brutal coup in 1980 and years of civil war have left gang violence and looting widespread.

GEOGRAPHY
A coastline of beaches and mangrove swamps rises to forested plateaus and highlands inland.

CLIMATE
High temperatures. There is only one wet season, from May to October, except in the extreme southeast.

PEOPLE & SOCIETY
The key social distinction used to be between Americo-Liberians – descendants of freed slaves – and the indigenous tribal peoples. However, political assimilation and intermarriage have eased tensions. Intertribal tension is now a much more serious problem fueling the civil war which ravaged the country from 1990 to 2003.

◆ **INSIGHT:** *Liberia is named after the people liberated from slavery who arrived from the US in the 1800s*

THE ECONOMY
War caused economic collapse. Rubber is key export. Bans now lifted on timber and diamond exports. Revenue from merchant shipping licenses. Debt burden. Income well below prewar levels. Vast iron ore reserves.

FACTFILE

OFFICIAL NAME: Republic of Liberia
DATE OF FORMATION: 1847
CAPITAL: Monrovia
POPULATION: 4.1 million
TOTAL AREA: 43,000 sq. miles
(111,370 sq. km)
DENSITY: 110 people per sq. mile

LANGUAGES: Kpelle, Vai, Bassa, Kru, Grebo, Kissi, Gola, Loma, English*
RELIGIONS: Christian 40%, traditional beliefs 40%, Muslim 20%
ETHNIC MIX: Indigenous tribes (12 groups) 49%, Kpellé 20%, Bassa 16%, Gio 8%, Krou 7%
GOVERNMENT: Presidential system
CURRENCY: Liberian dollar = 100 cents

Libya

Situated on north Africa's Mediterranean coast, Libya was declared a revolutionary state in 1969 by Colonel Gaddafi. Civil war to oust his regime began during the 2011 "Arab Spring."

GEOGRAPHY

Apart from the coastal strip and a mountain range in the south, Libya is desert or semidesert.

CLIMATE

Hot and arid. The coastal area has a temperate climate, with mild, wet winters and hot, dry summers.

PEOPLE & SOCIETY

Once a nation of nomads and livestock herders, it is almost 80% urban. Revolution wiped out private enterprise and the middle classes. Jews and European settlers were banished, and Islam and African unity were promoted. Years of political marginalization and sanctions ended after Libya offered compensation for terrorist bombings and ended its Weapons of Mass Destruction (WMD) program. Rebels quickly seized the east in early 2011, but took months to reach Tripoli in spite of international assistance.

THE ECONOMY

Oil is key export. Dates, olives, and fruit grow in oases, but most food is imported. Corruption and mismanagement. Recent instability.

INSIGHT: *90% of Libya is still desert, despite grand irrigation projects*

FACTFILE

OFFICIAL NAME: Libyan Republic (post Gaddafi regime)

DATE OF FORMATION: 1951

CAPITAL: Tripoli

POPULATION: 6.5 million

TOTAL AREA: 679,358 sq. miles (1,759,540 sq. km)

DENSITY: 10 people per sq. mile

LANGUAGES: Arabic*, Tuareg

RELIGIONS: Muslim (mainly Sunni) 97%, other 3%

ETHNIC MIX: Arab and Berber 97%, other 3%

GOVERNMENT: Transitional regime

CURRENCY: Libyan dinar = 1000 dirhams

Liechtenstein

Perched in the Alps between Switzerland and Austria, the state of Liechtenstein became an independent principality of the Holy Roman Empire in 1719. It has close links with Switzerland.

GEOGRAPHY

The upper Rhine Valley covers the western third of the country. The mountains and narrow valleys of the eastern Alps make up the remainder.

CLIMATE

Warm, dry summers. Winters are cold, with heavy snow in the mountains from December to March.

PEOPLE & SOCIETY
The principality's role as a financial center accounts for its many foreign residents (a third of the population). Half of the workforce are cross-border commuters. Living standards are high, with few social tensions. Linked by a customs union since 1924, Switzerland handles Liechtenstein's foreign affairs and defense issues.

 INSIGHT: *Women in Liechtenstein obtained the vote only in 1984*

THE ECONOMY
Banking secrecy (now modified) and low taxes help attract foreign investment. Anti-money-laundering rules are recent. Diversified exports include precision instruments, dental products, and chemicals.

2000m/6562ft	
1000m/3281ft	
500m/1640ft	
200m/656ft	
Sea Level	

Ruggell
Mauren
Bendern
Planken
Schaan
AUSTRIA
VADUZ
SWITZERLAND
Triesenberg
Triesen
Balzers

0   4 km
0   4 miles

FACTFILE

OFFICIAL NAME: Principality of Liechtenstein
DATE OF FORMATION: 1719
CAPITAL: Vaduz
POPULATION: 35,236
TOTAL AREA: 62 sq. miles (160 sq. km)
DENSITY: 568 people per sq. mile

LANGUAGES: German^, Alemannish dialect, Italian
RELIGIONS: Roman Catholic 79%, other 13%, Protestant 8%
ETHNIC MIX: Liechtensteiner 66%, other 12%, Swiss 10%, Austrian 6%, German 3%, Italian 3%
GOVERNMENT: Parliamentary system
CURRENCY: Swiss franc = 100 rappen/centimes

Lithuania

Lying on the eastern coast of the Baltic Sea, Lithuania is the largest of the Baltic states. The first Soviet republic to declare independence from Moscow in 1991, it joined the EU in 2004.

GEOGRAPHY
Mostly flat with moors, bogs, and an intensively farmed central lowland. Numerous lakes and forested sandy ridges in the east.

CLIMATE
Coastal location moderates continental extremes. Cold winters, cool summers, and steady rainfall.

PEOPLE & SOCIETY
Homogeneous population, with Lithuanians forming a large majority. Only 3500 Jews, known as Litvaks, remain in Lithuania. Strong Roman Catholic tradition and historic links with Poland. There are better relations among ethnic groups than in other Baltic states and interethnic marriages are fairly common. However, ethnic Russians and Poles see a threat from "Lithuanianization." A large income gap has grown since independence.

THE ECONOMY
High-tech and heavy industries: engineering, shipbuilding, food processing. Bounced back from deep recession in 2009. Litas pegged to euro. Inflation and debt levels delaying euro's adoption.

INSIGHT: *The "amber coast" of Lithuania produces most of the world's amber – fossilized resin*

FACTFILE

OFFICIAL NAME: Republic of Lithuania

DATE OF FORMATION: 1991

CAPITAL: Vilnius

POPULATION: 3.3 million

TOTAL AREA: 25,174 sq. miles (65,200 sq. km)

DENSITY: 131 people per sq. mile

LANGUAGES: Lithuanian*, Russian

RELIGIONS: Roman Catholic 79%, other 15%, Russian Orthodox 4%, Protestant 2%

ETHNIC MIX: Lithuanian 85%, Polish 6%, Russian 5%, other 3%, Belarussian 1%

GOVERNMENT: Parliamentary system

CURRENCY: Litas = 100 centu

Luxembourg

Part of the plateau of the Ardennes in western Europe, Luxembourg is one of Europe's richest states. A tax haven and banking center, it is also home to key EU institutions.

GEOGRAPHY
Dense Ardennes forests in the north, with a low, open plateau to the south. Undulating terrain throughout.

CLIMATE
The climate is moist, with warm summers and mild winters. Snow is common only in the Ardennes.

PEOPLE & SOCIETY
Ethnic tensions are rare, despite a large proportion of foreigners (over a third of residents). Integration has been straightforward; most are fellow western Europeans and Catholics, mainly from Italy and Portugal. Low unemployment and high salaries promote stability. Divorce rates are rising and marriage is becoming less common.

◆ **INSIGHT:** Luxembourg's capital is home to around 2000 investment funds and over 150 banks

THE ECONOMY
Traditional industries such as steelmaking have given way to the banking and service sectors. Low taxes and banking secrecy laws attract foreign investors.

500m/1640ft
200m/656ft
Sea Level

Clervaux
GERMANY
Ettelbrück
Echternach
Mersch
BELGIUM
●LUXEMBOURG
Pétange
Differdange
Esch-sur-Alzette
Dudelange
FRANCE

0   10 km
0   10 miles

FACTFILE

OFFICIAL NAME: Grand Duchy of Luxembourg

DATE OF FORMATION: 1867

CAPITAL: Luxembourg-Ville

POPULATION: 500,000

TOTAL AREA: 998 sq. miles (2586 sq. km)

DENSITY: 501 people per sq. mile

LANGUAGES: Luxembourgish*, German*, French*

RELIGIONS: Roman Catholic 97%, Protestant, Orthodox Christian, and Jewish 3%

ETHNIC MIX: Luxembourger 62%, foreign residents 38%

GOVERNMENT: Parliamentary system

CURRENCY: Euro = 100 cents

Macedonia

 Landlocked Macedonia was hit hard by the sanctions placed on its northern trading partners in the mid-1990s, and by violent conflict with ethnic Albanians in 2001.

GEOGRAPHY
Mainly mountainous or hilly, with deep river basins in the center. Plains in the northeast and southwest.

CLIMATE
Continental climate with wet springs and dry autumns. Heavy snowfalls in northern mountains.

PEOPLE & SOCIETY
Slav Macedonians are mostly Orthodox Christians, with some Muslims. Officially, Muslim Albanians account for 25% of the population, but they claim to number a third. In 2001 Albanian militants fought a bitter war against the government. A peace deal promised greater equality. A major stumbling block to EU and NATO accession is Greece's objection to the name Macedonia, in order to prevent any possibility of claims to historic "Macedonian" lands in north Greece.

THE ECONOMY
Steel, minerals, clothing, shoes, and tobacco exported. Slow transition to market economy. Organized crime and large gray economy. Investment boosted by EU candidate status.

◆ **INSIGHT:** *Ohrid is the deepest lake in Europe at 964 ft (294 m)*

FACTFILE

OFFICIAL NAME: Republic of Macedonia
DATE OF FORMATION: 1991
CAPITAL: Skopje
POPULATION: 2 million
TOTAL AREA: 9781 sq. miles (25,333 sq. km)
DENSITY: 201 people per sq. mile
LANGUAGES: Macedonian*, Albanian*, Turkish, Romani, Serbian
RELIGIONS: Orthodox Christian 65%, Muslim 29%, Roman Catholic 4%, other 2%
ETHNIC MIX: Macedonian 64%, Albanian 25%, Turkish 4%, Roma 3%, Serb 2%, other 2%
GOVERNMENT: Mixed presidential–parliamentary system
CURRENCY: Macedonian denar = 100 deni

Madagascar

Lying off east Africa in the Indian Ocean, the former French colony of Madagascar is the world's fourth-largest island. Power struggles erupted onto the streets in 2002 and 2009.

GEOGRAPHY

More than two-thirds of the country forms a savanna-covered plateau, which drops in the east through rainforests to the coast.

CLIMATE

Tropical and often hit by cyclones. Monsoons affect the east coast. The southwest is much drier.

PEOPLE & SOCIETY

People are Malay-Indonesian in origin, intermixed with later migrants from the African mainland. The main ethnic division is between the Merina of the central plateau and the poorer côtier (coastal) peoples. The Merina were the country's historic rulers, and remain the social elite.

◆ **INSIGHT:** *80% of Madagascar's plants and many of its animal species are found nowhere else*

THE ECONOMY

Most people are farmers. Cash crops are vanilla, coffee, and cloves. Garments and shrimp also exported. Political crises deter investors.

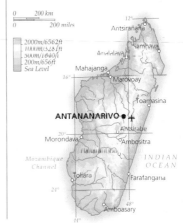

FACTFILE

OFFICIAL NAME: Republic of Madagascar

DATE OF FORMATION: 1960

CAPITAL: Antananarivo

POPULATION: 20.1 million

TOTAL AREA: 226,656 sq. miles (587,040 sq. km)

DENSITY: 90 people per sq. mile

LANGUAGES: Malagasy*, French*, English*

RELIGIONS: Traditional beliefs 52%, Christian (mainly Roman Catholic) 41%, Muslim 7%

ETHNIC MIX: Other Malay 46%, Merina 26%, Betsimisaraka 15%, Betsileo 12%, other 1%

GOVERNMENT: Transitional regime

CURRENCY: Ariary = 5 iraimbilanja

Malawi

A former colony of the UK, Malawi lies landlocked in southeast Africa, following the Great Rift Valley. Its name means "the land where the sun is reflected in the water like fire."

GEOGRAPHY

Lake Nyasa takes up one-fifth of the landscape. Highlands lie west of the lake. Much of the land is covered by forests and savanna.

CLIMATE

Mainly subtropical. The south is hot and humid. Highlands are cooler.

PEOPLE & SOCIETY

Most Malawians share a common Bantu origin. Unlike neighboring states, ethnicity has not been exploited for political ends. Multiparty elections in 1994 ended the 30-year dictatorship of Dr. Banda; a Muslim won the presidency, signaling that Banda's attempts to enforce Protestant dominance had failed. Around half of the population lives in poverty.

◆ INSIGHT: Lake Nyasa is 353 miles (568 km) in length and contains at least 500 species of fish

THE ECONOMY

Mainly subsistence farming. Tobacco accounts for half of export earnings. Tea and sugar are grown. Drought and corruption are problems.

FACTFILE

OFFICIAL NAME: Republic of Malawi
DATE OF FORMATION: 1964
CAPITAL: Lilongwe
POPULATION: 15.7 million
TOTAL AREA: 45,745 sq. miles (118,480 sq. km)
DENSITY: 432 people per sq. mile

LANGUAGES: Chewa, Lomwe, Yao, Ngoni, English*
RELIGIONS: Protestant 55%, Muslim 20%, Roman Catholic 20%, traditional beliefs 5%
ETHNIC MIX: Bantu 99%, other 1%
GOVERNMENT: Presidential system
CURRENCY: Malawi kwacha = 100 tambala

Malaysia

Malaysia stretches 1240 miles (2000 km) across southeast Asia from the Malay peninsula to Sabah in eastern Borneo. Federated in 1963, it included Singapore for two years.

GEOGRAPHY
The Malay Peninsula has central mountains, an eastern coastal belt, and fertile western plains. Swampy coastal plains rise to mountains on Borneo.

CLIMATE
Warm equatorial. Rainfall always heavy, but with distinct rainy seasons.

◆ **INSIGHT:** *Malaysia is southeast Asia's major tourist destination, with over 22 million visitors a year*

PEOPLE & SOCIETY
The key distinction is between Malays (Bumiputras, literally "sons of the soil") and the Chinese, who traditionally controlled most economic activity. Since the 1970s, Malays have been favored for education and jobs, in order to address this imbalance.

THE ECONOMY
Successful industrial base includes electronics, manufacturing, and heavy industry. Tourism is a major earner. Leading producer of palm oil, tin, and tropical hardwoods.

FACTFILE

OFFICIAL NAME: Federation of Malaysia
DATE OF FORMATION: 1963
CAPITALS: Kuala Lumpur; Putrajaya (administrative)
POPULATION: 27.9 million
TOTAL AREA: 127,316 sq. miles (329,750 sq. km)
DENSITY: 220 people per sq. mile

LANGUAGES: Bahasa Malaysia*, Malay, Chinese, Tamil, English
RELIGIONS: Muslim 61%, Buddhist 19%, Christian 9%, Hindu 6%, other 5%
ETHNIC MIX: Malay 53%, Chinese 26%, indigenous tribes 12%, Indian 8%, other 1%
GOVERNMENT: Parliamentary system
CURRENCY: Ringgit = 100 sen

Maldives

Set in the Indian Ocean, southwest of Sri Lanka, the Maldives is an archipelago of 1191 small coral islands, or atolls. 200 are inhabited. The word atoll comes from the Dhivehi word "atolu."

GEOGRAPHY
Consists of low-lying islands and coral atolls. The larger ones are covered in lush, tropical vegetation.

CLIMATE
Tropical. Rain falls throughout the year, but is heaviest June–November, during the monsoon. Violent storms occasionally hit the northern islands.

PEOPLE & SOCIETY
Maldivians, who are all Sunni Muslim, are descended from Sinhalese, Dravidian, Arab, and black ancestors. About 25% of the population live on Male'. Tourism has grown on separate resort islands away from residents. Politics has been controlled by a small group of influential families. However, a young elite pushed for reform: parties were legalized in 2005, and the presidential election in 2008 brought in a new regime.

THE ECONOMY
The fluctuating tourist industry is the economic mainstay. Fish, especially tuna, are the main export. Construction boom to repair 2004 tsunami damage.

INSIGHT:
The islands, which all lie below 4 ft (1.2 m), are threatened by rising sea levels, brought about by global warming and climatic changes

Ihavandippolhu Atoll

Faadhippolhu Atoll

Horsburgh Atoll

Male' Atoll

Ari Atoll

MALE'

Felidhu Atoll

Mulakatholhu Atoll

Kolhumadulu Atoll

Hadhdhunmathi Atoll

One and Half Degree Channel

INDIAN OCEAN

North Huvadhu Atoll

South Huvadhu Atoll

Equator

☐ Sea Level

0   100 km
0   100 miles

Addu Atoll
Gan

73°

6°

FACTFILE

OFFICIAL NAME: Republic of Maldives
DATE OF FORMATION: 1965
CAPITAL: Male'
POPULATION: 300,000
TOTAL AREA: 116 sq. miles (300 sq. km)
DENSITY: 2586 people per sq. mile

LANGUAGES: Dhivehi* (Maldivian), Sinhala, Tamil, Arabic
RELIGIONS: Sunni Muslim 100%
ETHNIC MIX: All Maldivians are of Arab–Sinhalese–Malay descent
GOVERNMENT: Presidential system
CURRENCY: Rufiyaa = 100 laari

Mali

A former French colony, Mali is landlocked in the heart of west Africa. The 1991 coup ended the 23-year dictatorship of Moussa Traoré and ushered in multiparty elections from 1992.

GEOGRAPHY
The northern half lies in the Sahara. The inland delta of the Niger River flows through grassy savanna in the south.

CLIMATE
In the south, intensely hot, dry weather precedes the westerly rains. The north is almost rainless.

PEOPLE & SOCIETY
Most people live in the southern savanna region and are farmers, herders, or river fishermen. The Bambara tribe are culturally and politically dominant. A few nomadic Fulani and Tuareg herders travel the northern plains. There is tension between the peoples of the south and Tuareg in the north. Women have little status; improving rights is controversial.

INSIGHT: *Tombouctou (Timbuktu) was the center of the 14th-century Malinké trading empire*

THE ECONOMY
Widespread poverty. Less than 2% of land can be cultivated. Vulnerable to drought. Gold, high-quality cotton, and livestock account for 90% of exports. Tourism potential, but recent Al-Qaeda in the Maghreb kidnappings are a deterrent.

FACTFILE

OFFICIAL NAME: Republic of Mali

DATE OF FORMATION: 1960

CAPITAL: Bamako

POPULATION: 13.3 million

TOTAL AREA: 478,764 sq. miles (1,240,000 sq. km)

DENSITY: 28 people per sq. mile

LANGUAGES: Bambara, Fulani, Senufo, Soninke, French*

RELIGIONS: Muslim (mainly Sunni) 90%, traditional beliefs 6%, Christian 4%

ETHNIC MIX: Bambara 52%, other 18%, Fulani 11%, Saracolé 7%, Soninka 7%, Tuareg 5%

GOVERNMENT: Presidential system

CURRENCY: CFA franc = 100 centimes

Malta

The densely populated Maltese archipelago lies between Africa and Europe. Controlled throughout its history by successive colonial powers, it gained independence from the UK in 1964.

GEOGRAPHY

The main island of Malta has low hills and a ragged coastline with numerous harbors, bays, sandy beaches, and rocky coves. The island of Gozo is more densely vegetated.

CLIMATE

Mediterranean climate. There are many hours of sunshine all year round, with very little rainfall.

PEOPLE & SOCIETY

Over the centuries, the Maltese have been subject to Arab, Sicilian, Spanish, French, and British influences. Today, the population is socially conservative and devoutly Roman Catholic – Malta only legalized divorce in 2011, the last European country except the Vatican to do so. Unemployment is high, particularly for women. Illegal migration from Africa has increased since Malta joined the EU in 2004.

THE ECONOMY

Tourism provides 25% of GDP. Joined eurozone in 2008. Developing offshore banking, high-tech industry. Semiconductors exported. Most goods have to be imported.

INSIGHT: *The Maltese language has Phoenician origins but features Arabic etymology and intonation*

FACTFILE

OFFICIAL NAME: Republic of Malta
DATE OF FORMATION: 1964
CAPITAL: Valletta
POPULATION: 400,000
TOTAL AREA: 122 sq. miles
(316 sq. km)
DENSITY: 3226 people per sq. mile

LANGUAGES: Maltese*, English*
RELIGIONS: Roman Catholic 98%, other and nonreligious 2%
ETHNIC MIX: Maltese 96%, other 4%
GOVERNMENT: Parliamentary system
CURRENCY: Euro = 100 cents

Marshall Islands

Under US rule as part of the UN Trust Territory of the Pacific Islands until independence in 1986, the Marshall Islands comprises a group of 34 widely scattered atolls.

GEOGRAPHY
Narrow coral rings with sandy beaches enclosing lagoons. Those in the south have thicker vegetation. Kwajalein is the world's largest atoll.

CLIMATE
Tropical oceanic, cooled year round by northeast trade winds.

PEOPLE & SOCIETY
Majuro, the capital city and commercial center, is home to almost half the population. Tensions are high due to poor living conditions. Life on the outlying islands is still traditional, based around subsistence agriculture and fishing. Society is matrilineal, with land and titles handed down through the mother's clan.

INSIGHT: *In 1954, Bikini Atoll was the site for the testing of the largest US H bomb – the 18. 22 megaton Bravo*

THE ECONOMY
Almost totally dependent on US aid and the rent paid by the US for its missile base on Kwajalein Atoll. High unemployment. Revenue from licenses to fish in Marshallese waters for tuna. Copra and coconut oil are the only significant agricultural exports.

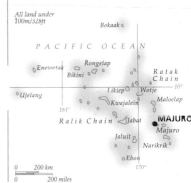

All land under 100m/328ft

PACIFIC OCEAN

Bokaak

Enewetak Rongelap
Bikini

Ujelang   Likiep   Wotje   Ratak Chain
           Kwajalein   Maloelap
161°   Ralik Chain   Jabat   MAJURO
                          Majuro
           Jaluit
                         Narikrik

Ebon

10°

170°

0   200 km
0   200 miles

FACTFILE

OFFICIAL NAME: Republic of the Marshall Islands

DATE OF FORMATION: 1986

CAPITAL: Majuro

POPULATION: 67,182

TOTAL AREA: 70 sq. miles (181 sq. km)

DENSITY: 960 people per sq. mile

LANGUAGES: Marshallese*, English*, Japanese, German

RELIGIONS: Protestant 90%, Roman Catholic 8%, other 2%

ETHNIC MIX: Micronesian 90%, other 10%

GOVERNMENT: Presidential system

CURRENCY: US dollar = 100 cents

Mauritania

Two-thirds of Mauritania's territory is desert – the only productive land is that drained by the Senegal River. The country has taken a strongly Arab direction since 1964.

 GEOGRAPHY

The Sahara, barren except for some scattered oases, covers the north. Savanna lands lie to the south.

 CLIMATE

The climate is generally hot and dry, aggravated by the dusty *harmattan* wind. Summer rain in the south, virtually none in the north.

PEOPLE & SOCIETY

The Maures control political and economic life. Family solidarity among nomadic peoples is particularly strong. Ethnic tension centers on the oppression of the black minority. Tens of thousands of blacks are estimated to be in illegal slavery. Coups have interrupted civilian rule in recent years.

 INSIGHT: *Slavery officially became illegal in Mauritania in 1980, but de facto slavery still persists*

THE ECONOMY

Agriculture and herding. Iron, copper, and gold mining. World's largest gypsum deposits. Offshore oil from 2006. Rich fishing grounds.

500m/1640ft
200m/656ft
Sea Level

ALGERIA

WESTERN SAHARA

Zouérat

Sahara

Nouâdhibou

Atâr

MALI

ATLANTIC OCEAN

Tidjikja

NOUAKCHOTT

Rosso

Kaédi   Kiffa

Néma

Senegal

SENEGAL

MALI

0   200 km
0   200 miles

FACTFILE

OFFICIAL NAME: Islamic Republic of Mauritania

DATE OF FORMATION: 1960

CAPITAL: Nouakchott

POPULATION: 3.4 million

TOTAL AREA: 397,953 sq. miles (1,030,700 sq. km)

DENSITY: 9 people per sq. mile

LANGUAGES: Hassaniyah Arabic*, Wolof, French

RELIGIONS: Sunni Muslim 100%

ETHNIC MIX: Maure 81%, Wolof 7%, Tukolor 5%, other 4%, Soninka 3%

GOVERNMENT: Presidential system

CURRENCY: Ouguiya = 5 khoums

Mauritius

The islands that make up Mauritius lie in the Indian Ocean east of Madagascar. They have enjoyed considerable economic success following recent industrial diversification and expansion.

GEOGRAPHY

The volcanic main island of Mauritius is ringed by coral reefs, and rises from the coast to a fertile central plateau. The outer islands – Rodriguez, the Agalega Islands, and the Cargados Carajos Shoals – lie some 300 miles (500 km) to the north.

CLIMATE

Warm and humid. Tropical storms are frequent December–March, the hottest and wettest months.

PEOPLE & SOCIETY

Most people are descendants of laborers brought over from India in the 19th century. A small minority of French descent form the wealthiest group. Creoles (descendants of African slaves) complain of discrimination. Literacy is high. Health care is free. Criminal offenses are usually traffic-related; little crime on outer islands.

THE ECONOMY

Clothing manufacture, tourism, and sugar. Loss of preferential trade terms for sugar and textiles. Offshore financial center. New outsourcing and ICT industries. Most food is imported.

INSIGHT: *The islands form part of the Mascarene Archipelago – once a land bridge between Asia and Africa*

FACTFILE

OFFICIAL NAME: Republic of Mauritius
DATE OF FORMATION: 1968
CAPITAL: Port Louis
POPULATION: 1.3 million
TOTAL AREA: 718 sq. miles (1860 sq. km)
DENSITY: 1811 people per sq. mile
LANGUAGES: French Creole, Hindi, Urdu, Tamil, Chinese, English*, French
RELIGIONS: Hindu 48%, Roman Catholic 24%, Muslim 17%, Protestant 9%, other 2%
ETHNIC MIX: Indo-Mauritian 68%, Creole 27%, Sino-Mauritian 3%, Franco-Mauritian 2%
GOVERNMENT: Parliamentary system
CURRENCY: Mauritian rupee = 100 cents

Mexico

Mexico stretches from the US border southward into the ancient Aztec and Mayan heartlands. Independence from Spain came in 1836. One in five Mexicans lives in the sprawling capital.

GEOGRAPHY

Coastal plains along the Pacific and Atlantic seaboards rise to a high arid central plateau. To the east and west are the Sierra Madre mountain ranges. Limestone lowlands form the projecting Yucatan peninsula.

CLIMATE

The plateau and high mountains are warm for much of the year. Pacific coast is tropical: storms occur mostly March–December. Northwest is dry.

PEOPLE & SOCIETY

Most Mexicans are *mestizos* of Spanish–Amerindian descent. Rural Amerindians are largely segregated from Hispanic society and most live in poverty, though the state promotes their culture. The Zapatista movement backs indigenous rights. Few women in male-dominated politics and business. Narcotics-related violent crime is rising.

THE ECONOMY

One of world's largest oil producers. Corn, fruit, vegetables, sugar are cash crops. NAFTA has boosted exports, but exposes farmers to subsidized US competition. Wealth disparity. Bounced back from 2008–2009 global downturn and swine flu crisis.

◆ INSIGHT: *More people cross the US–Mexican border each year – illegally or legally – than any other border in the world*

FACTFILE

OFFICIAL NAME: United Mexican States
DATE OF FORMATION: 1836
CAPITAL: Mexico City
POPULATION: 111 million
TOTAL AREA: 761,602 sq. miles
(1,972,550 sq. km
DENSITY: 150 people per sq. mile

LANGUAGES: Spanish*, Nahuatl, Mayan, Zapotec, Mixtec, Otomi, Totonac, Tzotzil
RELIGIONS: Roman Catholic 77%, other 14%, Protestant 6%, nonreligious 3%
ETHNIC MIX: *Mestizo* 60%, Amerindian 30%, European 9%, other 1%
GOVERNMENT: Presidential system
CURRENCY: Mexican peso = 100 centavos

Micronesia

The Federated States of Micronesia (FSM), situated in the western Pacific, comprise 607 islands and atolls grouped into four main island states: Pohnpei, Kosrae, Chuuk, and Yap.

GEOGRAPHY
Mixture of high volcanic islands with forested interiors, and low-lying coral atolls. Some of the islands have coastal mangrove swamps.

CLIMATE
Tropical, with high humidity. There is very heavy rainfall outside the January–March dry season.

◆ **INSIGHT:** *Chuuk's lagoon contains the sunken wrecks of over 100 Japanese ships and 270 planes from World War II*

PEOPLE & SOCIETY
Micronesians are physically, culturally, and linguistically diverse. Melanesians live on Yap, Polynesians in Pohnpei. The supply of electricity and running water is limited. Society is based on matrilineal clans.

THE ECONOMY
Dependent on US aid. Fishing licenses are a key source of foreign revenue. Tourism, fishing, betel nuts, copra are economic mainstays. Trust fund created to reduce aid reliance.

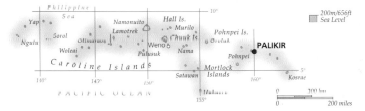

FACTFILE

OFFICIAL NAME: Federated States of Micronesia

DATE OF FORMATION: 1986

CAPITAL: Palikir (Pohnpei Island)

POPULATION: 106,836

TOTAL AREA: 271 sq. miles (702 sq. km)

DENSITY: 394 people per sq. mile

LANGUAGES: Trukese, Pohnpeian, Kosraean, Yapese, English*

RELIGIONS: Roman Catholic 50%, Protestant 47%, other 3%

ETHNIC MIX: Chuukese 49%, Pohnpeian 24%, other 14%, Kosraean 6%, Yapese 5%, Asian 2%

GOVERNMENT: Nonparty system

CURRENCY: US dollar = 100 cents

Moldova

The most densely populated of the former Soviet republics, Moldova has strong ethnic, linguistic, and cultural links with Romania, but relations with Russia remain paramount.

GEOGRAPHY

Steppes and hilly plains are drained by the Dniester and Prut rivers.

CLIMATE

Warm summers and relatively mild winters. Moderate rainfall is evenly spread throughout the year.

PEOPLE & SOCIETY

A shared heritage with Romania defines national identity, though in 1994 Moldovans voted against possible reunification with Romania. Most of the population is engaged in intensive agriculture. Transnistria is a breakaway state along the east bank of the Dniester, home to a largely ethnic Slav population. The Gagauz, in the south, have accepted autonomy.

◆ **INSIGHT:** *Vast underground wine vaults contain entire "streets" of bottles built into rock quarries*

THE ECONOMY

One of the two poorest countries in Europe. Mainly agricultural: produces wine, tobacco, fruit. Food processing and textiles. Depends on Russia for raw materials, fuel, exports. Instability.

FACTFILE

OFFICIAL NAME: Republic of Moldova
DATE OF FORMATION: 1991
CAPITAL: Chisinau
POPULATION: 3.6 million
TOTAL AREA: 13,067 sq. miles (33,843 sq. km)
DENSITY: 277 people per sq. mile

LANGUAGES: Moldovan*, Ukrainian, Russian
RELIGIONS: Orthodox Christian 93%, other 6%, Baptist 1%
ETHNIC MIX: Moldovan 84%, Ukrainian 7%, Gagauz 5%, Russian 2%, Bulgarian 1%, other 1%
GOVERNMENT: Parliamentary system
CURRENCY: Moldovan leu = 100 bani

Monaco

Monaco is a tiny principality on the Côte d'Azur. Its destiny changed radically when the casino was opened in 1863. Today, it promotes its image as an upmarket, glamorous destination.

GEOGRAPHY

A rocky promontory overlooking a narrow coastal strip that has been enlarged through land reclamation.

CLIMATE
Mediterranean. Summers are hot and dry; days with 12 hours of sunshine are not uncommon. Winters are mild and sunny.

PEOPLE & SOCIETY

Less than 20% of residents are Monégasques. Almost half are French, the rest Italian, American, British, Belgian, and others. Nationals enjoy considerable privileges, including housing subsidies to protect them from Monaco's high property prices, and the right of first refusal before a job can be offered to a foreigner. Women have equal status, but only acquired the vote in 1962. Prince Albert married South African swimmer Charlene Wittstock in 2011.

THE ECONOMY
Tourism, gambling, financial services. Banking secrecy laws and tax-haven conditions attract foreign investment. Close links and customs union with France (but not in EU). No resources: depends on imports.

◆ **INSIGHT:** *High-profile social and sporting events attract large crowds each spring, including the Rose Ball, Tennis Open, and Grand Prix*

FACTFILE

OFFICIAL NAME: Principality of Monaco
DATE OF FORMATION: 1861
CAPITAL: Monaco-Ville
POPULATION: 30,539
TOTAL AREA: 0.75 sq. miles (1.95 sq. km)
DENSITY: 40,719 people per sq. mile

LANGUAGES: French*, Italian, Monégasque, English
RELIGIONS: Roman Catholic 89%, Protestant 6%, other 5%
ETHNIC MIX: French 47%, other 21%, Italian 16%, Monégasque 16%
GOVERNMENT: Mixed monarchical–parliamentary system
CURRENCY: Euro = 100 cents

Mongolia

Landlocked between Russia and China, Mongolia is a huge, isolated, and sparsely populated nation. Over two-thirds of the country is part of the Gobi Desert.

 GEOGRAPHY

A mountainous steppe plateau in the north, with lakes in the north and west. The desert region of the Gobi dominates the south.

 CLIMATE

Continental. Mild summers and long, dry, very cold winters, with heavy snowfall. Temperatures can drop as low as −22°F (−30°C).

 PEOPLE & SOCIETY

Mongolia was unified by Genghis Khan in 1206 and was later absorbed into Manchu China. A majority of ethnic Mongolians live within China in Inner Mongolia. Tibetan Buddhism dominates. The traditional, nomadic way of life has been eroded as urban migration continues, spurred by ferocious winters, known as zud, which can devastate the rural economy.

THE ECONOMY

Rich deposits of oil, coal, copper, uranium, and other minerals remain largely untapped. Cashmere exports. Democracy, from 1990, brought a shift toward a market economy, but also rising poverty. State involvement in mining is an issue. Agriculture uses 40% of workforce, mainly as herders.

 INSIGHT: *Horseracing, wrestling, and archery are the national sports*

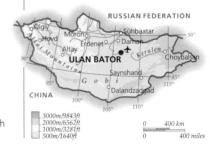

RUSSIAN FEDERATION

Ölgiy • Hovd • Mörön • Sühbaatar • Erdenet • Darhan • Altay • 50°
ULAN BATOR • Kerulen • Choybalsan
Altai Mountains • Saynshand • 45°
Gobi • Dalandzadgad • 115°
CHINA • 100° • 105° • 110°
90° • 95°

| 3000m/9843ft |
| 2000m/6562ft |
| 1000m/3281ft |
| 500m/1640ft |

0   400 km
0   400 miles

FACTFILE

OFFICIAL NAME: Mongolia
DATE OF FORMATION: 1924
CAPITAL: Ulan Bator
POPULATION: 2.7 million
TOTAL AREA: 604,247 sq. miles (1,565,000 sq. km)
DENSITY: 4 people per sq. mile

LANGUAGES: Khalkha Mongolian*, Kazakh
RELIGIONS: Tibetan Buddhist 50%, nonreligious 40%, Shamanist and Christian 6%, Muslim 4%
ETHNIC MIX: Khalkh 95%, Kazakh 4%, other 1%
GOVERNMENT: Mixed presidential–parliamentary system
CURRENCY: Tugrik (tögrög) = 100 möngö

Montenegro

Perched on the Adriatic coast, this tiny republic became a separate state in 2006, after 88 years of federation with its neighbors in various forms of the state of Yugoslavia.

GEOGRAPHY
A narrow coastal strip on the Adriatic. Fertile lowland plains around Lake Scutari. Mountainous interior with deep canyons.

CLIMATE
The lowlands have hot, dry summers and mild winters. Heavy snow in winter in the mountains.

PEOPLE & SOCIETY
Most Montenegrins are Orthodox Christians. They speak a language closely related to Serbian, using the same Cyrillic script. Muslim Albanians, who make up 80% of the population of the southern Ulcinj region, supported independence and are now asking for autonomy.

◆ INSIGHT: *Dark forests once cloaked Montenegro's mountains; its name means "Black Mountain"*

THE ECONOMY
Tourism (along Adriatic) drives growth. Bauxite reserves, aluminum industry. Economy dominated by black market; cigarette smuggling is rife. Return of foreign aid and investment. Approved in 2010 as candidate for EU membership. Uses euro, though not part of eurozone.

FACTFILE

OFFICIAL NAME: Montenegro
DATE OF FORMATION: 2006
CAPITAL: Podgorica
POPULATION: 600,000
TOTAL AREA: 5332 sq. miles (13,812 sq. km)
DENSITY: 113 people per sq. mile

LANGUAGES: Montenegrin*, Serbian, Albanian, Bosniak, Croatian
RELIGIONS: Orthodox Christian 74%, Muslim 18%, Roman Catholic 4%, other 4%
ETHNIC MIX: Montenegrin 43%, Serb 32%, other 12%, Bosniak 8%, Albanian 5%
GOVERNMENT: Parliamentary system
CURRENCY: Euro = 100 cents

Morocco

 Morocco is a former French colony in northwest Africa.
Since 1975, it has occupied the territory of Western Sahara, the future
of which is yet to be determined by UN-supervised referendum.

GEOGRAPHY
Fertile coastal plain is interrupted in
the east by the Rif Mountains. Atlas
Mountain ranges to the south. Beyond
lies the outer fringe of the Sahara.

CLIMATE
Ranges from temperate and warm
in the north, to semiarid in the south.
Cooler in the mountains.

PEOPLE & SOCIETY
The Berber minority descend from
north Africa's original inhabitants, and live
mainly in mountain villages. The Arab
majority inhabits the lowlands. Morocco
is unusual among Arab states in granting
Jews religious freedom and civil rights.
The king is spiritual leader and head of
state. During the 2011 "Arab Spring"
protesters called for more democracy.
Islamists have gained influence in politics.
Islamist militancy and the emergence
of terrorist cells are of concern.

THE ECONOMY
Major exporter of phosphates.
Investment in tourism and agriculture.
Fishing. Relations with EU strained over
illegal immigrants and cannabis trade.

INSIGHT: *Karueein University in Fès,
founded in 859 CE, is the world's
oldest existing educational institution*

FACTFILE
OFFICIAL NAME: Kingdom of Morocco
DATE OF FORMATION: 1956
CAPITAL: Rabat
POPULATION: 32.4 million
TOTAL AREA: 172,316 sq. miles (446,300 sq. km)
DENSITY: 188 people per sq. mile
LANGUAGES: Arabic*, Tamazight (Berber),
French, Spanish
RELIGIONS: Muslim (mainly Sunni) 99%,
other (mostly Christian) 1%
ETHNIC MIX: Arab 70%, Berber 29%,
European 1%
GOVERNMENT: Mixed monarchical–
parliamentary system
CURRENCY: Mor. dirham = 100 centimes

Mozambique

Mozambique lies on the southeast African coast. It was torn apart by a savage and devastating civil war between the Marxist government and a rebel faction between 1977 and 1992.

GEOGRAPHY
Largely a savanna-covered plateau. The coast is fringed by coral reefs and lagoons. The Zambezi River bisects the country.

CLIMATE
Tropical. Temperatures are hottest on the coast. Extremes of rainfall: drought and flood.

PEOPLE & SOCIETY
Tensions exist between north and south, rather than between ethnic groups. Life is centered on the extended family. Polygamy is fairly common. The country is struggling with the legacy of a war that killed around a million people, and the effects of frequent floods and droughts. Half the population lives in abject poverty.

INSIGHT: Maputo's busy port serves Zimbabwe and South Africa

THE ECONOMY
Extremely dependent on aid. Mineral potential. Cashew nuts, shrimp, cotton exported. Debt relief.

FACTFILE

OFFICIAL NAME: Republic of Mozambique
DATE OF FORMATION: 1975
CAPITAL: Maputo
POPULATION: 23.4 million
TOTAL AREA: 309,494 sq. miles
(801,590 sq. km)
DENSITY: 77 people per sq. mile

LANGUAGES: Makua, Xitsonga, Sena, Lomwe, Portuguese*
RELIGIONS: Traditional beliefs 56%, Christian 30%, Muslim 14%
ETHNIC MIX: Makua Lomwe 47%, Tsonga 23%, Malawi 12%, Shona 11%, Yao 4%, other 3%
GOVERNMENT: Presidential system
CURRENCY: New metical = 100 centavos

Myanmar (Burma)

Forming the eastern shores of the Bay of Bengal and the Andaman Sea in southeast Asia, Myanmar suffers from isolation, political repression, and ethnic conflict.

GEOGRAPHY
The fertile Irrawaddy basin lies at the center. Mountains to the west, Shan plateau to the east. Tropical rainforest covers much of the land.

CLIMATE
Tropical. Hot summers, with high humidity, and warm winters.

PEOPLE & SOCIETY
The military, in power from 1962, paid little regard to human rights, and didn't tolerate opposition. The National League for Democracy won elections in 1990, but was kept from power. Elections in 2010, nominally restoring civilian rule, were dominated by the new military-backed party. Ethnic minorities are fighting for independence.

◆ **INSIGHT:** *Myanmar is one of the world's biggest teak exporters, though reserves are diminishing rapidly*

THE ECONOMY
Corrupt, mismanaged, subject to sanctions – but gas, teak, and gems are exported. One of world's largest illegal opium producers. Goods sold on black market carry high prices.

FACTFILE

OFFICIAL NAME: Union of Myanmar
DATE OF FORMATION: 1948
CAPITAL: Nay Pyi Taw
POPULATION: 50.5 million
TOTAL AREA: 261,969 sq. miles (678,500 sq. km)
DENSITY: 199 people per sq. mile

LANGUAGES: Burmese (Myanmar)*, Shan, Karen, Rakhine, Chin, Yangbye, Kachin, Mon
RELIGIONS: Buddhist 89%, Christian 4%, Muslim 4%, other 2%, Animist 1%
ETHNIC MIX: Burman (Bamah) 68%, other 12%, Shan 9%, Karen 7%, Rakhine 4%
GOVERNMENT: Presidential system
CURRENCY: Kyat = 100 pyas

Namibia

Located in southwestern Africa, Namibia gained independence from South Africa in 1990, after 24 years of armed struggle. It regained the territory of Walvis Bay in 1994.

GEOGRAPHY

The Namib Desert stretches along the coastal strip. Inland, a ridge of mountains rises to 8000 ft (2500 m). The Kalahari Desert lies in the east.

CLIMATE

Almost rainless. The coast is usually shrouded in thick fog, unless the hot, dry *berg* wind is blowing.

PEOPLE & SOCIETY
The Ovambo, the main ethnic group, live mainly in the more populous north. Some 100,000 whites, many of German descent, are centered around Windhoek and still control the economy. The minority San and Khoi bushmen are among the oldest human communities in the world. The ban on homosexuality is contentious.

◆ **INSIGHT:** *The Namib is the Earth's oldest, and one of its driest, deserts*

THE ECONOMY
Varied mineral resources, notably uranium and diamonds. Rich offshore fishing grounds. High unemployment. HIV/AIDS epidemic. One of Africa's most skewed distributions of wealth.

2000m/6562ft
1000m/3281ft
500m/1640ft
200m/656ft
Sea Level

0   200 km
0   200 miles

FACTFILE

OFFICIAL NAME: Republic of Namibia
DATE OF FORMATION: 1990
CAPITAL: Windhoek
POPULATION: 2.2 million
TOTAL AREA: 318,694 sq. miles (825,418 sq. km)
DENSITY: 7 people per sq. mile

LANGUAGES: Ovambo, Kavango, English*, Bergdama, German, Afrikaans
RELIGIONS: Christian 90%, traditional beliefs 10%
ETHNIC MIX: Ovambo 50%, other tribes 22%, Kavango 9%, Damara 7%, Herero 7%, other 5%
GOVERNMENT: Presidential system
CURRENCY: Namibian dollar = 100 cents

Nauru

Nauru lies in the Pacific, northeast of Australia.
Phosphate deposits gave its inhabitants huge temporary wealth,
but economic mismanagement has left them facing ruin.

GEOGRAPHY

A single low-lying coral atoll, with a fertile coastal belt. Coral cliffs encircle an elevated interior plateau.

CLIMATE

Equatorial, moderated by sea breezes. Occasional long droughts.

PEOPLE & SOCIETY

Native Nauruans are of mixed Micronesian and Polynesian origin. Most live in simple, traditional houses and spend their money on luxury cars and consumer goods. Welfare and education are free. A diet of imported processed foods has caused widespread obesity and diabetes. Mining was left to imported laborers, mainly from Kiribati, who lived in enclaves of male-only barracks and had few rights. Many young Nauruans leave to seek a better life in Australia or New Zealand.

THE ECONOMY

Phosphate revenues all but dried up. Sale of fishing rights sole resource. State trust fund invested badly overseas. Offshore banking facilities closed after international pressure.

INSIGHT: *Phosphate mining has left 80% of the island uninhabitable*

FACTFILE

OFFICIAL NAME: Republic of Nauru
DATE OF FORMATION: 1968
CAPITAL: None
POPULATION: 9322
TOTAL AREA: 8.1 sq. miles (21 sq. km)
DENSITY: 1151 people per sq. mile

LANGUAGES: Nauruan*, Kiribati, Chinese, Tuvaluan, English
RELIGIONS: Nauruan Congregational Church 60%, Roman Catholic 35%, other 5%
ETHNIC MIX: Nauruan 93%, Chinese 5%, other Pacific islanders 1%, European 1%
GOVERNMENT: Nonparty system
CURRENCY: Australian dollar = 100 cents

Nepal

Nepal, lying between India and China on the southern shoulder of the Himalayas, is one of the world's poorest countries. Its agricultural economy is heavily dependent on the monsoon.

GEOGRAPHY

Mainly mountainous. The area includes some of the highest mountains in the world, including Mount Everest. Flat, fertile river plains form the south.

CLIMATE
Warm monsoon season from July to October. The rest of the year is dry, sunny, and mild. Winter temperatures in the Himalayas average 14°F (–10°C).

PEOPLE & SOCIETY
Tensions are few between the diverse ethnic groups. Buddhist women, including Sherpas, face fewer social restrictions than Hindus. Trafficking of women and child labor are problems. Human rights violations rose during the 1999–2006 Maoist insurgency. The peace deal led to the abolition of the monarchy and Maoist victory in elections, but fractious coalitions mean instability continues.

THE ECONOMY
Agriculture employs 74% of people. Crops include rice and wheat. Tourism and investment affected by instability and Maoist insurgency. Reliant on aid. Hydropower potential.

INSIGHT: *Southern Nepal was the birthplace of Buddha (Prince Siddhartha Gautama) in 563 BCE*

FACTFILE

OFFICIAL NAME: Federal Democratic Republic of Nepal
DATE OF FORMATION: 1769
CAPITAL: Kathmandu
POPULATION: 29.9 million
TOTAL AREA: 54,363 sq. miles (140,800 sq. km)
DENSITY: 566 people per sq. mile

LANGUAGES: Nepali*, Maithili, Bhojpuri
RELIGIONS: Hindu 81%, Buddhist 11%, Muslim 4%, other (including Christian) 4%
ETHNIC MIX: Other 52%, Chhetri 16%, Hill Brahman 13%, Tharu 7%, Magar 7%, Tamang 5%
GOVERNMENT: Transitional regime
CURRENCY: Nepalese rupee = 100 paisa

Netherlands

Astride the delta of five major rivers in northwest Europe, the Netherlands built its historic wealth on maritime trade. Rotterdam is Europe's largest port.

GEOGRAPHY

Mainly flat, with 27% of the land below sea level and protected by dunes, dikes, and canals. There are a few low hills in the south and east.

CLIMATE

Mild, rainy winters and cool summers. Gales from the North Sea are common in fall and winter.

PEOPLE & SOCIETY

The Dutch have a long history of welcoming immigrants from former colonies and refugees seeking asylum. However, lack of integration is now raising fears about the failing asylum system, immigrant crime, and militant Islam. Population is mostly urban and the density is high. The state does not try to impose a particular morality on its citizens. Laws concerning sexuality, narcotics-taking, and euthanasia are among the world's most liberal.

THE ECONOMY

Major trading hub. High-profile multinationals. Diverse industrial base: chemicals, machinery, electronics, and metals. Costly social welfare system.

INSIGHT: *In 2002, the Netherlands became the first country in the world to legalize euthanasia*

FACTFILE

OFFICIAL NAME: Kingdom of the Netherlands

DATE OF FORMATION: 1648

CAPITALS: Amsterdam and The Hague

POPULATION: 16.7 million

TOTAL AREA: 16,033 sq. miles (41,526 sq. km)

DENSITY: 1275 people per sq. mile

LANGUAGES: Dutch*, Frisian

RELIGIONS: Roman Catholic 36%, other 34%, Protestant 27%, Muslim 3%

ETHNIC MIX: Dutch 82%, other 12%, Turkish 2%, Surinamese 2%, Moroccan 2%

GOVERNMENT: Parliamentary system

CURRENCY: Euro = 100 cents

New Zealand

Lying in the South Pacific, 990 miles (1600 km) southeast of Australia, New Zealand comprises North and South Islands, separated by the Cook Strait, and many smaller islands.

GEOGRAPHY
North Island, noted for hot springs and geysers, has the bulk of the population. South Island is mostly mountainous, with eastern lowlands.

CLIMATE
Generally temperate and damp. The far north is almost subtropical, whereas southern winters are cold.

PEOPLE & SOCIETY
Maoris were the first settlers, 1200 years ago. Today's majority European population is descended mainly from British migrants who settled after 1840. Maoris' living and education standards are generally lower than average. The government is continuing to negotiate the settlement of Maori land claims.

◆ INSIGHT: New Zealand was the first country to give women the vote (1893)

THE ECONOMY
Tourism is the biggest foreign-exchange earner. Modern agricultural sector; world's top exporter of dairy products. Hi-tech manufacturing. Open economy. Strong trade links.

FACTFILE

OFFICIAL NAME: New Zealand
DATE OF FORMATION: 1947
CAPITAL: Wellington
POPULATION: 4.3 million
TOTAL AREA: 103,737 sq. miles (268,680 sq. km)
DENSITY: 41 people per sq. mile

LANGUAGES: English*, Maori*
RELIGIONS: Anglican 24%, other 22%, Presbyterian 18%, nonreligious 16%, Roman Catholic 15%, Methodist 5%
ETHNIC MIX: European 75%, Maori 15%, other 7%, Samoan 3%
GOVERNMENT: Parliamentary system
CURRENCY: New Zealand dollar = 100 cents

Nicaragua

Nicaragua lies at the heart of Central America. The Sandinista revolution of 1978 led to 11 years of civil war between the left-wing Sandinistas and the right-wing US-backed Contras.

GEOGRAPHY

Extensive forested plains in the east. Central mountain region with many active volcanoes. The Pacific coastlands are dominated by lakes.

CLIMATE

Tropical. The lowlands are hot all year round. The mountains are cooler. Prone to occasional hurricanes.

PEOPLE & SOCIETY

Most people are *mestizo* (mixed Spanish–Amerindian), and there is a large white elite. Caribbean regions are home to communities of Miskito Amerindians and blacks, who gained autonomy in 1987. The revolution improved the status of women, but these gains have been undone by rampant poverty.

◆ INSIGHT: *Lake Nicaragua is the only freshwater lake in the world to contain marine animals*

THE ECONOMY

Textiles, coffee, meat, tobacco are main exports: affected by world price fluctuations. Remittances from abroad. Substantial debt relief has cut debt to around 60% of GDP. Corruption.

1000m/3281ft
500m/1640ft
200m/656ft
Sea Level

FACTFILE

OFFICIAL NAME: Republic of Nicaragua
DATE OF FORMATION: 1838
CAPITAL: Managua
POPULATION: 5.8 million
TOTAL AREA: 49,998 sq. miles
(129,494 sq. km)
DENSITY: 127 people per sq. mile)

LANGUAGES: Spanish*, English Creole, Miskito
RELIGIONS: Roman Catholic 80%, Protestant Evangelical 17%, other 3%
ETHNIC MIX: *Mestizo* 69%, White 17%, Black 9%, Amerindian 5%
GOVERNMENT: Presidential system
CURRENCY: Córdoba oro = 100 centavos

Niger

Niger lies in west Africa, upstream from Nigeria on the Niger River. One of the world's poorest states, it was ruled by one-party or military regimes until multipartyism was allowed in 1992.

GEOGRAPHY

The north and northeast regions are part of the Sahara. The Air Mountains in the center rise high above the desert. Savanna lies to the south.

CLIMATE

High temperatures persist for most of the year at around 95°F (35°C). The north is virtually rainless.

PEOPLE & SOCIETY

Tuareg nomads in the north feel excluded from politics and the benefits of development of their area's uranium resources. An early 1990s rebellion reignited briefly in 2007–2009. In the south, egalitarianism and a sense of community help to combat economic difficulties. Almost the entire urban population lives in slum conditions. Two-thirds of the population is under 25. Women have limited rights and restricted access to education.

THE ECONOMY

Vast uranium deposits. Frequent droughts and food shortages. Banditry. Expansion of Sahara. Oil potential.

INSIGHT: *The name Niger comes from the Tuareg word* n'eghirren, *which means "flowing water"*

FACTFILE

OFFICIAL NAME: Republic of Niger
DATE OF FORMATION: 1960
CAPITAL: Niamey
POPULATION: 15.9 million
TOTAL AREA: 489,188 sq. miles (1,267,000 sq. km)
DENSITY: 33 people per sq. mile

LANGUAGES: Hausa, Djerma, Fulani, Tuareg, Teda, French*
RELIGIONS: Muslim 99%, other (including Christian) 1%
ETHNIC MIX: Hausa 53%, Djerma and Songhai 21%, Tuareg 11%, Fulani 7%, Kanuri 6%, other 2%
GOVERNMENT: Presidential system
CURRENCY: CFA franc = 100 centimes

Nigeria

West Africa's biggest nation, Nigeria is a federation of 36 states and the capital, Abuja. Dominated by military governments since 1966, democracy returned in 1999.

GEOGRAPHY
Coastal area of beaches, swamps, and lagoons gives way to rainforest, and then to savanna on the high plateaus. Semidesert to the north.

CLIMATE
The south is hot, rainy and humid for most of the year. The arid north has one very humid wet season. The Jos Plateau and highlands are cooler.

PEOPLE & SOCIETY
Some 250 ethnic groups: tensions threaten national unity, with sporadic intercommunal violence. The northern states have introduced *sharia* (Islamic law) for their majority Muslim populations. Women have more economic independence in the south. In the Niger Delta, where 70% of people live on less than a dollar a day, militants are fighting for a share of the benefits of the region's oil wealth.

THE ECONOMY
Overdependent on oil, principal export since 1970s. Mismanagement and corruption. Foreign debt reduced.

INSIGHT: *Nigeria is Africa's most populous state – one in every seven Africans is Nigerian*

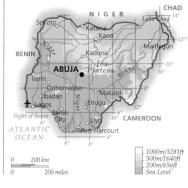

	1000m/3281ft
	500m/1640ft
	200m/656ft
	Sea Level

0   200 km
0   200 miles

FACTFILE

OFFICIAL NAME: Federal Republic of Nigeria
DATE OF FORMATION: 1960
CAPITAL: Abuja
POPULATION: 158 million
TOTAL AREA: 356,667 sq. miles (923,768 sq. km)
DENSITY: 450 people per sq. mile

LANGUAGES: Hausa, English*, Yoruba, Ibo
RELIGIONS: Muslim 50%, Christian 40%, traditional beliefs 10%
ETHNIC MIX: Other 29%, Hausa 21%, Yoruba 21%, Ibo 18%, Fulani 11%
GOVERNMENT: Presidential system
CURRENCY: Naira = 100 kobo

Norway

The Kingdom of Norway traces the rugged western coast of Scandinavia. Settlements are largely restricted to southern and coastal areas. Vast oil and natural gas revenues bring prosperity.

GEOGRAPHY
The western coast is indented with numerous fjords and features tens of thousands of islands. Mountains and plateaus cover most of the country.

CLIMATE
Mild coastal climate. Inland, the weather is more extreme, with warmer summers and cold, snowy winters.

PEOPLE & SOCIETY
Fairly homogeneous, but has welcomed refugees from Iraq, Somalia, Bosnia, Sri Lanka, and elsewhere. Strong family tradition despite high divorce rate. Fair-minded consensus promotes female equality, boosted by the generous childcare provision. Wealth is more evenly distributed than in most countries. Voted against joining the EU in 1994.

◆ **INSIGHT:** *Near Narvik, mainland Norway is only 4 miles (7 km) wide*

THE ECONOMY
Western Europe's top oil and natural gas producer: trust fund saves for post-oil future. Metal, chemical, and engineering industries. Generous aid donor. High cost of living.

FACTFILE

OFFICIAL NAME: Kingdom of Norway

DATE OF FORMATION: 1905

CAPITAL: Oslo

POPULATION: 4.9 million

TOTAL AREA: 125,181 sq. miles (324,220 sq. km)

DENSITY: 41 people per sq. mile

LANGUAGES: Norwegian* (*Bokmål* "book language" and *Nynorsk* "new Norsk"), Sámi

RELIGIONS: Evangelical Lutheran 88%, other and nonreligious 8%, Muslim 2%, Pentecostal 1%, Roman Catholic 1%

ETHNIC MIX: Norwegian 93%, other 6%, Sámi 1%

GOVERNMENT: Parliamentary system

CURRENCY: Norwegian krone = 100 øre

Oman

Oman occupies a strategic position on the Arabian Peninsula, at the entrance to the Persian Gulf. It is the least developed Gulf state, despite modest oil exports.

GEOGRAPHY
Mostly gravelly desert, with mountains in the north and south. Some narrow fertile coastal strips.

CLIMATE
Blistering heat in the west. Summer temperatures often climb above 113°F (45°C). Southern uplands receive rains June–September.

PEOPLE & SOCIETY
Urban drift has seen most Omanis move to northern towns. The majority are Ibadi Muslims who follow an appointed leader, the imam. Ibadism is not opposed to freedom for women, and a few women hold positions of authority. Baluchi from Pakistan are the largest group of foreign workers.

◆ INSIGHT: Until the late 1980s, Oman was closed to all but business or official visitors

THE ECONOMY
Oil and natural gas account for almost all export revenue. Commercially extractable reserves are limited. Other exports include fish, animals, and dates. Foreigners work in all sectors.

FACTFILE

OFFICIAL NAME: Sultanate of Oman
DATE OF FORMATION: 1951
CAPITAL: Muscat
POPULATION: 2.9 million
TOTAL AREA: 82,031 sq. miles (212,460 sq. km)
DENSITY: 35 people per sq. mile

LANGUAGES: Arabic*, Baluchi, Farsi, Hindi, Punjabi
RELIGIONS: Ibadi Muslim 75%, other Muslim and Hindu 25%
ETHNIC MIX: Arab 88%, Baluchi 4%, Persian 3%, Indian and Pakistani 3%, African 2%
GOVERNMENT: Monarchy
CURRENCY: Omani rial = 1000 baisa

Pakistan

Once a part of British India, Pakistan was created in 1947 in response to demands for an independent Muslim state. In 1971, Bangladesh (former East Pakistan) became a separate state.

GEOGRAPHY

Indus floodplain across east and south. Hindu Kush mountains in north. Semidesert plateau, mountains in west.

CLIMATE

Temperatures can soar to 122°F (50°C) in south and west, and fall to -4°F (-20°C) in the Hindu Kush.

PEOPLE & SOCIETY

Punjabis dominate government and the army. Tensions with minority groups, exacerbated by the vast gap between rich and poor. Strong family ties permeate politics and business. Relations with India are tense over Kashmir and terrorism. Islamist *taliban* insurgency in tribal areas on Afghan border: fighting has displaced millions.

◆ **INSIGHT:** *In 1988, Pakistan elected Benazir Bhutto as the first female prime minister in the Muslim world*

THE ECONOMY

Major cotton and rice producer, but unpredictable weather conditions often affect crop. Textiles. Instability. Corruption. Aid to fight terrorism and for earthquake reconstruction.

☐	5000m/16405ft
☐	4000m/13124ft
☐	3000m/9843ft
☐	2000m/6562ft
☐	1000m/3281ft
☐	500m/1640ft
☐	200m/656ft
☐	Sea Level

CHINA

ISLĀMĀBĀD
Khyber Pass
Peshawar
Rawalpindi
Sargodha
Faisalabad
Quetta
Multān
Bahāwalpur
Sukkur
Hyderabad
Karāchī
Arabian Sea

Siālkot
Gujrānwāla
Lahore
Punjab

AFGHANISTAN

IRAN   Baluchistan

INDIA

Sindh
Thar Desert

0   200 km
0   200 miles

FACTFILE

OFFICIAL NAME: Islamic Republic of Pakistan
DATE OF FORMATION: 1947
CAPITAL: Islamabad
POPULATION: 185 million
TOTAL AREA: 310,401 sq. miles (803,940 sq. km)
DENSITY: 621 people per sq. mile

LANGUAGES: Punjabi, Sindhi, Pashtu, Urdu*, Baluchi, Brahui
RELIGIONS: Sunni Muslim 77%, Shi'a Muslim 20%, Hindu 2%, Christian 1%
ETHNIC MIX: Punjabi 56%, Pathan (Pashtun) 15%, Sindhi 14%, Mohajir 7%, Baluchi 4%, other 4%
GOVERNMENT: Presidential system
CURRENCY: Pakistani rupee = 100 paisa

Palau

The 300-island Palau archipelago (known locally as Belau) lies in the western Pacific Ocean. It achieved independence in 1994, and is gradually reducing its aid dependence.

GEOGRAPHY
Terrain varies from thickly forested mountains to limestone and coral reefs. Babeldaob, the largest island, is volcanic, with many rivers and waterfalls.

CLIMATE
Hot and wet. Little variation in daily and seasonal temperatures. February–April is the dry season.

PEOPLE & SOCIETY
Native Palauans are a mix of the original Southeast Asian migrants and Pacific settlers. A modern influx from Asia has led to tension. 70% of the population lives on the island-city of Koror, prompting the construction of a new capital on Babeldoab. Native culture is preserved on outer islands despite strong influence from the US and Japan. Modekngei is a blend of Christianity and local beliefs.

THE ECONOMY
Tourism and fishing licenses are main earners. Coconuts, bananas, and taro. New 15-year US aid plan to 2024.

INSIGHT: *Palau's reefs contain 1500 species of fish and 700 types of coral*

FACTFILE
OFFICIAL NAME: Republic of Palau
DATE OF FORMATION: 1994
CAPITAL: Ngerulmud
POPULATION: 20,956
TOTAL AREA: 177 sq. miles (458 sq. km)
DENSITY: 107 people per sq. mile

LANGUAGES: Palauan*, English*, Japanese, Angaur, Tobi, Sonsorolese
RELIGIONS: Christian 66%, Modekngei 34%
ETHNIC MIX: Palauan 74%, Filipino 16%, other 6%, Chinese and other Asian 4%
GOVERNMENT: Nonparty system
CURRENCY: US dollar = 100 cents

Panama

A Spanish colony until 1821, Panama is the southernmost country in Central America. The colossal Panama Canal (which was under US control until 2000) links the Pacific and Atlantic oceans.

GEOGRAPHY
Lowlands along both coasts, with savanna-covered plains and rolling hills. Mountainous interior. Swamps and rainforests in the east.

CLIMATE
Hot and humid, with heavy rainfall in the May–December wet season. Cooler at high altitudes.

PEOPLE & SOCIETY
A multiethnic society, dominated by people of mixed Spanish–Amerindian origin (mestizo). Amerindians live in remote areas. The Panama Canal and former US military bases (the last of which closed in 1999) have given society a cosmopolitan outlook, but Catholicism and the extended family remain strong. Crime is high; money-laundering, narcotics trafficking, and corruption are rife.

THE ECONOMY
Colón Free Trade Zone: world's second-largest. Income from the canal (expansion project underway) and merchant ships sailing under flag of Panama. Banana and shrimp exports.

INSIGHT: The Panama Canal shortens the sea route between the east coast of the US and Japan by 3000 miles (1800 km)

FACTFILE

OFFICIAL NAME: Republic of Panama
DATE OF FORMATION: 1903
CAPITAL: Panama City
POPULATION: 3.5 million
TOTAL AREA: 30,193 sq. miles (78,200 sq. km)
DENSITY: 119 people per sq. mile
LANGUAGES: English Creole, Spanish*, Amerindian languages, Chibchan languages
RELIGIONS: Roman Catholic 84%, Protestant 15%, other 1%
ETHNIC MIX: Mestizo 70%, Black 14%, White 10%, Amerindian 6%
GOVERNMENT: Presidential system
CURRENCY: Balboa = 100 centésimos; US dollar is also legal tender

Papua New Guinea

A former Australian colony, Papua New Guinea (PNG) occupies the eastern section of the island of New Guinea and several other island groups. Much of the country is isolated.

GEOGRAPHY

Mountainous and forested mainland, with broad, swampy river valleys. 40 active volcanoes in the north. Around 600 outer islands.

CLIMATE

Hot and humid in lowlands, cooling toward highlands, where snow can fall on highest peaks.

PEOPLE & SOCIETY

Around 800 language groups and even more tribes. The main social distinction is between lowlanders, who have frequent contact with the outside world, and the very isolated, but increasingly threatened, highlanders. Great tensions exist between highland tribes, and vendettas can often last several generations. The island of Bougainville has been granted autonomy and promised an eventual referendum on independence.

THE ECONOMY

Minerals: significant quantities of gold, copper, oil, and natural gas. High government spending almost led to national bankruptcy in 2002.

INSIGHT: *PNG is home to the only known poisonous birds; contact with the feathers of some species of pitohui produces skin blisters*

FACTFILE

OFFICIAL NAME: Independent State of Papua New Guinea

DATE OF FORMATION: 1975

CAPITAL: Port Moresby

POPULATION: 6.9 million

TOTAL AREA: 178,703 sq. miles (462,840 sq. km)

DENSITY: 39 people per sq. mile

LANGUAGES: Pidgin English, Papuan, English*, Motu, c.800 native languages

RELIGIONS: Protestant 60%, Roman Catholic 37%, other 3%

ETHNIC MIX: Melanesian or mixed race 100%

GOVERNMENT: Parliamentary system

CURRENCY: Kina = 100 toea

Paraguay

Landlocked in central South America, and once a Spanish colony, Paraguay's postindependence history has included periods of military rule. Free elections held since 1993.

GEOGRAPHY
The Paraguay River divides the hilly and forested east from a flat alluvial plain, with marsh and semidesert scrub land in the west.

CLIMATE
Subtropical. The Gran Chaco is generally hotter and drier. All areas experience floods and droughts.

PEOPLE & SOCIETY
The population is mainly *mestizo* (mixed Spanish and native Guaraní origin). Most people are bilingual, though in rural areas Guaraní is more widely used. Cattle ranchers populate the Chaco, along with communities of the German-origin Mennonite Church. The army is politically active.

◆ **INSIGHT:** *The War of the Triple Alliance (1864–1870) killed almost 90% of Paraguay's male population*

THE ECONOMY
Agriculture: soybeans are the main export. Electricity exported from massive hydroelectric dams, including Itaipú (world's second-largest, jointly run with Brazil). Large informal economy. Corruption and smuggling.

FACTFILE

OFFICIAL NAME: Republic of Paraguay
DATE OF FORMATION: 1811
CAPITAL: Asunción
POPULATION: 6.5 million
TOTAL AREA: 157,046 sq. miles (406,750 sq. km)
DENSITY: 42 people per sq. mile

LANGUAGES: Guaraní*, Spanish*, German
RELIGIONS: Roman Catholic 90%, Protestant (including Mennonite) 10%
ETHNIC MIX: *Mestizo* 91%, other 7%, Amerindian 2%
GOVERNMENT: Presidential system
CURRENCY: Guaraní = 100 céntimos

Peru

Once the heart of the Inca Empire, before the Spanish conquest in the 16th century, Peru lies on the Pacific coast of South America, just south of the equator.

GEOGRAPHY
Coastal plain rises to Andes Mountains. Uplands, dissected by fertile valleys, lie east of the Andes. Tropical forest in extreme east.

CLIMATE
Coast is mainly arid. Middle slopes of the Andes are temperate; higher peaks are snow-covered. East is hot, humid, and very wet.

PEOPLE & SOCIETY
Though most people are Amerindians or mixed-race *mestizos*, society is dominated by a small group of Spanish descendants. Amerindians, and the small black community, suffer discrimination in towns, but access to information and political power are growing; the first Amerindian president was elected in 2001–2006. Clashes with left-wing militants killed almost 70,000 people between 1980 and 2000.

THE ECONOMY
Abundant mineral resources: notably copper and gold. Rich Pacific fish stocks. Illegal cocaine producer.

INSIGHT: *Lake Titicaca is the world's highest navigable lake*

FACTFILE

OFFICIAL NAME: Republic of Peru
DATE OF FORMATION: 1824
CAPITAL: Lima
POPULATION: 29.5 million
TOTAL AREA: 496,223 sq. miles (1,285,200 sq. km)
DENSITY: 60 people per sq. mile

LANGUAGES: Spanish*, Quechua*, Aymara
RELIGIONS: Roman Catholic 81%, other 19%
ETHNIC MIX: Amerindian 45%, *Mestizo* (European–Amerindian) 37%, White 15%, other 3%
GOVERNMENT: Presidential system
CURRENCY: New sol = 100 céntimos

Philippines

Lying in the western Pacific Ocean, the Philippines is the world's second-largest archipelago, with 7107 islands, of which 4600 are named but only around 1000 inhabited.

GEOGRAPHY
Larger islands are forested and mountainous. Over 20 active volcanoes. Frequent earthquakes.

CLIMATE
Tropical. Warm and humid all year round. Typhoons occur in the rainy season: June–October.

PEOPLE & SOCIETY
Over 100 ethnic groups, most of which are of Malay origin. The Catholic Church is a dominant cultural force; it opposes family-planning, despite high population growth. The Chinese minority has been established for 400 years. Women play a prominent part in society. High literacy levels. Islamist separatists and communist insurgents undermine stability.

◆ **INSIGHT:** Mass "People Power" demonstrations have brought down two presidents, in 1986 and 2001

THE ECONOMY
Coconuts, bananas, pineapples exported. Growing outsourcing center. Remittances from abroad. Corruption and poor infrastructure limit growth.

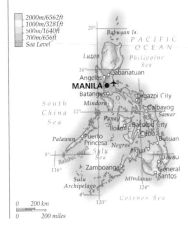

■	2000m/6562ft
■	1000m/3281ft
■	500m/1640ft
■	200m/656ft
■	Sea Level

0   200 km
0   200 miles

FACTFILE

OFFICIAL NAME: Republic of the Philippines
DATE OF FORMATION: 1946
CAPITAL: Manila
POPULATION: 93.6 million
TOTAL AREA: 115,830 sq. miles (300,000 sq. km)
DENSITY: 813 people per sq. mile

LANGUAGES: Filipino*, English*, Tagalog, Cebuano, Ilocano, Hiligaynon, many others
RELIGIONS: Roman Catholic 81%, Protestant 9%, Muslim 5%, other (including Buddhist) 5%
ETHNIC MIX: Other 34%, Tagalog 28%, Cebuano 13%, Ilocano 9%, Hiligaynon 8%, Bisaya 8%
GOVERNMENT: Presidential system
CURRENCY: Philippine peso = 100 centavos

Poland

Located in the heart of Europe, Poland has undergone massive social, economic, and political change since the collapse of communism in 1989. It joined the EU in 2004.

GEOGRAPHY

Lowlands, part of the North European Plain, cover most of the country. The Tatra Mountains run along the southern border.

CLIMATE

Rainfall peaks during the hot summers. Cold winters with snow, especially in mountains.

PEOPLE & SOCIETY

Ethnic homogeneity masks a number of tensions. Secular liberals criticize the semiofficial status of the Roman Catholic Church, and emerging wealth disparities are resented by those not profiting from the free market. The German minority in the west is growing more assertive.

◆ **INSIGHT:** *Wild wisent (European bison) live in the Bialowieza Forest straddling the Poland–Belarus border*

THE ECONOMY

Heavy industries dominate; services growing. Foreign investment reflects large potential market. Rapid privatization. Only EU state to avoid recession in 2007–2009 global downturn. Not adopting euro yet.

1000m/3281ft
500m/1640ft
200m/656ft
Sea Level

0   100 km
0   100 miles

FACTFILE

OFFICIAL NAME: Republic of Poland

DATE OF FORMATION: 1918

CAPITAL: Warsaw

POPULATION: 38 million

TOTAL AREA: 120,728 sq. miles (312,685 sq. km)

DENSITY: 323 people per sq. mile

LANGUAGES: Polish*

RELIGIONS: Roman Catholic 93%, other and nonreligious 5%, Orthodox Christian 2%

ETHNIC MIX: Polish 98%, other 2%

GOVERNMENT: Parliamentary system

CURRENCY: Zloty = 100 groszy

Portugal

Portugal, with its long Atlantic coast, lies on the western side of the Iberian Peninsula, which it shares with Spain. It is the most westerly country on the European mainland.

GEOGRAPHY

The Tagus River bisects the country roughly east to west, dividing mountainous north from lower and more undulating south.

CLIMATE

North is cool and moist. South is warmer, with dry, mild winters.

PEOPLE & SOCIETY

A homogeneous and stable society, which is losing some of its conservative traditions. History of immigration from former colonies, and recently from eastern Europe. Urban areas and the south are more socially liberal. The north is more responsive to traditional Roman Catholic values. Family ties remain important.

◆ **INSIGHT:** *Portugal is the world's leading producer of cork, which comes from the bark of the cork oak*

THE ECONOMY

Tourism. Exports of vegetables, fruit, wine, cars, and clothing. Mounting debt forced EU bailout in 2011 and tough cuts to reduce the budget deficit.

	1000m/3281ft
	500m/1640ft
	200m/656ft
	Sea Level

FACTFILE

OFFICIAL NAME: Republic of Portugal
DATE OF FORMATION: 1139
CAPITAL: Lisbon
POPULATION: 10.7 million
TOTAL AREA: 35,672 sq. miles (92,391 sq. km)
DENSITY: 301 people per sq. mile

LANGUAGES: Portuguese*
RELIGIONS: Roman Catholic 92%, Protestant 4%, nonreligious 3%, other 1%,
ETHNIC MIX: Portuguese 98%, African and other 2%
GOVERNMENT: Parliamentary system
CURRENCY: Euro = 100 cents

Qatar

Qatar projects from the Arabian Peninsula into the Persian Gulf. A founding member of OPEC, it is one of the region's wealthiest states due to oil and natural gas exports.

GEOGRAPHY
Flat, semiarid desert with dunes and salt pans. Vegetation is limited to small patches of scrub.

CLIMATE
Hot and humid. Temperatures in summer can soar to over 104°F (40°C). Rainfall is rare.

PEOPLE & SOCIETY
Only one in five residents is native-born; the rest are guest workers from across the Middle East, the Indian subcontinent, Southeast Asia, and north Africa. Qataris were once nomadic Bedouins, but since the advent of oil wealth, most now live in Doha and its suburbs, leaving the north dotted with abandoned villages. Women enjoy relative freedom; most wear the veil.

◆ **INSIGHT:** *There are twice as many men as women in Qatar*

THE ECONOMY
Steady supply of crude oil and huge natural gas reserves, plus related industries. All other raw materials and most foods are imported. Strong GDP growth. Economy is heavily dependent on foreign workforce.

FACTFILE

OFFICIAL NAME: State of Qatar
DATE OF FORMATION: 1971
CAPITAL: Doha
POPULATION: 1.5 million
TOTAL AREA: 4416 sq. miles (11,437 sq. km)
DENSITY: 353 people per sq. mile

LANGUAGES: Arabic*
RELIGIONS: Muslim (mainly Sunni) 95%, other 5%
ETHNIC MIX: Qatari 20%, other Arab 20%, Indian 20%, Nepalese 13%, Filipino 10%, other 10%, Pakistani 7%
GOVERNMENT: Monarchy
CURRENCY: Qatar riyal = 100 dirhams

Romania

Once dominated by Poles, Hungarians, and Ottomans, Romania has been slowly converting to a market economy since the 1989 overthrow of its communist regime. It joined the EU in 2007.

GEOGRAPHY
Carpathian Mountains encircle the Transylvanian plateau. Wide plains to the south and east. Danube River forms southern border.

CLIMATE
Continental. Summers are hot and humid, winters are cold and snowy. Very heavy spring rains.

PEOPLE & SOCIETY
Romanians are ethnically distinct from their Slav and Hungarian (Magyar) neighbors. Hungarians are the largest minority, living mainly in Transylvania. They are protected by the influence of Hungary, unlike the Roma, who suffer from discrimination. The overall population is shrinking.

◆ **INSIGHT:** *In 2001, Romania became the last country in Europe to lift its ban on homosexuality*

THE ECONOMY
Polluting, outdated heavy industries and unmechanized agricultural sector. Exports of textiles and metals led growth in 2000s. High budget deficits exposed economy in 2007–2009 global downturn: IMF bailout, austerity measures. Plans to join euro in 2015. Privatization continues.

FACTFILE

OFFICIAL NAME: Romania
DATE OF FORMATION: 1878
CAPITAL: Bucharest
POPULATION: 21.2 million
TOTAL AREA: 91,699 sq. miles (237,500 sq. km)
DENSITY: 238 people per sq. mile
LANGUAGES: Romanian*, Hungarian (Magyar), Romani, German
RELIGIONS: Romanian Orthodox 87%, Roman Catholic 5%, Protestant 5%, Greek Orthodox 1%, Uniate 1%, other 1%
ETHNIC MIX: Romanian 89%, Magyar 7%, Roma 3%, other 1%
GOVERNMENT: Presidential system
CURRENCY: New Romanian leu = 100 bani

Russian Federation

The Russian Federation was the core of the old Soviet Union, which broke up in 1991. Russia is still the world's largest state. Its diversity is a source of both strength and problems.

GEOGRAPHY
The Ural Mountains divide the European steppes and forests from the tundra and forests of Siberia. South-central deserts and mountains.

CLIMATE
Continental in European Russia, with warm summers and freezing winters. Elsewhere climate ranges from sub-arctic to Mediterranean and hot desert.

PEOPLE & SOCIETY
57 "nationalities" and 95 minorities in addition to ethnic Russians. Separatism suppressed. Population predicted to fall by 30% in 50 years. HIV/AIDS spreading.

THE ECONOMY
Vast resources (oil, gas, metals, timber). Inefficient industry, agriculture. Tax evasion. Black market and organized crime. Wealth disparities. 2009 recession.

INSIGHT: *The Trans-Siberian Railroad, running 5578 miles (9297 km) from Moscow to Vladivostok, is the longest in the world, traversing eight time zones*

3000m/9843ft
2000m/6562ft
1000m/3281ft
500m/1640ft
200m/656ft
Sea Level
Below Sea Level

0   1000 km
0   1000 miles

ARCTIC OCEAN

Barents Sea   Severnaya Zemlya

Bering Sea

Kaliningrad (Russ. Fed.)

FINLAND   Murmansk

Santk Peterburg (St Petersburg)

BELARUS

MOSCOW

UKRAINE   Nizhniy Novgorod

Perm'

Noril'sk

Magadan

Yakutsk

Sea of Okhotsk

GEORGIA   Volgograd

Groznyy

AZERB.

KAZAKHSTAN

Omsk   Tomsk

Siberia

Irkutsk   Chita

Trans-Siberian Railroad

MONGOLIA

Sakhalin

Vladivostok

Sea of Japan (East Sea)

CHINA

FACTFILE

OFFICIAL NAME: Russian Federation
DATE OF FORMATION: 1480
CAPITAL: Moscow
POPULATION: 140 million
TOTAL AREA: 6,592,735 sq. miles (17,075,200 sq. km)
DENSITY: 21 people per sq. mile

LANGUAGES: Russian*, Tatar, Ukrainian, other
RELIGIONS: Orthodox Christian 75%, Muslim 14%, other 11%
ETHNIC MIX: Russian 80%, other 12%, Tatar 4%, Ukrainian 2%, Chavash 1%, Bashkir 1%
GOVERNMENT: Mixed presidential–parliamentary system
CURRENCY: Russian rouble = 100 kopeks

Rwanda

Rwanda lies just south of the equator in east central
Africa, far from the nearest sea port. Since independence
from France in 1962, ethnic tensions have dominated politics.

GEOGRAPHY

A series of plateaus descend from
the ridge of volcanic peaks in the west
to the Akagera River on the eastern
border. The Great Rift Valley also passes
through this region.

CLIMATE

Tropical, though tempered by the
altitude. Two wet seasons are separated
by a dry season, from June to August.
Heaviest rain in the west.

PEOPLE & SOCIETY

For over 500 years the cattle-
owning Tutsi minority were politically
dominant over the land-owning Hutu. In
1959, violent revolt led to a reversal of
the roles. Ethnic tensions are fierce; in
the most recent violence, in 1994, over
800,000 people, mostly Tutsi, were
massacred in an act of state-backed
genocide; trials are ongoing. Most people
live at subsistence level.

THE ECONOMY

Rwanda is reliant on aid, but (given
stability) could become a big coffee and
tea producer. Exports tin, coltan, and iron
ore. Ecotourism is growing. Possible oil
and gas reserves. Landlocked: high
transportation costs.

INSIGHT: *Rwanda's parliament in
2008 was the first in the world to
have more women members than men*

FACTFILE

OFFICIAL NAME: Republic of Rwanda
DATE OF FORMATION: 1962
CAPITAL: Kigali
POPULATION: 10.3 million
TOTAL AREA: 10,169 sq. miles
(26,338 sq. km)
DENSITY: 1069 people per sq. mile

LANGUAGES: Kinyarwanda*, French*,
Kiswahili, English*
RELIGIONS: Christian 94%, Muslim 5%,
traditional beliefs 1%
ETHNIC MIX: Hutu 85%, Tutsi 14%, other
(including Twa) 1%
GOVERNMENT: Presidential system
CURRENCY: Rwanda franc = 100 centimes

St. Kitts & Nevis

A popular Caribbean tourist destination, St. Kitts and Nevis lies in the northern part of the Leeward Island chain. Nevis is the smaller and less developed of the two islands.

GEOGRAPHY
Volcanic in origin, with forested, mountainous interiors. Nevis has hot and cold springs.

CLIMATE
Tropical, tempered by trade winds. Little seasonal variation in temperature. Moderate rainfall.

PEOPLE & SOCIETY
The majority of the population are descended from former African slaves. There are small numbers of Europeans, and South Asians, and a community of Lebanese. Levels of emigration are high, and overseas remittances are an important source of national income. The government has pledged to retrain sugar workers. Native professionals and civil servants have largely replaced the former expatriate elite. The secessionist movement on Nevis remains an issue.

THE ECONOMY
Successful tourist industry is vulnerable to downturns in US market. Financial services. Once-key sugar industry closed down in 2005.

◆ **INSIGHT:** *Nevis has been renowned as a spa since the 18th century, and is known as the "Queen of the Caribbean"*

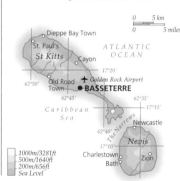

FACTFILE

OFFICIAL NAME: Federation of Saint Christopher and Nevis
DATE OF FORMATION: 1983
CAPITAL: Basseterre
POPULATION: 50,314
TOTAL AREA: 101 sq. miles (261 sq. km)
DENSITY: 362 people per sq. mile

LANGUAGES: English*, English Creole
RELIGIONS: Anglican 33%, Methodist 29%, other 22%, Moravian 9%, Roman Catholic 7%
ETHNIC MIX: Black 95%, mixed race 3%, White 1%, other and Amerindian 1%
GOVERNMENT: Parliamentary system
CURRENCY: East Caribbean dollar = 100 cents

St. Lucia

St. Lucia is one of the most beautiful of the Caribbean Windward Islands. Ruled by France and the UK at different times in its past, the island retains the influences of both.

GEOGRAPHY
Volcanic and mountainous, with some broad fertile valleys. The Pitons, ancient lava cones, rise from the sea on the forested west coast.

CLIMATE
Tropical, moderated by trade winds. May–October wet season brings daily warm showers. Rainfall is highest in the mountains.

PEOPLE & SOCIETY
The population is a tension-free mixture of descendants of Africans, Caribs, and Europeans. Family life and the Roman Catholic Church are important to most St. Lucians. In rural areas, women often head the households and run much of the farming. Plantation and hotel owners are the richest group. There is growing local resistance to overdevelopment of the island for tourism.

THE ECONOMY
Bananas are still biggest export, but struggling to compete since loss of preferential access to EU market. Successful tourism. Offshore banking.

INSIGHT: St. Lucia has two Nobel laureates, the most per capita in the world

FACTFILE

OFFICIAL NAME: Saint Lucia
DATE OF FORMATION: 1979
CAPITAL: Castries
POPULATION: 161,557
TOTAL AREA: 239 sq. miles (620 sq. km)
DENSITY: 685 people per sq. mile

LANGUAGES: English*, French Creole
RELIGIONS: Roman Catholic 90%, other 10%
ETHNIC MIX: Black 83%, Mulatto (mixed race) 13%, Asian 3%, other 1%
GOVERNMENT: Parliamentary system
CURRENCY: East Caribbean dollar = 100 cents

St. Vincent & the Grenadines

The islands of St. Vincent and the Grenadines form part of the Windward group in the Caribbean. St. Vincent is mostly volcanic, while the Grenadines are flat, mainly bare, coral reefs.

GEOGRAPHY

St. Vincent is mountainous and forested, with one of two active volcanoes in the Caribbean, La Soufrière. The Grenadines are 32 islands and cays, fringed by beaches.

CLIMATE

Tropical, with constant trade winds. Hurricanes are likely during the wet season in July–November.

PEOPLE & SOCIETY

Population is racially diverse; intermarriage has reduced tensions. Society is informal and relaxed, but family life is strongly influenced by the Christian Church. Locals fear that their traditional lifestyle is being threatened by the expanding tourist industry.

◆ **INSIGHT:** *The islands' precolonial inhabitants, the Carib, named them "Harioun" – home of the blessed*

THE ECONOMY

Dependent on agriculture and tourism. Bananas are the main cash crop. Tourism, targeted at the jet-set and cruise-ship markets, is concentrated on the Grenadines.

FACTFILE

OFFICIAL NAME: Saint Vincent and the Grenadines
DATE OF FORMATION: 1979
CAPITAL: Kingstown
POPULATION: 103,869
TOTAL AREA: 150 sq. miles (389 sq. km)
DENSITY: 793 people per sq. mile

LANGUAGES: English*, English Creole
RELIGIONS: Anglican 47%, Methodist 28%, Roman Catholic 13%, other 12%
ETHNIC MIX: Black 77%, Mulatto (mixed race) 19%, other 12%, Carib 2%, Asian 1%
GOVERNMENT: Parliamentary system
CURRENCY: East Caribbean dollar = 100 cents

Samoa

The Pacific islands of Samoa gained independence
from New Zealand in 1962. Four of the nine volcanic
islands are inhabited – Apolima, Manono, Savai'i, and Upolu.

 GEOGRAPHY
Comprises two large islands and
seven smaller ones. The two largest
islands have rainforested, mountainous
interiors surrounded by coastal lowlands
and coral reefs.

 CLIMATE
Tropical, with high humidity.
Cooler in May–November. Cyclone
season is December–March.

 PEOPLE & SOCIETY
Ethnic Samoans are the world's
second largest Polynesian group,
after the Maoris. Their way of life is
communal and formalized. Extended
family groups own 80% of the land.
Each family has an elected chief, who
looks after its political and social
interests. Large-scale migration to
the US and New Zealand reflects
the country's lack of jobs and the
attractions of a Western lifestyle.

 THE ECONOMY
Exports fish, coconut products
(oil, cream, copra), and nonu fruit.
Growth of tourism, offshore banking,
and light manufacturing (Japanese car
parts). Dependent on aid and expatriate
remittances. Rainforests are increasingly
exploited for timber.

◆ **INSIGHT:** *Samoa was named for
the sacred (sa) chickens (moa) of
Lu, son of Tagaloa, the god of creation*

FACTFILE

OFFICIAL NAME: Independent State
of Samoa
DATE OF FORMATION: 1962
CAPITAL: Apia
POPULATION: 200,000
TOTAL AREA: 1104 sq. miles
(2860 sq. km)

DENSITY: 183 people per sq. mile
LANGUAGES: Samoan*, English*
RELIGIONS: Christian 99%, other 1%
ETHNIC MIX: Polynesian 91%,
Euronesian (mixed European and
Polynesian) 7%, other 2%
GOVERNMENT: Parliamentary system
CURRENCY: Tala = 100 sene

San Marino

Perched on the slopes of Monte Titano in the Italian Appennines, San Marino has maintained its independence since the 4th century CE, but Italy effectively controls most of its affairs.

GEOGRAPHY

Distinctive limestone outcrop of Monte Titano dominates wooded hills and pastures near Italy's Adriatic coast.

CLIMATE

High altitude and sea breezes moderate a Mediterranean climate. Hot summers and cool, wet winters.

PEOPLE & SOCIETY

Territory is divided into nine "castles," or districts. Tightly knit society, with 16 centuries of tradition. Strict immigration rules require 30-year residence before applying for citizenship. Living standards are similar to those in northern Italy. About 20,000 Sammarinesi live abroad, most in Italy.

INSIGHT: *Sales of postage stamps and coins contribute around 10% of the national income*

THE ECONOMY

Tourism, banking, manufacturing, and investment all hit by 2008–2009 global downturn. Banking transparency has improved. Lower tax rates than Italy. Wine, cheese, olive oil, textiles, and ceramics are exported. Also relies on Italian subsidy and infrastructure.

500m/1640ft
200m/656ft
Sea Level

0   4 km
0   4 miles

FACTFILE

OFFICIAL NAME: Republic of San Marino

DATE OF FORMATION: 1631

CAPITAL: San Marino

POPULATION: 31,817

TOTAL AREA: 23.6 sq. miles (61 sq. km)

DENSITY: 1326 people per sq. mile

LANGUAGES: Italian*

RELIGIONS: Roman Catholic 93%, other and nonreligious 7%

ETHNIC MIX: Sammarinese 88%, Italian 10%, other 2%

GOVERNMENT: Parliamentary system

CURRENCY: Euro = 100 cents

São Tomé & Príncipe

A former Portuguese colony, São Tomé and Príncipe comprises two main islands and surrounding islets, off the west coast of Africa. Elections in 1991 ended 15 years of Marxism.

GEOGRAPHY

Islands scattered across the equator. São Tomé and Príncipe are heavily forested and mountainous.

CLIMATE
Hot and humid, but cooled by the Benguela Current. Plentiful rainfall.

PEOPLE & SOCIETY

Population is mostly black, though Portuguese culture pre-dominates. Blacks run the political parties. Society is well integrated and free from racial prejudice. Príncipe assumed autonomous status in 1995. There is a growing business class. The extended family offers the main form of social security. One of Africa's highest aid to population ratios

◆ **INSIGHT:** *The population is entirely of immigrant descent: the islands were uninhabited when colonized in 1470*

THE ECONOMY
Cocoa provides 95% of export earnings. Coconuts, pepper, coffee also farmed. Tourism potential. Offshore oil may come onstream in 2014.

```
1000m/3281ft
500m/1640ft
200m/656ft
Sea Level
```

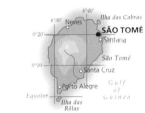

FACTFILE

OFFICIAL NAME: Democratic Republic of São Tomé and Príncipe

DATE OF FORMATION: 1975

CAPITAL: São Tomé

POPULATION: 179,506

TOTAL AREA: 386 sq. miles (1001 sq. km)

DENSITY: 484 people per sq. mile

LANGUAGES: Portuguese Creole, Portuguese*

RELIGIONS: Roman Catholic 84%, other 16%

ETHNIC MIX: Black 90%, Portuguese and Creole 10%

GOVERNMENT: Presidential system

CURRENCY: Dobra = 100 céntimos

Saudi Arabia

Occupying most of the Arabian Peninsula, Saudi Arabia covers an area the size of western Europe. It is the world's largest oil producer and has a major petrochemicals industry.

GEOGRAPHY

Mostly desert or semidesert plateau. Mountain ranges in the west run parallel to the Red Sea and drop steeply to a coastal plain.

CLIMATE

In summer, temperatures often soar above 118°F (48°C), but in winter they may fall below freezing. Rainfall is rare.

PEOPLE & SOCIETY

Most Saudis are Sunni Muslims who embrace *sharia* (Islamic law) and follow the strictly orthodox Wahhabi interpretation of Islam in their daily lives. Women are obliged to wear the veil, cannot hold a driver's license, and have no role in public life. The al-Sa'ud family rules with absolute power. Supported by the religious establishment, it controls all political life and makes few concessions to any calls for wider public participation.

THE ECONOMY

Vast oil and natural gas reserves. A third of workers are foreign. Attractive jobs for young Saudis are scarce, however.

◆ **INSIGHT:** *Three million Muslims a year make the hajj (pilgrimage) to the holy city of Mecca. Only practicing Muslims are allowed inside the city*

FACTFILE

OFFICIAL NAME: Kingdom of Saudi Arabia

DATE OF FORMATION: 1932

CAPITALS: Riyadh

POPULATION: 26.2 million

TOTAL AREA: 756,981 sq. miles (1,960,582 sq. km)

DENSITY: 32 people per sq. mile

LANGUAGES: Arabic*

RELIGIONS: (Native population) Sunni Muslim 85%, Shi'a Muslim 15%

ETHNIC MIX: Arab 72%, foreign (mostly south or southeast Asian) 20%, Afro-Asian 8%

GOVERNMENT: Monarchy

CURRENCY: Saudi riyal = 100 halalat

Senegal

Senegal's capital, Dakar, stands on the westernmost cape
of Africa. After independence from France, Senegal became a
single-party state, but it has had multiparty elections since 1981.

 GEOGRAPHY
Arid semidesert in the north. The
south is mainly savanna bushland. Plains
in the southeast.

CLIMATE
Tropical, with humid rainy
conditions June–October, and a drier
season December–May. The coast is
cooled by northern trade winds.

PEOPLE & SOCIETY
Interethnic marriage has reduced
ethnic tensions. Groups can be identified
regionally. Dakar is a Wolof area, with
the Serer concentrated to the east and
southeast of Dakar. The Senegal River is
dominated by the Peul and Toucouleur.
The Diola (Jola) in Casamance have felt
politically excluded, prompting a long-
running secessionist struggle; a cease-fire
has held since 2004. A large diaspora has
raised global awareness of Senegalese
culture and music.

THE ECONOMY
Good infrastructure, particularly
port at Dakar. Fishing (though stocks
diminishing). Remittances. Phosphate
mining. Groundnuts. Development of
tourism. Oil potential off Casamance.

INSIGHT: *Senegal's name derives
from the Muslim Zenega Berbers who
invaded in the 1300s*

FACTFILE

OFFICIAL NAME: Republic of Senegal
DATE OF FORMATION: 1960
CAPITAL: Dakar
POPULATION: 12.9 million
TOTAL AREA: 75,749 sq. miles
(196,190 sq. km)
DENSITY: 174 people per sq. mile

LANGUAGES: Wolof, Serer, Pulaar, Diola,
Mandinka, Malinké, Soninké, French[A]
RELIGIONS: Sunni Muslim 95%, Christian
(mainly Catholic) 4%, traditional beliefs 1%
ETHNIC MIX: Wolof 43%, Serer 15%,
other 14%, Peul 14%, Toucouleur 9%, Diola 5%
GOVERNMENT: Presidential system
CURRENCY: CFA franc = 100 centimes

Serbia

The central and eastern region of what was once Yugoslavia, Serbia was a pariah state until Slobodan Milosevic was ousted in 2000. Montenegro broke away in 2006, and Kosovo in 2008.

GEOGRAPHY

Landlocked since secession of Montenegro. Fertile Danube plain in the north, rolling uplands in the center and southeast. Mountains in southwest.

CLIMATE

Continental in north, with wet springs and warm summers. Colder winters with heavy snow in south.

PEOPLE & SOCIETY

Serbs are Orthodox Christian, and their language uses Cyrillic script. The Catholic Magyars (Hungarians) live mainly in Vojvodina, which has been granted some autonomy. Society was severely shaken in the 1990s by interethnic conflict. EU integration is more likely to progress now that Serbia has cooperated in the apprehension of suspected war criminals.

 INSIGHT: *The medieval Serbian Empire reached into northern Greece*

THE ECONOMY

Recovering from sanctions and 1999 NATO bombing: GDP is only just back to pre-1990 level. Reserves of coal, oil. Strong industrial base. Privatization ongoing. Foreign investment growing. Danube is a key transportation link.

FACTFILE

OFFICIAL NAME: Republic of Serbia

DATE OF FORMATION: 2006

CAPITAL: Belgrade

POPULATION: 9.9 million

TOTAL AREA: 29,905 sq. miles (77,453 sq. km)

DENSITY: 331 people per sq. mile

LANGUAGES: Serbian*, Hungarian (Magyar)

RELIGIONS: Orthodox Christian 85%, other 6%, Roman Catholic 6%, Muslim 3%

ETHNIC MIX: Serb 83%, other 10%, Magyar 4%, Bosniak 2%, Roma 1%

GOVERNMENT: Parliamentary system

CURRENCY: Serbian dinar = 100 para

Seychelles

Formerly a UK colony, the Seychelles comprises 115 islands in the Indian Ocean. After 14 years as a one-party state, multiparty elections were introduced in 1993.

GEOGRAPHY

Mostly low-lying coral atolls, but 40, including the largest, Mahé, are mountainous and are the only granitic midocean islands in the world.

CLIMATE

Tropical oceanic climate. Hot and humid. Rainy season December–May

PEOPLE & SOCIETY

The islands were uninhabited when French settlers arrived in the 18th century. Today, the population is homogeneous – a result of inter-marriage between ethnic groups. Almost 90% of people live on Mahé. Living standards are among Africa's highest. Poverty is rare and the welfare system caters to all.

INSIGHT: *The Seychelles' unique species include the coco-de-mer palm, which produces the world's largest seeds*

THE ECONOMY

Tourism is main sector, based on appeal of beaches and exotic wildlife. Tuna is fished and canned for export. Re-export trade. All domestic requirements are imported. Virtually no mineral resources. High debt-servicing burden. Lack of foreign exchange.

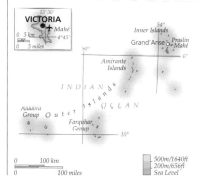

FACTFILE

OFFICIAL NAME: Republic of Seychelles

DATE OF FORMATION: 1976

CAPITAL: Victoria

POPULATION: 89,188

TOTAL AREA: 176 sq. miles (455 sq. km)

DENSITY: 858 people per sq. mile

LANGUAGES: French Creole*, English*, French*

RELIGIONS: Roman Catholic 82%, Anglican 6%, other (including Muslim) 6%, other Christian 4%, Hindu 2%

ETHNIC MIX: Creole 89%, Indian 5%, other 4%, Chinese 2%

GOVERNMENT: Presidential system

CURRENCY: Seychelles rupee = 100 cents

Sierra Leone

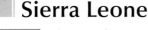

The west African state of Sierra Leone achieved independence from the UK in 1961. Today, trying to recover from ten years of devastating civil war, it is one of the world's poorest nations.

GEOGRAPHY

Flat plain, running the length of the coast, stretches inland for 83 miles (133 km). Beyond, forests rise to highlands near neighboring Guinea in the northeast.

CLIMATE

Hot tropical weather, with very high rainfall and humidity. The dusty, northeastern *harmattan* wind blows November–April.

PEOPLE & SOCIETY

Mende and Temne are the major ethnic groups. Freetown's citizens are largely descended from slaves freed from Britain and the US, resulting in a strongly Anglicized Creole culture in the capital. The countryside is less developed. A brutal civil war broke out in 1991 and was not properly resolved until a 2001 peace agreement. Two million people were displaced during the conflict.

THE ECONOMY

Aid is vital: reconstruction will take years. Diamond exports, though smuggling is rife. Rutile and bauxite also mined. Coffee and cocoa are cash crops, but most farming is subsistence.

◆ **INSIGHT:** *The British philanthropist Granville Sharp set up a settlement for freed slaves in Freetown in 1787*

FACTFILE

OFFICIAL NAME: Republic of Sierra Leone

DATE OF FORMATION: 1961

CAPITAL: Freetown

POPULATION: 5.8 million

TOTAL AREA: 27,698 sq. miles (71,740 sq. km)

DENSITY: 210 people per sq. mile

LANGUAGES: Mende, Temne, Krio, English*

RELIGIONS: Muslim 60%, Christian 30%, traditional beliefs 10%

ETHNIC MIX: Mende 35%, Temne 32%, other 21%, Limba 8%, Kuranko 4%

GOVERNMENT: Presidential system

CURRENCY: Leone = 100 cents

Singapore

Linked to the southernmost tip of the Malay peninsula by a causeway, Singapore was established as a trading settlement in 1819. It is now one of Asia's most important commercial centers.

GEOGRAPHY

Little remains of the original vegetation on Singapore Island. The other 54 much smaller islands are little more than swampy jungle.

CLIMATE

Equatorial. Hot and humid, with heavy rainfall all year round.

PEOPLE & SOCIETY

Dominated by the Chinese, who make up three-quarters of the community. The old English-speaking Straits Chinese and newer Mandarin-speakers are now well integrated. Malays are generally the poorest group. The population is skilled and industrious; there is a significant foreign workforce. Society is highly regulated; official campaigns aim to improve public behavior. Crime is low and punishment can be severe. Living standards are among the world's highest.

THE ECONOMY

Wealth from success as entrepôt and center of high-tech industries, such as electronics and pharmaceuticals. Leads research in new biotechnologies. All food, energy, and water imported. Worst-ever recession in 2008–2009.

INSIGHT: *Chewing gum was banned outright from 1992 to 2004*

FACTFILE

OFFICIAL NAME: Republic of Singapore

DATE OF FORMATION: 1965

CAPITAL: Singapore

POPULATION: 4.8 million

TOTAL AREA: 250 sq. miles (648 sq. km)

DENSITY: 20,339 people per sq. mile

LANGUAGES: Mandarin*, Malay*, Tamil*, English*

RELIGIONS: Buddhist 55%, Taoist 22%, Muslim 16%, Hindu, Christian, and Sikh 7%

ETHNIC MIX: Chinese 74%, Malay 14%, Indian 9%, other 3%

GOVERNMENT: Parliamentary system

CURRENCY: Singapore dollar = 100 cents

Slovakia

Landlocked in central Europe, Slovakia became a separate state in 1993, splitting ex-communist Czechoslovakia in two. It joined the EU in 2004 and the eurozone five years later.

GEOGRAPHY

The Tatra Mountains stretch along the northern border with Poland. Southern lowlands include the fertile Danube plain.

CLIMATE

Continental. Moderately warm summers and steady rainfall. Cold winters with heavy snowfalls.

PEOPLE & SOCIETY
The majority Slovaks are the dominant group. The Magyars (Hungarians) seek protection of their language and culture, backed by Hungary. Magyar parties exist in the political mainstream, and on occasion form part of the ruling coalition. Ethnic Czechs have dual citizenship. Roma are unrepresented and face significant discrimination. Rural eastern regions are least developed.

THE ECONOMY
Heavy industry, especially cars. Exports hit by 2007–2009 global downturn. Inexpensive workforce. Rising foreign investment. High unemployment, budget deficits. Successful privatizations.

◆ **INSIGHT:** *From 1526 to 1784 Bratislava, then known as Pozsony, served as the capital of Hungary*

FACTFILE

OFFICIAL NAME: Slovak Republic
DATE OF FORMATION: 1993
CAPITAL: Bratislava
POPULATION: 5.4 million
TOTAL AREA: 18,859 sq. miles
(48,845 sq. km)
DENSITY: 285 people per sq. mile

LANGUAGES: Slovak*, Hungarian (Magyar), Czech
RELIGIONS: Roman Catholic 69%, other 13%, nonreligious 13%, Greek Catholic (Uniate) 4%, Orthodox Christian 1%
ETHNIC MIX: Slovak 86%, Magyar 10%, Roma 2%, Czech 1%, other 1%
GOVERNMENT: Parliamentary system
CURRENCY: Euro = 100 cents

Slovenia

Lying at the junction of central Europe and the Balkans, Slovenia seceded from socialist Yugoslavia in 1991. In 2004, it became the first former Yugoslav state to join the EU.

GEOGRAPHY

Alpine terrain with hills and mountains. Forests cover almost half the country's area. There is a short coastline on the Adriatic Sea.

CLIMATE

Mediterranean climate on the small coastal strip. The alpine interior has continental extremes.

PEOPLE & SOCIETY

Long historical association with western Europe, accounts for the "Alpine" rather than "Balkan" outlook of Slovenia's people, despite close similarities to other former Yugoslavs. The absence of sizable Serb or Croat minorities made for a relatively peaceful secession from Yugoslavia. There are small communities of Italians and Magyars (Hungarians) in the southwest and east respectively.

THE ECONOMY

First new EU member to join eurozone (in 2007). Export-oriented, so vulnerable to global economic trends. Competitive manufacturing industry. Sizable state-owned sector remains.

INSIGHT: *A wheel found in a marsh in 2003 is claimed to be the world's oldest, pre-dating 3000 BCE*

1000m/3281ft
500m/1640ft
200m/656ft
Sea Level

HUNGARY

Murska
Sobota

AUSTRIA

Maribor   Ptuj

Jesenice
Kranj   Celje

ITALY   LJUBLJANA

Nova Gorica   Krško
Brežice

Postojna

Adriatic
Sea   CROATIA

0   25 km
0   25 miles

FACTFILE

OFFICIAL NAME: Republic of Slovenia
DATE OF FORMATION: 1991
CAPITAL: Ljubljana
POPULATION: 2 million
TOTAL AREA: 7820 sq. miles (20,253 sq. km)
DENSITY: 256 people per sq. mile

LANGUAGES: Slovenian*
RELIGIONS: Roman Catholic 58%, other 28%, Atheist 10%, Orthodox Christian 2%, Muslim 2%
ETHNIC MIX: Slovene 83%, other 12%, Serb 2%, Croat 2%, Bosniak 1%
GOVERNMENT: Parliamentary system
CURRENCY: Euro = 100 cents

Solomon Islands

The Solomons archipelago comprises several hundred coral reef islands scattered in the southwestern Pacific. Most of the population live on the six largest islands.

GEOGRAPHY

The six largest islands are volcanic, mountainous, and thickly forested. Flat coastal plains provide the only cultivable land.

CLIMATE

Northern islands are hot and humid all year round; farther south a cool season develops. November–April wet season brings cyclones.

PEOPLE & SOCIETY

Almost all Solomon Islanders are Melanesian. Animist beliefs exist alongside Christianity. Tensions are regional; Guadalcanal natives (Isatabu) fought against immigrant Malaitan workers in the 1998–2000 conflict, displacing thousands and ruining the economy. In 2003, Australian-led peacekeepers arrived. A new devolved "state system" has granted outlying islands more autonomy and brought a semblance of stability.

THE ECONOMY

Subsistence farming and fishing sustain 75% of people. Cash crops are copra and cocoa. Gold deposits. Civil conflict bankrupted the government, closed the main gold mine, and cut trade links. Forests have been depleted.

INSIGHT: *The battle for Japanese-held Guadalcanal was the first major US offensive in the Pacific War during World War II*

FACTFILE

OFFICIAL NAME: Solomon Islands
DATE OF FORMATION: 1978
CAPITAL: Honiara
POPULATION: 500,000
TOTAL AREA: 10,985 sq. miles (28,450 sq. km)
DENSITY: 46 people per sq. mile
LANGUAGES: English*, Pidgin English, Melanesian Pidgin, c. 120 others
RELIGIONS: Church of Melanesia (Anglican) 34%, Roman Catholic 19%, other 19%, South Seas Evangelical Church 17%, Methodist 11%
ETHNIC MIX: Melanesian 93%, Polynesian 4%, Micronesian 2%, other 1%
GOVERNMENT: Parliamentary system
CURRENCY: Solomon Is. dollar = 100 cents

Somalia

A semiarid state occupying the Horn of Africa, Somalia was formed from the Italian and British colonies of Somaliland. Conflict has left it without effective government since 1991.

GEOGRAPHY

Highlands in the north, flatter scrub-covered land to the south. Coastal areas are more fertile.

CLIMATE

Very dry, except for the north coast, which is hot and humid. The interior has among the world's highest average annual temperatures.

PEOPLE & SOCIETY

The clan system forms the basis of all commercial, political, and social life. Most people are ethnic Somali. The minority Bantu are traditionally seen as socially inferior. Since the 1991 coup, Somalia has lacked a strong central authority. Somaliland has declared independence, while Puntland claims autonomy. Islamist militias now control most of the country: some have joined the latest attempt at a transitional government, but fighting continues.

THE ECONOMY

Ongoing war. All goods, except arms, are in short supply. Piracy, banditry. Few natural resources. Prone to drought; latest famine declared in 2011. Somaliland is more stable, but its trade is hampered by lack of international recognition.

INSIGHT: *Until 1973, Somali was an unwritten language*

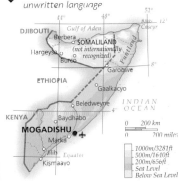

FACTFILE

OFFICIAL NAME: Somalia
DATE OF FORMATION: 1960
CAPITAL: Mogadishu
POPULATION: 9.4 million
TOTAL AREA: 246,199 sq. miles (637,657 sq. km)
DENSITY: 39 people per sq. mile

LANGUAGES: Somali*, Arabic*, English, Italian
RELIGIONS: Sunni Muslim 99%, Christian 1%
ETHNIC MIX: Somali 85%, other 15%
GOVERNMENT: Transitional regime
CURRENCY: Somali shilin = 100 senti

South Africa

After 80 years of white minority rule, South Africa held
its first multiracial, multiparty elections in 1994. Victory for the
blacks marked the symbolic overturning of long years of apartheid.

GEOGRAPHY

Much of the interior is grassy *veld*.
Desert in the west and far north.
Mountains east, south, and west.

CLIMATE

Warm, temperate, and dry.
Cape Town has a Mediterranean climate.
Semiarid in the west.

PEOPLE & SOCIETY

The majority black population now
dominates politically, but the minority
white community still controls the
economy. A small black middle class is
growing, but unemployment among
blacks remains high. Nearly six million
people are HIV-positive, but the fight
against AIDS is hampered by social
attitudes. Violent crime is a problem.

◆ **INSIGHT:** *Over the last century,
South Africa has produced over
half of the world's gold*

THE ECONOMY

Africa's largest, most developed
economy. Leading mineral producer,
notably metals, diamonds, coal. Tourism
is also key. Wealth gap has widened: jobs,
housing, and better access to basic
services are needed to fight poverty.

2000m/6562ft
1000m/3281ft
500m/1640ft
Sea Level

ZIMBABWE
BOTSWANA
MOZAMBIQUE
Limpopo
PRETORIA/
TSHWANE
Middelburg
Kalahari
SWAZILAND
Soweto
Johannesburg
NAMIBIA
Desert
Vryburg
Piet Retief
Upington
Vaal
Kroonstad
Orange
Kimberley
LESOTHO
Pietermaritzburg
BLOEMFONTEIN
Northern Karoo
Durban
Middelburg
INDIAN
OCEAN
CAPE
TOWN
Great Karoo
Beaufort West
East London
Drakensberg
George
Port Elizabeth
Cape of
Good Hope

0   400 km
0   400 miles

FACTFILE

OFFICIAL NAME: Republic of South Africa
DATE OF FORMATION: 1934
CAPITALS: Pretoria / Tshwane; Cape Town;
Bloemfontein
POPULATION: 50.5 million
TOTAL AREA: 471,008 sq. miles (1,219,912 sq. km)
DENSITY: 107 people per sq. mile

LANGUAGES: English*, isiZulu*, isiXhosa*,
Afrikaans*, 7 other official languages*
RELIGIONS: Christian 68%, animist and
traditional beliefs 29%, Muslim 2%, Hindu 1%
ETHNIC MIX: Black 80%, White 9%,
Colored 9%, Asian 2%
GOVERNMENT: Presidential system
CURRENCY: Rand = 100 cents

South Sudan

A long civil war in Sudan led to independence in 2011 for the mainly Christian southern part. The landlocked new state is poor and lacks vital infrastructure, despite its oil reserves.

GEOGRAPHY
The White Nile flows through South Sudan, from remote forest areas into the world's largest swamp, the Sudd.

CLIMATE
Tropical South Sudan's long, heavy rains result in some areas getting cut off. January to March is drier.

PEOPLE & SOCIETY
Most people are subsistence farmers. Village life is based on extended families; arranged marriages involve the payment of bride price. There are over 60 language groups. The Nilotic tribes include the Dinka and Nuer; the largest non-Nilotic group are the Azande on the Congolese border. Tribal divisions could threaten unity now the common cause of independence has been won. The Sudanese People's Liberation Movement, whose armed wing led the fighting, dominates politics.

THE ECONOMY
Needs foreign aid for humanitarian crisis and development. Issues over oil revenue and borders remain unresolved with Sudan, which controls sole oil export pipeline. Inherited foreign debt.

INSIGHT: *Decades of fighting from 1983 left over four million internally displaced*

500m/1640ft
200m/656ft
Sea Level

FACTFILE

OFFICIAL NAME: Republic of South Sudan
DATE OF FORMATION: 2011
CAPITAL: Juba
POPULATION: 8.3 million
TOTAL AREA: 248,777 sq. miles
(644,329 sq. km)
DENSITY: 33 people per sq. mile

LANGUAGES: Arabic, Dinka, Nuer, Zande, Bari, Shilluk, Lotuko
RELIGIONS: Over half of the population follow Christian or traditional beliefs
ETHNIC MIX: Dinka 40%, Nuer 15%, Bari 10%, Azande 10%, Shilluk 10%, Arab 10%, other 5%
GOVERNMENT: Presidential system
CURRENCY: South Sudan pound = 100 piastres

Spain

At its unification under Ferdinand and Isabella in 1492, Spain occupied a pivotal position between Europe, Africa, the North Atlantic, and the Mediterranean.

GEOGRAPHY

Mountain ranges in the north, center, and south, with a huge central plateau. Mediterranean lowlands. Verdant valleys in the northwest.

CLIMATE

Maritime in north. Hotter and drier in south. The central plateau has an extreme climate.

PEOPLE & SOCIETY

A vigorous ethnic regionalism, suppressed under Franco's fascist regime, now flourishes. There are 17 autonomous regions. People remain churchgoing, though Roman Catholic teachings on social issues are often flouted. Spanish women are increasingly emancipated, with strong political representation.

 INSIGHT: *Over 3000 festivals and feasts take place each year in Spain*

THE ECONOMY

Exports food, wine. Few natural resources. Large fishing fleet. Tourism and motor industry hit by global downturn; highest unemployment in EU since abrupt end of construction boom. Austerity measures aim to cut debt and deficits. A target for economic migrants from Africa.

FACTFILE

OFFICIAL NAME: Kingdom of Spain

DATE OF FORMATION: 1492

CAPITAL: Madrid

POPULATION: 45.3 million

TOTAL AREA: 194,896 sq. miles (504,782 sq. km)

DENSITY: 235 people per sq. mile

LANGUAGES: Spanish*, Catalan*, Galician*, Basque*

RELIGIONS: Roman Catholic 96%, other 4%

ETHNIC MIX: Castilian Spanish 72%, Catalan 17%, Galician 6%, Basque 2%, Roma 1%, other 2%

GOVERNMENT: Parliamentary system

CURRENCY: Euro = 100 cents

Sri Lanka

The teardrop-shaped island of Sri Lanka is separated from India by the Palk Strait. Ethnic Tamil rebels — the Tamil Tigers — were defeated in 2009, after a brutal 26-year civil war.

GEOGRAPHY
The main island is dominated by rugged central highlands. Fertile northern plains are dissected by rivers. Much of the land is tropical jungle.

CLIMATE
Tropical, with breezes on the coast and cooler air in highlands. Northeast is driest and hottest.

PEOPLE & SOCIETY
The Sinhalese are mostly Buddhist, while Tamils are mostly Hindu. Moors are the Muslim descendants of Arab traders. Tamils were the minority group favored by the British colonists. Majority-Sinhalese power since independence in 1948 fueled tensions, erupting into civil war in 1983. The eventual government victory in 2009 made this the only rebel insurgency ever defeated in modern times.

THE ECONOMY
Garment industry. Remittances. Major tea exporter. Civil war drained government funds, deterred investors and tourists. Tsunami damage in 2004.

◆ **INSIGHT:** *Sri Lanka elected the world's first woman prime minister, Sirimavo Bandaranaike, in 1960*

FACTFILE

OFFICIAL NAME: Democratic Socialist Republic of Sri Lanka
DATE OF FORMATION: 1948
CAPITAL: Colombo / Sri Jayewardenapura Kotte
POPULATION: 20.4 million
TOTAL AREA: 25,332 sq. miles (65,610 sq. km)
DENSITY: 816 people per sq. mile

LANGUAGES: Sinhala*, Tamil*, English
RELIGIONS: Buddhist 69%, Hindu 15%, Muslim 8%, Christian 8%
ETHNIC MIX: Sinhalese 74%, Tamil 18%, Moor 7%, other 1%
GOVERNMENT: Mixed presidential–parliamentary system
CURRENCY: Sri Lanka rupee = 100 cents

Sudan

The secession of the black African south in 2011 left Sudan as Africa's third-largest country. Darfur in the west is suffering a terrible humanitarian crisis.

GEOGRAPHY

Lies within the upper Nile basin. Mostly arid plains. Highlands border the Red Sea in the northeast.

CLIMATE

North is hot, arid desert with constant dry winds. Rainy season lasting a few months in the south.

PEOPLE & SOCIETY

About two million people are nomads. There are many ethnic groups. Islamic law, imposed by the Arab majority, restricts women's freedoms and alienated the non-Muslim south, which finally seceded in 2011 after prolonged conflict. Ethnic violence by Arab militias in Darfur since 2003 has killed 300,000 people and created a huge refugee crisis within Sudan and in neighboring Chad and CAR. President Bashir faces an international arrest warrant for crimes against humanity.

THE ECONOMY

Oil reserves reduced by secession of South. Cotton, sesame, gum arabic. Violence and drought hamper farming. Millions of people displaced. Large debt.

INSIGHT: *Sudan has more pyramids than Egypt: over 200 structures remain from ancient Nubian kingdoms on the Nile*

■ 2000m/6562ft	
■ 1000m/3281ft	
■ 500m/1640ft	
■ 200m/656ft	
□ Sea Level	

0   400 km
0   400 miles

FACTFILE

OFFICIAL NAME: Republic of the Sudan
DATE OF FORMATION: 1956
CAPITAL: Khartoum
POPULATION: 34 million
TOTAL AREA: 718,722 sq. miles (1,861,481 sq. km)
DENSITY: 47 people per sq. mile

LANGUAGES: Arabic*, Nubian, Beja, Fur
RELIGIONS: Nearly the whole population is Muslim (mainly Sunni)
ETHNIC MIX: Arab 60%, other 18%, Nubian 10%, Beja 8%, Fur 3%, Zaghawa 1%
GOVERNMENT: Presidential system
CURRENCY: New Sudanese pound = 100 piastres

Suriname

Suriname is a former Dutch colony on the north coast of
South America. Democracy was restored in 1991, after almost 11 years
of military rule. The Netherlands is still the main supplier of aid.

GEOGRAPHY
Mostly covered by tropical
rainforest. Coastal plain rises to central
plateaus and the Guiana Highlands.

CLIMATE
Tropical. Hot and humid, but
cooled by trade winds. High rainfall,
especially in the interior.

PEOPLE & SOCIETY
The Dutch brought laborers
from South Asia and Java. Independence
saw mass emigration: over 300,000
Surinamese live in the Netherlands.
Of those left, over 85% live near the
coast, the rest in scattered rainforest
communities. Indigenous Amerindians
only number a few thousand. *Bosnegers* –
descended from runaway African slaves –
fought the military government in the
late 1980s. Under civilian rule, each
group has had a political party
representing its interests.

THE ECONOMY
Alumina and gold are the key
exports. Rice and bananas are main cash
crops. Oil production and tourism are
growing. Excessive bureaucracy.

◆ **INSIGHT:** *In a 1667 Anglo-Dutch deal,
Holland gained Suriname but lost New
Amsterdam (now New York)*

1000m/3281ft
500m/1640ft
200m/656ft
Sea Level

0   200 km
0   200 miles

FACTFILE

OFFICIAL NAME: Republic of Suriname
DATE OF FORMATION: 1975
CAPITAL: Paramaribo
POPULATION: 500,000
TOTAL AREA: 63,039 sq. miles (163,270 sq. km)
DENSITY: 8 people per sq. mile
LANGUAGES: Sranan (Creole), Dutch*, Hindi,
Javanese, Sarnami, Saramaccan, Chinese, Carib

RELIGIONS: Christian 48%, Hindu 27%,
Muslim 20%, traditional beliefs 5%
ETHNIC MIX: East Indian 27%, Creole 18%,
Black 15%, Javanese 15%, mixed race 13%,
other 6%, Amerindian 4%, Chinese 2%
GOVERNMENT: Parliamentary system
CURRENCY: Surinamese dollar = 100 cents

Swaziland

The tiny southern African kingdom of Swaziland is crippled with HIV/AIDS and economically dependent on South Africa. Vocal demands for multiparty democracy have been ignored.

GEOGRAPHY

Mainly high plateaus and mountains. Rolling grasslands and low scrub plains to the east. Pine forests on western border.

CLIMATE

Temperatures rise and rainfall declines as the land descends eastward, from high to low grassy *veld*.

PEOPLE & SOCIETY

One of Africa's most conservative states, though there is pressure from urban-based modernizers. Political system promotes Swazi tradition and is dominated by powerful monarchy. Women face discrimination. Swaziland has the world's highest prevalence of HIV/AIDS: chastity is urged to combat its spread.

◆ **INSIGHT:** *Polygamy is practiced in Swaziland – when King Sobhuza died in 1982, he left 100 widows*

THE ECONOMY
Sugarcane is the main cash crop. Wood pulp and soft drink concentrates are also exported. Loss of workforce to HIV/AIDS, and high cost of health care.

FACTFILE

OFFICIAL NAME: Kingdom of Swaziland

DATE OF FORMATION: 1968

CAPITAL: Mbabane

POPULATION: 1.2 million

TOTAL AREA: 6704 sq. miles (17,363 sq. km)

DENSITY: 181 people per sq. mile

LANGUAGES: English*, siSwati*, isiZulu, Xitsonga

RELIGIONS: Traditional beliefs 40%, other 30%, Roman Catholic 20%, Muslim 10%

ETHNIC MIX: Swazi 97%, other 3%

GOVERNMENT: Monarchy

CURRENCY: Lilangeni = 100 cents

Sweden

The largest Scandinavian country by both population and area, Sweden has one of the world's most extensive welfare systems and is among the leading proponents of equal rights for women.

GEOGRAPHY
Heavily forested, with many lakes. Northern plateau extends beyond the Arctic Circle. Southern lowlands are widely cultivated.

CLIMATE
Southern coasts warmed by Gulf Stream. Northern areas have more extreme continental climate.

PEOPLE & SOCIETY
The nuclear family forms the basis of society, but the marriage rate is one of the lowest in the world, and cohabitation is now common. The model welfare system is paid for by a high tax burden. Women are well represented at all levels. A minority of 20,000 Sámi lives in the far north. Most industries and the bulk of population are based in and around the southern cities. An EU member since 1995, Sweden has voted not to join the euro.

THE ECONOMY
Companies of global importance, including Volvo, Saab, SFK, Ericsson. Highly developed infrastructure. Up-to-date technology. Skilled workforce.

◆ **INSIGHT:** Sweden has maintained a position of armed neutrality since 1815

FACTFILE

OFFICIAL NAME: Kingdom of Sweden
DATE OF FORMATION: 1523
CAPITAL: Stockholm
POPULATION: 9.3 million
TOTAL AREA: 173,731 sq. miles (449,964 sq. km)
DENSITY: 59 people per sq. mile
LANGUAGES: Swedish*, Finnish, Sámi

RELIGIONS: Evangelical Lutheran 75%, other 13%, other Protestant 5%, Muslim 5%, Roman Catholic 2%
ETHNIC MIX: Swedish 86%, foreign-born or first-generation immigrant 12%, Finnish and Sámi 2%
GOVERNMENT: Parliamentary system
CURRENCY: Swedish krona = 100 öre

Switzerland

One of the world's most prosperous countries, Switzerland sits at the center of Europe. It has retained its neutral status through every major European conflict since 1815.

GEOGRAPHY

Mostly mountainous, with river valleys. The Alps cover 60% of its area; the Jura in the west cover 10%. Lowlands lie along the east–west axis.

CLIMATE

Most rain falls in the warm summer months. Winters are snowy, but milder and foggy away from the mountains. Avalanches are a problem.

PEOPLE & SOCIETY

Switzerland is composed of distinct German-Swiss, French-Swiss, and Italian-Swiss linguistic groups. In the east, a 35,000-strong minority speaks Romansch. The country is divided into 26 autonomous cantons (states), each with control over housing and economics. Public referenda are widely used to decide policy. Society is conservative; marriage is common but divorce is above the EU average rate.

THE ECONOMY

Diversified economy relies on services – the banking sector manages over a quarter of the world's offshore private wealth – and specialized industries (engineering, watches, etc).

◆ **INSIGHT:** *Famed for its neutrality, Switzerland only joined the UN in 2002, and remains outside the EU*

FACTFILE

OFFICIAL NAME: Swiss Confederation

DATE OF FORMATION: 1291

CAPITAL: Bern

POPULATION: 7.6 million

TOTAL AREA: 15,942 sq. miles (41,290 sq. km)

DENSITY: 495 people per sq. mile

LANGUAGES: German*, Swiss-German, French*, Italian*, Romansch*

RELIGIONS: Roman Catholic 42%, Protestant 35%, other and nonreligious 19%, Muslim 4%

ETHNIC MIX: German 64%, French 20%, other 9.5%, Italian 6%, Romansch 0.5%

GOVERNMENT: Parliamentary system

CURRENCY: Swiss franc = 100 rappen/centimes

Syria

Stretching from the eastern Mediterranean to the Tigris River, Syria's borders are regarded as an artificial creation of French colonial rule by many Syrians. Foreign relations are turbulent.

GEOGRAPHY

A short stretch of coastal plain is backed by a low range of hills. The Euphrates River cuts through a vast interior desert plateau.

CLIMATE

Mediterranean coastal climate. Inland areas are arid. In winter, snow is common on the mountains.

PEOPLE & SOCIETY

Most Syrians live within 60 miles (100 km) of the coast. 90% are Muslim, including the politically dominant Shi'a Alawis. In the north and west are groups of Kurds, Armenians, and Turkic-speaking peoples. Some 460,000 Palestinian refugees live in Syria, and over a million Iraqis have fled here since 2003. There is a growing gulf between rich and poor. Fierce repression of pro-democracy protests in 2011 drew international condemnation.

THE ECONOMY

Oil, though production is falling. Natural gas. High defense spending. Large public sector. Agriculture: fruit, cotton, and grain. Under US sanctions.

INSIGHT: Syria is an ancient land; there are at least 3500 as yet unexcavated archaeological sites

FACTFILE

OFFICIAL NAME: Syrian Arab Republic
DATE OF FORMATION: 1941
CAPITAL: Damascus
POPULATION: 22.5 million
TOTAL AREA: 71,498 sq. miles (184,180 sq. km)
DENSITY: 317 people per sq. mile

LANGUAGES: Arabic*, French, Kurdish, Armenian, Circassian, Assyrian, Aramaic
RELIGIONS: Sunni Muslim 74%, Alawi 12%, Christian 10%, Druze 3%, other 1%
ETHNIC MIX: Arab 90%, Kurd 9%, Armenian, Turkmen, and Circassian 1%
GOVERNMENT: One-party state
CURRENCY: Syrian pound = 100 piastres

Taiwan

The republic of Taiwan (formerly Formosa) is on an island 80 miles (130 km) off the southeast coast of mainland China, which still considers it to be a renegade province.

GEOGRAPHY
Mountain region covers two-thirds of the island. Highly fertile lowlands and coastal plains.

CLIMATE
Tropical monsoon. Hot and humid. Typhoons July–September. Snow falls in mountains in winter.

PEOPLE & SOCIETY
Most Taiwanese are Han Chinese, descendants of the 1644 migration of the Ming dynasty from the mainland. The modern republic was created in 1949, when the nationalist Kuomintang was expelled from the mainland following Communist victory in the civil war. 100,000 emigrés established themselves as a ruling class. Initial resentment has subsided as a new Taiwan-born generation has taken over the reins of power. The aboriginal minority suffers discrimination.

THE ECONOMY
Successful economy of small, adaptable companies. High-tech goods: TVs, computers, and semiconductors. Rising trade, investment with China.

◆ **INSIGHT:** *Taiwan lost its seat at the UN to Beijing in 1971: both claim to represent "China"*

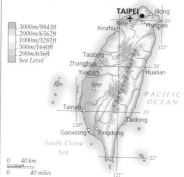

3000m/9843ft
2000m/6562ft
1000m/3281ft
500m/1640ft
200m/656ft
Sea Level

TAIPEI · Jilong
Pate · Hsintien
Xinzhu
Taizong
Zhanghua
Yuanlin · Hualian
Jiayi
PACIFIC OCEAN
Tainan
Taidong
Gaoxiong · Pingdong
South China Sea

0   40 km
0   40 miles

FACTFILE

OFFICIAL NAME: Republic of China (ROC)
DATE OF FORMATION: 1949
CAPITAL: Taipei
POPULATION: 23.1 million
TOTAL AREA: 13,892 sq. miles (35,980 sq. km)
DENSITY: 1852 people per sq. mile
LANGUAGES: Amoy Chinese, Mandarin Chinese*, Hakka Chinese
RELIGIONS: Buddhist, Confucianist, and Taoist 93%, Christian 5%, other 2%
ETHNIC MIX: Han Chinese (pre-20th-century migration) 84%, Han Chinese (20th-century migration) 14%, Aboriginal 2%
GOVERNMENT: Presidential system
CURRENCY: Taiwan dollar = 100 cents

Tajikistan

Tajikistan lies landlocked on the western slopes of the Pamirs in central Asia. Soon after the breakup of the USSR in 1991, civil war erupted between ruling communists and Islamists.

GEOGRAPHY

Mainly mountainous: bare slopes of the Pamir ranges, with fast-flowing rivers, cover most of the country. Small but fertile Fergana Valley in northwest.

CLIMATE

Continental extremes in the valleys. Bitterly cold winters in the mountains. Rainfall is low

PEOPLE & SOCIETY

Unlike the other former Soviet republics of central Asia, Tajikistan is dominated by a people of Persian (Iranian) origin rather than Turkic origin. The main ethnic conflict is with the Turkic Uzbek minority. Russians are discriminated against; most fled in the 1992–1997 civil war, and standards of living fell dramatically. Islamist militants are active. Two million people work abroad, primarily in Russia.

THE ECONOMY

Mass poverty. Declining cotton revenue. Also exports aluminum. Uranium deposits. Transit route for illicit Afghan opium. Corruption. Needs reforms to attract foreign investment.

INSIGHT: *Carpet-making, an ancient tradition learned from Persia, is still a major source of revenue*

FACTFILE

OFFICIAL NAME. Republic of Tajikistan
DATE OF FORMATION: 1991
CAPITAL: Dushanbe
POPULATION: 7.1 million
TOTAL AREA: 55,251 sq. miles
(143,100 sq. km)
DENSITY: 129 people per sq. mile

LANGUAGES: Tajik*, Uzbek, Russian
RELIGIONS: Sunni Muslim 95%, Shi'a Muslim 3%, other 2%
ETHNIC MIX: Tajik 80%, Uzbek 15%, other 3%, Kyrgyz 1%, Russian 1%
GOVERNMENT: Presidential system
CURRENCY: Somoni = 100 diram

Tanzania

The east African state of Tanzania was formed in 1964 by the union of Tanganyika and the Zanzibar islands. A third of its area is game reserve or national park.

GEOGRAPHY
The mainland is mostly a high plateau lying to the east of the Great Rift Valley. Forested coastal plain. Highlands in the north and south.

CLIMATE
Tropical on the coast and Zanzibar. Semiarid on central plateau, semitemperate in the highlands. March–May rains.

PEOPLE & SOCIETY
99% of people belong to one of 120 small ethnic Bantu groups. Arabs, Asians, and Europeans make up the remaining population. Use of Kiswahili as the lingua franca has eliminated ethnic rivalries. The majority of Tanzanians are subsistence famers.

◆ **INSIGHT:** At 19,340 ft (5895 m), Kilimanjaro in northeast Tanzania is Africa's highest mountain

THE ECONOMY
Reliant on agriculture, including forestry and cattle. Coffee, cotton, tea, cashew nuts, sisal, and cloves are cash crops. Gold, diamonds, and gems mined. Safari and beach tourism. Debt relief.

FACTFILE

OFFICIAL NAME: United Republic of Tanzania
DATE OF FORMATION: 1964
CAPITAL: Dodoma
POPULATION: 45 million
TOTAL AREA: 364,898 sq. miles (945,087 sq. km)
DENSITY: 132 people per sq. mile

LANGUAGES: Kiswahili*, Sukuma, Chagga, Nyamwezi, Hehe, Makonde, Yao, English*
RELIGIONS: Christian 63%, Muslim 35%, other 2%
ETHNIC MIX: Native African (over 120 tribes) 99%, European, Asian, and Arab 1%
GOVERNMENT: Presidential system
CURRENCY: Tanzanian shilling = 100 cents

Thailand

Thailand lies at the heart of mainland southeast Asia.
Continuing rapid industrialization has resulted in massive congestion
in the capital and a serious depletion of natural resources.

 GEOGRAPHY
One-third is low plateau, drained
by tributaries of the Mekong River.
Central plain is the most fertile area.

 CLIMATE
Tropical. Hot, humid March–May;
monsoon rains May–October; cooler
season November–March.

 PEOPLE & SOCIETY
Buddhism is a national binding
force. 600,000 hill tribes-people, with
their own languages, live in the north and
northeast. The Chinese minority is the
most assimilated in the region. Malay
Islamists in the undeveloped far south
are fighting for secession. Politics has
been unstable since the 2006 fall of
populist Prime Minister Thaksin.

 INSIGHT: *Thailand, meaning "land of
the free," is the only SE Asian nation
never to have been colonized*

THE ECONOMY
Successful manufacturing. Natural
gas reserves. Leading exporter of rice
and rubber. Tourism, though sex industry
harms image. 2004 tsunami damage.

	2000m/6562ft
	1000m/3281ft
	500m/1640ft
	200m/656ft
	Sea Level

FACTFILE

OFFICIAL NAME: Kingdom of Thailand

DATE OF FORMATION: 1238

CAPITAL: Bangkok

POPULATION: 68.1 million

TOTAL AREA: 198,455 sq. miles
(514,000 sq. km)

DENSITY: 345 people per sq. mile

LANGUAGES: Thai*, Chinese, Malay, Khmer,
Mon, Karen, Miao

RELIGIONS: Buddhist 95%, Muslim 4%,
other (including Christian) 1%

ETHNIC MIX: Thai 83%, Chinese 12%, Malay 3%,
Khmer and other 2%

GOVERNMENT: Parliamentary system

CURRENCY: Baht = 100 satang

Togo

Togo lies sandwiched between Ghana and Benin in west Africa. General Eyadema ruled from 1967–2005; his son succeeded him. Lomé port is an important entrepôt for regional trade.

GEOGRAPHY
Central forested region bounded by savanna lands to the north and south. Mountain range stretches southwest to northeast.

CLIMATE
Coast hot and humid; drier inland. Rainy season March–July, with heaviest falls in the west.

PEOPLE & SOCIETY
Harsh resentment between Ewe in the south and Kabye in the north. Kabye control the military, but the north is less developed than the south. Extended family is important. Tribalism and nepotism are key factors in everyday life. Some ethnic groups, such as the Mina, have matriarchal societies.

◆ **INSIGHT:** *The "Nana Benz," the entrepreneurial market-women of Lomé, control Togo's retail trade*

THE ECONOMY
Most people are farmers. Self-sufficient in staple foods. Togo's main cash crops are coffee and cocoa: cotton has declined. Its phosphate deposits are the most mineral-rich in the world, but easily extractable reserves are depleted and the sector needs investment.

500m/1640ft
200m/656ft
Sea Level

0   50 km
0   50 miles

FACTFILE

OFFICIAL NAME: Republic of Togo
DATE OF FORMATION: 1960
CAPITAL: Lomé
POPULATION: 6.8 million
TOTAL AREA: 21,924 sq. miles (56,785 sq. km)
DENSITY: 324 people per sq. mile

LANGUAGES: Ewe, Kabye, Gurma, French*
RELIGIONS: Christian 47%, traditional beliefs 33%, Muslim 14%, other 6%
ETHNIC MIX: Ewe 46%, other African 41%, Kabye 12%, European 1%
GOVERNMENT: Presidential system
CURRENCY: CFA franc = 100 centimes

Tonga

 Tonga is a South Pacific archipelago of 170 islands; only 45 of these islands are inhabited. The king retains significant powers though some democratic reforms were introduced in 2011.

 GEOGRAPHY
Easterly islands are generally low and fertile. Those in the west are higher and volcanic in origin.

CLIMATE
Tropical oceanic. Temperatures range between 68°F (20°C) and 86°F (30°C) all year round. Heavy rainfall, especially February–March

 PEOPLE & SOCIETY
Tonga is the last remaining Polynesian monarchy. All land belongs to the crown, but is administered by nobles who allot it to the common people. Respect for traditional values is high, though younger, Westernized Tongans are starting to question some attitudes. The first elected commoner became prime minister in 2006.

 INSIGHT: *Unique in the Pacific, Tonga was never brought under foreign rule*

THE ECONOMY
Squashes and vanilla exported. Remittances. Potential for tourism and fisheries. Capital's business district destroyed in 2006 prodemocracy riots.

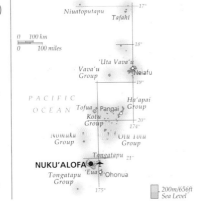

FACTFILE

OFFICIAL NAME: Kingdom of Tonga
DATE OF FORMATION: 1970
CAPITAL: Nuku'alofa
POPULATION: 105,916
TOTAL AREA: 289 sq. miles (748 sq. km)
DENSITY: 381 people per sq. mile
LANGUAGES: English*, Tongan*

RELIGIONS: Free Wesleyan 41%, other 17%, Roman Catholic 16%, Church of Jesus Christ of Latter-Day Saints 14%, Free Church of Tonga 12%
ETHNIC MIX: Tongan 98%, other 2%
GOVERNMENT: Monarchy
CURRENCY: Pa'anga (Tongan dollar) = 100 seniti

Trinidad & Tobago

The two islands of the former UK colony of Trinidad and Tobago are the most southerly of the Caribbean Windward Islands, lying just 9 miles (15 km) off the coast of Venezuela.

GEOGRAPHY

Both islands are hilly and wooded. Trinidad has a rugged mountain range in the north, and swamps on its east and west coasts.

CLIMATE

Tropical, with July–December wet season. Escapes the region's hurricanes, which pass to the north.

PEOPLE & SOCIETY

Trinidad's East Indian community is the Caribbean's largest and holds onto its Muslim and Hindu heritage. There are tensions with the mainly Christian blacks; political parties are divided along race lines. Blacks form the majority on Tobago. High rates of kidnapping and murder are an issue.

◆ **INSIGHT:** *Trinidad and Tobago is the birthplace of steel bands and Calypso music*

THE ECONOMY

Oil and natural gas: it provides 40% of US imports of liquefied natural gas, but reserves are declining fast. Associated industries: second-largest producer of methanol. Tourism on wildlife-rich Tobago.

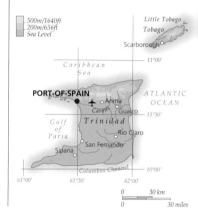

FACTFILE

OFFICIAL NAME: Republic of Trinidad and Tobago

DATE OF FORMATION: 1962

CAPITAL: Port-of-Spain

POPULATION: 1.3 million

TOTAL AREA: 1980 sq. miles (5128 sq. km)

DENSITY: 656 people per sq. mile

LANGUAGES: English Creole, English*, Hindi, French, Spanish

RELIGIONS: Roman Catholic 26%, Hindu 23%, other 23%, Protestant 22%, Muslim 6%

ETHNIC MIX: East Indian 40%, Black 38%, mixed race 20%, White, Chinese 1%, other 1%

GOVERNMENT: Parliamentary system

CURRENCY: Trin. & Tob. dollar = 100 cents

Tunisia

A French north African colony until 1956, Tunisia was relatively liberal in social terms, but in 2011 protesters ousted the dictatorial president, triggering the "Arab Spring" across the region.

GEOGRAPHY
Mountains in the north are surrounded by plains. Vast, low-lying salt pans in the center. To the south lies the Sahara Desert.

CLIMATE
Summer temperatures are high. The north is often wet and windy in winter. Far south is arid.

PEOPLE & SOCIETY
The population is almost entirely of Arab-Berber descent, with Jewish and Christian minorities. Many still live in extended family groups, in which three or four generations are represented. Women have better rights than in most other Arab countries and make up over 30% of the workforce. Parliamentary and municipal quotas aim to increase their representation in politics. A low birth rate is a result of a long-standing family planning policy.

THE ECONOMY
Competitive and diversified. Expanding manufacturing. Exports olives, dates, citrus fruit, phosphates. Tourism hurt by instability. Free trade with EU.

INSIGHT: *Tunisia was the center of trading empires from the 9th century BCE*

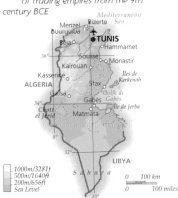

FACTFILE

OFFICIAL NAME: Republic of Tunisia
DATE OF FORMATION: 1956
CAPITAL: Tunis
POPULATION: 10.4 million
TOTAL AREA: 63,169 sq. miles
(163,610 sq. km)
DENSITY: 173 people per sq. mile

LANGUAGES: Arabic*, French
RELIGIONS: Muslim (mainly Sunni) 98%, Christian 1%, Jewish 1%
ETHNIC MIX: Arab and Berber 98%, Jewish 1%, European 1%
GOVERNMENT: Transitional regime
CURRENCY: Tunisian dinar = 1000 millimes

Turkey

Lying partly in the region of eastern Thrace in Europe, but mostly in Asia, Turkey's position gives it significant influence in the Mediterranean, the Black Sea, and the Middle East.

GEOGRAPHY
Asian Turkey (Anatolia) is dominated by two mountain ranges, separated by a high, semidesert plateau. Coastal regions are fertile.

CLIMATE
Coast has a Mediterranean climate. Interior has cold, snowy winters and hot, dry summers.

PEOPLE & SOCIETY
Despite racial diversity, Turkey has a strong sense of national identity, and close links with other Turkic states. Kurds, the largest minority, based in the southeast, have waged a violent campaign for greater autonomy intermittently since 1984. Islamist parties are challenging Turkey's cherished identity as a secular state. It has applied to join the EU, though progress will be slow.

THE ECONOMY
Liberalized economy, boosted by self-sufficient agriculture, and textiles, tourism, and manufacturing sectors. Route of Asian oil pipelines to Europe.

INSIGHT: *Turkey had two of the seven wonders of the ancient world: the tomb of King Mausolus at Halicarnassus (now Bodrum), and the temple of Artemis at Ephesus*

FACTFILE
OFFICIAL NAME: Republic of Turkey
DATE OF FORMATION: 1923
CAPITAL: Ankara
POPULATION: 75.7 million
TOTAL AREA: 301,382 sq. miles (780,580 sq. km)
DENSITY: 255 people per sq. mile

LANGUAGES: Turkish*, Kurdish, Arabic, Circassian, Armenian, Greek, Georgian, Ladino
RELIGIONS: Muslim (mainly Sunni) 99%, other 1%
ETHNIC MIX: Turkish 70%, Kurdish 20%, other 8%, Arab 2%
GOVERNMENT: Parliamentary system
CURRENCY: Turkish lira = 100 kurus

Turkmenistan

Stretching from the Caspian Sea into the central Asian desert, Turkmenistan has had less upheaval than most ex-Soviet states, under President Niyazov's dictatorial rule (1991–2006).

GEOGRAPHY
Low Garagum Desert covers 80% of the country. Mountains on southern border with Iran. Fertile Amu Darya Valley in north.

CLIMATE
Arid desert climate with extreme summer heat, but sub freezing winter temperatures.

PEOPLE & SOCIETY
Before Russia annexed the area in 1884, the Turkmen were a largely nomadic tribal people. Today, the tribal unit remains strong, with population clustered around desert oases. Relations with Uzbek and Russian minorities have become tense in recent years due to the "Turkmenization" of government, education, and religion. Political reform since Niyazov's sudden death in 2006 is slowly dismantling the old regime

THE ECONOMY
State-controlled, though there is some private investment. Natural gas and oil are main resources. Overintensive farming of cotton. Black market.

INSIGHT: President Niyazov created an elaborate personality cult, styling himself as Turkmenbashi – "head" of all Turkmen

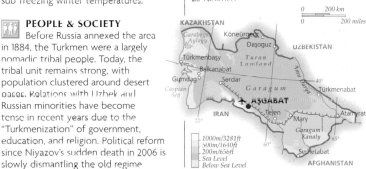

FACTFILE

OFFICIAL NAME: Turkmenistan
DATE OF FORMATION: 1991
CAPITAL: Asgabat
POPULATION: 5.2 million
TOTAL AREA: 188,455 sq. miles (488,100 sq. km)
DENSITY: 28 people per sq. mile

LANGUAGES: Turkmen*, Uzbek, Russian, Kazakh, Tatar
RELIGIONS: Sunni Muslim 89%, Orthodox Christian 9%, other 2%
ETHNIC MIX: Turkmen 85%, other 6%, Uzbek 5%, Russian 4%
GOVERNMENT: One-party state
CURRENCY: New manat = 100 tenge

Tuvalu

One of the world's smallest, most isolated states, Tuvalu lies in the central Pacific. The nine islands were linked to the Gilbert Islands (Kiribati) as a UK colony until independence.

GEOGRAPHY

A series of coral atolls, none more than 15 ft (4.6 m) above sea level. Poor soils restrict vegetation to bush, coconut palms, and breadfruit trees.

CLIMATE

Hot all year round. Heavy annual rainfall. Hurricane season brings many violent storms.

PEOPLE & SOCIETY

People are mostly Polynesian. Around half the population lives on Funafuti, where government jobs are based. Life is communal and traditional. Most people live by subsistence farming, digging pits out of the coral to grow crops. Fresh water is precious, due to frequent droughts.

◆ **INSIGHT:** Low-lying Tuvalu, like the Maldives, is set to disappear with rising sea levels

THE ECONOMY

World's smallest economy. Remittances from Tuvaluan seafarers. Sale of fishing licenses. Copra, stamps, and coins exported. Income from trust fund and the lease of .tv Internet suffix.

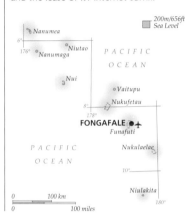

FACTFILE

OFFICIAL NAME: Tuvalu
DATE OF FORMATION: 1978
CAPITAL: Fongafale, on Funafuti Atoll
POPULATION: 10,544
TOTAL AREA: 10 sq. miles (26 sq. km)
DENSITY: 1054 people per sq. mile

LANGUAGES: Tuvaluan, Kiribati, English*
RELIGIONS: Church of Tuvalu 97%, Baha'i 1%, Seventh-day Adventist 1%, other 1%
ETHNIC MIX: Polynesian 96%, Micronesian 4%
GOVERNMENT: Nonparty system
CURRENCY: Australian dollar and Tuvaluan dollar = 100 cents each

Uganda

Landlocked in east Africa, Uganda has a history of ethnic strife. Under President Museveni, steps have been taken to restore peace and to rebuild the economy and democracy.

GEOGRAPHY

Predominantly a large plateau with the Ruwenzori mountain range and the Great Rift Valley in the west. Lake Victoria lies to the southeast. Vegetation is of savanna type.

CLIMATE

Altitude and the influence of the lakes modify the equatorial climate. Rain falls throughout the year; spring is the wettest period.

PEOPLE & SOCIETY

Mostly rural population comprising 13 main ethnic groups. President Museveni has worked hard to break down ethnic animosities, but a noticeable north–south divide persists, with most development in the south. After two decades of brutal clashes (1987–2008), the Ugandan army is still pursuing remnants of the Lord's Resistance Army across the DRC, South Sudan, and the CAR.

THE ECONOMY

Resource-rich, but undeveloped and poor. Exports coffee, fish, tea, and flowers. Oil exploration. Hydroelectric power is reducing oil imports. Great potential from mining. Debt relief.

INSIGHT: *Lake Victoria is the world's third-largest lake*

FACTFILE

OFFICIAL NAME: Republic of Uganda
DATE OF FORMATION: 1962
CAPITAL: Kampala
POPULATION: 33.8 million
TOTAL AREA: 91,135 sq. miles (236,040 sq. km)
DENSITY: 439 people per sq. mile

LANGUAGES: Luganda, Nkole, Chiga, Lango, Acholi, Teso, Lugbara, English*
RELIGIONS: Christian 85%, Muslim (mainly Sunni) 12%, other 3%
ETHNIC MIX: Other 50%, Baganda 17%, Banyakole 10%, Basoga 9%, Iteso 7%, Bakiga 7%
GOVERNMENT: Presidential system
CURRENCY: New Uganda shilling = 100 cents

Ukraine

The former "breadbasket of the Soviet Union," Ukraine lies on the north coast of the Black Sea. Politics is divided between pro-Russian sentiments and pro-European nationalism.

 GEOGRAPHY
Mainly fertile steppes and forests. Carpathian Mountains in west, Crimean chain in south. Pripet Marshes in northwest.

 CLIMATE
Mainly continental climate, with distinct seasons. Southern Crimea has Mediterranean climate.

 PEOPLE & SOCIETY
Over 90% of people in the west are Ukrainian, but in cities in the east and south, and in Crimea, Russians form a majority. The government is wary of Crimean separatism. Tatars have been returning there since the Soviet Union's collapse and now comprise around 12% of the local population. Over five million people in Ukraine, Belarus, and Russia live in areas "contaminated" by the 1986 Chornobyl nuclear disaster.

$ THE ECONOMY
Minerals: 5% of global reserves. Slow reform of land laws, holding back agriculture. Oil/natural gas transit from Russia and the Caspian to Europe: natural gas price disputes with Russia. Political instability.

◆ **INSIGHT:** *Ukraine means "on the border," referring to its position on the edge of the old Russian Empire*

FACTFILE

OFFICIAL NAME: Ukraine
DATE OF FORMATION: 1991
CAPITAL: Kiev
POPULATION: 45.4 million
TOTAL AREA: 223,089 sq. miles (603,700 sq. km)
DENSITY: 195 people per sq. mile

LANGUAGES: Ukrainian*, Russian, Tatar
RELIGIONS: Christian (mainly Orthodox) 95%, other 5%
ETHNIC MIX: Ukrainian 78%, Russian 17%, other 5%
GOVERNMENT: Presidential system
CURRENCY: Hryvna = 100 kopiykas

United Arab Emirates

Bordering the Gulf on the northern coast of the Arabian
Peninsula, the seven states of the UAE are Abu Dhabi, Dubai,
Sharjah, Ajman, Umm al Qaywayn, Ras al Khaymah, and Fujayrah.

GEOGRAPHY

Mostly flat, semiarid desert with
dunes, salt pans, and occasional oases.
Cities are watered by extensive
irrigation systems.

CLIMATE

Summers are humid, despite
minimal rainfall. Sand-laden *shamal*
winds blow in winter and spring.

PEOPLE & SOCIETY

Emirians, who make up just a
quarter of the population, are mostly
Sunni Muslims of Bedouin descent, and
largely city dwellers. In theory, women
enjoy equal rights with men. Poverty
is rare and there is no income tax.
The 1970s oil boom encouraged the
immigration of workers, mostly from
Asia. Western expatriates are permitted
a virtually unrestricted lifestyle.
Islamism, however, is a growing
force among the young.

THE ECONOMY

Major oil and natural gas exporter;
plentiful reserves. Dynamic Dubai: free
trade zone, financial center (but 2008
global downturn caught overextended
banks). Water is scarce. Imports most
food. Some emirates are less developed.

INSIGHT: *Mina Jabal Ali, in Dubai, is
the largest man-made port in the world*

FACTFILE

OFFICIAL NAME: United Arab Emirates

DATE OF FORMATION: 1971

CAPITAL: Abu Dhabi

POPULATION: 4.7 million

TOTAL AREA: 32,000 sq. miles
(82,880 sq. km)

DENSITY: 146 people per sq. mile

LANGUAGES: Arabic*, Farsi, Indian and
Pakistani languages, English

RELIGIONS: Muslim (mainly Sunni) 96%,
Christian, Hindu, and other 4%

ETHNIC MIX: Asian 60%, Emirian 25%,
other Arab 12%, European 3%

GOVERNMENT: Monarchy

CURRENCY: UAE dirham = 100 fils

United Kingdom

Separated from continental Europe by the English Channel, the UK consists of Great Britain (England, Wales, and Scotland), several smaller islands, and Northern Ireland.

 GEOGRAPHY

Rugged uplands dominate the landscape of Scotland, Wales, and northern England. All of the peaks in the United Kingdom over 4000 ft (1219 m) are in highland Scotland. The Pennine mountains, known as the "backbone of England," run the length of northern England. Lowland England rises into several ranges of rolling hills, and there is an interconnected system of rivers and canals. Over 600 islands, many uninhabited, lie west and north of the Scottish mainland.

 CLIMATE

Generally mild, temperate, and highly changeable. Rain is fairly well distributed throughout the year. The west is generally wetter than the east, and the south warmer than the north. Winter snow is common in upland areas.

PEOPLE & SOCIETY

Scottish and Welsh people have a stronger sense of separate identity than the English; the creation of the Scottish Parliament and Welsh Assembly has given them greater political autonomy. Devolved government in Northern Ireland remains problematic. Other ethnic minorities account for 5% of the population; more than half of them were born in the UK. Asian women in particular can be socially isolated. Asians and West Indians in most cities face deprivation and social stress, but white working-class youths were also evident when innercity rioting erupted in 2011. Income inequality is greater now than in 1884, when records began. In key areas such as policing, multiethnic recruitment has made little progress. Marriage is in decline. Over 40% of all births occur outside marriage, but most of them to cohabiting couples. Single-parent households account for just over a quarter of all families.

FACTFILE

OFFICIAL NAME: United Kingdom of Great Britain and Northern Ireland

DATE OF FORMATION: 1707

CAPITAL: London

POPULATION: 61.9 million

TOTAL AREA: 94,525 sq. miles (244,820 sq. km)

DENSITY: 664 people per sq. mile

LANGUAGES: English*, Welsh, Scottish Gaelic

RELIGIONS: Anglican 45%, other and nonreligious 37%, Roman Catholic 9%, Presbyterian 4%, Muslim 3%, Methodist 2%

ETHNIC MIX: English 80%, Scottish 9%, other 5%, Welsh 3%, Northern Irish 3%

GOVERNMENT: Parliamentary system

CURRENCY: Pound sterling = 100 pence

$ THE ECONOMY

World leader in financial services, pharmaceuticals, and defense industries. Strong multinationals. Precision engineering and high-tech industries, including biotechnology and telecommunications. Energy sector based on declining North Sea oil and natural gas reserves. Innovative in computer software development. Flexible working practices. Long-term decline of manufacturing sector, particularly heavy industries and car manufacture, partially offset by rise in financial and other services.

Nonparticipant in euro. High levels of government, corporate, and consumer debt: banks made major losses in 2007–2009 global downturn. Bailouts and stimulus packages pushed the government's finances further into the red. Tackling the deficit by cuts in spending puts pressure on growth strategy and social programs, with rising unemployment.

◆ **INSIGHT:** *The UK has no formal written constitution, but a stable government system based on Parliament, which originated as a check on royal power in the 13th century*

Shetlands Is.
Lerwick

Orkney Is.

Outer Hebrides

Stornoway

— 58°

Inverness

Aberdeen

Scotland

Inner Hebrides

Oban

Dundee

Glasgow

Edinburgh — 56°

Londonderry

Newcastle upon Tyne

Northern Ireland

Belfast

Carlisle

North Sea

Isle of Man

— 54°

IRELAND

Blackpool

Leeds

Liverpool

Blackburn

Manchester

Sheffield

England

Derby

Birmingham

Leicester

Norwich

Cambridge — 52°

Wales

Oxford

Thames

LONDON

Swansea

Cardiff

Reading

Bristol

Dover

Celtic Sea

Southampton

— 2°

ATLANTIC OCEAN

Exeter

Plymouth

— 50°

English Channel

8°   6°   4°   2°   0°

1000m/3281ft
500m/1640ft
200m/656ft
Sea Level

0   100 km
0   100 miles

United States of America

Stretching across the most temperate part of North America, and with many natural resources, the US is the world's leading economic power and third-largest country.

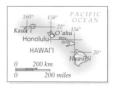

GEOGRAPHY

The US has a varied topography. Forested mountains stretch from New England in the far northeast, giving way to lowlands and swamps in the extreme south. The central plains are dominated by the Mississippi–Missouri River system and the Great Lakes on the Canadian border. The Rocky Mountains in the west contain active volcanoes and drop to the coast across the earthquake-prone San Andreas Fault. The southwest is arid desert. Mountainous Alaska is mostly Arctic tundra.

CLIMATE

There are four main climatic zones. The north and east are continental and temperate, with heavy rainfall, warm summers, and cold winters. Florida and the Deep South are tropical and prone to hurricanes. The southwest is arid desert, with searing summer heat and low rainfall. Southern California is Mediterranean, with hot summers and mild winters.

INSIGHT: *The United States of America has the world's oldest constitution. Drafted in 1787, it has operated continuously ever since, albeit with numerous amendments*

3000m/9843ft
2000m/6562ft
1000m/3281ft
500m/1640ft
200m/656ft
Sea Level

0   400 km
0   400 miles

United States of America

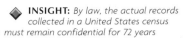

◆ **INSIGHT:** *By law, the actual records collected in a United States census must remain confidential for 72 years*

PEOPLE & SOCIETY

Although the demographic, economic, and cultural dominance of White Americans is firmly entrenched after over 400 years of settlement, the ethnic balance of the country is shifting. Barack Obama, whose father was African, became the first non-White US president in 2009. The African-American community, originally uprooted by the slave trade, has a strong consciousness. Less well organized socially but more numerous, and faster-growing, the Hispanic community is predicted to number over 25% of the population by 2050. Native Americans, dispossessed in the 19th century, are now among the poorest people. Constitutionally, state and religion are clearly separated. Conservative Christianity, however, is increasingly dominant politically. Living standards are high, but bad diet and insufficient exercise have left over a third of Americans obese.

THE ECONOMY

World's largest economy: huge resource base; well-established high-tech, engineering, and entertainment industries; global spread of US culture. Decline of manufacturing as jobs lost to low-wage economies. The combination of tax cuts to boost consumer spending and a rising defense budget for the "war on terrorism" drove the budget into a record deficit after 2001. Oil production was hit in 2005 by Hurricane Katrina, causing global price hikes. The "subprime" mortgage lending crisis of 2007 sent global stock markets plummeting. In 2008, Lehman Brothers bank crashed spectacularly, while other giants in the financial sector received huge bailouts. Further tax cuts and billion-dollar spending packages in 2009 attempted to lift the economy back out of recession, but widened an already-gaping budget deficit. Pressure for sharp spending cuts conflicts with concern about faltering growth.

FACTFILE

OFFICIAL NAME: United States of America
DATE OF FORMATION: 1776
CAPITAL: Washington, D.C.
POPULATION: 318 million
TOTAL AREA: 3,717,792 sq. miles
(9,626,091 sq. km)
DENSITY: 90 people per sq. mile

LANGUAGES: English, Spanish, other
RELIGIONS: Protestant 52%, Roman Catholic 25%, other 20%, Jewish 2%, Muslim 1%
ETHNIC MIX: White 62%, Hispanic 13%, African American 13%, other 7%, Asian 4%, Native American 1%
GOVERNMENT: Presidential system
CURRENCY: US dollar = 100 cents

Uruguay

Situated in southeastern South America, Uruguay returned
to civilian government in 1985, after 12 years of military rule.
Most land is used for farming: Uruguay is a major wool exporter.

GEOGRAPHY
Low, rolling grasslands cover 80%
of the country. Narrow coastal plain.
Alluvial floodplain in southwest. Five
rivers flow westward and drain into
the Uruguay River.

CLIMATE
Temperate throughout the
country. Warm summers, mild winters,
and moderate rainfall.

PEOPLE & SOCIETY
Uruguayans are largely second-or
third-generation Italians or Spaniards.
Wealth derived from cattle ranching
enabled the country to establish the
first welfare state in South America.
Waves of emigration occurred during
the economic decline of the 1960s, the
period of military rule, and the 1999–2002
economic crisis. Though a Roman Catholic
country, Uruguay is liberal in its attitude
to religion and all forms are tolerated.

THE ECONOMY
Exports wool, meat, hides, rice,
wood, soy. Well-educated workforce.
Banking services. Mineral potential.

INSIGHT: *Uruguay's rich pastures
are ideal for raising livestock; animal
products bring in over 40% of export earnings*

200m/656ft
Sea Level

0   100 km
0   100 miles

FACTFILE

OFFICIAL NAME: Eastern Republic
of Uruguay
DATE OF FORMATION: 1828
CAPITAL: Montevideo
POPULATION: 3.4 million
TOTAL AREA: 68,039 sq. miles
(176,220 sq. km)

DENSITY: 50 people per sq. mile
LANGUAGES: Spanish*
RELIGIONS: Roman Catholic 66%, other and
nonreligious 30%, Jewish 2%, Protestant 2%
ETHNIC MIX: White 90%, *Mestizo* (European–
Amerindian) 6%, Black 4%
GOVERNMENT: Presidential system
CURRENCY: Urug. peso = 100 centésimos

Uzbekistan

Sharing what is left of the Aral Sea with neighboring Kazakhstan, Uzbekistan lies on the ancient Silk Road between Asia and Europe. It is the most populous central Asian republic.

GEOGRAPHY

Arid and semiarid plains in much of the west. Fertile, irrigated farmland in the east lies below the peaks of the western Pamirs.

CLIMATE

Harsh continental climate. Summers can be extremely hot and dry; winters are cold.

PEOPLE & SOCIETY

Complex ethnic makeup. Ex-Communists are in firm control, but traditional social patterns based on clan, religion, and region have reemerged. Constitutional measures aim to control the influence of Islam: activities against Islamists have drawn international condemnation. Most people live in the fertile east. Birth rates are high, and the status of women continues to be low.

THE ECONOMY

Highly regulated. Reserves of natural gas, oil, coal, gold (has one of the world's largest gold mines), and other minerals. Cash crop is cotton: requires much irrigation. Grain imports necessary.

INSIGHT: *The Aral Sea has shrunk to just a tenth of its former size, due to diversion of rivers for irrigation*

FACTFILE

OFFICIAL NAME: Republic of Uzbekistan
DATE OF FORMATION: 1991
CAPITAL: Tashkent
POPULATION: 27.8 million
TOTAL AREA: 172,741 sq. miles
(447,400 sq. km)
DENSITY: 161 people per sq. mile

LANGUAGES: Uzbek*, Russian, Tajik, Kazakh
RELIGIONS: Sunni Muslim 88%, Orthodox Christian 9%, other 3%
ETHNIC MIX: Uzbek 80%, other 6%, Russian 6%, Tajik 5%, Kazakh 3%
GOVERNMENT: Presidential system
CURRENCY: Som = 100 tiyin

Vanuatu

An archipelago of 82 islands and islets in the South Pacific, Vanuatu was ruled jointly by the UK and France from 1906 until independence in 1980. Politics is democratic but volatile.

GEOGRAPHY
Mountainous and volcanic, with coral beaches and dense rainforest. Cultivated land along the coasts.

CLIMATE
Tropical. Temperatures and rainfall decline from north to south.

PEOPLE & SOCIETY
Indigenous Melanesians form a majority. Ni-Vanuatu culture is traditional; local social and religious customs are strong, despite centuries of missionary influence. Subsistence farming and fishing are the main activities. 80% of the population lives on the 12 main islands. Women have lower social status than men and payment of bride price is common.

◆ **INSIGHT:** With 105 indigenous tongues, Vanuatu has the world's highest per capita density of languages

THE ECONOMY
Reliant on aid. Main export is copra; diversifying into beef, timber, kava. Tourism. Offshore banking: rules tightened after international pressure.

FACTFILE

OFFICIAL NAME: Republic of Vanuatu

DATE OF FORMATION: 1980

CAPITAL: Port Vila

POPULATION: 200,000

TOTAL AREA: 4710 sq. miles (12,200 sq. km)

DENSITY: 42 people per sq. mile

LANGUAGES: Bislama (Melanesian pidgin)*, English*, French*, other indigenous languages

RELIGIONS: Presbyterian 37%, other 19%, Anglican 15%, Roman Catholic 15%, traditional beliefs 8%, Seventh-day Adventist 6%

ETHNIC MIX: ni-Vanuatu 94%, European 4%, other 2%

GOVERNMENT: Parliamentary system

CURRENCY: Vatu = 100 centimes

Vatican City

The Vatican City, or Holy See, the seat of the Roman Catholic Church, is a walled enclave in the Italian city of Rome. It is the world's smallest fully independent state.

GEOGRAPHY
The Vatican's territory includes 10 other buildings in Rome, plus the papal residence. The Vatican Gardens cover half the City's area.

CLIMATE
Mild winters with regular rainfall. Hot, dry summers with occasional thunderstorms.

PEOPLE & SOCIETY
The Vatican has about 800 permanent inhabitants, including over 100 lay persons. Thousands of lay staff are also employed. Citizenship can be acquired through long-term residence and holding a position within the City. The reigning pope has supreme legislative and judicial powers, and holds office for life. Though the Vatican City is officially neutral, papal opinion has a great influence on the world's 1.2 billion Roman Catholics.

$ THE ECONOMY
Investments and voluntary contributions made by Catholics worldwide (known as Peter's Pence) are backed up by tourist revenue and the issue of Vatican stamps and coins.

◆ **INSIGHT:** *The Vatican City is the spiritual center for one in six of the world's population*

FACTFILE

OFFICIAL NAME: State of the Vatican City
DATE OF FORMATION: 1929
CAPITAL: Vatican City
POPULATION: 832
TOTAL AREA: 0.17 sq. miles (0.44 sq. km)
DENSITY: 4894 people per sq. mile

LANGUAGES: Italian*, Latin*
RELIGIONS: Roman Catholic 100%
ETHNIC MIX: Cardinals are from many nationalities, but Italians form the largest group. Most resident lay persons are Italian. The current pope is from Germany.
GOVERNMENT: Papal state
CURRENCY: Euro = 100 cents

Venezuela

Lying on the southern shores of the Caribbean, Venezuela was the first of Spain's colonies to seek independence. Despite large oil reserves, many Venezuelans still live in poverty.

GEOGRAPHY

Andes Mountains and the Maracaibo lowlands in the northwest. Central grassy plains are drained by the Orinoco River system. Forested Guiana Highlands in the southeast.

CLIMATE

Tropical. Hot and humid. Uplands are cooler. Orinoco plains are alternately parched or flooded.

PEOPLE & SOCIETY

Venezuela is historically a "melting pot," with immigrants from Europe and all over Latin America. The few indigenous Amerindians live in remote areas. Venezuela has one of the most urbanized societies in the region, with most of its population living in the northern cities. President Chávez's left-wing rhetoric raises opposition within Venezuela from urban society, and from the US.

THE ECONOMY

Oil accounts for 80% of exports. Reserves of coal, gold, other minerals. Nationalization program is enlarging the inefficient, corruption-prone state sector and deterring foreign investors.

INSIGHT: *Venezuela's Angel Falls is the world's tallest waterfall, with a total drop of 3210 ft (979 m)*

FACTFILE

OFFICIAL NAME: Bolivarian Republic of Venezuela

DATE OF FORMATION: 1830

CAPITAL: Caracas

POPULATION: 29 million

TOTAL AREA: 352,143 sq. miles (912,050 sq. km)

DENSITY: 85 people per sq. mile

LANGUAGES: Spanish*, Amerindian languages

RELIGIONS: Roman Catholic 96%, Protestant 2%, other 2%

ETHNIC MIX: *Mestizo* (European–Amerindian) 69%, White 20%, Black 9%, Amerindian 2%

GOVERNMENT: Presidential system

CURRENCY: Bolívar fuerte = 100 céntimos

Vietnam

French rule of Vietnam ended in 1954. Divided at 17°N, the US-backed South fought the Communist North. Reunified after the North's 1975 victory, it is run as a single-party state.

 GEOGRAPHY
A heavily forested mountain range separates the northern Red River delta lowlands from the Mekong Delta in the south.

 CLIMATE
Cool winters in north; south is tropical, with even temperatures.

PEOPLE & SOCIETY
Ethnic Vietnamese dominate; the Chinese minority was viewed as a corrupt bourgeoisie by the victorious Communists after the war. Mountain-based minorities *(montagnards)* were also sidelined; tensions persist over the settling of highlands by lowlanders. Women play an active role in society. There is no political or press freedom.

◆ **INSIGHT:** *Intense US bombing and defoliant spraying in the 1962–1975 Vietnam War has scarred the landscape*

 THE ECONOMY
Liberal economic policy *(doi moi)* from 1986: now one of fastest-growing economies. Major rice exporter. Cheap labor. Strong manufacturing: textiles, electrical goods. Diverse resource base.

CHINA
Red River
22°
LAOS
HANOI
Hang Gai
Nam Định
Hai Phong
Gulf
of
Tongking
18°
0   100 km
0   100 miles
Vinh

2000m/6562ft
1000m/3281ft
500m/1640ft
200m/656ft
Sea Level

Huế
Đà Nẵng
South
China
Sea
CAMBODIA
Quy Nhon
14°
Mekong
Nha Trang
Đà Lạt
Long Xuyên
Hồ Chí Minh
Gulf
of
Thailand
Cần Thơ
Mekong
Delta
Vung Tau
10°
104°
108°

FACTFILE

OFFICIAL NAME: Socialist Republic of Vietnam
DATE OF FORMATION: 1976
CAPITAL: Hanoi
POPULATION: 89 million
TOTAL AREA: 127,243 sq. miles (329,560 sq. km)
DENSITY: 708 people per sq. mile

LANGUAGES: Vietnamese*, Chinese, Thai, Khmer, Muong, Nung, Miao, Yao, Jarai
RELIGIONS: Other 74%, Buddhist 14%, Roman Catholic 7%, Cao Dai 3%, Protestant 2%
ETHNIC MIX: Vietnamese 86%, other 8%, Tay 2%, Thai 2%, Muong 2%
GOVERNMENT: One-party state
CURRENCY: Dông = 10 hao = 100 xu

Yemen

Located in southern Arabia, Yemen was formerly two countries: the People's Democratic Republic of Yemen (south and east) and the Yemen Arab Republic (northwest) were united in 1990.

GEOGRAPHY
Mountainous west with a fertile strip along the Red Sea. Arid desert and mountains elsewhere.

CLIMATE
Desert climate, modified by altitude, which affects temperatures by as much as 54°F (30°C).

PEOPLE & SOCIETY
Almost entirely of Arab and Bedouin descent, most Yemenis are Sunni Muslims, of the Shafi sect. In rural and northern areas, tribalism and Islamic orthodoxy are strong and most women wear the veil. Tension continues between cosmopolitan Aden and the more conservative north. Islamists have a growing political role. Popular protests as part of the 2011 "Arab Spring" pressed for regime change. Foreigners are subject to sporadic attacks and kidnappings.

THE ECONOMY
Instability deters investment. Considerable oil and natural gas reserves. Agriculture is the largest employer: qat (mild narcotic), coffee, and cotton.

INSIGHT: Mokha, on the Red Sea, gave its name to the first coffee beans exported to Europe in the 1600s

3000m/9843ft
2000m/6562ft
1000m/3281ft
500m/1640ft
200m/656ft
Sea Level

0   100 km
0   100 miles

SAUDI ARABIA

OMAN

Ar Rub' al Khali

Say'ūn

SANA
Al Hudaydah   Sayhūt
Ash Shihr
16°   Bayt al Faqih   Al Mukallā
Red   Ta'izz   Hadramawt
Sea
Al Mukha   Aden   Suquṭra
(Mokha)   (Aden)   Gulf of Aden   'Abd al Kūrī
44°   48°   12°
52°

FACTFILE

OFFICIAL NAME: Republic of Yemen
DATE OF FORMATION: 1990
CAPITAL: Sana
POPULATION: 24.3 million
TOTAL AREA: 203,849 sq. miles (527,970 sq. km)
DENSITY: 112 people per sq. mile

LANGUAGES: Arabic*
RELIGIONS: Sunni Muslim 55%, Shi'a Muslim 42%, Christian, Hindu, and Jewish 3%
ETHNIC MIX: Arab 99%, Afro-Arab, Indian, Somali, and European 1%
GOVERNMENT: Presidential system
CURRENCY: Yemeni rial = 100 fils

Zambia

Bordered to the south by the Zambezi River, Zambia lies at the heart of southern Africa. In 1991, it made a peaceful transition from single-party rule to multiparty democracy.

GEOGRAPHY

A high savanna plateau, broken by mountains in northeast. Vegetation mainly trees and scrub.

CLIMATE

Tropical, with three seasons: cool and dry, hot and dry, and wet. Southwest is prone to drought.

PEOPLE & SOCIETY

There are more than 70 different ethnic groups, but there are fewer tensions than in many African states. Major groups are the Bemba (in the northeast), Tonga (south), Nyanja (east), and Lozi (west). There are also thousands of refugees, mostly from the DRC and Angola. A National Gender Policy was issued in 2000 to redress inequalities between the sexes. The standard of living has fallen in real terms since independence. One in seven adults is infected with HIV/AIDS.

THE ECONOMY

Copper: output has risen since 2000, when decades of falling global prices ended. New agricultural exports, notably flowers. Debt relief.

◆ **INSIGHT:** *Spray from Musi-o-Tunya (Victoria Falls) can be seen up to 20 miles (35 km) away*

FACTFILE

OFFICIAL NAME: Republic of Zambia
DATE OF FORMATION: 1964
CAPITAL: Lusaka
POPULATION: 13.3 million
TOTAL AREA: 290,584 sq. miles (752,614 sq. km)
DENSITY: 47 people per sq. mile

LANGUAGES: Bemba, Tonga, Nyanja, Lozi, Lala-Bisa, Nsenga, English*
RELIGIONS: Christian 63%, traditional beliefs 36%, Muslim and Hindu 1%
ETHNIC MIX: Bemba 34%, other African 26%, Tonga 16%, Nyanja 14%, Lozi 9%, European 1%
GOVERNMENT: Presidential system
CURRENCY: Zambian kwacha = 100 ngwee

Zimbabwe

Situated in southern Africa, Zimbabwe achieved
independence from the UK in 1980. President Robert Mugabe,
in power since then, has become increasingly authoritarian.

GEOGRAPHY
High plateaus in center bordered by
Zambezi River in the north and Limpopo
in the south. Rivers crisscross central area.

CLIMATE
Tropical, though moderated by the
high altitude. Wet season November–
March. Drought is common in the
eastern highlands.

PEOPLE & SOCIETY
Two main ethnic groups: Shona
in the north and east, and Ndebele in
the south. Shona outnumber Ndebele
by four to one. Whites are generally
far more affluent than blacks. Official
efforts to redress this imbalance
(such as land redistribution) have
become increasingly aggressive.
The political opposition to Mugabe
joined him in a fractious unity
government from 2009 in an
attempt to rebuild the country.

THE ECONOMY
Undermined by mismanagement,
corruption, and international isolation.
High unemployment. Abandoned own
currency in 2009 after hyperinflation.

INSIGHT: *The ruins of the*
1000-year-old city of Great
Zimbabwe, after which the country is
named, are near modern-day Masvingo

FACTFILE

OFFICIAL NAME: Republic of Zimbabwe

DATE OF FORMATION: 1980

CAPITAL: Harare

POPULATION: 12.6 million

TOTAL AREA: 150,803 sq. miles (390,580 sq. km)

DENSITY: 84 people per sq. mile

LANGUAGES: Shona, isiNdebele, English*

RELIGIONS: Syncretic 50%, Christian 25%,
traditional beliefs 24%, other 1%

ETHNIC MIX: Shona 71%, Ndebele 16%,
other African 11%, White 1%, Asian 1%

GOVERNMENT: Presidential system

CURRENCY: Zimbabwe dollar suspended in
2009; US dollar, South African rand, euro, UK
pound, and Botswanan pula are legal tender

Overseas territories

Despite the rapid process of global decolonization since World War II, around eight million people in more than 50 territories around the world continue to live under the protection of Australia, Denmark, France, the Netherlands, New Zealand, Norway, the UK, or the USA. These remnants of former colonial empires may have persisted for economic, strategic, or political reasons and are administered by the protecting country in a variety of ways.

AUSTRALIA

Australia's overseas territories have not been an issue since Papua New Guinea became independent in 1975. Consequently, there is no overriding policy toward them.

Ashmore & Cartier Is. *Ref: 124 A3*
STATUS: External territory
CLAIMED: 1931
POPULATION: None
AREA: 2 sq miles (5.2 sq km)

Christmas Island *Ref: 123 E5*

STATUS: External territory
CLAIMED: 1958
CAPITAL: The Settlement
POPULATION: 1402
AREA: 52 sq miles (135 sq km)

Cocos Islands *Ref: 123 D5*
STATUS: External territory
CLAIMED: 1955
CAPITAL: West Island
POPULATION: 596
AREA: 5.5 sq miles (14 sq km)

Coral Sea Islands *Ref: 126 B4*
STATUS: External territory
CLAIMED: 1969
POPULATION: 8 (Meteorologists)
AREA: 1.2 sq miles (3 sq km)

Heard & McDonald Is. *Ref: 123 C7*
STATUS: External territory
CLAIMED: 1947
POPULATION: None
AREA: 161 sq miles (417 sq km)

Norfolk Island *Ref: 124 D4*

STATUS: External territory
CLAIMED: 1774
CAPITAL: Kingston
POPULATION: 2169
AREA: 13 sq miles (34 sq km)

DENMARK

The Faeroes and Greenland have had home rule since 1948 and 1979 respectively.

Faeroe Islands *Ref: 65 F5*

STATUS: External territory
CLAIMED: 1380
CAPITAL: Tórshavn
POPULATION: 49,267
AREA: 540 sq miles (1399 sq km)

Greenland *Ref: 64 D3*

STATUS: External territory
CLAIMED: 1380
CAPITAL: Nuuk
POPULATION: 57,670
AREA: 836,109 sq miles (2,166,086 sq km)

Overseas territories

FRANCE

France's relations with *L'Outre-Mer* stress interdependence rather than independence. *Départements* have their own governments. *Collectivités* have some autonomy.

Clipperton Island *Ref: 135 F3*
STATUS: Dependency of French Polynesia
CLAIMED: 1935
POPULATION: None
AREA: 3.4 sq miles (9 sq km)

French Guiana *Ref: 41 H3*
STATUS: Overseas department
CLAIMED: 1817
CAPITAL: Cayenne
POPULATION: 225,651
AREA: 35,135 sq miles (91,000 sq km)

French Polynesia *Ref: 127 H1*
STATUS: Overseas collectivity
CLAIMED: 1843
CAPITAL: Papeete
POPULATION: 300,000
AREA: 1608 sq miles (4165 sq km)

French Southern & Antarctic Lands
Ref: 123 B6
STATUS: Overseas territory
CLAIMED: 1772, 1840, 1843, 1924
CAPITAL: Port-aux-Français
POPULATION: 140
AREA: 169,800 sq miles (439,781 sq km)

Guadeloupe *Ref: 37 G4*
STATUS: Overseas department
CLAIMED: 1635
CAPITAL: Basse-Terre
POPULATION: 404,000
AREA: 629 sq miles (1628 sq km)

Martinique *Ref: 37 G4*
STATUS: Overseas department
CLAIMED: 1635
CAPITAL: Fort-de-France
POPULATION: 400,000
AREA: 425 sq miles (1100 sq km)

Mayotte *Ref: 61 G2*
STATUS: Overseas department
CLAIMED: 1843
CAPITAL: Mamoudzou
POPULATION: 194,159
AREA: 144 sq miles (374 sq km)

New Caledonia *Ref: 126 D5*
STATUS: Special collectivity
CLAIMED: 1853
CAPITAL: Nouméa
POPULATION: 300,000
AREA: 7347 sq miles (19,100 sq km)

Réunion *Ref: 61 H4*
STATUS: Overseas department
CLAIMED: 1638
CAPITAL: Saint-Denis
POPULATION: 800,000
AREA: 970 sq miles (2500 sq km)

St Barthélemy *Ref: 37 G3*
STATUS: Overseas collectivity
CLAIMED: 1878
CAPITAL: Gustavia
POPULATION: 8823
AREA: 8 sq miles (21 sq km)

St Martin *Ref: 37 E5*
STATUS: Overseas collectivity
CLAIMED: 1648
CAPITAL: Marigot
POPULATION: 33,164
AREA: 20 sq miles (53 sq km)

Overseas territories

St Pierre & Miquelon *Ref: 21 G4*
STATUS: Overseas collectivity
CLAIMED: 1604
CAPITAL: Saint-Pierre
POPULATION: 5888
AREA: 93 sq miles (242 sq km)

Wallis & Futuna *Ref: 127 E4*
STATUS: Overseas collectivity
CLAIMED: 1842
CAPITAL: Mata'Utu
POPULATION: 15,398
AREA: 106 sq miles (274 sq km)

NETHERLANDS

These islands were once part of the Dutch West Indies. They are now self-governing.

Aruba *Ref: 37 E5*
STATUS: Constituent country
CLAIMED: 1636
CAPITAL: Oranjestad
POPULATION: 106,113
AREA: 75 sq miles (194 sq km)

Bonaire *Ref: 37 E5*

STATUS: Special municipality
CLAIMED: 1816
CAPITAL: Kralendijk
POPULATION: 15,800
AREA: 113 sq miles (294 sq km)

Curaçao *Ref: 37 E5*
STATUS: Constituent country
CLAIMED: 1815
CAPITAL: Willemstad
POPULATION: 142,180
AREA: 171 sq miles (444 sq km)

Saba *Ref: 37 G3*
STATUS: Special municipality
CLAIMED: 1816
CAPITAL: The Bottom
POPULATION: 2,000
AREA: 5 sq miles (13 sq km)

Sint-Eustatius *Ref: 37 G3*
STATUS: Special municipality
CLAIMED: 1784
CAPITAL: Oranjestad
POPULATION: 3100
AREA: 8 sq miles (21 sq km)

Sint-Maarten *Ref: 37 G3*
STATUS: Constituent country
CLAIMED: 1648
CAPITAL: Phillipsburg
POPULATION: 37,429
AREA: 13 sq miles (34 sq km)

NEW ZEALAND

New Zealand remains responsible for its territories' foreign policy and defense.

Cook Islands *Ref: 127 G4*

STATUS: Associated territory
CLAIMED: 1901
CAPITAL: Avarua
POPULATION: 11,124
AREA: 91 sq miles (235 sq km)

Niue *Ref: 127 F5*

STATUS: Associated territory
CLAIMED: 1901
CAPITAL: Alofi
POPULATION: 1311
AREA: 102 sq miles (264 sq km)

Overseas territories

Tokelau *Ref: 127 F3*
STATUS: Dependent territory
CLAIMED: 1926
CAPITAL: None
POPULATION: 1384
AREA: 4 sq miles (10 sq km)

NORWAY

There is a NATO base on Jan Mayen.
Bouvet Island is a nature reserve.

Bouvet Island *Ref: 49 D7*
STATUS: Dependency
CLAIMED: 1928
POPULATION: None
AREA: 22 sq miles (58 sq km)

Jan Mayen *Ref: 65 F3*
STATUS: Dependency
CLAIMED: 1929
POPULATION: 18 (Meteorologists)
AREA: 147 sq miles (381 sq km)

Peter I. Island *Ref: 136 A3*
STATUS: Dependency
CLAIMED: 1931
POPULATION: None
AREA: 69 sq miles (180 sq km)

Svalbard *Ref: 65 F2*
STATUS: Dependency
CLAIMED: 1920
CAPITAL: Longyearbyen
POPULATION: 2019
AREA: 24,289 sq miles (62,906 sq km)

UNITED KINGDOM

The UK's dependencies are locally governed
by a mix of elected and appointed officials.

Anguilla *Ref: 37 G3*

STATUS: Overseas territory
CLAIMED: 1650
CAPITAL: The Valley
POPULATION: 15,094
AREA: 37 sq miles (96 sq km)

Ascension Island *Ref: 49 C5*
STATUS: Dependency of St Helena
CLAIMED: 1673
CAPITAL: Georgetown
POPULATION: 880
AREA: 34 sq miles (88 sq km)

Bermuda *Ref: 17 L6*

STATUS: Overseas territory
CLAIMED: 1612
CAPITAL: Hamilton
POPULATION: 68,679
AREA: 20 sq miles (53 sq km)

British Indian Ocean Territory
Ref: 122 C4 STATUS: Overseas territory

CLAIMED: 1814
CAPITAL: Diego Garcia
POPULATION: 4000
AREA: 23 sq miles (60 sq km)

British Virgin Islands *Ref: 37 F3*

STATUS: Overseas territory
CLAIMED: 1672
CAPITAL: Road Town
POPULATION: 25,383
AREA: 59 sq miles (153 sq km)

Cayman Islands *Ref: 36 B3*

STATUS: Overseas territory
CLAIMED: 1670
CAPITAL: George Town
POPULATION: 51,384
AREA: 100 sq miles (259 sq km)

Overseas territories

Falkland Islands *Ref: 47 D7*

STATUS: Overseas territory
CLAIMED: 1832
CAPITAL: Stanley
POPULATION: 3140
AREA: 4699 sq miles (12,173 sq km)

Gibraltar *Ref: 74 D5*

STATUS: Overseas territory
CLAIMED: 1713
CAPITAL: Gibraltar
POPULATION: 28,956
AREA: 2.5 sq miles (6.5 sq km)

Guernsey *Ref: 71 D8*

STATUS: Crown dependency
CLAIMED: 1066
CAPITAL: St. Peter Port
POPULATION: 65,068
AREA: 25 sq miles (65 sq km)

Isle of Man *Ref: 71 C5*

STATUS: Crown dependency
CLAIMED: 1765
CAPITAL: Douglas
POPULATION: 84,655
AREA: 221 sq miles (572 sq km)

Jersey *Ref: 71 D8*

STATUS: Crown dependency
CLAIMED: 1066
CAPITAL: St. Helier
POPULATION: 94,161
AREA: 45 sq miles (116 sq km)

Montserrat *Ref: 37 G4*

STATUS: Overseas territory
CLAIMED: 1632
CAPITAL: Plymouth (uninhab.)
POPULATION: 5140
AREA: 40 sq miles (102 sq km)

Pitcairn Islands *Ref: 125 G4*

STATUS: Overseas territory
CLAIMED: 1887
CAPITAL: Adamstown
POPULATION: 48
AREA: 18 sq miles (47 sq km)

Saint Helena *Ref: 49 D5*

STATUS: Overseas territory
CLAIMED: 1673
CAPITAL: Jamestown
POPULATION: 7700
AREA: 47 sq miles (122 sq km)

South Georgia & the South Sandwich Islands *Ref: 49 C7*

STATUS: Overseas territory
CLAIMED: 1775
POPULATION: None
AREA: 1387 sq miles (3592 sq km)

Tristan da Cunha *Ref: 49 D6*

STATUS: Dependency of St. Helena
CLAIMED: 1612
CAPITAL: Edinburgh
POPULATION: 264
AREA: 38 sq miles (98 sq km)

Turks & Caicos Islands *Ref: 37 E2*

STATUS: Overseas territory
CLAIMED: 1766
CAPITAL: Cockburn Town
POPULATION: 44,819
AREA: 166 sq miles (430 sq km)

UNITED STATES

Commonwealth territories are self-governing and an integral part of the US. Unincorporated territories have varying degrees of autonomy.

Overseas territories

American Samoa *Ref: 127 F4*

STATUS: Unincorp. territory
CLAIMED: 1900
CAPITAL: Pago Pago
POPULATION: 67,242
AREA: 75 sq miles (195 sq km)

Baker & Howland Islands *Ref: 127 E2*

STATUS: Unincorporated territory
CLAIMED: 1856
POPULATION: None
AREA: 0.5 sq miles (1.4 sq km)

Guam *Ref: 126 B1*

STATUS: Unincorp. territory
CLAIMED: 1898
CAPITAL: Hagåtña
POPULATION: 183,286
AREA: 212 sq miles (549 sq km)

Jarvis Island *Ref: 127 G2*

STATUS: Unincorporated territory
CLAIMED: 1856
POPULATION: None
AREA: 1.7 sq miles (4.5 sq km)

Johnston Atoll *Ref: 125 E1*

STATUS: Unincorporated territory
CLAIMED: 1858
POPULATION: None
AREA: 1 sq mile (2.8 sq km)

Kingman Reef *Ref: 127 F2*

STATUS: Unincorporated territory
CLAIMED: 1856
POPULATION: None
AREA: 0.4 sq miles (1 sq km)

Midway Islands *Ref: 134 D2*

STATUS: Unincorporated territory
CLAIMED: 1867
CAPITAL: None
POPULATION: 60
AREA: 2 sq miles (5.2 sq km)

Navassa Island *Ref: 36 D3*

STATUS: Unincorporated territory
CLAIMED: 1856
POPULATION: None
AREA: 2 sq miles (5.2 sq km)

Northern Mariana Islands *Ref: 124 C1*

STATUS: Comm. territory
CLAIMED: 1947
CAPITAL: Saipan
POPULATION: 46,050
AREA: 177 sq miles (457 sq km)

Palmyra Atoll *Ref: 127 G2*

STATUS: Incorporated territory
CLAIMED: 1898
POPULATION: None
AREA: 5 sq miles (12 sq km)

Puerto Rico *Ref: 37 F3*

STATUS: Comm. territory
CLAIMED: 1898
CAPITAL: San Juan
POPULATION: 4 million
AREA: 3515 sq miles (9104 sq km)

Virgin Islands *Ref: 37 F3*

STATUS: Unincorp. territory
CLAIMED: 1917
CAPITAL: Charlotte Amalie
POPULATION: 109,666
AREA: 137 sq miles (355 sq km)

Wake Island *Ref: 124 D1*

STATUS: Unincorporated territory
CLAIMED: 1898
CAPITAL: None
POPULATION: 150 (US air base)
AREA: 2.5 sq miles (6.5 sq km)

International organizations

This listing provides acronym definitions for the main international organizations concerned with worldwide economics, trade, and defense, plus an indication of membership.

ASEAN
Association of Southeast Asian Nations
ESTABLISHED: 1967
MEMBERS: Brunei, Cambodia, Indonesia, Laos, Malaysia, Myanmar, Philippines, Singapore, Thailand, Vietnam

CIS
Commonwealth of Independent States
ESTABLISHED: 1991
MEMBERS: Arm., Az., Belarus, Kaz., Kyrgy., Mold., Russia, Tajik., Turkmen.*, Ukraine*, Uzbek. *Unofficial members*

COMM *The Commonwealth of Nations*
ESTABLISHED: 1931; evolved out of the British Empire. Formerly known as the British Commonwealth of Nations.
MEMBERS: 54 *(Fiji currently suspended)*

EU *European Union*
ESTABLISHED: 1965; formerly known as EEC (European Economic Community) and EC (Economic Community)
MEMBERS: Austria, Belg., Bulg., Cyprus, Czech Rep., Denmark, Est., Fin., Fr., Ger., Greece, Hung., Ireland, Italy, Lat., Lith., Lux., Malta, Neth., Pol., Port., Rom., Slvka., Slvna., Spain, Swed., UK *(Croatia to join in 2013)*

G8 *Group of 8*
ESTABLISHED: 1994
MEMBERS: Canada, France, Germany, Italy, Japan, Russia, UK, US

IMF *International Monetary Fund*
(UN agency)
ESTABLISHED: 1945
MEMBERS: 187

NAFTA
North American Free Trade Agreement
ESTABLISHED: 1994
MEMBERS: Canada, Mexico, US

NATO
North Atlantic Treaty Organization
ESTABLISHED: 1949
MEMBERS: Albania, Belg., Bulg., Canada, Croatia, Czech Rep., Denmark, Est., France, Ger., Greece, Hung., Iceland, Italy, Lat., Lith., Lux., Neth., Norway, Poland, Port., Rom., Slovakia, Slovenia, Spain, Turkey, UK, US

OPEC *Organization of Petroleum Exporting Countries*
ESTABLISHED: 1960
MEMBERS: Algeria, Angola, Ecuador, Iran, Iraq, Kuwait, Libya, Nigeria, Qatar, Saudi Arabia, United Arab Emirates, Venezuela

UN *United Nations*
ESTABLISHED: 1945
MEMBERS: 193; all nations are represented, except Taiwan and Kosovo. The Vatican City has "observer status" only.

WTO *World Trade Organization*
ESTABLISHED: 1995
MEMBERS: 153 *(including the EU)*

Abbreviations

This glossary provides a comprehensive guide to the abbreviations used in this atlas.

abbrev. abbreviation
Afgh. Afghanistan
Amh. Amharic
anc. ancient
Ar. Arabic
Arm. Armenia/Armenian
Aus. Austria
Aust. Australia
Az. Azerbaijan

Bas. Basque
Bel. Belorussian
Belg. Belgium/Belgian
Bos. & Herz. Bosnia & Herzegovina
Bul. Bulgarian
Bulg. Bulgaria
Bur. Burmese

C Central
C. Cape
Cam. Cambodian
Cast. Castilian
Chin. Chinese
Comm. Commonwealth
Cord. Cordillera (Sp. mts.)
Cz. Czech
Czech Rep. Czech Republic

D.C. District of Columbia
Dan. Danish
Dominican Rep. Dominican Republic

E East
Emb. Embalse
Eng. English
Eq. Guinea Equatorial Guinea
Est. Estonia/Estonian

Faer. Faeroese
Fin. Finland/Finnish
Flem. Flemish

Fr. France/French
Geo. Georgia
Geor. Georgian
Ger. Germany/German
Gk. Greek

Heb. Hebrew
Hung. Hungary/Hungarian

I. Island
Ind. Indonesia, Indonesian
Is. Islands
It. Italian

Kaz. Kazakhstan/Kazakh
Kep. Kepulauan (Ind. island group)
Kir. Kirghiz
Kor. Korean
Kos. Kosovo
Kurd. Kurdish
Kyrgy. Kyrgyzstan

L. Lake, Lago
Lat. Latvia
Latv. Latvian
Leb. Lebanon
Liech. Liechtenstein
Lith. Lithuania/Lithuanian
Lux. Luxembourg

Mac. Macedonia
Med. Sea Mediterranean Sea
Mon. Montenegro
Mold. Moldova
Mt. Mount/Mountain
Mts. Mountains

N North
N. Korea North Korea
Neth. Netherlands
NW Northwest
NZ New Zealand

P. Pulau (Ind. island)
Peg. Pegunungan (Ind. mountain range)
Per. Persian
Pol. Poland/Polish
Port. Portugal, Portuguese

prev. previously
R. River, Rio, Río
Res. Reservoir
Rom. Romania/Romanian
Rus. Russian
Russ. Fed. Russian Federation

S South
S. Korea South Korea
SA South Africa
SCr. Serbian and Croatian
Serb. Serbia
Slvka. Slovakia
Slvna. Slovenia
Som. Somali
Sp. Spanish
St, St. Saint
Str. Strait
Swed. Swedish
Switz. Switzerland

Tajik. Tajikistan
Th. Thai
Turk. Turkish
Turkm. Turkmen
Turkmen. Turkmenistan

U.A.E. United Arab Emirates
UK United Kingdom
Ukr. Ukrainian
Uninhab. Uninhabitable
Unincorp. Unincorporated
Urug. Uruguayan
US United States of America
Uzb. Uzbek
Uzbek. Uzbekistan

var. variant
Vdkhr. Vodokhranilishche (Rus. reservoir)
Vdskh. Vodoskhovyshche (Ukr. reservoir)
Ven. Venezuela

W West
W. Sahara Western Sahara
Wel. Welsh

Yugo. Yugoslavia

Zamb. Zambian

A

Aabenraa Denmark 67 A8
Aachen Germany 76 A4
Aalborg Denmark 67 B7
Aalst Belgium 69 B5
Aba Nigeria 57 G5
Ābādān Iran 102 C4
Abadan Turkmenistan *prev.*
  Bezmein, Büzmeýin
  104 B3
Abashiri Japan 112 D2
Abéché Chad 58 D3
Aberdeen Scotland, UK 70 D3
Aberdeen South Dakota, USA
  25 E2
Aberdeen Washington, USA
  26 A2
Aberystwyth Wales, UK 71 C6
Abhā Saudi Arabia 103 B6
Abidjan Côte d'Ivoire 56 D5
Abilene Texas, USA 29 F3
Abomey Benin 57 G4
Abu Dhabi *capital of* United
  Arab Emirates *var.* Abū Ẓaby
  103 D5
Abuja *capital of* Nigeria
  57 G4
Abū Ẓaby *see* Abu Dhabi
Acapulco Mexico 33 E5
Acarai Mountains *mountain
  range* Brazil/Guyana 41 F3
Acarigua Venezuela 40 D1
Accra *capital of* Ghana 57 E5
Acklins Island *island* Bahamas
  36 D2
Aconcagua, Cerro *peak*
  Argentina 46 B4
A Coruña Spain *Cast.* La
  Coruña 74 C1
ACT *see* Australian Capital
  Territory
Adalia *see* Antalya
Adalia, Gulf of *see* Antalya
  Körfezi
'Adan Yemen *Eng.* Aden
  103 B7
Adana Turkey *var.* Seyhan
  98 D4

Adapazarı Turkey *var.* Sakarya
  98 B2
Ad Dahnā' *desert* Saudi Arabia
  103 C5
Ad Dakhla Western Sahara
  52 A4
Ad Dawḥah *see* Doha
Addis Ababa *capital of* Ethiopia
  Amh. Ādīs Ābeba 55 C5
Adelaide Australia 131 B6
Adélie, Terre d' *territory*
  Antarctica 136 C4
Aden *see* 'Adan
Aden, Gulf of *sea feature*
  Indian Ocean 122 A3
Adige *river* Italy 78 C2
Ādīs Ābeba *see* Addis Ababa
Adıyaman Turkey 99 E4
Adriatic Sea Mediterranean
  Sea 78 D4
Aegean Sea Mediterranean
  Sea *Gk.* Aigaío Pélagos, *Turk.*
  Ege Denizi 87 D5
Aeolian Islands *see* Isole Eolie
Afghanistan *country* C Asia
  104–105
Africa 50–51
Africa, Horn of *physical region*
  Ethiopia/Somalia 122 A3
Afyon Turkey *prev.*
  Afyonkarahisar 98 B3
Afyonkarahisar *see* Afyon
Agadez Niger 57 G3
Agadir Morocco 52 B2
Agassiz Fracture Zone *tectonic
  feature* Pacific Ocean
  135 E4
Agen France 73 B6
Āgra India 116 D3
Agrigento Italy 79 C7
Agrínio Greece 87 B5
Aguarico *river* Ecuador/Peru
  40 B4
Aguascalientes Mexico 32 D4
Ahaggar *mountains* Algeria
  var. Hoggar 53 E4
Ahmadābād India 116 C4
Ahvāz Iran 102 C4
Ahvenanmaa *see* Åland
Aigaío Pélagos *see* Aegean Sea
Aintab *see* Gaziantep

Aïr, Massif de l' *region* Niger
  57 G2
Aix-en-Provence France
  73 D6
Ajaccio Corse, France 73 E7
Ajdābiyā Libya 53 G2
Ajmer India 116 D3
Akaba *see* Al 'Aqabah
Akchâr *desert* Mauritania
  56 C2
Akimiski Island *island* Canada
  20 C3
Akita Japan 112 D3
Akjoujt Mauritania 56 C2
Akmola *see* Astana
Akmolinsk *see* Astana
Akpatok Island *island* Canada
  21 E1
Akra Kanestron *see* Palioúri,
  Akrotírio
Akron Ohio, USA 22 D3
Aksai Chin *disputed region*
  China/India 108 B4
Aktau Kazakhstan *prev.*
  Shevchenko 96 A4
Akureyri Iceland 65 E4
Akyab *see* Sittwe
Alabama *state* USA 30 D3
Alacant *see* Alicante
Alajuela Costa Rica 34 D4
Alamogordo New Mexico, USA
  28 D3
Åland *island group* Finland *Fin.*
  Ahvenanmaa 67 D6
Al 'Aqabah Jordan *var.* Akaba
  101 B7
Alaska *state* USA 18
Alaska, Gulf of *sea feature*
  Pacific Ocean 16 C3
Alaska Range *mountain range*
  Alaska, USA 18 C3
Albacete Spain 75 E3
Alba Iulia Romania 90 B4
Albania *country* SE Europe 83
Albany Australia 129 B7
Albany Georgia, USA 31 E3
Albany New York, USA
  23 F3
Albany Oregon, USA 26 A3
Albany *river* Canada 20 B3

Al Başrah Iraq var. Basra
102 C4

Al Baydāʾ Libya 53 G2

Albert, Lake lake Uganda/Dem.
Rep. Congo 59 E5

Alberta province Canada 19 E4

Albi France 73 C6

Albuquerque New Mexico, USA
28 D2

Alcácer do Sal Portugal 74 C4

Aldabra Group island group
Seychelles 61 G2

Aleg Mauritania 56 C3

Aleksandriya see Oleksandriya

Aleksandropolʼ see Gyumri

Aleksinac Serbia 82 E4

Alençon France 72 D3

Alessandria Italy 78 B2

Ålesund Norway 67 A5

Aleutian Basin undersea
feature Bering Sea 134 D1

Aleutian Islands islands Alaska,
USA 18 A3

Aleutian Trench undersea
feature Pacific Ocean 134 D1

Alexander Island island
Antarctica 136 A3

Alexandra New Zealand 133 B7

Alexandretta see İskenderun

Alexandria see Al Iskandarīyah

Alexandria Louisiana, USA
30 B3

Alexandroúpoli Greece 86 D3

Al Fāshir see El Fasher

Alföld see Great Hungarian
Plain

Algarve region Portugal 74 C4

Algeciras Spain 74 D5

Algeria country N Africa
52-53

Alghero Italy 79 A5

Algiers capital of Algeria
52 D1

Al Ḥasakah Syria 100 D2

Al Ḥudaydah Yemen 103 B7

Al Ḥufūf Saudi Arabia 103 C5

Alicante Spain Cat. Alacant
75 F4

Alice Springs Australia
130 A4

Al Iskandarīyah Egypt Eng.
Alexandria 54 B1

Al Ismāʿīlīya Egypt Eng. Ismalia
54 B1

Al Jawf Saudi Arabia 102 B4

Al Jazīrah region Iraq/Syria
100 E2

Al Jīzah Egypt var. El Giza 54 B1

Al Karak Jordan 101 B6

Al Khalīl see Hebron

Al Khārijah Egypt var.
El Khārga 54 B2

Al Khums Libya 53 F2

Al Khurṭūm see Khartoum

Alkmaar Netherlands 68 C2

Al Kufrah Libya 53 H4

Al Lādhiqīyah Syria Eng.
Latakia 100 B3

Allahābād India 117 E4

Allenstein see Olsztyn

Allentown Pennsylvania, USA
37 F4

Alma-Ata capital of Kazakhstan
Rus./Kaz. Almaty 96 C5

Al Madīnah Saudi Arabia Eng.
Medina 102 A5

Al Mafraq Jordan 101 B5

Almalyk Uzbekistan Uzb.
Olmaliq 105 E2

Al Manāmah see Manama

Al Marj Libya 53 G2

Almaty see Alma-Ata

Al Mawṣil Iraq Eng. Mosul
102 B3

Almelo Netherlands 68 E3

Almería Spain 75 E5

Al Minyā Egypt 54 B2

Al Mukallā Yemen 103 C7

Alofi capital of Niue 127 F5

Alor, Kepulauan island group
Indonesia 121 E5

Alps mountain range C Europe
62 D4

Al Qāhirah see Cairo

Al Qāmishlī Syria var. Kamishli
100 E1

Al Qunayṭirah Syria 100 B4

Altai Mountains mountain
range C Asia 108 C2

Altamura Italy 79 E5

Altar, Desierto de Desert
Mexico/USA var. Sonoran
Desert 32 A1

Altay China 108 C2

Altay Mongolia 108 D2

Altun Shan mountain range
China 108 C3

Alturas California, USA 26 B4

Al Uqsur Egypt Eng. Luxor
54 B2

Alytus Lithuania Pol. Olita
89 B5

Amadeus, Lake seasonal lake
Australia 129 E5

Amakusa-nada island group
Japan 113 A6

Amami-Ō-shima island Japan
113 A8

Amarillo Texas, USA 29 E2

Amazon river South America
38 C3

Amazon Basin region C South
America 42 D2

Ambanja Madagascar 61 G2

Ambarchik Russian Federation
97 G2

Ambato Ecuador 40 A4

Amboasary Madagascar 61 F4

Ambon Indonesia 121 F4

Ambositra Madagascar 61 G3

Ambriz Angola 60 B1

Amdo China 108 C4

Ameland island Netherlands
68 D1

American Falls Reservoir
Reservoir Idaho, USA 26 E4

American Samoa external
territory USA, Pacific Ocean
127 F4

Amersfoort Netherlands 68 D3

Amga river Russian Federation
95 F2

Amiens France 72 C3

Amindivi Islands island group
India 114 C2

Amirante Islands island group
Seychelles 61 H1

Amman capital of Jordan
101 B5

Ammassalik Greenland var.
Angmagssalik 64 D4

Ammochostos see Gazimağusa
Āmol Iran 102 C3
Amorgós island Greece 87 D6
Amritsar India 116 D2
Amsterdam capital of Netherlands 68 C3
Amsterdam Island island French Southern and Antarctic Territories 123 C6
Am Timan Chad 58 C3
Amu Darya river C Asia 104 D3
Amundsen Gulf sea feature Canada 19 E2
Amundsen Plain undersea feature Pacific Ocean 136 B4
Amundsen Sea Antarctica 97 G4
Amur river E Asia 97 G4 107 E1
Anabar river Russian Federation 95 E2
Anadolu Dağları see Doğu Karadeniz Dağlarıı
Anadyr' Russian Federation 97 H1
Anápolis Brazil 43 F4
Anatolia region SE Europe 85 G3
Anchorage Alaska, USA 18 C3
Ancona Italy 78 C3
Andalucía región Spain 74 D4
Andaman Islands island group India 115 H2 119 A5
Andaman Sea Indian Ocean 122 D3
Andes mountain range South America 39 B6
Andijon Uzbekistan Rus. Andizhan 105 F2
Andhra Pradesh state India 115 E1
Andizhan see Andijon
Andorra country SW Europe 73 B6
Andorra la Vella capital of Andorra 73 B6
Ándros island Greece 87 D5
Andros Island island Bahamas 36 C1
Angara river C Asia 95 D3
Ángel de la Guarda, Isla island Mexico 32 B2
Angel Falls see Salto Ángel

Angeles Philippines 121 E1
Ángel, Salto waterfall Venezuela Eng. Angel Falls 41 F2
Ångermanälven river Sweden 66 C4
Angers France 72 B4
Anglesey island Wales, UK 71 C5
Angmagssalik see Ammassalik
Angola country C Africa 60
Angola Basin undersea feature Atlantic Ocean 49 D6
Angora see Ankara
Angoulême France 73 B5
Angren Uzbekistan 105 E2
Anguilla external territory UK, West Indies 37
Anhui province China var. Anhwei, Wan 111 C5
Anhwei see Anhui
Anjouan island Comoros 61 F2
Ankara capital of Turkey prev. Angora 98 C3
Annaba Algeria 53 E1
An Nafūd desert region Saudi Arabia 102 B4
An Najaf Iraq var. Najaf 102 B4
Annapolis Maryland, USA 23 F4
Ann Arbor Michigan, USA 22 C3
Annecy France 73 D5
Anshan China 110 D4
Ansongo Mali 57 E3
Antakya Turkey var. Hatay 98 D4
Antalaha Madagascar 61 G2
Antalya Turkey prev. Adalia 98 B4
Antalya, Gulf of see Antalya Körfezi
Antalya Körfezi sea feature Mediterranean Sea Eng. Gulf of Antalya, var. Gulf of Adalia 98 B4
Antananarivo capital of Madagascar prev. Tananarive 61 G3
Antarctica 136
Antarctic Peninsula peninsula Antarctica 136 A2
Antequera Spain 74 D5

Anticosti, Île d' island Canada 21 F3
Antigua island Antigua & Barbuda 37 G3
Antigua & Barbuda country West Indies 37
Anti-Lebanon mountains Lebanon/Syria 100 B4
Antipodes Islands island group New Zealand 124 D5
Antofagasta Chile 46 B2
Antsirañana Madagascar 61 G2
Antsohihy Madagascar 61 G2
Antwerp see Antwerpen
Antwerpen Belgium Eng. Antwerp 69 C5
Anyang China 110 C4
Aoga-shima island Japan 113 D6
Aomori Japan 112 D3
Aoraki peak New Zealand var. Cook, Mount 133 B6
Aosta Italy 78 A2
Aoukâr Plateau Mauritania 56 D3
Apeldoorn Netherlands 68 D3
Apennines see Appennino
Apia capital of Samoa 127 F4
Appalachian Mountains mountain range E USA 17 D5
Appennino mountain range Italy Eng. Apennines 78 C4
Apure river Venezuela 40 D2
Aqaba see Al 'Aqabah
Aqaba, Gulf of sea feature Red Sea Ar. Khalīj al 'Aqabah 101 A8
'Aqabah, Khalīj al see Aqaba, Gulf of
Āqchah Afghanistan var. Āqcheh 104 D3
Āqcheh see Āqchah
Arabian Basin undersea feature Indian Ocean 122 B3
Arabian Peninsula peninsula Asia 85 H5 94 B5 103 C5
Arabian Sea Indian Ocean 122 B3
Aracaju Brazil 43 H3
Arad Romania 90 B4

Aṭ Ṭā'if Saudi Arabia 102 B6
Attapu Laos 119 E5
Attawapiskat Canada 20 C3
Attawapiskat *river* Canada 20 B3
Attu Island *island* Alaska, USA 18 A2
Auch France 73 B6
Auckland New Zealand 132 D3
Auckland Islands *island group* New Zealand 124 D5
Augsburg Germany 77 C6
Augusta Australia 129 B7
Augusta Georgia, USA 31 E2
Augusta Maine, USA 23 G2
Aurillac France 73 C5
Aurora Colorado, USA 24 D4
Aurora Illinois, USA 22 B3
Aussig *see* Ústí nad Labem
Austin Texas, USA 29 G4
Australasia 124-125
Australes, Îles *island group* French Polynesia 125 F4
Austral Fracture Zone *tectonic feature* Pacific Ocean 125 H4
Australia *country* Pacific Ocean 124
Australian Alps Australia 131 D7
Australian Capital Territory *territory* Australia *abbrev.* A.C.T. *131* D6
Austria *country* C Europe 77
Auxerre France 72 C4
Avarua *capital of* Cook Islands 127 G5
Aveiro Portugal 74 C2
Avignon France 73 D6
Ávila Spain 74 D2
Avilés Spain 74 D1
Awbārī Libya 53 F3
Axel Heiberg Island *island* Canada 19 F1
Axios *see* Vardar
Ayacucho Peru 42 B4
Aydarko'l Ko'li *lake* Uzbekistan *var.* Aydarkül 104 D2
Aydarkül *see* Aydarko'l Ko'li
Aydın Turkey 98 A3

Ayer's Rock *see* Uluru
Ayr Scotland, UK 70 C4
Ayutthaya Thailand 119 C5
Ayvalık Turkey 98 A3
Azaouâd *desert* Mali 57 E2
A'zāz Syria 100 B2
Azerbaijan *country* SW Asia 99 G2
Azores *islands* Portugal, Atlantic Ocean 48 C3
Azov, Sea of Black Sea *Ukr.* Azovs'ke More, *Rus.* Azovskoye More 93 A6 91 G4
Azovs'ke More *see* Azov, Sea of
Azovskoye More *see* Azov, Sea of
Azul Argentina 46 D4
Azur, Côte d' *coastal region* France 73 E6
Az Zarqā' Jordan 101 B5
Az Zāwiyah Libya 53 F2

B

Baalbek Lebanon *var.* Ba'labakk 100 B4
Babeldaob *island* Palau 124 B2
Babruysk Belarus *Rus.* Bobruysk 89 D6
Babuyan Channel *channel* Philippines 121 E1
Bacan, Pulau *island* Indonesia 121 F4
Bačka Topola Serbia 82 D3
Bacău Romania 90 C4
Badajoz Spain 74 C4
Baden Switzerland 77 E6
Bādiyat ash Shām *see* Syrian Desert
Baffin Bay *sea feature* Atlantic Ocean 48 B1
Baffin Island *island* Canada 19 G2
Bafing *river* Africa 56 C3
Bafoussam Cameroon 58 B4
Bagdad *see* Baghdad
Bagé Brazil 44 C4

Baghdad *capital of* Iraq *var.* Bagdad, *Ar.* Baghdād 102 B3
Baghdād *see* Baghdad
Baghlān Afghanistan 105 E3
Bago Myanmar *prev.* Pegu 118 B4
Bagoé *river* Côte d'Ivoire/Mali 56 D4
Baguio Philippines 121 E1
Bahamas *country* West Indies, Atlantic Ocean 36
Baharden *see* Baharly
Baharly Turkmenistan *prev.* Baharden, Räherden, Bakharden, Bakherden 104 B3
Bahāwalpur Pakistan 116 C3
Bäherden *see* Baharly
Bahía Blanca Argentina 47 C5
Bahia, Islas de la *islands* Honduras 34 D2
Bahir Dar Ethiopia 54 C4
Bahrain *country* SW Asia 103 C5
Baia Mare Romania 90 B3
Baikal, Lake *see* Baykal, Ozero
Bairiki *capital of* Kiribati 127 E2
Baishan China 110 E3
Baja Hungary 81 C7
Baja California *peninsula* Mexico *Eng.* Lower California 32 B2
Bajo Nuevo *island* Colombia 35 F2
Baker Oregon, USA 26 C3
Baker & Howland Islands *external territory* USA, Pacific Ocean 125 E2
Bakersfield California, USA 27 C7
Bakharden *see* Baharly
Bakherden *see* Baharly
Bākhtarān *see* Kermānshāh
Bakı *see* Baku
Baku *capital of* Azerbaijan *Az.* Bakı, *var.* Baky 99 H2
Baky *see* Baku
Balabac Strait *sea feature* South China Sea/Sulu Sea 120 D2

Ba'labakk *see* Baalbek
Balakovo Russian Federation 93 C6
Bālā Murghāb Afghanistan 104 D4
Balaton *lake* Hungary *var.* Lake Balaton, *Ger.* Plattensee 81 C7
Balaton, Lake *see* Balaton
Balbina, Represa *Reservoir* Brazil 42 D2
Baleares, Islas *island group* Spain *Eng.* Balearic Islands 75 H3
Balearic Islands *see* Baleares, Islas
Bali *island* Indonesia 120 D5
Balıkesir Turkey 98 A3
Balikpapan Indonesia 120 D4
Balkanabat Turkmenistan *prev.* Nebitdag 104 B2
Balkan Mountains *mountain range* Bulgaria *Bul.* Stara Planina 86 C2
Balkhash Kazakhstan 96 C5
Balkhash, Lake *see* Balkhash, Ozero
Balkhash, Ozero *lake* Kazakhstan *Eng.* Lake Balkhash 94 C3
Ballarat Australia 131 C7
Balsas *river* Mexico 33 E5
Bălţi Moldova 90 D3
Baltic Port *see* Paldiski
Baltic Sea Atlantic Ocean 67 C7
Baltimore Maryland, USA 23 F4
Baltischport *see* Paldiski
Baltiski *see* Paldiski
Bamako *capital of* Mali 56 D3
Bambari Central African Republic 58 D4
Bamenda Cameroon 58 B4
Banaba *island* Kiribati *prev.* Ocean Island 127 E2
Bandaaceh Indonesia 120 A3
Banda, Laut *see* Banda Sea
Banda Sea *sea feature* Pacific Ocean *Ind.* Laut Banda 121 F4
Bandar-e 'Abbās Iran 102 D4
Bandar-e Būshehr Iran 102 C4

Bandar Lampung Indonesia *prev.* Tanjungkarang 120 C4
Bandar Seri Begawan *capital of* Brunei 120 D3
Bandon Oregon, USA 26 A3
Bandundu Dem. Rep. Congo 59 C6
Bandung Indonesia 120 C5
Bangalore India 114 D2
Banggai, Kepulauan *island group* Indonesia 121 E4
Banghāzī Libya *Eng.* Benghazi 53 G2
Bangka, Palau *island* Indonesia 120 C4
Bangkok *capital of* Thailand *Th.* Krung Thep 119 C5
Bangladesh *country* S Asia 117
Bangor Northern Ireland, UK 71 B5
Bangor Maine, USA 23 G2
Bangui *capital of* Central African Republic 59 C5
Bani *river* Mali 56 D3
Banī Suwayf Egypt *var.* Beni Suef 54 B1
Banja Luka Bosnia & Herzegovina 82 B3
Banjarmasin Indonesia 120 D4
Banjul *capital of* Gambia 56 B3
Banks Island *island* Canada 19 E2
Banks Islands *island group* Vanuatu, Pacific Ocean 126 D4
Banks Peninsula *peninsula* New Zealand 133 C6
Banks Strait *sea feature* Tasman Sea 131 C7
Danská Bystrica Slovakia *Ger.* Neusohl, *Hung.* Besztercebánya 81 C6
Bantry Bay *sea feature* Ireland 71 A6
Banyo Cameroon 58 B4
Banzare Seamounts *undersea feature* Indian Ocean 123 C7
Baotou China 109 F3
Baranavichy Belarus *Rus.* Baranovichi, *Pol.* Baranowicze 89 C6

Baranovichi *see* Baranavichy
Baranowicze *see* Baranavichy
Barbados *country* West Indies 37 H4
Barbuda *island* Antigua & Barbuda 37 G3
Barcaldine Australia 130 C4
Barcelona Spain 75 G2
Barcelona Venezuela 41 E1
Barcolod City Philippines 121 E2
Bareilly India 117 E3
Barentsburg Svalbard 65 F2
Barentsøya *island* Svalbard 65 G2
Barents Sea Arctic Ocean 122 H5
Bari Italy 79 E5
Barinas Venezuela 40 D2
Barisan, Pegunungan *mountains* Indonesia 120 B4
Barkly Tableland *plateau* Australia 130 B3
Barlavento, Ilhas de *island group* Cape Verde *var.* Windward Islands 56 A2
Bar-le-Duc France 72 D3
Barlee, Lake *lake* Australia 130 B5
Barlee Range *mountain range* Australia 128 B4
Barnaul Russian Federation 96 D4
Barnstaple England, UK 71 C7
Barquisimeto Venezuela 40 D1
Barra *island* Scotland, UK 70 B3
Barranquilla Colombia 40 B1
Barrier Range *mountain range* Australia 131 C5
Barrow *river* Ireland 71 B6
Barstow California, USA 27 C7
Bartang *river* Tajikistan 105 F3
Bartica Guyana 41 G2
Baruun-Urt Mongolia 109 F2
Barwon River *river* Australia 131 D5
Barysaw Belarus *Rus.* Borisov 89 D5
Basarabeasca Moldova 90 D4
Basel Switzerland 77 B6
Basra *see* Al Başrah

Bassein *see* Pathein
Basse-Terre *capital of* Guadeloupe 37 G4
Basseterre *capital of* St Kitts & Nevis 37 G3
Bass Strait *sea feature* Australia 131 C7
Bastia Corse, France 73 E7
Bastogne Belgium 69 D7
Bata Equatorial Guinea 58 A5
Batangas Philippines 121 E2
Bătdâmbâng Cambodia 119 D5
Bath England, UK 71 D6
Dathurst Canada 21 F4
Bathurst Island *island* Australia 128 D2
Bathurst Island *island* Canada 19 F2
Bâṭin, Wādī al *dry watercourse* Asia 102 C4
Batman Turkey *var.* Iluh 99 E4
Batna Algeria 53 E1
Baton Rouge Louisiana, USA 30 B3
Batticaloa Sri Lanka 115 E3
Batumi Georgia 99 F2
Bauru Brazil 44 D2
Bavarian Alps *mountains* Austria/Germany 77 C6
Bayamo Cuba 36 C2
Bayan Har Shan *mountain range* China 108 D4
Bayanhongor Mongolia 108 D2
Bay City Michigan, USA 22 C3
Baydhabo Somalia 55 D6
Baykal, Ozero *lake* Russian Federation *Eng.* Lake Baikal 95 E3
Bayonne France 73 A6
Baýramaly Turkmenistan 104 C3
Bayrūt *see* Beirut
Beaufort Sea Arctic Ocean 137 F2
Beaufort West South Africa 60 D5
Beaumont Texas, USA 29 H4
Beauvais France 72 C3
Béchar Algeria 52 C2
Be'er Sheva' Israel 101 A6

Beijing *capital of* China *var.* Peking 110 C4
Beira Mozambique 61 E3
Beirut *capital of* Lebanon *var.* Beyrouth, Bayrūt 100 B4
Beja Portugal 74 C4
Béjaïa Algeria 53 E1
Bek-Budi *see* Karshi
Békéscsaba Hungary 81 D7
Belarus *country* E Europe *var.* Belorusia 89
Belau *see* Palau
Belcher Islands *islands* Canada 20 C2
Beledweyne Somalia 55 D5
Belém Brazil 43 F2
Belfast Northern Ireland, UK 71 B5
Belfort France 72 E4
Belgaum India 114 C1
Belgium *country* W Europe 69
Belgorod Russian Federation 93 A5
Belgrade *capital of* Serbia *SCr.* Beograd 82 D3
Belitung, Pulau *island* Indonesia 120 C4
Belize *country* Central America 34
Belize City Belize 34 C1
Belle Île *island* France 72 A4
Belle Isle, Strait of *sea feature* Canada 21 G3
Bellevue Washington, USA 26 B2
Bellingham Washington, USA 26 B1
Bellingshausen Sea Antarctica 136 A3
Bello Colombia 40 B2
Bellville South Africa 60 C5
Belmopan *capital of* Belize 34 C1
Belo Horizonte Brazil 45 F1
Belorussia *see* Belarus
Belostok *see* Białystok
Beloye More Arctic Ocean *Eng.* White Sea 63 F1
Belyy, Ostrov *island* Russian Federation 137 H4

Bend Oregon, USA 26 B3
Bendery *see* Tighina
Bendigo Australia 131 C7
Benevento Italy 79 D5
Bengal, Bay of *sea feature* Indian Ocean 122 D3
Bengbu China 111 D5
Benghazi *see* Banghāzī
Bengkulu Indonesia 120 B4
Benguela Angola 60 B2
Beni *river* Bolivia 42 C4
Benidorm Spain 75 F4
Beni-Mellal Morocco 52 C2
Denin *country* N Africa *prev.* Dahomey 57
Benin, Bight of *sea feature* W Africa 57 F5
Benin City Nigeria 57 F5
Beni Suef *see* Banī Suwayf
Ben Nevis *mountain* Scotland, UK 70 C3
Benue *river* Cameroon/Nigeria 57 G4
Beograd *see* Belgrade
Berat Albania 83 D6
Berbera Somalia 54 D4
Berbérati Central African Republic 58 C5
Berdyans'k Ukraine 91 G4
Bereket Turkmenistan *prev.* Gazandzhyk, *var.* Kazandzhik, *Turkm.* Gazanjyk 104 B2
Berezina *see* Byerazino
Bergamo Italy 78 B2
Bergen Norway 67 A5
Bergse Maas *river* Netherlands 68 D4
Bering Sea Pacific Ocean 134 D1
Bering Strait *sea feature* Bering Sea/Chukchi Sea 134 D1
Berkeley California, USA 27 B6
Berlin *capital of* Germany 76 D3
Bermejo *river* Argentina 46 D3
Bermuda *external territory* UK, Atlantic Ocean 48 B3
Bern *capital of* Switzerland *Fr.* Berne 77 B7
Berne *see* Bern

Berner Alpen *mountain range* Switzerland 77 B7

Bertoua Cameroon 59 B5

Besançon France 72 D4

Besztercebánya *see* Banská Bystrica

Bethlehem West Bank 101 A5

Beyrouth *see* Beirut

Béziers France 73 C6

Bezmein *see* Abadan

Bhamo Myanmar 118 B2

Bhāvnagar India 116 C4

Bhōpal India 116 D4

Bhutan *country* S Asia 117

Biak, Pulau *island* Indonesia 121 G4

Białystok Poland *Rus.* Belostok 80 E3

Biel Switzerland 77 B7

Bielefeld Germany 76 B4

Bielitz-Biala *see* Bielsko-Biała

Bielsko-Biała Poland *Ger.* Bielitz-Biala 81 C5

Bié Plateau *upland* Angola 51 C6

Bighorn Mountains *mountains* C USA 24 C2

Bignona Senegal 56 B3

Big Spring Texas, USA 29 E3

Bihać Bosnia & Herzegovina 82 B3

Bihār *state* India 117 F3

Bijelo Polje Montenegro 82 D4

Bikāner India 116 C3

Bila Tserkva Ukraine 91 E2

Bilbao Spain 75 E1

Billings Montana, USA 24 C2

Bilma, Grand Erg de *desert* Niger 57 G3

Biloela Australia 130 D4

Biloxi Mississippi, USA 30 C3

Biltine Chad 58 D3

Binghamton New York, USA 23 F3

Birāk Libya 53 F3

Birātnagar Nepal 117 F3

Birmingham England, UK 71 D6

Birmingham Alabama, USA 30 D2

Bîr Mogreïn Mauritania 56 C1

Birsen *see* Biržai

Biržai Lithuania *Ger.* Birsen 88 C4

Biscay, Bay of *sea feature* Atlantic Ocean 62 C4

Bishkek *capital of* Kyrgyzstan *prev.* Frunze, Pishpek 105 F2

Bishop California, USA 27 C6

Biskra Algeria 53 E2

Bismarck North Dakota, USA 25 E2

Bismarck Archipelago *island group* Papua New Guinea 126 B3

Bismarck Sea *sea* Pacific Ocean 124 B2

Bissau *capital of* Guinea-Bissau 56 B4

Bitola Macedonia 83 F6

Bitterroot Range *mountains* NW USA 26 D2

Biwa-ko *lake* Japan 113 C5

Bizerte Tunisia 53 E1

Bjelovar Croatia 82 B2

Bjørnøya *island* N Norway *Eng.* Bear Island 65 G3

Black Drin *river* Albania/ Macedonia 83 D5

Black Forest *see* Schwarzwald

Black Hills *mountains* C USA 24 D3

Blackpool England, UK 71 D5

Black River *river* China/Vietnam 118 D3

Black Sea Asia/Europe 63 F4

Black Volta *river* Ghana/Côte d'Ivoire 57 E4

Blackwater *river* Ireland 71 A6

Blagoevgrad Bulgaria 86 C3

Blagoveshchensk Russian Federation 91 G4

Blanca, Bahía *sea feature* Argentina 39 D5

Blanche, Lake *lake* Australia 131 B5

Blantyre Malawi 61 E2

Blenheim New Zealand 133 D5

Blida Algeria 52 D1

Bloemfontein South Africa 60 D4

Blois France 72 C4

Bloomington Indiana, USA 22 C4

Bluefields Nicaragua 35 E3

Blue Mountains *mountains* W USA 26 C2

Blue Nile *river* Ethiopia/Sudan 54 C4

Blumenau Brazil 44 D3

Bo Sierra Leone 56 C4

Boa Vista Brazil 42 D1

Boa Vista *island* Cape Verde 56 A3

Bobo-Dioulasso Burkina Faso 56 D4

Bobruysk *see* Babruysk

Boca de la Serpiente *see* Serpent's Mouth, The

Bochum Germany 76 B4

Bodø Norway 66 C3

Bodrum Turkey 98 A4

Bogor Indonesia 120 C5

Bogotá *capital of* Colombia 40 B3

Bo Hai *sea feature* Yellow Sea 110 D4

Bohemian Forest *region* Germany 77 D5

Bohol Sea *Sea* Philippines 121 E2

Boise Idaho, USA 26 D3

Boké Guinea 56 C4

Bokhara *see* Buxoro

Bol Chad 58 B3

Bolivia *country* C South America 42–43

Bologna Italy 78 C3

Bolton England, UK 71 D5

Bolzano Italy *Ger.* Bozen 78 C2

Boma Dem. Rep. Congo 59 B7

Bombay *see* Mumbai

Bomu *river* Central African Republic/Dem. Rep. Congo 59 D5

Bonaire *external territory* Netherlands, West Indies 37 E5

Bongo, Massif des — Bryan

Bongo, Massif des *upland* Central African Republic 58 D4

Bongor Chad 58 C3

Bonn Germany 76 B4

Boosaaso Somalia 54 E4

Borås Sweden 67 B7

Bordeaux France 73 B5

Borger Texas, USA 29 E2

Borisov *see* Barysaw

Borlänge Sweden 67 C6

Borneo *island* SE Asia 120-121

Bornholm *island* Denmark 67 C8

Bosanski Šamac Bosnia & Herzegovina 82 C3

Bosna *river* Bosnia & Herzegovina 82 C3

Bosna I Hercegovina, Federacija Admin. region *republic* Bosnia and Herzegovina 82 C4

Bosnia & Herzegovina *country* SE Europe 82-83

Bosporus *sea feature* Turkey *Turk.* İstanbul Boğazi 98 B2

Bossangoa Central African Republic 58 C4

Bosten Hu *Lake* China 108 C3

Boston Massachusetts, USA 23 G3

Bothnia, Gulf of *sea feature* Baltic Sea 67 C5

Botoşani Romania 90 C3

Botswana *country* southern Africa 60

Bouar Central African Republic 58 C4

Bougainville Island *island* Papua New Guinea 126 C3

Bougouni Mali 56 D4

Boulder Colorado, USA 24 C4

Boulogne-sur-Mer France 72 C2

Bourges France 72 C4

Bourgogne *region* France *Eng.* Burgundy 72 D4

Bourke Australia 131 C5

Bournemouth England, UK 71 D7

Bouvet Island *external territory* Norway, Atlantic Ocean 49 D7

Bowen Australia 130 D3

Bowling Green Kentucky, USA 22 C5

Bozeman Montana, USA 24 B2

Bozen *see* Bolzano

Brač *island* Croatia 82 B4

Bradford England, UK 71 D5

Braga Portugal 74 C2

Bragança Portugal 74 C2

Brahmaputra *river* Asia 117 G3

Brăila Romania 90 D4

Brainerd Minnesota, USA 25 F2

Brandon Canada 19 F5

Brasília *capital of* Brazil 43 F4

Braşov Romania 90 C4

Bratislava *capital of* Slovakia *Ger.* Pressburg, *Hung.* Pozsony 81 C6

Bratsk Russian Federation 97 E4

Braunau am Inn Austria 77 D6

Braunschweig Germany *Eng.* Brunswick 76 C4

Brazil *country* South America 42-43

Brazil Basin *undersea feature* Atlantic Ocean 49 C5

Brazilian Highlands *upland* Brazil 43 G4

Brazos *river* SW USA 29 G3

Brazzaville *capital of* Congo 59 B6

Brecon Beacons *hills* Wales, UK 71 C6

Breda Netherlands 68 C4

Bregenz Austria 77 B7

Bremen Germany 76 B3

Bremerhaven Germany 76 B3

Brescia Italy 78 B2

Breslau *see* Wrocław

Brest Belarus *Pol.* Brześć nad Bugiem, *prev.* Brześć Litewski, *Rus.* Brest-Litovsk 89 B6

Brest France 72 A3

Brest-Litovsk *see* Brest

Bretagne *region* France *Eng.* Brittany 72 A3

Brezhnev *see* Naberezhnyye Chelny

Bria Central African Republic 58 D4

Bridgetown *capital of* Barbados 37 H4

Brig Switzerland 77 B5

Brighton England, UK 71 E7

Brindisi Italy 79 E5

Brisbane Australia 131 E5

Bristol England, UK 71 D6

British Columbia *province* Canada 18-19

British Indian Ocean Territory *external territory* UK, Indian Ocean 122 C4

British Isles *islands* W Europe 70-71

British Virgin Islands *external territory* UK, West Indies 37

Brittany *see* Bretagne

Brno Czech Republic *Ger.* Brünn 81 B5

Broken Arrow Oklahoma, USA 29 G1

Broken Hill Australia 131 B6

Broken Ridge *undersea feature* Indian Ocean 123 D6

Bromberg *see* Bydgoszcz

Brooks Range *mountains* Alaska, USA 18 D2

Brookton Australia 129 B6

Broome Australia 128 C3

Brownfield Texas, USA 29 E2

Brownsville Texas, USA 29 G5

Bruges *see* Brugge

Brugge Belgium *Fr.* Bruges 69 A5

Brunei *country* E Asia 120 D3

Brünn *see* Brno

Brunswick Georgia, USA 31 E3

Brunswick *see* Braunschweig

Brusa *see* Bursa

Brussel *see* Brussels

Brussels *capital of* Belgium *Fr.* Bruxelles, *Flem.* Brussel 69 C6

Brüx *see* Most

Bruxelles *see* Brussels

Bryan Texas, USA 29 G3

Bryansk Russian Federation 93 A5 96 A2
Brześć Litewski see Brest
Brześć nad Buglem see Brest
Bucaramanga Colombia 40 C2
Buchanan Liberia 56 C5
Bucharest capital of Romania 90 C5
Budapest capital of Hungary 81 C6
Budweis see České Budějovice
Buenaventura Colombia 40 B3
Buenos Aires capital of Argentina 46 D4
Buenos Aires, Lago lake Argentina/Chile 47 B6
Buffalo New York, USA 23 E3
Bug river E Europe 90 C1
Bujumbura capital of Burundi prev. Usumbura 55 B7
Bukavu Dem. Rep. Congo 59 E6
Bukhara see Buxoro
Bulawayo Zimbabwe 60 D3
Bulgan Mongolia 109 E2
Bulgaria country E Europe 86
Bumba Dem. Rep. Congo 59 D5
Bunbury Australia 129 B6
Bundaberg Australia 130 E4
Bunia Dem. Rep. Congo 59 E5
Buraydah Saudi Arabia 103 B5
Burē Ethiopia 54 C4
Burgas Bulgaria 86 E2
Burgos Spain 75 F2
Burgundy see Bourgogne
Burketown Australia 130 B3
Burkina Faso country W Africa 57
Burlington Iowa, USA 25 G4
Burlington Vermont, USA 23 F2
Burma see Myanmar
Burnie Tasmania 131 C8
Burns Oregon, USA 26 C3
Bursa Turkey prev. Brusa 98 B3
BūrSa'īd Egypt Eng. Port Said 54 B1
Burtnieku Ezers lake Latvia 88 C3
Buru, Pulau island Indonesia 121 E4

Burundi country C Africa 55
Busan South Korea prev. Pusan 110 E4
Busselton Australia 129 B7
Butembo Dem. Rep. Congo 59 E5
Buton, Pulau island Indonesia 121 E4
Butte Montana, USA 24 B2
Butuan Philippines 121 F2
Buxoro Uzbekistan var. Bokhara, Rus. Bukhara 104 D2
Büyükağrı Dağı see Ararat, Mount
Buzău Romania 90 C4
Büzmeýin see Abadan
Byarezino river Belarus Rus. Berezina 89 D6
Bydgoszcz Poland Ger. Bromberg 80 C3
Byerazino river Belarus Rus. Berezina 89 D6
Byzantium see İstanbul

C

Caazapá Paraguay 44 C3
Cabanatuan Philippines 121 F1
Cabimas Venezuela 40 C1
Cabinda exclave Angola 60 B1
Cabot Strait sea feature Atlantic Ocean 21 G4
Čačak Serbia 82 D4
Cáceres Spain 74 D3
Cachoeiro de Itapemirim Brazil 45 F1
Cadiz Philippines 121 E2
Cádiz Spain 74 D5
Caen France 72 B3
Cagayan de Oro Philippines 121 F2
Cagliari Italy 79 A5
Cahors France 73 B5
Cairns Australia 130 D3
Cairo capital of Egypt Ar. Al Qāhirah, var. El Qāhira 54 B1
Čakovec Croatia 82 B2
Calabar Nigeria 57 G5
Calabria region Italy 79 D6
Calafate see El Calafate

Calais France 72 C2
Calais Maine, USA 23 H1
Calama Chile 46 B2
Calbayog Philippines 121 F2
Calcutta see Kolkata
Caldas da Rainha Portugal 74 B3
Caldwell Idaho, USA 27 C3
Caleta Olivia Argentina 47 C6
Calgary Canada 19 E5
Cali Colombia 40 A3
Calicut India see Kozhikode 114 D2
California state USA 26 27
California, Golfo de sea feature Pacific Ocean Eng. California, Gulf of 32 B2 123 F2
Callabonna, Lake lake Australia 131 B5
Callao Peru 42 A3
Caltanissetta Italy 79 C7
Camagüey Cuba 36 C2
Cambodia country SE Asia Cam. Kampuchea 119
Cambridge England, UK 71 E6
Cambridge New Zealand 132 D2
Cameroon country W Africa 58–59
Campbell Plateau undersea feature Pacific Ocean 134 C5
Campeche Mexico 33 G4
Campeche, Bahía de sea feature Mexico Eng. Gulf of Campeche 33 G4
Campina Grande Brazil 43 H3
Campinas Brazil 45 E4
Campo Grande Brazil 44 C1
Campos Brazil 45 F2
Canada country North America 16–17
Canada Basin undersea feature Arctic Ocean var. Laurentian Basin 137 F2
Canadian River river SW USA 29 E2
Çanakkale Turkey 98 A3
Çanakkale Boğazı see Dardanelles
Canarias, Islas islands Spain Eng. Canary Islands 50 A2

Cévennes *mountains* France 73 C6

Ceylon *see* Sri Lanka

Ceylon Plain *undersea feature* Indian Ocean 122 C4

Chad *country* C Africa 58

Chad, Lake *lake* C Africa 58 D3

Chāgai Hills *mountains* Pakistan 116 A2

Chagos-Laccadive Plateau *undersea feature* Indian Ocean 122 C4

Chagos Trench *undersea feature* Indian Ocean 122 C4

Chalkída Greece 87 C5

Challenger Deep *undersea feature* Pacific Ocean 134 B3

Châlons-en-Champagne France 72 D3

Chambéry France 73 D5

Champaign Illinois, USA 22 B4

Chañaral Chile 46 B2

Chandigarh India 116 D2

Chang, Ko *island* Thailand 119 C5

Changchun China 110 D3

Chang Jiang *river* China *var.* Yangtze 111 B6

Changsha China 111 C6

Chaniá Greece 87 C7

Channel Islands *island group* California, USA 27 B8

Channel Islands *islands* UK 71 D8

Channel-Port-aux-Basques Canada 21 G4

Channel Tunnel France/UK 71 E7

Chapala, Lago de *lake* Mexico 32 D4

Chardzhev *see* Türkmenabat

Chardzhou *see* Türkmenabat

Chari *river* C Africa 58 C3

Chārīkār Afghanistan 105 E4

Chärjew *see* Türkmenabat

Charleroi Belgium 69 C6

Charleston South Carolina, USA 31 F2

Charleston West Virginia, USA 22 D5

Charleville Australia 130 C4

Charlotte North Carolina, USA 31 F1

Charlotte Amalie *capital of* Virgin Islands 37 F3

Charlottesville Virginia, USA 23 E5

Charlottetown Canada 21 G4

Charters Towers Australia 130 D3

Chartres France 72 C3

Châteauroux France 72 C4

Chatham Islands *islands* New Zealand 134 D4

Chattanooga Tennessee, USA 30 D1

Chauk Myanmar 118 A3

Chaves Portugal 74 C2

Cheboksary Russian Federation 93 C5

Cheboygan Michigan, USA 22 C2

Chech, Erg *desert* Algeria/ Mali 56 D1

Che-chiang *see* Zhejiang

Cheju-do *see* Jeju-do

Cheju Strait *see* Jeju Strait

Chekiang *see* Zhejiang

Cheleken *see* Hazar

Chelyabinsk Russian Federation 96 C3

Chemnitz Germany *prev.* Karl-Marx-Stadt 78 D4

Chenāb *river* Pakistan 116 C2

Chengdu China 111 B5

Chennai India *prev.* Madras 115 E2

Cherbourg France 72 B3

Cherepovets Russian Federation 92 B4

Cherkasy Ukraine 91 E2

Cherkessk Russian Federation 93 A7

Chernigov *see* Chernihiv

Chernihiv Ukraine *Rus.* Chernigov 91 E1

Chernivtsi Ukraine *Rus.* Chernovtsy, *Rom.* Cernăuți 90 C3

Chernobyl' *see* Chornobyl'

Chernovtsy *see* Chernivtsi

Chernyakhovsk Kaliningrad, Russian Federation 88 B4

Chesapeake Bay *sea feature* USA 23 F5

Chester England, UK 71 D5

Cheyenne Wyoming, USA 24 D4

Chlang-hsi *see* Jiangxi

Chiang Mai Thailand 118 B4

Chiang-su *see* Jiangsu

Chiba Japan 113 D5

Chicago Illinois, USA 22 B3

Chiclayo Peru 42 A3

Chico California, USA 27 B5

Chicoutimi Canada 21 E4

Chifeng China *var.* Ulanhad 109 F2

Chihli *see* Hebei

Chihuahua Mexico 32 C2

Chile *country* S South America 46-47

Chile Basin *undersea feature* Pacific Ocean 135 G4

Chile Chico Chile 47 B6

Chile Rise *undersea feature* Pacific Ocean 135 G4

Chi-lin *see* Jilin

Chillán Chile 46 B4

Chiloé, Isla de *island* Chile 47 B6

Chimborazo *peak* Ecuador 38 A3

Chimbote Peru 42 A3

Chimkent *see* Shymkent

Chimoio Mozambique 61 E3

China *country* E Asia 108-109

Chinandega Nicaragua 34 C3

Chindwinn *river* Myanmar 118 A2

Chinghai *see* Qinghai

Chingola Zambia 60 D2

Chinook Trough *undersea feature* Pacific Ocean 134 D1

Chíos Greece 87 D5

Chíos *island* Greece *prev.* Khios 87 D5

Chirchik Uzbekistan *Uzb.* Chirchiq 105 E2

Chirchiq *see* Chirchik

Chiriquí, Golfo de *sea feature* Panama 35 E5

Chişinău *capital of* Moldova, *var.* Kishinev 90 D3

Chita Russian Federation 97 F4

Chitré Panama 35 F5

Chittagong Bangladesh 117 G4

Chitungwiza Zimbabwe 60 D3

Choluteca Honduras 34 C3

Choma Zambia 60 D3

Chona *river* Russian Federation 95 E2

Chon Buri Thailand 119 C5

Ch'ŏngjin North Korea 110 E3

Chongqing *province* China *var.* Chungking 111 B5

Chonos, Archipiélago de los *island group* Chile 47 B6

Chornobyl' Ukraine *Rus.* Chernobyl' 91 E1

Choûm Mauritania 56 C2

Choybalsan Mongolia 109 F2

Christchurch New Zealand 133 C6

Christmas Island *external territory* Australia, Indian Ocean 122 D5

Christmas Island *see* Kiritimati

Christmas Ridge *undersea feature* Pacific Ocean 125 F1

Chuan *see* Sichuan

Chubut *river* Argentina 47 B6

Chudskoye Ozero *see* Peipus, Lake

Chui *see* Chuy

Chukchi Plain *undersea feature* Arctic Ocean 137 G2

Chukchi Sea Arctic Ocean *Rus.* Chukotskoye More 137 F1

Chukotskoye More *see* Chukchi Sea

Chula Vista California, USA 27 C8

Chulym *river* Russian Federation 94 D3

Chumphon Thailand 119 C6

Chungking *see* Chongqing

Chuquicamata Chile 46 B2

Chur Switzerland 77 B7

Churchill Canada 19 G4

Chuuk Islands *island group* Micronesia 126 B1

Chuy Brazil *var.* Chuí 44 C5

Cienfuegos Cuba 36 B2

Cieza Spain 75 F4

Cilacap Indonesia 120 C5

Cincinnati Ohio, USA 22 C4

Ciudad Bolívar Venezuela 41 E2

Ciudad del Este Paraguay 44 C3

Ciudad de México *see* Mexico City

Ciudad Guayana Venezuela 41 E2

Ciudad Juárez Mexico 32 C1

Ciudad Obregón Mexico 32 B2

Ciudad Ojeda Venezuela 40 C1

Ciudad Real Spain 75 E3

Ciudad Valles Mexico 33 E3

Ciudad Victoria Mexico 33 E3

Clarence *river* New Zealand 133 C5

Clarion Fracture Zone *tectonic feature* Pacific Ocean 125 G1

Clarksville Tennessee, USA 30 D1

Clearwater Florida, USA 31 E4

Clermont Australia 130 D4

Clermont-Ferrand France 73 C5

Cleveland Ohio, USA 22 D3

Clipperton Fracture Zone *tectonic feature* Pacific Ocean 125 G2

Clipperton Island *external territory* France, Pacific Ocean 135 F3

Cloncurry Australia 130 C3

Clovis New Mexico, USA 29 E2

Cluj-Napoca Romania 90 B3

Clutha *river* New Zealand 133 B7

Coast Ranges *mountain range* W USA 26 A5

Coats Island *island* Canada 20 C1

Coats Land *physical region* Antarctica 136 B2

Coatzacoalcos Mexico 33 G4

Cobán Guatemala 34 B2

Cochabamba Bolivia 42 C4

Cochin India *see* Kochi 114 D3

Cochrane Canada 20 C4

Cochrane Chile 47 B6

Coco *river* Honduras/Nicaragua 34 D2

Cocos Basin *undersea feature* Indian Ocean 122 D4

Cocos Islands *external territory* Australia, Indian Ocean 122 D5

Cod, Cape *coastal feature* NE USA 23 G3

Coeur d'Alene Idaho, USA 26 C2

Coffs Harbour Australia 131 E6

Coihaique Chile 47 B6

Coimbatore India 114 D3

Coimbra Portugal 74 C3

Colchester England, UK 71 E6

Colmar France 72 E4

Cologne *see* Köln

Colombia *country* N South America 40-41

Colombo *administrative capital* of Sri Lanka 115 E4

Colón Panama 35 F4

Colón, Archipiélago de *see* Galapagos Islands

Colorado *state* USA 24 C4

Colorado *river* USA 16 B5

Colorado *river* Argentina 47 C5

Colorado Plateau *upland region* S USA 28 B1

Colorado Springs Colorado, USA 24 D4

Columbia South Carolina, USA 31 F2

Columbia *river* NW USA 26 C1

Columbus Georgia, USA 30 D3

Columbus Mississippi, USA 30 C2

Columbus Nebraska, USA 25 E4

Columbus Ohio, USA 22 D4

Comayagua Honduras 34 C2

Comilla Bangladesh 117 G4

Communism Peak *peak* Tajikistan *Rus.* Pik Kommunizma, *prev.* Stalin Peak, Garmo Peak 105 F3

Como, Lago di *lake* Italy 78 B2

Comodoro Rivadavia Argentina 47 C6

Comoros *country* Indian Ocean 61

Conakry *capital of* Guinea 56 C4

Concepción Chile 47 B5

Concepción Paraguay 44 B2

Conchos *river* Mexico 32 C2

Concord New Hampshire, USA 22 G2

Concordia E Argentina 46 D3

Congo *country* C Africa 59

Congo *river* C Africa *var.* Zaire 51 C5

Congo Basin *drainage basin* C Africa 59 C5

Congo, Democratic Republic of *country* C Africa 59

Connecticut *state* USA 23 G3

Constance, Lake *river* C Europe 77 B6

Constantine Algeria 53 E1

Constantinople *see* Istanbul

Constanţa Romania 90 D5

Coober Pedy Australia 131 A5

Cook, Mount *see* Aoraki

Cook Islands *external territory* New Zealand, Pacific Ocean 127 G4

Cook Strait *sea feature* New Zealand 133 D5

Cooktown Australia 130 D2

Cooma Australia 131 D7

Coos Bay Oregon, USA 26 A3

Cootamundra Australia 131 D6

Copenhagen *capital of* Denmark 67 B7

Copiapó Chile 46 B3

Coppermine *see* Kugluktuk

Coquimbo Chile 46 B3

Corabia Romania 90 B5

Coral Sea Pacific Ocean 130 E3

Coral Sea Islands *external territory* Australia, Coral Sea 130 E3

Corantijn *see* Courantyne

Cordillera Cantábrica *mountain range* Spain 74 D1

Córdoba Argentina 46 C3

Córdoba Spain 74 D4

Cordova Alaska, USA 18 D3

Corfu *see* Kérkyra

Corinth *see* Kórinthos

Corinth, Gulf of *see* Korinthiakós Kólpos

Corinto Nicaragua 34 C3

Cork Ireland 71 B6

Corner Brook Canada 21 G3

Coro Venezuela 40 D1

Coronel Oviedo Paraguay 44 C2

Corpus Christi Texas, USA 29 G5

Corrib, Lough *lake* Ireland 71 A5

Corrientes Argentina 46 D3

Corse *island* France *Eng.* Corsica 73 E7 84 D2

Corsica *see* Corse

Çorum Turkey 90 D2

Corvallis Oregon, USA 26 A3

Cosenza Italy 79 D6

Costa Blanca *coastal region* Spain 75 F4

Costa Brava *coastal region* Spain 75 H2

Costa Rica *country* Central America 34-35

Côte d'Ivoire *country* W Africa *Eng.* Ivory Coast 56 D4

Cottbus Germany 76 D4

Council Bluffs Iowa, USA 25 F4

Courantyne *river* Guyana / Suriname *var.* Corantijn 41 G3

Courland Lagoon *sea feature* Baltic Sea 88 B4

Coventry England, UK 71 D6

Covilhã Portugal 74 C3

Cowan, Lake *lake* Australia 129 C6

Cozumel, Isla de *island* Mexico 33 H3

Cracow *see* Kraków

Craiova Romania 90 B5

Cremona Italy 78 B2

Cres *island* Croatia 82 A3

Crescent City California, USA 26 A4

Crete *see* Kriti

Crete, Sea of Mediterranean Sea *Gk.* Kritikó Pélagos 87 D7

Crimea *see* Krym

Cristóbal Panama 48 A4

Croatia *country* SE Europe 82

Croker Island *island* Australia 128 E2

Crotone Italy 79 E6

Crozet Basin *undersea feature* Indian Ocean 123 B6

Crozet Islands *island group* Indian Ocean 123 B7

Crystal Brook Australia 131 B6

Cuanza *river* Angola 60 B2

Cuba *country* West Indies 36

Cubango *see* Okavango

Cúcuta Colombia 40 C2

Cuenca Ecuador 40 A5

Cuenca Spain 75 E3

Cuernavaca Mexico 33 E4

Cuiabá Brazil 43 E4

Culiacán Mexico 32 C3

Cumaná Venezuela 41 E1

Cumberland Maryland, USA 23 E4

Cunene *river* Angola/Namibia 60 B3

Cunnamulla Australia 131 C5

Curaçao *external territory* Netherlands, West Indies 37 E5

Curicó Chile 46 B4

Curitiba Brazil 44 D3

Cusco Peru *prev.* Cuzco 42 B4

Cuttack India 117 F5

Cuxhaven Germany 76 B3

Cuyuni *river* Guyana/Venezuela 41 F2

Cuzco *see* Cusco

Elx *see* Elche
Ely Nevada USA 27 D5
Emden Germany 76 B3
Emerald Australia 130 D4
Emmen Netherlands 68 E2
Empty Quarter *see* Ar Rub' al
Khali
Ems *river* Germany/Netherlands
76 B3
Encarnación Paraguay 44 C3
Enderbury Island *atoll* Kiribati
136 C2
Enderby Land *region*
Antarctica 136 C2
Enderby Plain *undersea feature*
Indian Ocean 123 B7
England *national region* UK
70–71
English Channel *sea feature*
Atlantic Ocean 71 D7
Enguri *river* Georgia *Rus.* Inguri
99 F1
Enid Oklahoma, USA 29 F1
Ennedi *plateau* Chad 58 D2
Enns *river* Austria 77 D6
Enschede Netherlands
68 E3
Ensenada Mexico 32 A1
Entebbe Uganda 55 B6
Enugu Nigeria 57 G5
Eolie, Isole *island group* Italy
Eng. Lipari Islands, *var.*
Aeolian Islands 79 D6
Eperies *see* Prešov
Eperjes *see* Prešov
Épinal France 72 E4
Equatorial Guinea *country* W
Africa 59
Erdenet Mongolia 109 E2
Erechim Brazil 44 D3
Erenhot China 109 F2
Erevan *see* Yerevan
Ereğli Turkey 98 C4
Erfurt Germany 76 C4
Erie Pennsylvania, USA 22 D3
Erie, Lake *lake* Canada/USA
17 D5
Eritrea *country* E Africa 54
Erivan *see* Yerevan
Erlangen Germany 77 C5

Ernākulam India 114 D3
Er Rachidia Morocco 52 C2
Erzerum *see* Erzurum
Erzgebirge *mountain range*
Czech Republic/Germany *var.*
Krušné Hory 77 D5
Erzincan Turkey 99 E3
Erzurum Turkey *prev.* Erzerum
99 F3
Esbjerg Denmark 67 A7
Esch-sur-Alzette Luxembourg
69 D8
Escuintla Guatemala 34 B2
Eşfahān Iran 102 C3
Esh Sham *see* Damascus
Eskişehir Turkey 98 B3
Esmeraldas Ecuador 40 A4
Esperance Australia 129 C6
Espíritu Santo *island* Vanuatu
124 D3
Espoo Finland 67 D6
Esquel Argentina 47 B6
Essaouira Morocco 52 B2
Essen Germany 76 A4
Essequibo *river* Guyana 41 G3
Estelí Nicaragua 34 D3
Estevan Canada 19 F5
Estonia *country* E Europe
88 D2
Ethiopia *country* E Africa 54–55
Ethiopian Highlands *upland*
E Africa 50 D4
Etna, Mount *peak* Sicily, Italy
79 D7
Etosha Pan *salt basin* Namibia
60 C3
Eucla Australia 129 D6
Eugene Oregon, USA 26 A3
Eugene Washington, USA
26 B1
Euphrates *river* SW Asia 102 C4
Europe 62–63
Evansville Indiana, USA 22 B5
Everest, Mount *peak* China/
Nepal 108 B3
Everett Washington, USA 26 B1
Everglades, The *wetlands*
Florida, USA 31 C7
Évvoia *island* Greece 87 C5
Exeter England, UK 71 C7

Exmoor *region* England,
UK 71 C7
Exmouth Australia 128 A4
Exmouth Gulf *gulf* Australia
128 A4
Exmouth Plateau *undersea
feature* Indian Ocean 123 E5
Eyre North, Lake *salt lake*
Australia 131 F7
Eyre Peninsula *peninsula*
Australia 131 A6
Eyre South, Lake *salt lake*
Australia 131 B5

F

Fada N'gourma Burkina Faso
57 E4
Faeroe Islands *external
territory* Denmark, Atlantic
Ocean *Faer.* Føroyar, *Dan.*
Færøerne 65 F5
Færøerne *see* Faeroe Islands
Faguibine, Lac *lake* Mali 57 E3
Fairbanks Alaska, USA 18 D3
Fairlie New Zealand 133 B6
Faisalābād Pakistan 116 C2
Faīzābād Afghanistan *prev.*
Feyzābād 105 E3
Falkland Islands *external
territory* UK, Atlantic Ocean
47 D7
Fallon Nevada, USA 27 C5
Falun Sweden 67 C6
Famagusta *see* Gazimağusa
Farafangana Madagascar 61 G4
Farāh Afghanistan 104 C5
Farasān, Jazā'ir *island group*
Saudi Arabia 103 B6
Farewell, Cape *headland* New
Zealand 132 C4
Farewell, Cape *see* Nunap Isua
Farghona *see* Farg'ona
Farg'ona Uzbekistan *prev.*
Novyy Margilan, *Uzb.*
Farghona 105 F2
Fargo North Dakota, USA 25 E2
Farkhor Tajikistan 105 E3
Farmington New Mexico, USA
28 C1
Faro Portugal 74 C4

Farquhar Group *island group*
Seychelles 61 G2

Farvel, Cap *see* Nunap Isua

Faxaflói *bay* Iceland 64 D5

Faya Chad 58 C2

Fayetteville Arkansas, USA
30 A1

Fayetteville North Carolina,
USA 31 F1

Fdérik Mauritania 56 C1

Fear, Cape *coastal feature*
North Carolina, USA 31 G2

Fehmarn *island* Germany 76 C2

Fehmarn Belt *sea feature*
Germany 76 C2

Feira de Santana Brazil 43 G3

Fellin *see* Viljandi

Fengtien *see* Liaoning

Fenoarivo *see* Fenoarivo
Atsinanana

Fenoarivo Atsinanana
Madagascar *prev.* Fenoarivo
61 G3

Fens, The *wetland* England, UK
71 E6

Fergana *see* Farg'ona

Ferizaj Kosovo *prev.* Uroševac
83 D5

Ferrara Italy 78 C3

Ferrol Spain 74 C1

Fès Morocco *Eng.* Fez 52 C2

Feyzābād *see* Faīzābād

Fez *see* Fès

Fianarantsoa Madagascar 61 G3

Fier Albania 83 D6

Figueira da Foz Portugal 74 C3

Figueres Spain 75 G2

Figuig Morocco 52 D2

Fiji *country* Pacific Ocean 127

Finland *country* N Europe
66-67

Finland, Gulf of *sea feature*
Baltic Sea 67 E6

Fiordland *physical region* New
Zealand 133 A7

Firenze Italy *Eng.* Florence
78 C3

Fishguard Wales, UK 71 C6

Fitzroy *river* Australia 128 C3

Fitzroy Crossing Australia
128 D3

Fiume *see* Rijeka

Flagstaff Arizona, USA 28 B2

Flanders *region* Belgium 69 A5

Flensburg Germany 76 B2

Flinders Island *island* Australia
131 C7

Flinders Ranges *mountain
range* Australia 131 B6

Flinders River *river* Australia
130 C3

Flin Flon Canada 19 F5

Flint Michigan, USA 22 C3

Flint Island *island* Kiribati
127 H4

Florence Alabama, USA 30 C2

Florence South Carolina, USA
31 F2

Florence *see* Firenze

Florencia Colombia 40 B3

Flores Guatemala 34 B1

Flores *island* Indonesia 121 E5

Flores, Laut *see* Flores Sea

Flores Sea Pacific Ocean *Ind.*
Laut Flores 121 E5

Florianópolis Brazil 44 D3

Florida *state* USA 31 E4

Florida, Straits of *sea feature*
Bahamas/USA 31 F5 36 B1

Florida Keys *island chain*
Florida, USA 31 F5

Flórina Greece 86 B3

Flushing *see* Vlissingen

Foča Bosnia & Herzegovina
82 C4

Focşani Romania 90 C4

Foggia Italy 79 D5

Fogo *island* Cape Verde 56 A3

Foligno Italy 78 C4

Fongafale *capital of* Tuvalu
127 E3

Fonseca, Gulf of *sea feature*
El Salvador/Honduras 34 C3

Forlì Italy 78 C3

Formentera *island* Spain 75 G4

Former Yugoslav Republic of
Macedonia *see* Macedonia

Formosa Argentina 46 D2

Formosa *see* Taiwan

Formosa Strait *see*
Taiwan Strait

Fóroyar *see* Faeroe Islands

Fortaleza Brazil 43 H2

Fortescue River *river* Australia
128 B4

Fort Collins Colorado, USA
24 D4

Fort-de-France *capital of*
Martinique 37 G4

Forth *river* Scotland, UK 70 C4

Forth, Firth of *inlet* Scotland,
UK 70 D4

Fort Lauderdale Florida, USA
31 F5

Fort McMurray Canada 19 F4

Fort Myers Florida, USA 31 E4

Fort Peck Lake *lake* Montana,
USA 24 C1

Fort Saint John Canada 19 E4

Fort Smith Canada 19 E4

Fort Smith Arkansas, USA
30 A1

Fort Wayne Indiana, USA
22 C4

Fort William Scotland, UK
70 C3

Fort Worth Texas, USA 29 G3

Foveaux Strait *sea feature* New
Zealand 133 A7

Fox Glacier New Zealand
133 B6

Franca Brazil 45 E1

France *country* W Europe
72-73

Francistown Botswana 60 D3

Frankfort Kentucky, USA
22 C5

Frankfurt *see* Frankfurt am
Main

Frankfurt am Main Germany
Eng. Frankfurt 77 B5

Frankfurt an der Oder
Germany 76 D5

Fränkische Alb *mountains*
Germany 77 C6

Frantsa-Iosifa, Zemlya *islands*
Russian Federation *Eng.*
Franz Josef Land 137 G4

Franz Josef Land *see* Frantsa-
Iosifa, Zemlya

Fraser Island *island* Australia
130 E4

Frauenburg *see* Saldus
Fray Bentos Uruguay 44 B5
Fredericksburg Virginia, USA
23 E4
Fredericton Canada 21 F4
Frederikshavn Denmark
67 B7
Fredrikstad Norway 67 B6
Freeport Bahamas 36 C1
Freeport Texas, USA 29 G4
Freetown *capital of*
Sierra Leone 56 C4
Freiburg im Breisgau Germany
77 B6
Fremantle Australia 129 B6
French Guiana *external
territory* France, N South
America 41
French Polynesia *external
territory* France, Pacific
Ocean 135 E3
**French Southern and
Antarctic Territories** *French
overseas territory* Indian
Ocean *Fr.* Terres Australes
et Antarctiques Françaises
123 C7
Fresnillo Mexico 32 D1
Fresno California, USA 27 B6
Fobisher Bay *see* Iqaluit
Frome, Lake *salt lake* Australia
131 B5
Frunze *see* Bishkek
Fu-chien *see* Fujian
Fuerte Olimpo Paraguay
44 B1
Fuerteventura *island* Spain
52 A3
Fuhkien *see* Fujian
Fujian *province* China *var.*
Fu-chien, Fuhkien, Fukien,
Min 111 D6
Fukien *see* Fujian
Fukui Japan 113 C5
Fukuoka Japan 113 A6
Fukushima Japan 112 D4
Fulda Germany 77 C5
Fünfkirchen *see* Pécs
Fushun China 110 D3
Furnas, Represa de *Reservoir*
Brazil 45 E1
Fuxin China 110 D3

Fujian China *prev.* Linchuan
111 D6
FYR Macedonia *see* Macedonia

G

Gaalkacyo Somalia 55 E5
Gabès Tunisia 53 E2
Gabon *country* W Africa 59
Gaborone *capital of* Botswana
60 D4
Gabrovo Bulgaria 86 D2
Gadsden Alabama, USA 30 D2
Gaeta, Golfo di *sea feature*
Italy 79 C5
Gafsa Tunisia 53 E2
Gagnoa Côte d'Ivoire
56 D5
Gagra Georgia 99 E1
Gairdner, Lake *lake* Australia
131 B6
Galapagos Fracture Zone
tectonic feature Pacific Ocean
135 F3
Galapagos Islands *islands*
Ecuador, Pacific Ocean
var. Tortoise Islands, *Sp.*
Archipiélago de Colón
135 G3
Galapagos Rise *undersea
feature* Pacific Ocean
135 G3
Galaţi Romania 90 D4
Galesburg Illinois, USA 22 B4
Galicia *region* Spain 74 C1
Galilee, Sea of *see* Tiberias, Lake
Galle Sri Lanka 115 E4
Gallego Rise *undersea feature*
Pacific Ocean 135 F3
Gallipoli Italy 79 E5
Gällivare Sweden 66 D3
Gallup New Mexico, USA
28 C2
Galveston Texas, USA
29 G4
Galway Ireland 71 A5
Gambia *country* W Africa 56
Gambia *River* Africa 56 C3
Gambier, Îles *island group*
French Polynesia 135 E4

Gan *see* Gansu
Gan *see* Jiangxi
Gäncä Azerbaijan *Rus.*
Gyandzha, *prev.* Kirovabad,
Yelisavetpol 99 G2
Gand *see* Gent
Gander Canada 21 H3
Gandía Spain 75 F3
Ganges *river* S Asia 116 F4
Ganges Fan *Undersea feature*
Bay of Bengal 122 D3
Ganges, Mouths of the
wetlands Bangladesh/India
117 G4
Gangtok India 117 G3
Gansu *province* China *var.* Gan,
Kansu 111 B5
Gao Mali 57 E3
Gaoual Guinea 56 C4
Gaoxiong Taiwan *prev.*
Kaohsiung 111 D7
Gar China *var.* Shiquanhe
108 A4
Garagum Kanaly *canal*
Turkmenistan *prev.*
Karakumskiy Kanal 104 C3
Garagum *desert* Turkmenistan
var. Kara Kum, Karakumy
104 C2
Garda, Lago di *lake* Italy
78 B2
Gardēz Afghanistan *prev.*
Gardiz 105 E4
Gardiz *see* Gardēz
Garissa Kenya 55 C6
Garmo Peak *see* Communism
Peak
Garonne *river* France 73 B5
Garoowe Somalia 55 E5
Garoua Cameroon 58 B4
Gary Indiana, USA 22 B3
Gaspé Canada 21 F4
Gastonia North Carolina, USA
31 E1
Gävle Sweden 67 C5
Gaya India 117 F4
Gaza Gaza Strip 101 A6
Gazandzhyk *see* Bereket
Gazanjyk *see* Bereket
Gaza Strip *disputed territory*
SW Asia 101 A6

Gaziantep — Grampian Mountains

Guayaquil Ecuador 40 A4
Guayaquil, Golfo do *sea feature* Ecuador/Peru 40 A5
Guernsey *island* Channel Islands 71 D8
Güney Dogu Toroslar *mountain range* SE Turkey 99 F3
Guiana Highlands *upland* N South America 38 C2
Guider Cameroon 58 B4
Guimarães Portugal 74 C2
Guinea *country* W Africa 56
Guinea, Gulf of *sea feature* Atlantic Ocean 49 D5
Guinea-Bissau *country* W Africa 56
Guiyang China 111 B6
Guizhou *province* China *var.* Kuei-chou, Kweichow, Qian 111 B6
Gujarāt *state* India 116 C4
Gujrānwāla Pakistan 116 C2
Gujrāt Pakistan 116 C2
Gulf, The *sea feature* Arabian Sea *var.* Persian Gulf 122 B2
Gulfport Mississippi, USA 30 C3
Gulu Uganda 55 B6
Gumbinnen *see* Gusev
Gunnbjørn Fjeld *mountain* Greenland 64 D4
Guri, Embalse de *Reservoir* Venezuela 41 E2
Gusau Nigeria 57 F3
Gusev Kaliningrad, Russian Federation *prev.* Gumbinnen 88 B4
Gushgy *see* Serhetabat
Guwāhāti India 117 G3
Guyana *country* NE South America 41
Gwalior India 116 D3
Gwangju South Korea *prev.* Kwangju 111 E4
Gyandzha *see* Gäncä
Gyangzê China 108 C5
Győr Hungary *Ger.* Raab 81 C6

Gyumri Armenia *Rus.* Kumayri, *prev.* Leninakan, Aleksandropol'99 F2
Gyzylarbat *see* Serdar

H

Ha'apai Group *islands* Tonga 127 F5
Haapsalu Estonia *Ger.* Hapsal 88 C2
Haarlem Netherlands 68 C3
Haast New Zealand 133 B6
Hachijō-jima *island* Japan 113 C7
Hachinohe Japan 112 D3
Hadejia *river* Nigeria 57 G3
Ḥaḍramawt *Mountain range* Yemen 103 C7
Hagåtña Guam 126 B1
Hague, The *see* 's-Gravenhage
Haibowan *see* Wuhai
Haicheng China 110 D4
Haifa *see* Hefa
Hailar *see* Hulun Buir
Hainan *island* China *var.* Hainan Dao 106 D3 111 C8
Hainan *province* China *var.* Qiong 111 C7
Hainan Dao *see* Hainan Dao
Hai Phong Vietnam 118 D3
Haiti *country* West Indies 36
Hajdarken *see* Khaydarkan
Hakodate Japan 112 D3
Ḥalab Syria 100 B2
Ḥalāniyāt, Juzur al *Island group* Oman 103 D6
Halden Norway 67 B6
Halfmoon Bay New Zealand 133 A7
Halifax Canada 21 F4
Halle Germany 76 C4
Hallein Austria 77 D7
Halls Creek Australia 128 D3

Halmahera, Pulau *island* Indonesia 121 F3
Halmahera Sea *Sea* Indonesia 121 F4
Halmstad Sweden 67 B7
Hamada Japan 113 B5
Hamadān Iran 102 C3
Ḥamāh Syria 100 B3
Hamamatsu Japan 113 C5
Hamar Norway 67 B5
Hamburg Germany 76 C3
Hämeenlinna Finland 67 D5
HaMelah, Yam *see* Dead Sea
Hamersley Range *mountain range* Australia 128 B4
Hamhŭng North Korea 110 E4
Hami China 108 C3
Hamilton Canada 20 D5
Hamilton New Zealand 132 D3
Hamm Germany 76 B4
Hammerfest Norway 66 D2
Handan China 110 C4
HaNegev *desert region* Israel *Eng.* Negev 101 A6
Hangayn Nuruu *mountain range* Mongolia 108 D2
Hangzhou China 111 D5
Hannover Germany *Eng.* Hanover 76 B4
Hanoi *capital of* Vietnam 118 D3
Hanover *see* Hannover
Hanzhong China 111 B5
Hapsal *see* Haapsalu
Ḥaraḍ Yemen 103 C5
Harare *capital of* Zimbabwe 61 E3
Harbin China 110 E3
Hargeysa Somalia 55 D5
Hari *river* Indonesia 120 B3
Harīrūd *river* C Asia 104 D4
Harper Liberia 56 D5
Harrisburg Pennsylvania, USA 23 E4
Harstad Norway 66 C2
Hartford Connecticut, USA 23 G3
Har Us Nuur *lake* Mongolia 108 C2
Hasselt Belgium 69 D5

Hastings New Zealand 132 E4
Hastings Nebraska, USA 24 E4
Hatay see Antakya
Hatteras, Cape coastal feature North Carolina, USA 31 G1
Hattiesburg Mississippi, USA 30 C3
Hat Yai Thailand 119 C7
Haugesund Norway 67 A6
Hauraki Gulf gulf New Zealand 132 D2
Havana capital of Cuba Sp. La Habana 36 B2
Havelock North Carolina, USA 31 G1
Havre Montana, USA 24 C1
Havre-Saint-Pierre Canada 21 F3
Hawai'i state USA 135 E2
Hawai'ian Islands islands USA 125 E1
Hawai'ian Ridge undersea feature Pacific Ocean 134 D2
Hawera New Zealand 132 D4
Hawke Bay bay New Zealand 132 E4
Hawler see Arbīl
Hawthorne Nevada, USA 27 C6
Hay River Canada 19 E4
Hays Kansas, USA 25 F4
Hazar Turkmenistan prev. Cheleken 104 A2
Heard & McDonald Islands islands Indian Ocean 123 C7
Hebei province China var. Hopeh, Hopei, Ji; prev. Chihli 110 C4
Hebron West Bank var. Al Khalīl, El Khalīl, Heb. Hevron 101 D7
Heerenveen Netherlands 68 D2
Heerlen Netherlands 69 D6
Hefa Israel prev. Haifa 101 A5
Hefei China 111 D5
Hei see Heilongjiang
Heidelberg Germany 77 B5
Heilbronn Germany 77 B5
Heilongjiang province China var. Hei, Hei-lung-chiang 110 E3

Hei-lung-chiang see Heilongjiang
Helena Montana, USA 24 B2
Hells Canyon valley Idaho/ Oregon USA 26 C3
Helmand river Afghanistan 104 C5
Helmond Netherlands 69 D5
Helsingborg Sweden 67 B7
Helsinki capital of Finland 67 D6
Henan province China var. Honan, Yu 111 C5
Hengduan Shan mountain range China 111 A6
Hengelo Netherlands 68 E3
Hengyang China 111 C6
Henzada see Hinthada
Herāt Afghanistan 104 C4
Hermansverk Norway 67 A5
Hermosillo Mexico 32 B2
Herning Denmark 67 A7
Heywood Islands island group Australia 128 C3
Hiiumaa island Estonia Ger. Dagden, Swed. Dagö 88 C2
Hildesheim Germany 76 C4
Hilversum Netherlands 68 C3
Himalayas mountain range S Asia 106 B2
Himora Ethiopia 54 C4
Ḥimṣ Syria 100 B3
Hinchinbrook Island island Australia 130 D3
Hindu Kush mountain range C Asia 105 E4
Hinthada Myanmar prev. Henzada 118 A4
Hiroshima Japan 113 B5
Hitachi Japan 112 D4
Hjørring Denmark 67 A7
Hlybokaye Belarus Rus. Glubokoye 89 D5
Hobart Tasmania 131 C8
Hobbs New Mexico, USA 29 E3
Hô Chi Minh Vietnam var. Ho Chi Minh City, prev. Saigon 119 E6
Ho Chi Minh City see Hô Chi Minh

Hodeida see Al Ḥudaydah
Hoek van Holland Netherlands 68 B4
Hoggar see Ahaggar
Hohe Tauern mountain range Austria 77 C7
Hohhot China 109 F3
Hokitika New Zealand 133 B5
Hokkaidō island Japan 112 D2
Holguín Cuba 36 C2
Holland see Netherlands
Hollabrunn Austria 77 E6
Holon Israel 101 A5
Holyhead Wales, UK 71 C5
Hombori Mopti, Mali 57 E3
Homyel' Belarus Rus. Gomel' 89 E7
Honan see Henan
Honduras country Central America 34-35
Honduras, Gulf of sea feature Caribbean Sea 34 C2
Hønefoss Norway 67 B6
Hông Gai Vietnam 118 E3
Hong Kong China var. Xianggang 111 C6
Honiara capital of Solomon Islands 126 C3
Honshū island Japan 112 D3
Hoorn Netherlands 68 C2
Hopa Turkey 99 E2
Hopedale Canada 21 F2
Hopeh see Hebei
Hopei see Hebei
Hopkinsville Kentucky, USA 22 B5
Horki Belarus Rus. Gorki 89 E5
Horlivka Ukraine Rus. Gorlovka 90 G3
Horn, Cape see Hornos, Cabo
Hornos, Cabo Eng Cape Horn coastal feature Chile 47 C8
Horsham Australia 131 C7
Hospitalet see L'Hospitalet de Llobregat
Hot Springs Arkansas, USA 30 B2
Houston Texas, USA 29 G4
Hovd Mongolia 108 C2
Hövsgöl Nuur lake Mongolia 108 D1

Hradec Králové Czech Republic
Ger. Königgrätz 81 B5

Hrodna Belarus *Rus.* Grodno
89 B5

Huacho Peru 42 A3

Huainan China 111 D5

Huambo Angola 60 B2

Huancayo Peru 42 B3

Huang He *river* China *Eng.*
Yellow River 110 C4

Huánuco Peru 42 B3

Huaraz Peru 42 B3

Hubei *province* China 111 C5

Hubli India 114 C2

Hudson *river* NE USA 23 F3

Hudson Bay *sea feature*
Canada 16 C4

Hudson Strait *sea feature*
Canada 16 H3

Huế Vietnam 118 E4

Huehuetenango Guatemala
34 B2

Huelva Spain 74 C4

Huesca Spain 75 F2

Hughenden Australia 130 C4

Hull *see* Kingston upon Hull

Hulun Buir China *var.* Hailar
109 F1

Hulun Nur *lake* China 109 F1

Humboldt *river* W USA 27 C5

Hunan *province* China *var.*
Xiang 111 C6

Hungarian Plain *plain* C Europe
85 E2

Hungary *country* C Europe 81

Huntington Beach California,
USA 27 C8

Huntington West Virginia, USA
22 D5

Huntsville Alabama, USA 30 D2

Hurghada Egypt 54 B2

Huron, Lake *lake* Canada/USA
22 D2

Hurunui *river* New Zealand
133 C5

Húsavík Iceland 65 E4

Huvadhu Atoll *island* Maldives
114 C5

Hvar *island* Croatia 82 B4

Hyargas Nuur *lake* Mongolia
108 D2

Hyderābād India 114 D1,
116 B3

Hyères, Îles d' *islands* France
73 D6

I

Iaşi Romania 90 D3

Ibadan Nigeria 57 F4

Ibagué Colombia 40 B3

Ibarra Ecuador 40 A4

Iberian Peninsula *peninsula*
SW Europe 84 B3

Ibérico, Sistema *Mountain
range* Spain 75 F2

Ibiza *island* Spain *Cat.* Eivissa
75 G4

Ica Peru 42 B4

İçel *see* Mersin

Iceland *country* Atlantic Ocean
65 E4

Idaho *state* USA 26

Idaho Falls Idaho, USA 26 E3

Idfū Egypt 54 B2

Idlib Syria 100 B2

Ieper Belgium *Fr.* Ypres 69 A6

Ifôghas, Adrar des *upland* Mali
var. Adrar des Iforas 57 F2

Iforas, Adrar des *see* Ifôghas,
Adrar des

Iglau *see* Jihlava

Iglesias Italy 79 A5

Iguaçu *River* Argentina/Brazil
44 C3

Iguidi, 'Erg *desert* Algeria/
Mauritania 56 D1

Ihavananthapuram *island*
Maldives 114 C4

Ihosy Madagascar 61 G4

Iisalmi Finland 66 E4

IJssel *river* Netherlands 68 D3

IJsselmeer *lake* Netherlands
prev. Zuider Zee 68 D2

Ikaria *island* Greece 87 D5

Iki *island* Japan 113 A6

Ilagan Philippines 121 E1

Ilebo Dem. Rep. Congo 59 C6

Ili *River* China/Kazakhstan
94 D3

Iligan Philippines 121 F2

Illapel Chile 46 B3

Illinois *state* USA 22 B4

Iloilo Philippines 121 E2

Ilorin Nigeria 57 F4

Iluh *see* Batman

Imatra Finland 67 E5

Imperatriz Brazil 43 F2

Impfondo Congo 59 C5

Imphāl India 117 H4

Independence Missouri, USA
25 F4

India *country* S Asia 114-115,
116-117

Indian Ocean 122-123

Indiana *state* USA 22 C4

Indianapolis Indiana, USA
22 C4

Indigirka *river* Russian
Federation 95 F2

Indonesia *country* SE Asia
120-121

Indonesian Borneo *see*
Kalimantan

Indore India 116 D4

Indus *river* S Asia 116 C1

Indus Cone *see.* Indus Fan

Indus Fan *var.* Indus Cone.
Undersea feature Arabian
Sea 122 B3

Indus, Mouths of the *wetlands*
Pakistan 116 B4

Ingolstadt Germany 77 C6

Inguri *see* Enguri

Inhambane Mozambique 61 E4

Inn *river* C Europe 77 D6

Innaanganeq *headland*
Greenland 64 C1

Inner Islands *islands* Seychelles
61 H1

Inner Mongolia *autonomous
region* China 109 F3

Innsbruck Austria 77 C7

I-n-Sâkâne, Erg *Desert* Mali
57 E2

I-n-Salah Algeria 52 D3

Insein Myanmar 118 B4

Inukjuak Canada *prev.* Port
Harrison 20 D2

Inuvik Canada 19 E3

Invercargill New Zealand 133 A7

Inverness Scotland, UK 70 C3
Investigator Ridge undersea feature Indian Ocean 122 D4
Ioánnina Greece 86 A4
Iónia Nisiá island group Greece Eng. Ionian Islands 87 A5
Ionian Islands see Iónia Nisiá
Ionian Sea Mediterranean Sea 87 A6
Íos island Greece 87 D6
Iowa state USA 25 F3
Ipoh Malaysia 120 B3
Ipswich England, UK 71 E6
Iqaluit Canada prev. Frobisher Bay 19 H3
Iquique Chile 46 B1
Iquitos Peru 42 B2
Irákleio Greece 87 D7
Iran country SW Asia 102-103
Iranian Plateau upland Iran 102 D4
Iraq country SW Asia 102
Irbid Jordan 101 B5
Ireland country W Europe 70-71
Irian Jaya see Papua
Irish Sea British Isles 71 C5
Irkutsk Russian Federation 97 E4
Iron Mountain Michigan, USA 22 B2
Ironwood Michigan, USA 22 B1
Irrawaddy river Myanmar 118 B2
Irrawaddy, Mouths of the wetlands Myanmar 118 A4
Irtysh River Asia 94 C3
Iruña see Pamplona
Ishim River Kazakhstan/Russian Federation 94 C3
Isiro Dem. Rep. Congo 59 E5
İskenderun Turkey Eng. Alexandretta 98 D4
Iskür river Bulgaria 86 C1
Iskür, Yazovir Reservoir Bulgaria 86 C2
Islay island Scotland, UK 70 B4
Islāmābād capital of Pakistan 116 C1
Ismaila see Al Ismā'īlīya
Isnā Egypt 54 B2

Ísparta Turkey 98 B4
Israel country SW Asia 100-101
Issyk-Kul, Ozero lake Kyrgyzstan 105 G2
İstanbul Turkey var. Stambul, prev. Constantinople, Byzantium, Bul. Tsarigrad 98 B2
İstanbul Boğazı see Bosporus
Itabuna Brazil 43 G4
Itagüí Colombia 40 B2
Italy country S Europe 78-79
Ittoqqortoormiit Greenland 65 E3
Iturup island Japan/Russian Federation (disputed) 112 F1
Ivanhoe Australia 131 C6
Ivano-Frankivs'k Ukraine 90 C2
Ivanovo Russian Federation 92 B4
Ivittuut Greenland 64 B4
Ivory Coast see Côte d'Ivoire
Ivujivik Canada 20 D1
Iwaki Japan 112 D4
Izabal, Lago de lake Guatemala 34 C2
Izhevsk Russian Federation 93 C5 96 B3
İzmir Turkey prev. Smyrna 98 A3
İzmit Turkey var. Kocaeli 98 B2
Izu-shotō island group Japan 113 D6

J

Jabal ash Shifā desert Saudi Arabia 102 A4
Jabalpur India 116 F4
Jackson Mississippi, USA 30 C2
Jacksonville Florida, USA 31 E3
Jacksonville Texas, USA 29 G3
Jacmel Haiti 36 D3
Jaén Spain 75 E4
Jaffna Sri Lanka 115 E3
Jagdaqi China 109 G1
Jiangxi province China 111 C6
Jaipur India 116 D3

Jajce Bosnia & Herzegovina 82 C4
Jakarta capital of Indonesia 120 C5
Jakobstad Finland 66 D4
Jakobstadt see Jēkabpils
Jalālābād Afghanistan 105 E4
Jalal-Abad see Dzhalal-Abad
Jalandhar India 116 D2
Jalapa see Xalapa
Jamaame Somalia 55 D6
Jamaica country West Indies 36
Jamālpur Bangladesh 117 G4
Jambi Indonesia 120 B4
James Bay sea feature Canada 20 C4
Jammu & Kashmir disputed region India/Pakistan 116 D2
Jāmnagar India 116 B4
Jan Mayen external territory Norway, Arctic Ocean 65 F3
Japan country E Asia 112-113
Japan, Sea of Pacific Ocean 112 B3
Jarvis Island external territory USA, Pacific Ocean 125 F2
Java see Jawa
Java Sea Pacific Ocean var. Laut Jawa 122 D4
Java Trench undersea feature Indian Ocean 122 D4
Jawa island Indonesia var. Java 120 C5
Jawa, Laut see Java Sea
Jayapura Indonesia 121 H4
Jaz Mūriān, Hāmūn-e lake Iran 102 E4
Jedda see Jiddah
Jefferson City Missouri, USA 25 G4
Jeju-do island South Korea prev. Cheju do 111 E5
Jeju Strait sea feature South Korea prev. Cheju Strait 111 E5
Jēkabpils Latvia Ger. Jakobstadt 88 C4
Jelgava Latvia Ger. Mitau 88 C3
Jember Indonesia 120 D5
Jena Germany 76 C4

Jenīn var. Janīn, Jinīn; anc.
Engannim. West Bank 101 D6
Jérémie Haiti 36 D3
Jerevan see Yerevan
Jericho West Bank 101 B5
Jerid, Chott el salt lake Africa
84 D4
Jersey island Channel Islands
71 D8
Jerusalem capital of Israel
101 B5
Jhelum Pakistan 116 C2
Ji see Hebei
Ji see Jilin
Jiangsu province China var.
Chiang-su, Kiangsu, Su
111 D5
Jiangxi province China var.
Chiang-hsi, Gan, Kiangsi
111 C6
Jiaxing Zhejiang, China 111 D5
Jibuti see Djibouti
Jiddah Saudi Arabia Eng. Jedda
103 A5
Jiftlik Post West Bank
101 D7
Jihlava Czech Republic Ger.
Iglau 81 B5
Jilin province China var. Chi-lin,
Girin, Ji, Kirin 110 E3
Jilin China 110 E3
Jīma Ethiopia 55 C5
Jin see Shanxi
Jinan China 111 C4
Jingdezhen China 111 D5
Jinhua China 111 D5
Jining see Ulan Qab
Jinotega Nicaragua 34 D3
Jinsha Jiang river China 108 D5
Jinzhou China 110 D4
Jīzān Saudi Arabia 103 B6
João Pessoa Brazil 43 H3
Jodhpur India 116 C3
Joensuu Finland 67 E5
Johannesburg South Africa
60 D4
Johnston Atoll US
unincorporated territory
Pacific Ocean 125 E1
Johor Bahru Malaysia 120 C3
Joinville Brazil 44 D3

Joliet Illinois, USA 22 B3
Jönköping Sweden 67 B7
Jonquière Canada 21 E4
Jordan country SW Asia
100-101
Jordan river SW Asia 101 B5
Joseph Bonaparte Gulf gulf
Australia 128 D2
Jos Plateau upland Nigeria
57 G4
Juan Fernandez, Islas islands
Chile 46 A4
Juàzeiro Brazil 43 G3
Juàzeiro do Norte Brazil 43 G3
Juba capital of South Sudan
55 B5
Júcar river Spain 75 E3
Judenburg Austria 77 D7
Juigalpa Nicaragua 34 D3
Juiz de Fora Brazil 43 G5 45 F2
Juneau Alaska, USA 18 D4
Junggar Pendi desert China
108 C2
Junin Argentina 46 D4
Jura mountains France/
Switzerland 77 A7
Jura island Scotland, UK 70 B4
Jurbarkas Lithuania Ger.
Jurburg, var. Georgenburg
88 B4
Jurburg see Jurbarkas
Juruá river Brazil/Peru 42 C2
Juticalpa Honduras 34 D2
Jutland see Jylland
Juventud, Isla de la island
Cuba 36 B2
Jylland peninsula Denmark
Eng. Jutland 67 A7
Jyväskylä Finland 67 D5

K

K2 peak China/Pakistan
Eng. Mount Godwin Austen
116 D1
Kaachka see Kaka
Kaahka see Kaka
Kabale Uganda 55 B6
Kabinda Dem. Rep. Congo 59 D7

Kābol see Kabul
Kabul capital of Afghanistan
Per. Kābol 105 E4
Kachch, Gulf of sea feature
Arabian Sea 116 B4
Kachch, Rann of wetland India/
Pakistan var. Rann of Kutch
116 B4
Kadugli Sudan 54 B4
Kaduna Nigeria 57 G4
Kaédi Mauritania 56 C3
Kâghet Physical region
Mauritania 56 D1
Kagoshima Japan 113 A6
Kahramanmaraş Turkey var.
Marash, Maraş 98 D4
Kai, Kepulauan island group
Indonesia 121 G4
Kaifeng China 111 C5
Kaikohe New Zealand 132 C2
Kaikoura New Zealand 133 C5
Kainji Reservoir Reservoir
Nigeria 57 F4
Kairouan Tunisia 53 E1
Kaiserslautern Germany
77 B5
Kaitaia New Zealand 132 C2
Kajaani Finland 66 E4
Kaka Turkmenistan prev.
Kaakhka, var. Kaachka 104 C3
Kakhovka Ukraine 91 F4
Kakhovs'ka Vodoskhovyshche
Reservoir Ukraine 91 F3
Kalahari Desert desert
southern Africa 60 C4
Kalamariá Greece 86 C3
Kalámata Greece 87 B6
Kalāt see Qalāt
Kalbarri Australia 129 A5
Kalemie Dem. Rep. Congo
59 E7
Kalgoorlie Australia 129 C6
Kalimantan geopolitical region
Indonesia Eng. Indonesian
Borneo 120 D4
Kaliningrad external territory
Russian Federation 96 A2
Kaliningrad Kaliningrad,
Russian Federation prev.
Königsberg 88 A4
Kalinkavichy Belarus Rus.
Kalinkovichi 89 D7

L

Leskovac — Lord Howe Rise

Lorient France 72 A4
Los Alamos New Mexico, USA 28 D1
Los Angeles California, USA 27 C7
Loslau see Wodzisław Śląski
Los Mochis Mexico 32 C3
Losonc see Lučenec
Losontz see Lučenec
Lot *river* France 73 B5
Louangphrabang Laos 118 C3
Loubomo Congo 59 B6
Louisiana *state* USA 30 B3
Louisville Kentucky, USA 22 C5
Louisville Ridge *undersea feature* Pacific Ocean 125 E4
Lovech Bulgaria 86 C2
Lower California see Baja California
Lower Hutt New Zealand
Loxa see Loksa
Loyauté, Îles *island group* New Caledonia 126 D5
Loznica Serbia 82 C3
Lu see Shandong
Luanda *capital of* Angola 60 B1
Luanshya Zambia 60 D2
Lubango Angola 60 B2
Lubbock Texas, USA 29 E2
Lübeck Germany 76 C3
Lublin Poland *Rus.* Lyublin 80 E4
Lubny Ukraine 91 F2
Lubumbashi Dem. Rep. Congo 59 E8
Lucapa Angola 60 C1
Lucena Philippines 120 E2
Lučenec Slovakia *Hung.* Losonc, *Ger.* Losontz 81 D6
Lucerne see Luzern
Lucknow India 117 E3
Lüderitz Namibia 60 C4
Ludhiāna India 116 D2
Lugano Switzerland 77 B7
Lugo Spain 74 C1
Luhans'k Ukraine 91 H3
Luleå Sweden 66 D4
Lumsden New Zealand 133 A7
Lüneburg Germany 76 C3
Luninyets Belarus 89 C6

Luoyang *var.* Honan, Lo-yang. China 110 C4
Lusaka *capital of* Zambia 60 D2
Lushnjë Albania 83 D6
Lūt, Baḩrat see Dead Sea
Luts'k Ukraine 90 C1
Luxembourg *country* W Europe 69 D8
Luxembourg *capital of* Luxembourg 69 D8
Luxor see Al Uqşur
Luzern Switzerland *Fr.* Lucerne 77 B7
Luzon *island* Philippines 121 E1
Luzon Strait *sea feature* Philippines/Taiwan 107 E3
L'viv Ukraine *Rus.* L'vov 90 C2
L'vov see L'viv
Lyepyel' Belarus *Rus.* Lepel' 89 D5
Lyon France 73 D5
Lyublin see Lublin

M

Ma'ān Jordan 101 B6
Maas see Meuse
Maastricht Netherlands 69 D6
Macao *external territory* Portugal, E Asia *var.* Macau 111 C7
Macapá Brazil 43 F1
Macau see Macao
Macdonnell Ranges *mountains* Australia 130 A4
Macedonia *country* SE Europe officially Former Yugoslav Republic of Macedonia, *abbrev.* FYR Macedonia 83
Maceió Brazil 43 H3
Machala Ecuador 40 A5
Mackay Australia 130 D4
Mackay, Lake *lake* Australia 128 C4
Mackenzie *river* Canada 19 E4
Mackenzie Bay *sea feature* Atlantic Ocean 136 D3

Macleod, Lake *lake* Australia 128 A4
Mâcon France 72 D5
Macon Georgia, USA 31 E2
Madagascar *country* Indian Ocean 61
Madagascar Basin *undersea feature* Indian Ocean 123 B5
Madagascar Plateau *undersea feature* Indian Ocean 123 A6
Madang Papua New Guinea 126 B3
Madeira *river* Bolivia/Brazil 42 D2
Madeira *island group* Portugal 52 A2
Madhya Pradesh *state* India 117 E4
Madison Wisconsin, USA 22 B3
Madiun *prev.* Madioen. Indonesia 120 D5
Madona Latvia *Ger.* Modohn 88 D3
Madras see Chennai
Madre de Dios *river* Bolivia/ Peru 42 C3
Madrid *capital of* Spain 75 E3
Madurai India 114 D3
Magadan Russian Fed. 97 G3
Magallanes see Punta Arenas
Magallanes, Estrecho de see Magellan, Strait of
Magdalena *river* Colombia 40 B2
Magdeburg Germany 76 C4
Magelang Indonesia 120 C5
Magellan, Strait of *sea feature* S South America *Sp.* Estrecho de Magallanes 47 B8
Maggiore, Lake *lake* Italy/ Switzerland 78 B2
Mahajanga Madagascar 61 G3
Mahalapye Botswana 60 D4
Mahānādi *river* India 117 F5
Mahārashtra *state* India 116 D5
Mahé *island* Seychelles 61 H1
Mahilyow Belarus *Rus.* Mogilëv 89 E6
Mährisch-Ostrau see Ostrava

Maicao Colombia 40 C1
Maiduguri Nigeria 57 H4
Maïmanah Afghanistan *prev.*
  Meymaneh 104 D4
Maine *state* USA 23 G1
Maine, Gulf of *gulf* USA 23 G2
Mainz Germany 77 B5
Maio *Island* Cape Verde 56 A3
Maíz, Islas del *islands*
  Nicaragua 35 E3
Majorca *see* Mallorca
Majuro *island* Marshall Islands
  126 F1
Makarska Croatia 82 B4
Makarov Basin *undersea
  feature* Arctic Ocean 137 G3
Makassar Indonesia *prev.*
  Ujungpandang 121 E4
Makassar Strait *strait* Indonesia
  120 D4
Makeyevka *see* Makiyivka
Makhachkala Russian
  Federation 93 B7 96 A4
Makiyivka Ukraine *Rus.*
  Makeyevka 91 G5
Makkah Saudi Arabia *Eng.*
  Mecca 103 A5
Makkovik Canada 21 F2
Malabo *capital of* Equatorial
  Guinea 59 A5
Malacca, Strait of *sea feature*
  Indonesia/ Malaysia
  106 C4 119 C18 120 B3
Maladzyechna Belarus *Rus.*
  Molodechno, *Pol.*
  Molodeczno 89 C5
Málaga Spain 74 D5
Malakal South Sudan 55 B5
Malang Indonesia 120 D5
Malanje Angola 60 C2
Malatya Turkey 99 E3
Malawi *country* southern
  Africa 61 E3
Malay Peninsula *peninsula*
  Malaysia/Thailand 119 D8
Malaysia *country* Asia 120
Malden Island *atoll* Kiribati
  125 F2
Maldives *country* Indian Ocean
  114 C4
Male' *capital of* Maldives
  114 C4

Malekula *island* Vanuatu 124 D3
Mali *country* W Africa 57
Malindi Kenya 55 C7
Mallorca *island* Spain *Eng.*
  Majorca 75 H3
Malmö Sweden 67 B7
Malta *country* Mediterranean
  Sea 79 C8
Malta Montana, USA 24 C1
Malta Channel *sea feature*
  Mediterranean Sea 79 C7
Maluku *island group*
  Indonesia *var.* Moluccas
  107 E4 121 F4
Maluku, Laut Pacific Ocean
  Eng. Molucca Sea 121 F4
Mamberamo *river* Indonesia
  121 H4
Mamoudzou *capital of*
  Mayotte 61 G2
Man, Isle of *island* UK 71 C5
Manado Indonesia 121 F3
Managua *capital of* Nicaragua
  34 D3
Manama *capital of* Bahrain *Ar.*
  Al Manāmah 103 C5
Mananjary Madagascar 61 G3
Manaus Brazil 42 D2
Manchester England, UK
  71 D5
Manchester New Hampshire,
  USA 23 G2
Manchurian Plain *plain* E Asia
  107 E1
Mandalay Myanmar 118 B3
Mangalia Romania 90 D5
Mangalore India 114 C2
Manicouagan, Réservoir
  Reservoir Canada 21 E3
Manihiki *atoll* Cook Islands
  125 F3
Maniitsoq Greenland 64 C3
Manila *capital of* Philippines
  121 E1
Manisa Turkey *prev.* Saruhan
  98 A3
Manitoba *province* Canada
  19 G4
Manizales Colombia 40 B3
Manjimup Australia 129 B7
Mannar Sri Lanka 115 E3

Mannar, Gulf of *sea feature*
  Indian Ocean 114 D3
Mannheim Germany 77 B5
Manono Dem. Rep. Congo
  59 E7
Mansel Island *island* Canada
  20 C1
Mansfield Ohio, USA 22 D4
Manta Ecuador 40 A4
Mantes-la-Jolie France 72 C3
Mantova Italy *Eng.* Mantua
  78 B2
Mantua *see* Mantova
Manurewa New Zealand
  132 D3
Manzhouli China 109 F1
Mao Chad 58 B3
Maoke, Pegunungan
  mountains Indonesia
  121 H4
Maputo *capital of*
  Mozambique 61 E4
Mar, Serra do *mountains* Brazil
  38 D4
Maracaibo Venezuela 40 C1
Maracaibo, Lago de *inlet*
  Venezuela 40 C1
Maracay Venezuela 40 D1
Maradi Niger 57 F3
Marāgheh Iran 102 C3
Marajó, Ilha de *island* Brazil
  43 F2
Marañón *river* Peru 42 B2
Maraş *see* Kahramanmaraş
Marash *see* Kahramanmaraş
Marbella Spain 74 D5
Marble Bar Australia 128 B4
Mar Chiquita, Laguna *salt lake*
  Argentina 46 C3
Mardān Pakistan 116 C1
Mar del Plata Argentina 47 D5
Mardin Turkey 99 E4
Margarita, Isla de *island*
  Venezuela 41 E1
Märgow, Dasht-e- *desert*
  Afghanistan 104 C5
Mariana Trench *undersea
  feature* Pacific Ocean
  124 B1 126 B1
Marias, Islas *islands* Mexico
  32 C4

Miranda de Ebro Spain 75 E1
Mirim, Lake see Mirim Lagoon
Mirim Lagoon *lagoon* Brazil/
Uruguay *var.* Mirim, Lake
44 C5
Mirtóo Pelagos *sea feature*
Mediterranean Sea 87 C6
Miskitos Cayos *islands*
Nicaragua 35 E2
Miskolc Hungary 81 D6
Mişrātah Libya 53 F2
Mississippi *state* USA 30 C2
Mississippi *river* USA 16 C5
Mississippi Delta *wetlands* USA
30 C4
Missoula Montana, USA 24 B2
Missouri *state* USA 25 G4
Missouri *river* USA 17 C5
Mistassini, Lake *lake* Canada
20 D3
Mitau see Jelgava
Mitchell S Dakota, USA
25 E3
Mitchell River *river* Australia
130 C3
Mitilini Greece 86 D4
Mito Japan 112 D4
Mitrovicë Kosovo *prov.*
Kosovska Mitrovica 83 D5
Mits'iwa Eritrea *var.* Massawa
54 C4
Mitumba, Monts *Mountain
range* Dem. Rep. Congo 59 F7
Miyazaki Japan 113 B6
Mjøsa *lake* Norway 67 B5
Mljet *island* Croatia 83 C5
Mmabatho South Africa 60 D4
Mo Norway 66 C3
Mobile Alabama, USA 30 C3
Moçambique Mozambique
61 F2
Mocimboa da Praia
Mozambique 61 F2
Mocoa Colombia 40 B4
Mocuba Mozambique 61 E3
Modena Italy 78 B3
Modesto California, USA 27 B6
Modohn see Madona
Modriča Bosnia & Herzegovina
82 C3

Mogadiscio see Mogadishu
Mogadishu *capital of* Somalia
Som. Muqdisho, *It.*
Mogadiscio 55 D6
Mogilëv see Mahilyow
Mo i Rana Norway 66 C3
Mojave California, USA 27 C7
Mojave Desert *desert* W USA
27 C7
Moldavia see Moldova
Molde Norway 66 A4
Moldova *country* E Europe *var.*
Moldavia 90
Molodechno see Maladzyechna
Molodeczno see Maladzyechna
Molotov see Perm'
Moluccas see Maluku
Molucca Sea see Maluku, Laut
Mombasa Kenya 55 C7
Monaco *country* W Europe
73 E6
Monclova Mexico 33 E2
Moncton Canada 21 F4
Mongo Chad 58 C3
Mongolia *country* NE Asia
108-109
Monroe Louisiana, USA 30 B2
Monrovia *capital of* Liberia
56 C5
Mons Belgium 69 B6
Montague Seamount *undersea
feature* Atlantic Ocean 45 H1
Montana *state* USA 24 C2
Montauban France 73 C6
Mont Blanc *peak* France/Italy
62 D4
Mont-de-Marsan France
72 B6
Monte Cristi Dominican
Republic 37 E3
Montego Bay Jamaica 36 C3
Montenegro *Country*
SE Europe 83 D5
Monterey California, USA
27 B6
Montería Colombia 40 B2
Montero Bolivia 42 D4
Monterrey Mexico 33 E2
Montes Claros Brazil 43 G4
Montevideo *capital of* Uruguay
44 C5

Montgomery Alabama, USA
30 D2
Monthey Switzerland 77 A7
Montpelier Vermont, USA
23 F2
Montpellier France 73 C6
Montréal Canada 21 E4
Montserrat *external territory*
UK, West Indies 37
Monywa Myanmar 118 A3
Monza Italy 78 B2
Moora Australia 129 B6
Moore, Lake *lake* Australia
129 B6
Moorhead Minnesota, USA
25 E2
Moosonee Canada 20 C3
Mopti Mali 57 E3
Morava *river* C Europe 82 E4
Moravská Ostrava see Ostrava
Moray Firth *inlet* Scotland, UK
70 C3
Moree Australia 131 D5
Morelia Mexico 33 E4
Morena, Sierra *mountain
range* Spain 74 D4
Murghāb, Daryā-ye *river*
Afghanistan/Turkmenistan
104 D4
Morioka Japan 112 D3
Mornington Abyssal Plain
undersea feature Pacific
Ocean 135 G5
Morocco *country* N Africa 52
Morogoro Tanzania 55 C7
Mörön Mongolia 108 D2
Morondava Madagascar 61 F3
Moroni *capital of* Comoros
61 F2
Morotai, Pulau *island* Indonesia
121 F3
Morova *river* Poland 80 C6
Morris Jesup, Kap *headland*
Greenland 65 E1
Moscow *capital of* Russian
Federation *Rus.* Moskva
92 B4 96 B2
Mosel see Moselle
Mosel *river* W Europe *Fr.*
Moselle 77 A5
Moselle *river* W Europe *Ger.*
Mosel 72 E4

Mosgiel New Zealand 133 B7
Moshi Tanzania 55 C7
Moskva *see* Moscow
Mosquito Coast *coastal region* Nicaragua 35 E3
Moss Norway 67 B6
Mossendjo Congo 59 B6
Mossoró Brazil 43 H2
Most Czech Republic *Ger.* Brüx 80 A4
Mostaganem Algeria 52 D1
Mostar Bosnia & Herz. 82 C4
Mosul *see* Al Mawşil
Motril Spain 75 E5
Motueka New Zealand 133 C5
Moulins France 72 C4
Moulmein *see* Mawlamyine
Moundou Chad 58 C4
Mount Gambier Australia 131 B7
Mount Isa Australia 130 B4
Mount Magnet Australia 129 B5
Mount Vernon Illinois, USA 22 B5
Mouscron Belgium 69 A6
Moyobamba Peru 42 B2
Moyu China 108 B2
Mozambique *country* SE Africa 61
Mozambique Channel *sea feature* Indian Ocean 61 F3
Mozyr' *see* Mazyr
Mpika Zambia 61 E2
Mtwara Tanzania 55 C8
Muang Không Laos 119 D5
Muang Xaignabouri *see* Xaignabouri
Mudanjiang China 110 E3
Mufulira Zambia 60 D2
Muğla Turkey 98 A4
Mulhouse France 72 E4
Mull *island* Scotland, UK 70 B3
Muller, Pegunungan *mountains* Indonesia 120 C3
Multān Pakistan 116 C2
Mumbai India *var.* Bombay 117 C5
München Germany *Eng.* Munich 77 C6

Muncie Indiana, USA 22 C4
Munich *see* München
Münster Germany 76 B4
Muqdisho *see* Mogadishu
Mur *river* C Europe 77 E7
Murchison River *river* Australia 129 B5
Murcia Spain 75 F4
Mureş *river* Hungary/Romania 81 D7
Murfreesboro Tennessee, USA 30 D1
Murgab Tajikistan 105 F3
Murgap *river* Turkmenistan *var.* Murghab 104 C3
Murghab *see* Murgap
Müritz *lake* Germany 76 D3
Murmansk Russian Federation 92 C2 96 C1
Murray *river* Australia 131 B6
Murray Fracture Zone *tectonic feature* Pacific Ocean 135 E2
Murray Ridge *Undersea feature* Arabian Sea 122 B3
Murwillumbah Australia 131 E5
Murzuq Libya 53 F3
Muş Turkey 99 F3
Muscat *capital of* Oman *Ar.* Masqaţ 103 D5
Musgrave Ranges *mountain range* Australia 129 D5
Musters, Lago *lake* Argentina 46 C6
Mu Us Shadi *Desert* China 109 E3
Mvonioǎlv *river* Finland/ Sweden 66 D3
Mwali *island* Comoros 61 F2
Mwanza Tanzania 55 B6
Mwene-Ditu Dem. Rep. Congo 59 D7
Mweru, Lake *lake* Dem. Rep. Congo/Zambia 59 D7
Myanmar *country* SE Asia *var.* Myanmar 118-119
Myeik Myanmar *prev.* Mergui 119 B5
Mykolayiv Ukraine *Rus.* Nikolayev 91 E4
Mykonos *island* Greece 87 D5

Mysore India 114 D2
Mzuzu Malawi 61 E2

N

Naberezhnyye Chelny Russian Federation *prev.* Brezhnev 93 C5
Nablus West Bank *var.* Nābulus, *Heb.* Shekhem 101 D6
Nābulus *see* Nablus
Nacala Mozambique 61 F2
Naga Philippines 120 E2
Nagano Japan 112 C4
Nagasaki Japan 113 A6
Nägercoil India 114 D3
Nagorno-Karabakh *region* Azerbaijan 99 G2
Nagoya Japan 113 C5
Nägpur India 116 D4
Nagqu China 108 C5
Nagykanizsa Hungary *Ger.* Grosskanizsa 81 C7
Nagyszombat *see* Trnava
Naha Japan 113 A8
Nain Canada 21 F2
Nairobi *capital of* Kenya 55 C6
Najaf *see* An Najaf
Najrän Saudi Arabia 103 B6
Nakamura Japan 113 B6
Nakhichevan' *see* Naxçıvan
Nakhon Ratchasima Thailand 119 C5
Nakhon Sawan Thailand 119 C5
Nakhon Si Thammarat Thailand 119 C6
Nakuru Kenya 55 C6
Nal'chik Russian Federation 96 A4
Namangan Uzbekistan 105 E2
Nam Co *lake* China 108 C4
Nam Đinh Vietnam 118 D3
Namib Desert *desert* Namibia 60 B3
Namibe Angola 60 B2
Namibia *country* southern Africa 60
Nampa Idaho, USA 26 C3

New Ireland — North Island

Okhotsk, Sea of Pacific Ocean 134 C1

Okinawa *island* Japan 113 A8

Oki-shotō *island group* Japan 113 B5

Oklahoma *state* USA 29 F1

Oklahoma City Oklahoma, USA 29 F2

Okushiri-tō *island* Japan 112 C2

Okāra Pakistan 116 C2

Öland *island* Sweden 67 C7

Olavarría Argentina 46 D4

Olbia Italy 79 B5

Oldenburg Germany 76 B3

Oleksandriya Ukraine *Rus.* Aleksandriya 91 E3

Olenëk Russian Federation 97 E3

Ölgiy Mongolia 108 C2

Olhão Portugal 74 C4

Olita *see* Alytus

Olmaliq *see* Almalyk

Olmütz *see* Olomouc

Olomouc Czech Republic *Ger.* Olmütz 81 C5

Olsztyn Poland *Ger.* Allenstein 80 D2

Olt *river* Romania 90 B5

Olympia Washington, USA 26 B2

Omaha Nebraska, USA 25 F4

Oman *country* SW Asia 103 D6

Oman, Gulf of *sea feature* Indian Ocean 103 E5, 122 B3

Omdurman Sudan 54 B4

Omsk Russian Federation 96 C4

Onega *river* Russian Federation 92 C4

Onega, Lake *see* Onezhskoye Ozero

Onezhskoye Ozero *lake* Russian Federation *Eng.* Lake Onega 92 B3

Ongole India 115 E2

Onitsha Nigeria 57 F5

Onslow Australia 128 A4

Ontario *province* Canada 18 B3

Ontario, Lake *lake* Canada/USA 17 D5

Oostende Belgium *Eng.* Ostend 69 A5

Opole Poland *Ger.* Oppeln 80 C4

Oporto *see* Porto

Oppeln *see* Opole

Oradea Romania 90 B3

Oran Algeria 52 D1

Orange River *river* southern Africa 60 C4

Oranjestad Aruba 37 E5

Orantes *River* Asia 100 B3

Ordu Turkey 98 D3

Ordzhonikidze *see* Vladikavkaz

Örebro Sweden 67 C6

Oregon *state* USA 26

Orël Russian Federation 83 A5

Orem Utah, USA 24 B4

Orenburg Russian Federation 93 C6 96 B4

Orense *see* Ourense

Orestiáda Greece 86 D3

Orinoco *river* Colombia/ Venezuela 41 E3

Oristano Italy 79 A5

Orkney *islands* Scotland, UK 70 C2

Orlando Florida, USA 31 E4

Orléans France 72 C4

Örnsköldsvik Sweden 67 C5

Orontes *river* SW Asia 100 B3

Orosirá Rodópis *see* Rhodope Mountains

Orsha Belarus 89 E5

Orsk Russian Federation 93 D6 96 B4

Oruro Bolivia 42 C4

Ōsaka Japan 113 C5

Osborn Plateau *undersea feature* Indian Ocean 123 C5

Ösel *see* Saaremaa

Osh Kyrgyzstan 105 F2

Oshawa Canada 20 D5

Oshkosh Wisconsin, USA 22 B2

Osijek Croatia 82 C3

Oslo *capital* of Norway 67 B6

Osmaniye Turkey 98 D4

Osnabrück Germany 76 B3

Osorno Chile 47 B5

Oss Netherlands 68 D4

Ossora Russian Federation 97 H2

Ostend *see* Oostende

Östersund Sweden 67 C5

Ostrava Czech Republic *Ger.* Mährisch-Ostrau, *prev.* Moravská Ostrava 81 C5

Ostrołęka Poland 80 D3

Ostrowiec Świętokrzyski Poland 80 D4

Ōsumi-shotō *island group* Japan 113 A7

Otago Peninsula *peninsula* New Zealand 133 B7

Otaru Japan 112 D2

Oti *river* Africa 57 E4

Otranto, Strait of *sea feature* Albania/Italy 79 E5

Ottawa *capital* of Canada 20 D4

Ottawa *river* Canada 20 D4

Ou *river* Laos 118 C3

Ouachita *river* SE USA 30 B2

Ouagadougou *capital* of Burkina Faso 57 E3

Ouarâne *desert* Mauritania 56 D2

Ouargla Algeria 53 E2

Ouessant, Île d' *island* France 72 A3

Ouésso Congo 59 C5

Oujda Morocco 52 D2

Oulu Finland 66 D4

Oulu *river* Finland 66 D4

Oulujärvi *lake* Finland 66 E4

Ounasjoki *river* Finland 66 D3

Our *river* W Europe 69 E7

Ourense Spain *Cast.* Orense 74 C2

Ourinhos Brazil 44 D2

Ourthe *river* Belgium 69 D6

Outer Hebrides *island group* UK *var.* Western Isles 70 B3

Outer Islands *island group* Seychelles 61 H2

Ouyen Australia 131 C6

Oviedo Spain 74 D1

Owando Congo 59 C6

Owen Fracture Zone *tectonic feature* Arabian Sea 122 B3

Owensboro Kentucky, USA 22 B5

Oxford England, UK 71 D6

Oxnard California, USA 29 C7

Oyem Gabon 59 B5

Oyo Nigeria 57 F4

Ozark Plateau *plain* Arkansas/ Missouri, USA 25 G5

Ózd Hungary 81 D6

P

Paamiut Greenland 64 B4

Pachuca Mexico 33 E4

Pacific-Antarctic Ridge *undersea feature* Pacific Ocean 136 B5

Pacific Ocean 134-135

Padang Indonesia 120 B4

Paderborn Germany 76 B4

Padova Italy *Eng.* Padua 78 C2

Padre Island *island* Texas, USA 29 G5

Padua *see* Padova

Paducah Kentucky, USA 22 B5

Paeroa Waikato, New Zealand 132 D3

Pafos *see* Paphos

Pag *island* Croatia 82 A3

Pago Pago *capital of* American Samoa 127 F4

Paide Estonia *Ger.* Weissenstein 88 D2

Paihia New Zealand 132 D2

Painted Desert *desert* SW USA 28 C1

País Valenciano *cultural region* Spain 75 F3

Pakistan *country* S Asia 116

Pakokku Myanmar 118 A3

Palagruža *island* Croatia 83 B5

Palau *country* Pacific Ocean *var.* Belau 124 B2 126

Palawan *island* Philippines 121 E2

Palawan Passage *passage* Philippines 121 E2

Paldiski Estonia *prev.* Baltiski, *Eng.* Baltic Port, *Ger.* Baltischport 88 C2

Palembang Indonesia 120 C4

Palencia Spain 74 D2

Palermo Italy 79 C6

Palıkır *capital of* Micronesia 126 C2

Palioúri, Akrotírio *coastal feature* Greece *var.* Akra Kanestron 86 C4

Palk Strait *sea feature* India/Sri Lanka 115 E3

Palliser, Cape *headland* New Zealand 133 D5

Palm Springs California, USA 27 D8

Palma Spain 75 G3

Palmer Land *physical region* Antarctica 136 A3

Palmerston North New Zealand 132 D4

Palmyra *see* Tudmur

Palmyra Atoll *external territory* USA, Pacific Ocean 125 F2

Palu Indonesia 121 E4

Pamir *river* Afghanistan/ Tajikistan 105 F3

Pamirs *mountains* Tajikistan 105 F3

Pampa Texas, USA 29 E2

Pampas *region* South America 46 C4

Pamplona Spain *var.* Iruña 75 F1

Panaji India 114 C2

Panama *country* Central America 35

Panamá, Golfo de *sea feature* Panama 35 F5

Panama Canal *canal* Panama 35 F4

Panama City *capital of* Panama 35 F5

Panama City Florida, USA 30 D3

Pančevo Serbia 82 D3

Panevėžys Lithuania 88 C4

Pantanal *region* Brazil 38 C4

Pantelleria *island* Italy 79 B7

Papeete *capital of* French Polynesia 127 H4

Paphos Cyprus *var.* Pafos 98 C5

Papua *province* Indonesia *prev.* Irian Jaya 121 H4

Papua New Guinea *country* Pacific Ocean 126

Paracel Islands *disputed territory* Asia 120 D1

Paragua *river* Venezuela 41 E3

Paraguay *country* South America 44

Paraguay *river* C South America 38 C4 44 B2

Parakou Benin 57 F4

Paramaribo *capital of* Suriname 41 G2

Paraná Argentina 46 D4

Paraná *river* C South America 46 D3

Paranaíba Brazil 43 G2

Paraparaumu New Zealand 132 D4

Pardubice Czech Republic *Ger.* Pardubitz 81 B5

Pardubitz *see* Pardubice

Parepare Indonesia 121 E4

Paris *capital of* France 72 C3

Paris Texas, USA 29 G2

Parma Italy 78 B3

Pärnu Estonia *Rus.* Pyarnu, *prev.* Pernov, *Ger.* Pernau 88 C2

Pärnu *river* Estonia 87 D6

Pasadena California, USA 27 C7

Pasadena Texas, USA 29 G4

Passo Fundo Brazil 44 D3

Pasto Colombia 40 B4

Patagonia *region* S South America 47 C6

Pathein Myanmar *prev.* Bassein 118 A4

Patna India 117 F3

Patos, Lagoa dos *lagoon* Brazil 44 D4

Pátra Greece 87 B5

Pattani Thailand 119 C7

Pattaya Thailand 119 C5

Patuca *river* Honduras 34 D2

Pau France 73 B6

Pavlodar Kazakhstan 96 C4

Pavlograd *see* Pavlohrad

Pavlohrad Ukraine *Rus.* Pavlograd 91 G3

Paysandú Uruguay 44 B4

Pazardzhik — Piraiévs

Pressburg see Bratislava

Preston England, UK 71 D5

Pretoria capital of South Africa see Tshwane 60 D4

Préveza Greece 86 A4

Prijedor Bosnia & Herzegovina 82 B3

Prilep Macedonia 83 E5

Prince Albert Canada 19 F5

Prince Edward Island province Canada 21 F4

Prince Edward Islands island group South Africa 123 A7

Prince George Canada 19 E5

Prince of Wales Island island Canada 19 F2

Prince Rupert Canada 18 D4

Princess Charlotte Bay bay Australia 130 C2

Princess Elizabeth Land region Antarctica 136 C3

Principe island Sao Tome & Principe 59 A5

Pripet river Belarus/Ukraine 90 C1

Pripet Marshes wetlands Belarus/Ukraine 90 C1

Prishtinë capital of Kosovo 83 D5

Prizren Kosovo 83 D5

Prome see Pyay

Prossnitz see Prostějov

Prostějov Czech Republic Ger. Prossnitz 81 C5

Provence region France 73 D6

Providence Rhode Island, USA 23 G3

Providencia, Isla de island Colombia 35 E3

Provo Utah, USA 24 B4

Prudhoe Bay Alaska, USA 18 D2

Przheval'sk see Karakol

Pskov Russian Federation 92 A4

Pskov, Lake lake Estonia/ Russian Federation Est. Pihkva Järv, Rus. Pskovskoye Ozero 88 D3

Pskovskoye Ozero see Pskov, Lake

Ptich' see Ptsich

Ptsich river Belarus Rus. Ptich' 89 D7

Pucallpa Peru 42 B3

Puebla Mexico 33 F4

Pueblo Colorado, USA 22 D4

Puerto Aisén Chile 47 B6

Puerto Barrios Guatemala 34 C2

Puerto Carreño Colombia 40 D2

Puerto Cortés Honduras 34 C2

Puerto Deseado Argentina 47 C6

Puerto Maldonado Peru 42 C4

Puerto Montt Chile 47 B5

Puerto Natales Chile 47 B7

Puerto Plata Dominican Republic 37 E3

Puerto Princesa Philippines 120 E2

Puerto Rico external territory USA, West Indies 37 F3

Puerto San Julián Argentina 47 C7

Puerto Suárez Bolivia 42 D4

Puerto Vallarta Mexico 32 D4

Pula Croatia 82 A3

Pul-e Khumri Afghanistan prev. Pol-e Khomri 105 E4

Pune India prev. Poona 114 C1

Puno Peru 42 C4

Punta Arenas Chile prev. Magallanes 47 B7

Puntarenas Costa Rica 34 D4

Purmerend Netherlands 68 C3

Purus river Brazil/Peru 42 C3

Pusan see Busan

Putrajaya capital of Malaysia 120 B3

Putumayo river NW South America 38 B3

Pyapon Myanmar 118 B4

Pyarnu see Pärnu

Pyay Myanmar prev. Prome 118 A4

Pyongyang capital of North Korea 110 E4

Pyramid Lake lake Nevada, USA 25 C5

Pyrenees mountain range SW Europe 62 C4

Q

Qaanaaq Greenland var. Thule 64 D1

Qäbatiya West Bank 101 D7

Qaidam Pendi basin China 108 D4

Qalāt Afghanistan prev. Kalāt 104 D5

Qalqilya West Bank 101 D7

Qamdo China 108 D5

Qandahār see Kandahār

Qaqortoq Greenland 64 C4

Qara Qum see Karakumy

Qarshi see Karshi

Qasigiannguit Greenland 64 C3

Qatar country SW Asia 103 D5

Qattara Depression see Qaṭṭārah, Munkhafaḍ al

Qaṭṭārah, Munkhafaḍ al desert basin Egypt Eng. Qattara Depression 54 A1

Qausuittuq see Resolute

Qeqertarsuaq Greenland 64 B3

Qeqertarsuaq island Greenland 64 B3

Qian see Guizhou

Qilian Shan mountain range China 108 D4

Qimusseriarsuaq bay Greenland 64 C2

Qinā Egypt 54 B2

Qingdao China 110 D4

Qinghai province China var. Chinghai, Koko Nor, Qing, Tsinghai 108 D4

Qinghai Hu lake China var. Koko Nor 108 D4

Qingzang Gaoyuan plateau China Eng. Plateau of Tibet 110 A4

Qiong see Hainan

Qiqihar China 110 D3

Qira China 108 B4

Qitai China 108 C3

Rhodes *see* Ródos
Rhodope Mountains *mountain range* Bulgaria/Greece *Gk.* Orosirá Rodópis, *Bul.* Despoto Planina 86 C3
Rhône *river* France/Switzerland 62 C4
Ribeirão Preto Brazil 45 E1
Riberalta Bolivia 42 C3
Rîbnița Moldova 90 D3
Richfield Utah, USA 24 B4
Richland Washington, USA 24 C2
Richmond Kentucky, USA 22 C5
Richmond New Zealand 133 C5
Richmond Virginia, USA 23 E5
Richmond Range *mountain range* New Zealand 133 C5
Ricobayo, Embalse de *reservoir* Spain 74 D2
Riga *capital of* Latvia *Latv.* Rīga 88 C3
Riga, Gulf of *sea feature* Baltic Sea 88 C3
Riihimäki Finland 67 D5
Rijeka Croatia *It.* Fiume 82 A3
Rimah, Wādī ar *dry watercourse* Saudi Arabia 103 B5
Rimini Italy 78 C3
Rîmnicu Vîlcea *see* Râmnicu Vâlcea
Riobamba Ecuador 40 A4
Rio Branco Brazil 42 C3
Rio Cuarto Argentina 46 C4
Rio de Janeiro Brazil 45 F2
Rio Gallegos Argentina 47 C7
Rio Grande Brazil 44 D4
Rio Grande *river* N America 16 B6
Rio Grande Rise *undersea feature* Atlantic Ocean 49 C6
Río Verde Mexico 33 E3
Rishiri-tō *island* Japan 112 D1
Rivas Nicaragua 34 D3
Rivera Uruguay 44 C4
Riverside California, USA 27 C8
Riverton New Zealand 133 A7
Rivne Ukraine *Rus.* Rovno 90 C2

Riyadh *capital of* Saudi Arabia *Ar.* Ar Riyāḍ 103 C5
Rize Turkey 99 E2
Rkiz Mauritania 56 C3
Road Town *capital of* British Virgin Islands 37 F3
Roanne France 73 D5
Roanoke Virginia, USA 23 E5
Roanoke *river* SE USA 31 G1
Robinson Range *mountain range* Australia 129 B5
Rochester Minnesota, USA 25 F3
Rochester New York, USA 23 E3
Rockford Illinois, USA 22 B3
Rockhampton Australia 130 D4
Rock Island Illinois, USA 22 B3
Rock Springs Wyoming, USA 24 C3
Rockstone Guyana 41 G2
Rocky Mountains *mountain range* Canada/USA 18-19 D4
Rodez France 73 C6
Ródhos *see* Ródos
Ródos *island* Greece *var.* Ródhos, *Eng.* Rhodes 87 E6
Ródos Greece *Eng.* Rhodes 87 E6
Rodosto *see* Tekirdağ
Roeselare Belgium 69 A5
Roma Australia 131 D5
Roma *see* Rome
Romania *country* SE Europe 90
Rome *capital of* Italy *It.* Roma 78 C4
Rome Georgia, USA 30 D2
Rønne Denmark 67 B8
Ronne Ice Shelf *ice feature* Antarctica 136 B3
Roosendaal Netherlands 68 C4
Rosario Argentina 46 D4
Roseau *capital of* Dominica 37 G4
Rosenau *see* Rožňava
Rositten *see* Rēzekne
Ross Ice Shelf *ice feature* Antarctica 136 B4
Ross Sea Antarctica 136 B4

Rostak *see* Ar Rustāq
Rostock Germany 76 C2
Rostov-na-Donu Russian Federation 96 A3
Roswell New Mexico, USA 28 D2
Rotorua New Zealand 132 D3
Rotorua, Lake *lake* New Zealand 132 D3
Rotterdam Netherlands 68 C4
Rouen France 72 C3
Rovaniemi Finland 66 D3
Rovno *see* Rivne
Rovuma *river* Mozambique/Tanzania 61 F2
Roxas City Philippines 121 E2
Rožňava Slovakia *Ger.* Rosenau, *Hung.* Rozsnyó 81 D6
Rozsnyó *see* Rožňava
Ruatoria New Zealand 132 E3
Ruawai New Zealand 132 D2
Rudnyy Kazakhstan 96 C4
Rudolf, Lake *see* Lake Turkana
Rügen *headland* Germany 76 D2
Rukwa, Lake *lake* Tanzania 55 B7
Rumbek South Sudan 55 B5
Rundu Namibia 60 C3
Ruoqiang China 108 C3
Ruse Bulgaria 86 D1
Russian Federation *country* Europe/Asia 92-93 96-97
Rustavi Georgia 99 F2
Rutland Vermont, USA 23 F2
Rutog China 108 B4
Rwanda *country* C Africa 55
Ryazan' Russian Federation 93 B5 96 B3
Rybinskoye Vodokhranilishche *Reservoir* Russian Federation *Eng.* Rybinsk Reservoir 92 B4
Rybnik Poland 81 C5
Ryūkyū-rettō *island group* Japan 113 A8

Ryukyu Trench *Undersea feature* East China Sea 134 B2

Rzeszow Poland 81 E5**Saale** *river* Germany 76 C4

S

Saarbrücken Germany 77 A5

Saare *see* Saaremaa

Saaremaa *island* Estonia *var.* Saare, Sarema, *Ger.* Ösel, *var.* Oesel 88 C2

Šabac Serbia 82 C3

Sabadell Spain 75 G2

Sabah *cultural region* Borneo 120 D3

Sab'atayn, Ramlat as *desert* Yemen 103 C7

Sabhā Libya 53 F3

Sabzevār Iran 102 D3

Sacramento California, USA 27 B6

Şa'dah Yemen 103 B6

Sado *island* Japan 112 C4

Safi Morocco 52 B2

Saginaw Michigan, USA 22 C4

Sahara *desert* N Africa 50 B3

Sahel *region* W Africa 50 B3

Saïda Lebanon *anc.* Sidon 100 B4

Saidpur Bangladesh 117 G3

Saigon *see* Hô Chi Minh

Saimaa *lake* Finland 67 E5

Saint-Brieuc France 72 A3

Saint Catherines Canada 20 D5

Saint-Chamond France 73 D5

St Christopher & Nevis *see* St Kitts & Nevis

St Cloud Minnesota, USA 25 F2

St-Denis *capital of* Réunion 61 H4

Saintes France 72 B5

Saint-Étienne France 73 D5

Saint George Australia 131 D5

St. George's *capital of* Grenada 37 G5

St Helena *external territory* UK, Atlantic Ocean 49 D5

St Helier *capital* Jersey 71 D8

Saint-Jean, Lake *lake* Canada 21 E4

Saint John Canada 21 F4

St John's *country capital* Antigua and Barbuda 37 G3

Saint John's Canada 21 H3

St Joseph Missouri, USA 25 F4

St Kitts & Nevis *country* West Indies *var.* St Christopher & Nevis 37

St.-Laurent-du-Maroni French Guiana 41 H2

Saint Lawrence *river* Canada 21 F4

Saint Lawrence, Gulf of *sea feature* Canada 21 F3

St Lawrence Island *island* Alaska, USA 18 C2

Saint-Lô France 73 B3

Saint Louis Senegal 56 B3

St Louis Missouri, USA 25 G4

St Lucia *country* West Indies 37

Saint-Malo France 72 B3

Saint-Nazaire France 72 B4

Saint Paul Minnesota, USA 25 F2

St-Paul, Île *island* French Southern and Antarctic Territories 123 C6

St Peter Port *capital of* Guernsey 71 D8

St Petersburg Russian Federation *Rus.* Sankt-Peterburg, *prev.* Leningrad, Petrograd 92 B3 96 B2

St Petersburg Florida, USA 31 E4

Saint Pierre & Miquelon *external territory* France, Atlantic Ocean 21 G4

St Vincent, Cape *see* São Vicente, Cabo de

St Vincent & The Grenadines *country* West Indies 37

Saipan *island country capital* Northern Mariana Islands 124 B1

Sakākah Saudi Arabia 102 B4

Sakakawea, Lake *lake* North Dakota, USA 24 D2

Sakarya *see* Adapazarı

Sakhalin *island* Russian Federation 97 H4

Sal *island* Cape Verde 56 A2

Salado *river* Argentina 46 C3

Şalālah Oman 103 D6

Salamanca Spain 74 D2

Sala y Gómez *island* Chile, Pacific Ocean 135 F4

Saldus Latvia *Ger.* Frauenburg 88 B3

Salekhard Russian Federation 96 D3

Salem India 114 D2

Salem Oregon, USA 26 A3

Salerno Italy 79 D5

Salerno, Golfo di *sea feature* Italy 79 D5

Salihorsk Belarus *Rus.* Soligorsk 89 C6

Salima Malawi 61 E2

Salinas California, USA 27 B6

Salisbury England, UK 71 D7

Salisbury Island *island* Canada 20 D1

Salonica *see* Thessaloniki

Salso *river* Italy 79 C7

Salt *see* As Salt

Salta Argentina 46 C2

Saltillo Mexico 33 E2

Salt Lake City Utah, USA 24 B4

Salto Uruguay 44 R4

Salton Sea *lake* California, USA 27 D8

Salvador Brazil 43 G4

Salween *river* SE Asia 111 A6

Salzburg Austria 77 D6

Salzgitter Germany 76 C4

Samara Russian Federation 93 C6 96 B3

Samarinda Indonesia 121 E4

Samarkand Uzbekistan 104 D2

Sambre *river* Belgium 69 B7

Samoa *country* Pacific Ocean 127 F4

Samobor Croatia 82 B3

Sámos *island* Greece 87 D5

Samothrace *see* Samothráki

Samothráki *island* Greece *Eng.* Samothrace 86 D3

Samsun Turkey 98 D2

Samui, Ko *island group* Thailand 119 C6

San *river* Poland 81 E5

Saña Peru 42 A3

Sana *capital of* Yemen *var.* Şan'ā' 103 B7

Sanandaj Sinneh. Iran 102 C3

San Andrés, Isla de *island* Colombia 35 E3

San Angelo Texas, USA 29 F3

San Antonio Chile 46 B4

San Antonio Texas, USA 29 F4

San Antonio *river* S USA 29 G4

San Antonio Oeste Argentina 47 C5

Sanāw Yemen 103 C6

San Bernardino California, USA 27 C7

San Carlos Uruguay 44 C5

San Carlos de Bariloche Argentina 47 B5

San Clemente Island *island* W USA 27 C8

San Cristóbal Venezuela 40 C2

San Diego California, USA 27 C8

Sandwich Island *see* Efate

San Fernando Trinidad & Tobago 37 G5

San Fernando Venezuela 40 D2

San Fernando de Noronha *island* Brazil 43 H2

San Francisco California, USA 27 B6

Sangir, Kepulauan *island group* Indonesia 121 F3

San Ignacio Belize 34 C1

San Joaquin Valley *valley* W USA 27 B6

San José *capital of* Costa Rica 34 D4

San Jose California, USA 27 B6

San José del Guaviare Colombia 40 C3

San Juan Argentina 46 B3

San Juan *river* Costa Rica/ Nicaragua 34 D4

San Juan *capital of* Puerto Rico 37 F3

San Juan Bautista Paraguay 44 B3

San Juan de los Morros Venezuela 40 D1

Sankt Martin *see* Martin

Sankt-Peterburg *see* St Petersburg

Sankt Pölten Austria 77 E6

Şanlıurfa Turkey *prev.* Urfa 98 E4

San Lorenzo Honduras 34 C3

San Luis Potosí Mexico 33 E3

San Marino *country* S Europe 78 C3

San Matías, Golfo *sea feature* Argentina 39 C6

San Miguel El Salvador 34 C3

San Miguel de Tucumán Argentina 46 C3

San Nicolas Island *island* W USA 27 B8

San Pedro Sula Honduras 34 C2

San Remo Italy 78 A3

San Salvador *capital of* El Salvador 34 C3

San Salvador de Jujuy Argentina 46 C2

San Sebastián Spain *Bas.* Donostia 75 E1

Santa Ana El Salvador 34 B2

Santa Ana California, USA 27 C8

Santa Barbara California, USA 27 B7

Santa Catalina Island *island* W USA 27 C8

Santa Clara Cuba 36 B2

Santa Cruz Bolivia 42 D4

Santa Cruz California, USA 27 B6

Santa Cruz Islands *island group* Solomon Islands 126 C4

Santa Fe Argentina 46 D3

Santa Fe New Mexico, USA 28 D2

Santa Maria Brazil 44 C4

Santa Marta Colombia 40 C1

Santander Spain 75 E1

Santanilla, Islas *islands* Honduras 35 E1

Santarém Brazil 43 E2

Santarém Portugal 74 C3

Santaren Channel *Channel* Bahamas 36 C2

Santa Rosa Argentina 47 C4

Santa Rosa California, USA 27 A6

Santa Rosa de Copán Honduras 34 C2

Santa Rosa Island *island* W USA 27 B8

Santiago *island* Cape Verde 56 A3

Santiago *capital of* Chile 46 B4

Santiago Dominican Republic 37 E3

Santiago Panama 35 F5

Santiago de Compostela Spain 74 C1

Santiago de Cuba Cuba 36 C3

Santiago del Estero Argentina 46 C3

Santo Antão *island* Cape Verde 56 A2

Santo Domingo *capital of* Dominican Republic 37 E3

Santo Domingo de los Colorados Ecuador 40 A4

Santorini *island* Greece 87 D6

Santos Brazil 45 E2

São Borja Brazil 44 C3

São Francisco *river* Brazil 43 G3

São José do Rio Preto Brazil 44 D1

São Luís Brazil 43 G2

São Nicolau *island* Cape Verde 56 A2

Saône *river* France 72 D4

São Paulo Brazil 43 F5 45 E2

São Tomé *capital of* Sao Tome & Principe 59 A5

São Tomé *island* Sao Tome & Principe 59 A5

Sao Tome & Principe *country* W Africa 59

São Vincente *island* Cape Verde 56 A2

São Vicente, Cabo de *coastal feature* Portugal *Eng.* Cape St Vincent 74 B4

Sapele Nigeria 57 F5

Sapporo Japan 112 D2

Saragossa *see* Zaragoza

Sarajevo *capital of* Bosnia & Herzegovina 82 C4
Sarandë Albania 83 D6
Saransk Russian Federation 93 B5
Saratov Russian Federation 93 B6
Sarawak *state* Malaysia 120 D3
Sardegna *island* Italy *Eng.* Sardinia 79 A5
Sardinia *see* Sardegna
Sarema *see* Saaremaa
Sargasso Sea Atlantic Ocean 48 B4
Sargodha Pakistan 116 C2
Sarh Chad 58 C4
Sārī Iran 102 D3
Saruhan *see* Manisa
Sasebo Japan 113 A6
Saskatchewan *province* Canada 19 F5
Saskatchewan *river* Canada 19 F5
Saskatoon Canada 19 F5
Sassandra *River* Côte d'Ivoire 56 D5
Sassari Italy 79 A5
Satu Mare Romania 90 B3
Saudi Arabia *country* SW Asia 102-103
Sault Sainte Marie Canada 20 C3
Sault Sainte Marie Michigan, USA 22 C1
Saurimo Angola 60 C2
Sava *river* SE Europe 82 C3
Savannah Georgia, USA 31 F3
Savannah *river* SE USA 31 E2
Savissivik Greenland 64 C2
Savona Italy 78 A3
Savu Sea *sea* Indonesia 120 E5
Sawhāj Egypt *var.* Sohâg 54 B2
Sawqirah Oman 103 D6
Saýat Turkmenistan 104 D3
Sayhūt Yemen 103 D7
Saynshand Mongolia 109 E2
Say 'ūn Yemen 103 C6
Scandinavia *geophysical region* Europe 48 D2

Schaffhausen Switzerland 77 B6
Schaulen *see* Šiauliai
Schefferville Canada 21 E2
Scheldt *river* W Europe 69 B5
Schiermonnikoog *island* Netherlands 68 D1
Schneidemühl *see* Piła
Schwäbische Alb *mountains* Germany 77 B6
Schwarzwald *Forested mountain region* Germany *Eng.* Black Forest 77 B6
Schwerin Germany 76 C3
Scilly, Isles of *islands* UK 71 B7
Scotia Sea Atlantic Ocean 136 A1
Scotland *national region* UK 70
Scottsbluff Nebraska, USA 24 D3
Scottsdale Arizona, USA 28 B2
Scranton Pennsylvania, USA 23 F3
Scutari, Lake *lake* Albania/ Montenegro 83 C5
Seddon New Zealand 133 C5
Seattle Washington, USA 26 B2
Ségou Mali 56 D3
Segovia Spain 75 E2
Segura *river* Spain 75 E4
Seikan Tunnel *tunnel* Japan 112 D3
Seinäjoki Finland 67 D5
Seine *river* France 72 C3
Selfoss Iceland 65 E5
Semara *see* Smara
Semarang Indonesia 120 D4
Semipalatinsk Kazakhstan 96 D4
Sendai Japan 112 D4
Senegal *country* W Africa 56
Senegal *river* Africa 56 C3
Sên, Stœng *river* Cambodia 119 D5
Seoul *capital of* South Korea *Kor.* Sŏul 110 E4
Sept-Îles Canada 21 F3
Seraing Belgium 69 D6
Seram, Pulau *island* Indonesia 121 F4

Serbia *country* SE Europe 82 D3
Serdar Turkmenistan *prev.* Gyzylarbat, *prev.* Kizyl-Arvat 104 B2
Serhetabat Turkmenistan *prev.* Gushgy, Kushka 104 C4
Serov Russian Federation 96 C3
Serpent's Mouth, The *sea feature* Trinidad & Tobago/ Venezuela *Sp.* Boca de la Serpiente 41 F1
Serra do Mar *mountains* Brazil 44 D3
Sérres Greece 86 C3
Setesdal *valley* Norway 67 A6
Sétif Algeria 53 E1
Setúbal Portugal 74 C4
Seul, Lake *lake* Canada 20 A3
Sevana Lich *lake* Armenia 99 G2
Sevastopol' Ukraine 91 F5
Severn *river* Canada 20 B3
Severn *river* England/Wales, UK 71 D6
Severnaya Dvina *river* Russian Federation *Eng.* Northern Dvina 92 C3
Severnaya Zemlya *island group* Russian Federation 137 H3
Sevilla Spain *Eng.* Seville 74 D4
Seville *see* Sevilla
Seychelles *country* Indian Ocean 61 G2 B4
Seydhisfjördhur Iceland 65 E4
Seýdi Turkmenistan *prev.* Neftezavodsk 104 D2
Seyhan *see* Adana
Sfax Tunisia 53 F2
's-Gravenhage *capital of* Netherlands *Eng.* The Hague 68 B3
Shaan *see* Shaanxi
Shaanxi *province* China *var.* Shaan, Shan-hsi, Shaanxi Sheng, Shenshi, Shensi 111 C5
Shaanxi Sheng *see* Shaanxi
Shache China 108 A3

Shackleton Ice Shelf — Skopje

Shackleton Ice Shelf *ice feature* Antarctica 136 D3
Shandong *province* China *var.* Lu, Shantung 110 D4
Shanghai China 111 D5
Shangrao China 111 D6
Shan-hsi *see* Shaanxi
Shannon *river* Ireland 71 B5
Shan Plateau *upland* Myanmar 118 B3
Shantou China 111 D6
Shantung *see* Shandong
Sharjah *see* Ash Shāriqah
Shawnee Oklahoma, USA 29 G2
Shdanov *see* Mariupol'
Shebeli *river* Ethiopia/Somalia 55 D5
Sheberghān *see* Shibirghān
Sheffield England, UK 71 D5
Shengking *see* Liaoning
Shenking *see* Liaoning
Shenshi *see* Shaanxi
Shensi *see* Shaanxi
Shenyang China 110 D3
Sherbrooke Canada 21 E4
Sheridan Wyoming, USA 22 C2
's-Hertogenbosch Netherlands 68 C4
Shetland *islands* Scotland, UK 70 D1
Shevchenko *see* Aktau
Shihezi China 108 C2
Shijiazhuang China 110 C4
Shikoku *island* Japan 113 B6
Shikoku Basin *undersea feature* Philippine Sea 134 B2
Shikotan *island* Japan/Russian Federation (disputed) 112 E2
Shikārpur Pakistan 116 B3
Shimonoseki Japan 113 A5
Shinano-gawa *river* Japan 112 C4
Shingū Japan 113 C5
Shinyanga Tanzania 55 B7
Shiquanhe *see* Gar
Shibirghān Afghanistan *prev.* Sherberghān 104 D3
Shīrāz Iran 102 D4
Shkodër Albania 83 D5
Shostka Ukraine 91 E1

Shreveport Louisiana, USA 30 A2
Shrewsbury England, UK 71 D6
Shumen Bulgaria 86 D2
Shymkent Kazakhstan *prev.* Chimkent 96 B5
Šiauliai Lithuania *Ger.* Schaulen 88 B4
Šibenik Croatia 82 B4
Siberia *region* Russian Federation 97 E3
Siberut, Pulau *island* Indonesia 120 B4
Sibiu Romania 90 B4
Sibolga Indonesia 120 B3
Sibu Malaysia 120 C3
Sibut Central African Republic 58 C4
Sibuyan Sea *sea* Philippines 121 E2
Sichuan *province* China *var.* Chuan, Ssu-ch'uan, Szechwan 111 B5
Sichuan Pendi *depression* China 111 B5
Sicilia *island* Italy *Eng.* Sicily 79 C7
Sicily, Strait of *sea feature* Mediterranean Sea 79 B7
Sicily *see* Sicilia
Sidi Bel Abbès Algeria 52 D1
Sidon *see* Saïda
Siednesibirskoye Ploskogor'ye *plateau* Russian Federation *Eng.* Central Siberian Plateau 97 E3
Siegen Germany 76 B4
Siena Italy 78 B3
Sierra Leone *country* W Africa 56
Sierra Madre del Sur *mountain range* Mexico 33 E5
Sierra Madre Occidental *mountain range* Mexico *var.* Western Sierra Madre 17 B6
Sierra Madre Oriental *mountain range* Mexico *var.* Eastern Sierra Madre 32 D2
Sierra Nevada *mountain range* Spain 75 E4
Sierra Nevada *mountain range* W USA 27 B6

Sighişoara Romania 90 C4
Siglufjördhur Iceland 65 E4
Siguiri Guinea 56 D4
Siirt Turkey 99 F3
Siling Co *lake* China 108 C5
Silkeborg Denmark 67 A7
Sillein *see* Žilina
Šilutė Lithuania 88 B4
Simeulue, Pulau *island* Indonesia 120 A3
Simferopol' Ukraine 91 F5
Simpson Desert *desert* Australia 130 C4
Sinai *desert* Egypt 54 B1
Sincelejo Colombia 40 B1
Sines Portugal 74 B4
Singapore *country* SE Asia 120
Singapore *capital of* Singapore 120 C3
Sinkiang *see* Xinjiang Uygur Zizhiqu
Sinnamary French Guiana 41 H2
Sinop Turkey 98 D2
Sint-Niklaas Belgium 69 B5
Sintra Portugal 74 B3
Sion Switzerland 77 B7
Sioux City Iowa, USA 25 F3
Sioux Falls South Dakota, USA 25 E3
Siracusa Italy *Eng.* Syracuse 79 D7
Siret *river* Romania/Ukraine 90 C4
Sirikit Reservoir *Reservoir* Thailand 118 C4
Sirte, Gulf of *see* Surt, Khalīj
Sisak Croatia 82 B3
Sisimiut Greenland 64 C3
Sittoung *river* Myanmar 118 B4
Sittwe Myanmar *prev.* Akyab 118 A3
Sivas Turkey 98 D3
Sjælland *island* Denmark 67 B7
Skagerrak *sea feature* Denmark/Norway 67 A6
Skellefteå Sweden 66 D4
Skopje *capital of* Macedonia 83 E5

Tampico — Terni

Ternopil' Ukraine *Rus.*
Ternopol' 90 C2
Ternopol' *see* Ternopil'
Terrassa Spain 75 G2
Terre Haute Indiana, USA 22 B4
**Terres Australes et
Antarctiques Françaises**
see French Southern and
Antarctic Territories
Terschelling *island* Netherlands
68 C1
Teruel Spain 75 F3
Teseney Eritrea 54 C4
Tessalit Mali 57 E2
Tete Mozambique 61 E3
Tétouan Morocco 52 C1
Tetovo Macedonia 83 D5
Tetschen *see* Děčín
Tevere *river* Italy 78 C4
Texas *state* USA 28-29 F3
Texarkana Arkansas, USA
30 A2
Texas City Texas, USA 29 G4
Texel *island* Netherlands 68 C2
Thailand *country* SE Asia 118-
119
Thailand, Gulf of *sea feature*
South China Sea 119 C6
Thames *river* England, UK 71 D6
Thar Desert *desert* India/
Pakistan 116 C3
Tharthār, Buḩayrat ath *lake*
Iraq 102 B3
Thásos *island* Greece 86 C3
Thaton Myanmar 118 B4
Theiss *see* Tisza
Thermaic Gulf *see* Thermaïkós
Kólpos
Thermaïkós Kólpos *sea feature*
Greece *Eng.* Thermaic Gulf
86 B4
Thessaloníki Greece *var.*
Salonica 86 B3
The Valley *dependent territory
capital* Anguilla 37 G5
Thimphu *capital of* Bhutan
117 G3
Thionville France 72 E3
Thiruvananthapuram India *see*
Trivandrum 114 D3
Thompson Canada 19 F4

Thorn *see* Toruń
Thorshavn *see* Tórshavn
Thracian Sea Greece *Gk.*
Thrakikó Pélagos 86 D3
Thrakikó Pélagos *see*
Thracian Sea
Three Kings Islands *island
group* New Zealand 132 C1
Thule *see* Qaanaaq
Thunder Bay Canada 20 B4
Thuner See *lake* Switzerland
77 B7
Thurso Scotland, UK 70 C2
Tianjin China *var.* Tientsin
110 D4
Tiberias, Lake *lake* Israel *var.*
Sea of Galilee, *Heb.* Yam
Kinneret, *Ar.* Baḩrat Ṭabarīyā
101 B5
Tibesti *mountains* Chad/Libya
50 C3
Tibet *autonomous region*
China *Chin.* Xizang 108 C5
Tibet, Plateau of *see* Qingzang
Gaoyuan
Tienen Belgium 69 C6
Tien Shan *mountain range* C
Asia 105 G2
Tientsin *see* Tianjin
Tierra del Fuego *island*
Argentina/Chile 47 C8
Tiflis *see* Tbilisi
Tighina Moldova *prev.* Bendery
90 D4
Tigris *river* SW Asia 94 B4
Tijuana Mexico 32 A1
Tiki Basin *undersea feature*
Pacific Ocean 135 E3
Tiksi Russian Federation 97 F2
Tilburg Netherlands 68 C4
Timaru New Zealand 133 B6
Timișoara Romania 90 A4
Timmins Canada 20 C4
Timor *island* Indonesia 121 F5
Timor Sea Indian Ocean 121 F5
Tindouf Algeria 52 B3
Tínos *island* Greece 87 D5
Tirana *capital of* Albania 83 D6
Tiraspol Moldova 90 D4
Tîrgoviște *see* Târgoviște
Tîrgu Mureş *see* Târgu Mureş

Tirol *region* Austria *var.* Tyrol
77 C7
Tiruchchirāppalli India 114 D3
Tisa *see* Tisza
Tisza *river* E Europe *Ger.* Theiss,
Cz./Rom./SCr. Tisa
81 D6
Titicaca, Lake *lake* Bolivia/Peru
42 C4
Tlemcen Algeria 52 D2
Toamasina Madagascar 61 G3
Toba, Danau *lake* Indonesia
120 B3
Tobago *island* Trinidad and
Tobago 37 G5
Toba Kākar Range *mountains*
Pakistan 116 B2
Tobruk *see* Ṭubruq
Tocantins *river* Brazil 43 F3
Tocopilla Chile 46 B2
Togo *country* W Africa 57 E4
Tokat Turkey 98 D3
Tokelau *external territory* New
Zealand, Pacific Ocean
127 F3
Tokmak Kyrgyzstan 105 F2
Tokuno-shima *island* Japan
113 A8
Tokushima Japan 113 B5
Tokyo *capital of* Japan 113 D5
Toledo Spain 75 E3
Toledo Ohio, USA 22 D4
Toledo Bend Reservoir
Reservoir S USA 29 H3
Toliara Madagascar 61 E3
Tol'yatti *prev.* Stavropol'
Russian Federation 93 C5
Tomakomai Japan 112 D2
Tombouctou Mali 57 E3
Tombua Angola 60 B2
Tomini, Gul of *sea feature*
Indonesia 121 E4
Tomsk Russian Federation
96 D4
Tonga *country* Pacific Ocean
127 E5
Tongatapu *island* Tonga
125 E3
Tongking, Gulf of *sea feature*
South China Sea *var.* Gulf of
Tonkin 111 B7

Tongliao — Tuguegarao

Waco — White Sea